Microsoft® Word 2016

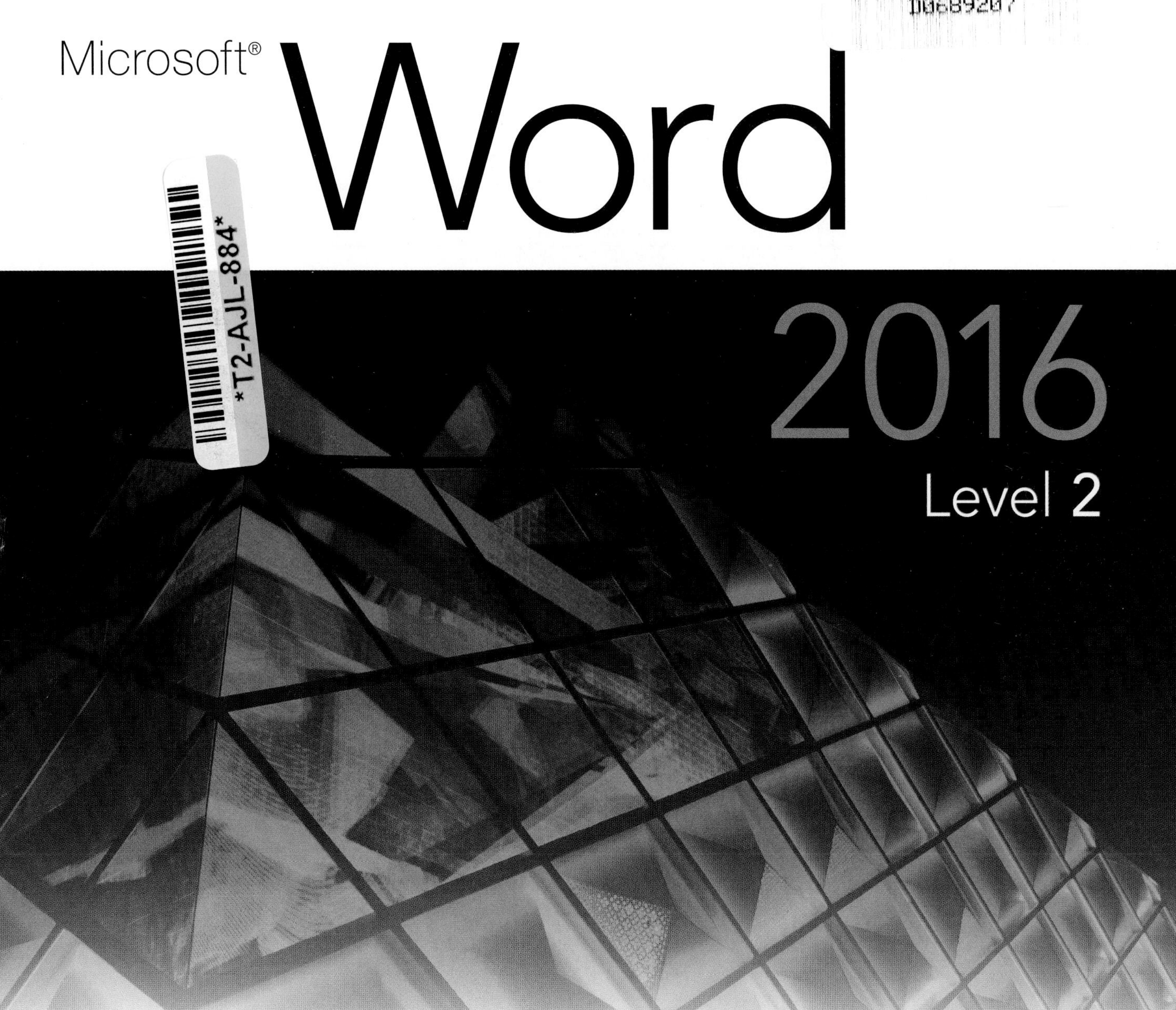

Level 2

Nita Rutkosky • Audrey Roggenkamp • Ian Rutkosky

PARADIGM
EDUCATION SOLUTIONS

St. Paul

Senior Vice President	Linda Hein
Editor in Chief	Christine Hurney
Director of Production	Timothy W. Larson
Production Editor	Jen Weaverling
Cover and Text Designer	Valerie King
Copy Editors	Communicáto, Ltd.
Senior Design and Production Specialist	Jack Ross
Design and Production Specialist	PerfecType
Assistant Developmental Editors	Mamie Clark, Katie Werdick
Testers	Janet Blum, Fanshawe College; Traci Post
Instructional Support Writers	Janet Blum, Fanshawe College; Brienna McWade
Indexer	Terry Casey
Vice President Information Technology	Chuck Bratton
Digital Projects Manager	Tom Modl
Vice President Sales and Marketing	Scott Burns
Director of Marketing	Lara Weber McLellan

Cover Photo Credits: © Photomall/Dreamstime.com.

ISBN 978-0-76386-923-6 (print)
ISBN 978-0-76386-924-3 (digital)

875 Montreal Way
St. Paul, MN 55102
Email: educate@emcp.com
Website: ParadigmCollege.com

Printed in the United States of America

23 22 21 20 19 18 17 2 3 4 5 6 7 8 9 10 11 12

Brief Contents

Contents

Preface

Benchmark Series: Microsoft® Word 2016 is designed for students who want to learn how to use this powerful word processing program to create professional-looking documents for school, work, and personal communication needs. After successfully completing a course using this textbook and digital courseware, students will be able to:

- Create and edit letters, flyers, announcements, and reports of varying complexity
- Apply appropriate formatting elements and styles to a range of document types
- Add graphics and other visual elements to enhance written communication
- Plan, research, write, revise, and publish documents to meet specific information needs
- Given a workplace scenario requiring a written solution, assess the communication purpose and then prepare the materials that achieve the goal efficiently and effectively

Upon completing the text, students can expect to be proficient in using Word to organize, analyze, and present information.

Well-designed textbook pedagogy is important, but students learn technology skills through practice and problem solving. Technology provides opportunities for interactive learning as well as excellent ways to quickly and accurately assess student performance. To this end, this textbook is supported with SNAP 2016, Paradigm's web-based training and assessment learning management system. Details about SNAP as well as additional student courseware and instructor resources can be found on page xiv.

Achieving Proficiency in Word 2016

Since its inception several Office versions ago, the *Benchmark Series* has served as a standard of excellence in software instruction. Elements of the *Benchmark Series* function individually and collectively to create an inviting, comprehensive learning environment that produces successful computer users. The following visual tour highlights the structure and features that comprise the highly popular *Benchmark* model.

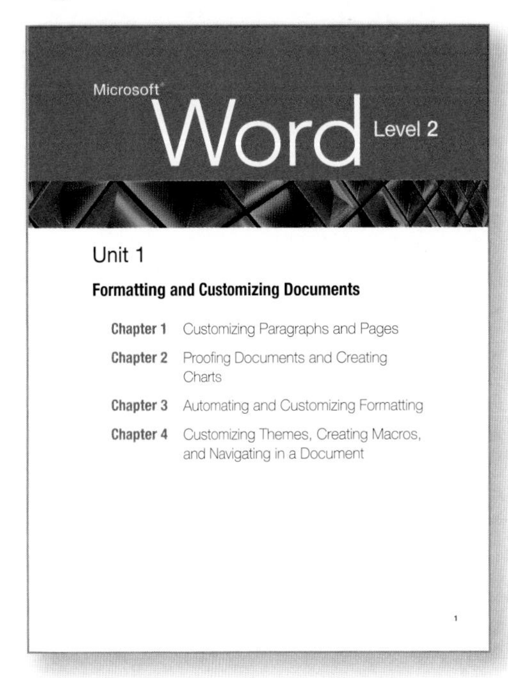

Microsoft
Word
Level 2
Unit 1
Formatting and Customizing Documents
Chapter 1 Customizing Paragraphs and Pages
Chapter 2 Proofing Documents and Creating Charts
Chapter 3 Automating and Customizing Formatting
Chapter 4 Customizing Themes, Creating Macros, and Navigating in a Document
1

Unit Openers display the unit's four chapter titles. *Word Level 2* contains two units; each unit concludes with a comprehensive unit performance assessment.

Student Textbook and eBook

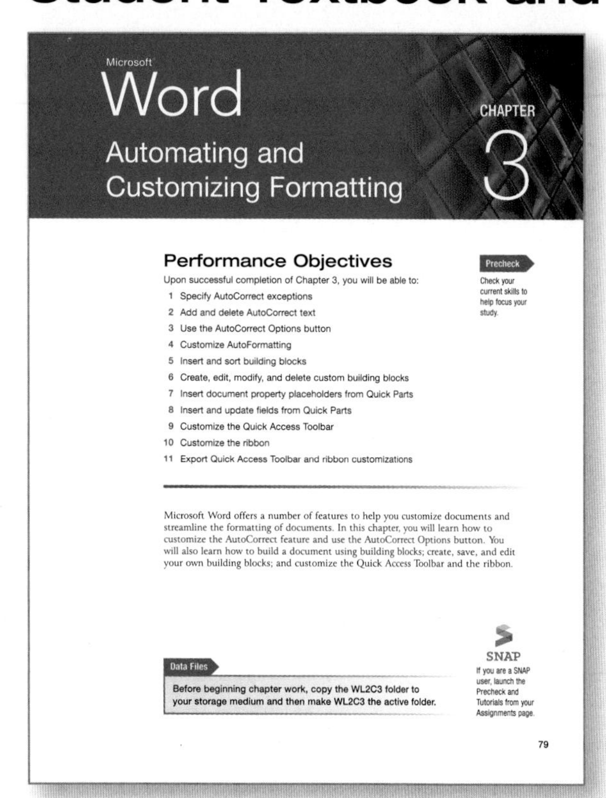

Microsoft
Word
Automating and Customizing Formatting
CHAPTER 3

Performance Objectives

Upon successful completion of Chapter 3, you will be able to:

1. Specify AutoCorrect exceptions
2. Add and delete AutoCorrect text
3. Use the AutoCorrect Options button
4. Customize AutoFormatting
5. Insert and sort building blocks
6. Create, edit, modify, and delete custom building blocks
7. Insert document property placeholders from Quick Parts
8. Insert and update fields from Quick Parts
9. Customize the Quick Access Toolbar
10. Customize the ribbon
11. Export Quick Access Toolbar and ribbon customizations

Precheck
Check your current skills to help focus your study.

Microsoft Word offers a number of features to help you customize documents and streamline the formatting of documents. In this chapter, you will learn how to customize the AutoCorrect feature and use the AutoCorrect Options button. You will also learn how to build a document using building blocks; create, save, and edit your own building blocks; and customize the Quick Access Toolbar and the ribbon.

Data Files
Before beginning chapter work, copy the WL2C3 folder to your storage medium and then make WL2C3 the active folder.

SNAP
If you are a SNAP user, launch the Precheck and Tutorials from your Assignments page.

79

Chapter Openers present the performance objectives and an overview of the skills taught.

Precheck quizzes allow students to check their current skills before starting chapter work.

Data Files are provided for each chapter from the ebook. A prominent note reminds students to copy the appropriate chapter data folder and make it active.

Students with SNAP access are reminded to launch the Precheck quiz and chapter tutorials from their SNAP Assignments page.

Projects Build Skill Mastery within Realistic Context

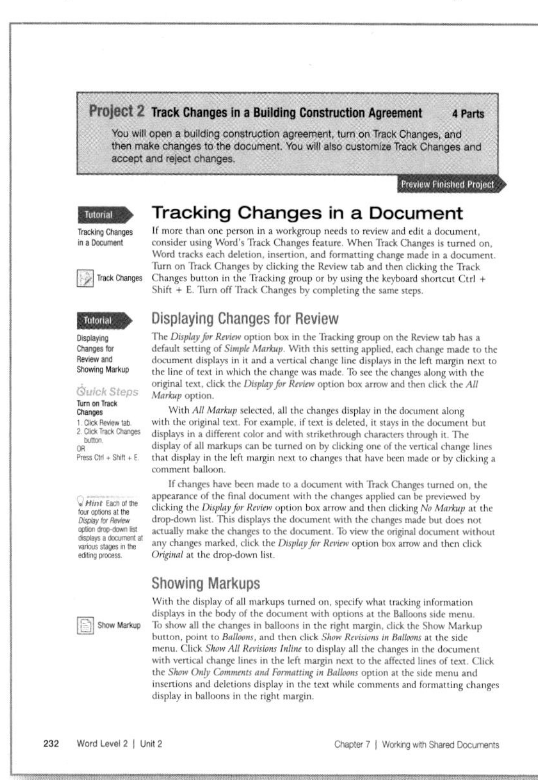

Project 2 Track Changes in a Building Construction Agreement 4 Parts

You will open a building construction agreement, turn on Track Changes, and then make changes to the document. You will also customize Track Changes and accept and reject changes.

Preview Finished Project

Tutorial
Tracking Changes in a Document

Track Changes

Tracking Changes in a Document

If more than one person in a workgroup needs to review and edit a document, consider using Word's Track Changes feature. When Track Changes is turned on, Word tracks each deletion, insertion, and formatting change made in a document. Turn on Track Changes by clicking the Review tab and then clicking the Track Changes button in the Tracking group or by using the keyboard shortcut Ctrl + Shift + E. Turn off Track Changes by completing the same steps.

Tutorial
Displaying Changes for Review and Showing Markup

Quick Steps
Turn on Track Changes
1. Click Review tab.
2. Click Track Changes button.
OR
Press Ctrl + Shift + E.

Displaying Changes for Review

The *Display for Review* option box in the Tracking group on the Review tab has a default setting of *Simple Markup*. With this setting applied, each change made to the document displays in it and a vertical change line displays in the left margin next to the line of text in which the change was made. To see the changes along with the original text, click the *Display for Review* option box arrow and then click the *All Markup* option.

With *All Markup* selected, all the changes display in the document along with the original text. For example, if text is deleted, it stays in the document but displays in a different color and with strikethrough characters through it. The display of all markups can be turned on by clicking one of the vertical change lines that display in the left margin next to changes that have been made or by clicking a comment balloon.

Hint Each of the four options at the *Display for Review* option drop-down list displays a document at various stages in the editing process.

If changes have been made to a document with Track Changes turned on, the appearance of the final document with the changes applied can be previewed by clicking the *Display for Review* option box arrow and then clicking *No Markup* at the drop-down list. This displays the document with the changes made but does not actually make the changes to the document. To view the original document without any changes marked, click the *Display for Review* option box arrow and then click *Original* at the drop-down list.

Show Markup

Showing Markups

With the display of all markups turned on, specify what tracking information displays in the body of the document with options at the Balloons side menu. To show all the changes in balloons in the right margin, click the Show Markup button, point to *Balloons*, and then click *Show Revisions in Balloons* at the side menu. Click *Show All Revisions Inline* to display all the changes in the document with vertical change lines in the left margin next to the affected lines of text. Click the *Show Only Comments and Formatting in Balloons* option at the side menu and insertions and deletions display in the text while comments and formatting changes display in balloons in the right margin.

232 Word Level 2 | Unit 2 Chapter 7 | Working with Shared Documents

Multipart Projects provide a framework for instruction and practice on software features. A project overview identifies tasks to accomplish and key features to use in completing the work.

Preview Finished Project shows how the file will look after students complete the project.

Tutorials provide interactive, guided training and measured practice.

Quick Steps provide feature summaries for reference and review.

Hint margin notes offer useful tips on how to use features efficiently and effectively.

Typically, a file remains open throughout all parts of the project. Students save their work incrementally. At the end of the project, students save and then close the file.

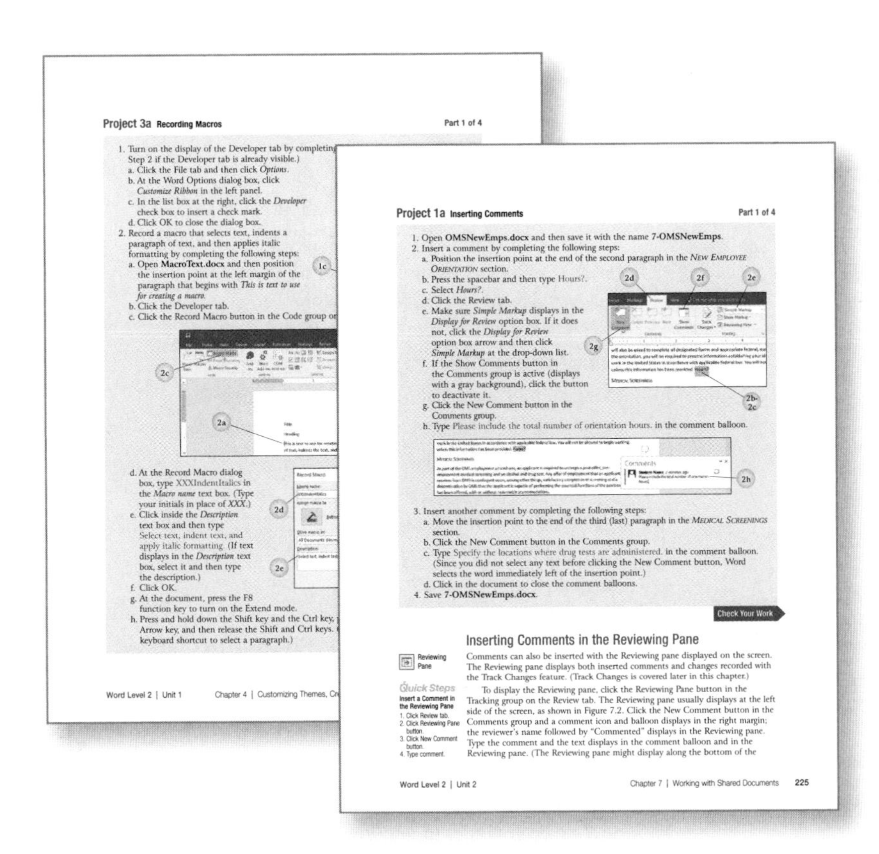

Step-by-Step Instructions guide students to the desired outcome for each project part. Screen captures illustrate what the screen should look like at key points.

Magenta Text identifies material to type.

Check Your Work allows students to confirm they have completed the project activity correctly.

Between project parts, the text presents instruction on the features and skills necessary to accomplish the next section of the project.

Chapter Review Tools Reinforce Learning

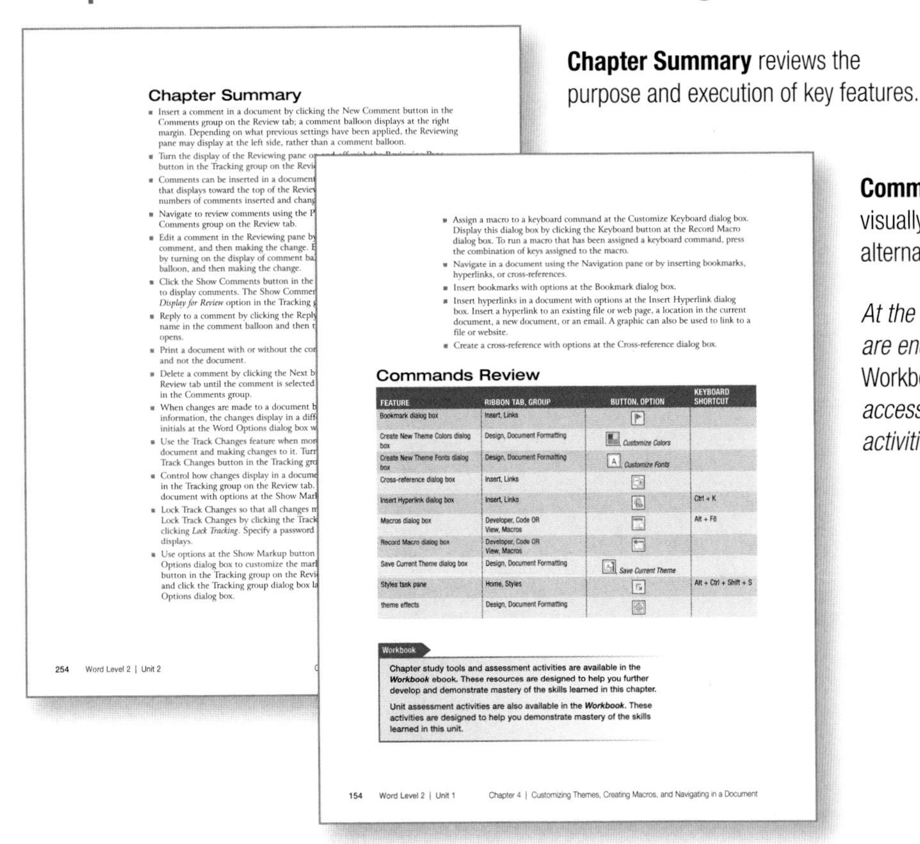

Chapter Summary
Commands Review
Workbook
Chapter study tools and assessment activities are available in the Workbook ebook. These resources are designed to help you further develop and demonstrate mastery of the skills learned in this chapter.
Unit assessment activities are also available in the Workbook. These activities are designed to help you demonstrate mastery of the skills learned in this unit.
154 Word Level 2 | Unit 1 Chapter 4 | Customizing Themes, Creating Macros, and Navigating in a Document
254 Word Level 2 | Unit 2

Chapter Summary reviews the purpose and execution of key features.

Commands Review summarizes visually the major features and alternative methods of access.

At the end of each chapter, students are encouraged to go to the Workbook *pages of the ebook to access study tools and assessment activities.*

Workbook eBook Activities Provide a Hierarchy of Learning Assessments

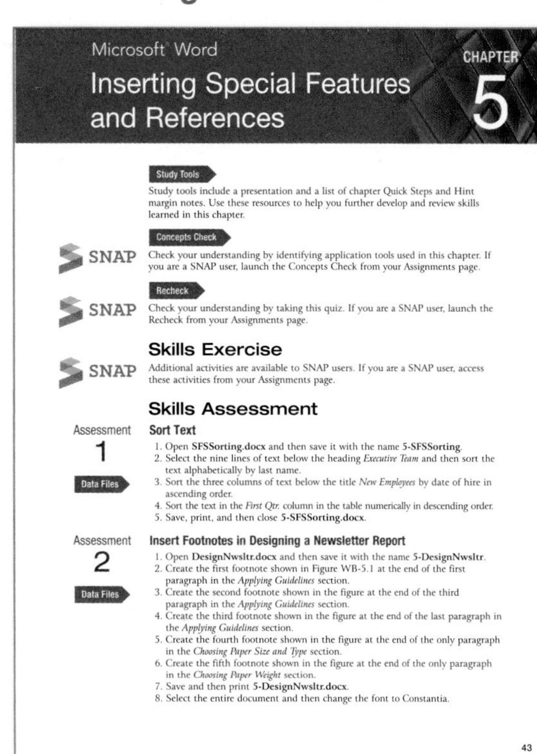

Microsoft Word
Inserting Special Features and References
CHAPTER 5

Study Tools
Study tools include a presentation and a list of chapter Quick Steps and Hint margin notes. Use these resources to help you further develop and review skills learned in this chapter.

Concepts Check
SNAP Check your understanding by identifying application tools used in this chapter. If you are a SNAP user, launch the Concepts Check from your Assignments page.

Recheck
SNAP Check your understanding by taking this quiz. If you are a SNAP user, launch the Recheck from your Assignments page.

Skills Exercise
SNAP Additional activities are available to SNAP users. If you are a SNAP user, access these activities from your Assignments page.

Skills Assessment

Assessment 1 — Data Files
Sort Text
1. Open **SFSSorting.docx** and then save it with the name **5-SFSSorting**.
2. Select the nine lines of text below the heading *Executive Team* and then sort the text alphabetically by last name.
3. Sort the three columns of text below the title *New Employees* by date of hire in ascending order.
4. Sort the text in the *First Qtr.* column in the table numerically in descending order.
5. Save, print, and then close **5-SFSSorting.docx**.

Assessment 2 — Data Files
Insert Footnotes in Designing a Newsletter Report
1. Open **DesignNwsltr.docx** and then save it with the name **5-DesignNwsltr**.
2. Create the first footnote shown in Figure WB-5.1 at the end of the first paragraph in the *Applying Guidelines* section.
3. Create the second footnote shown in the figure at the end of the third paragraph in the *Applying Guidelines* section.
4. Create the third footnote shown in the figure at the end of the last paragraph in the *Applying Guidelines* section.
5. Create the fourth footnote shown in the figure at the end of the only paragraph in the *Choosing Paper Size and Type* section.
6. Create the fifth footnote shown in the figure at the end of the only paragraph in the *Choosing Paper Weight* section.
7. Save and then print **5-DesignNwsltr.docx**.
8. Select the entire document and then change the font to Constantia.

43

Study Tools are presentations with audio support and a list of chapter Quick Steps and Hint margin notes designed to help students further develop and review skills learned in the chapter.

Concepts Check is an objective completion exercise that allows students to assess their comprehension and recall of application features, terminology, and functions.

Recheck concept quizzes for each chapter enable students to check how their skills have improved after completing chapter work.

Skills Exercises are available to SNAP 2016 users. SNAP will automatically score student work, which is performed live in the application, and provide detailed feedback.

Skills Assessment exercises ask students to develop both standard and customized types of word processing documents without how-to directions.

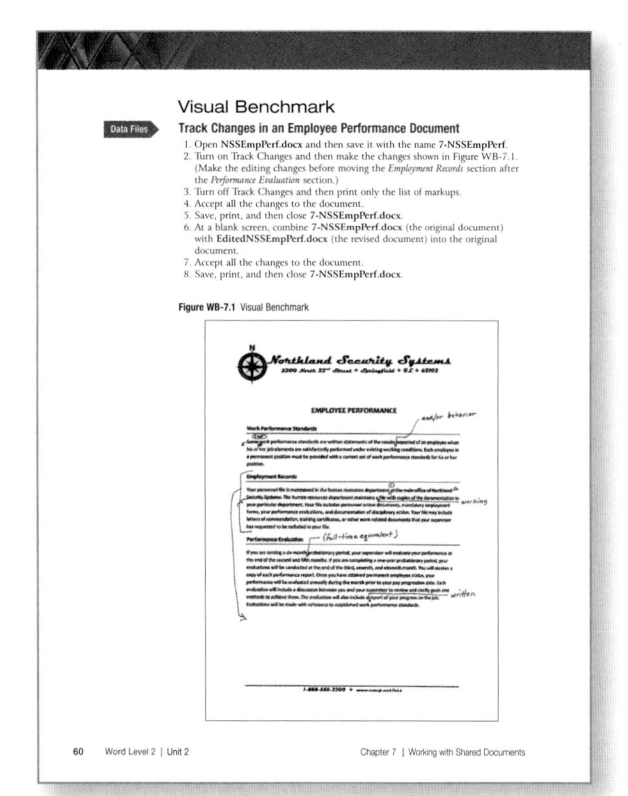

Visual Benchmark
Data Files
Track Changes in an Employee Performance Document
1. Open **NSSEmpPerf.docx** and then save it with the name **7-NSSEmpPerf**.
2. Turn on Track Changes and then make the changes shown in Figure WB-7.1. (Make the editing changes before moving the *Employment Records* section after the *Performance Evaluation* section.)
3. Turn off Track Changes and then print only the list of markups.
4. Accept all the changes to the document.
5. Save, print, and then close **7-NSSEmpPerf.docx**.
6. At a blank screen, combine **7-NSSEmpPerf.docx** (the original document) with **EditedNSSEmpPerf.docx** (the revised document) into the original document.
7. Accept all the changes to the document.
8. Save, print, and then close **7-NSSEmpPerf.docx**.

Figure WB-7.1 Visual Benchmark

60 Word Level 2 | Unit 2 — Chapter 7 | Working with Shared Documents

Visual Benchmark assessments test problem-solving skills and mastery of application features.

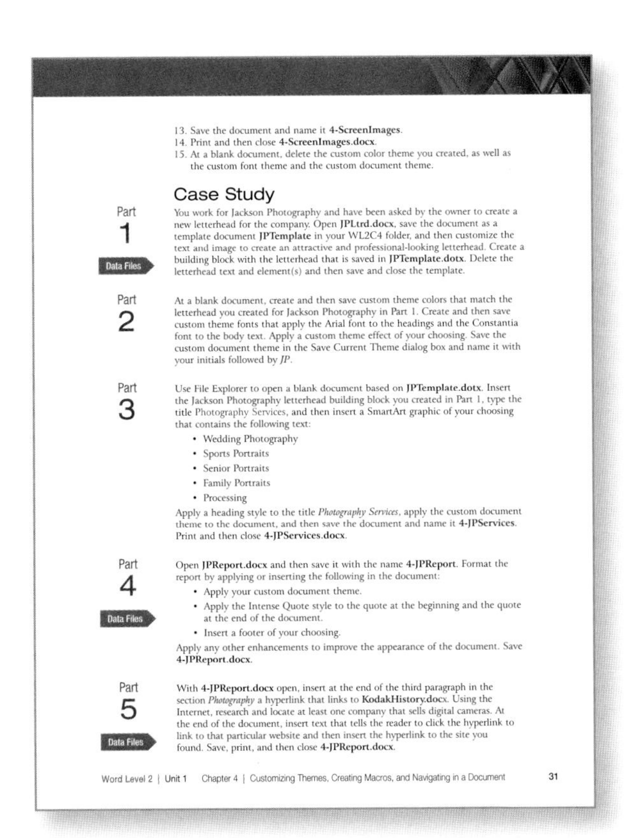

13. Save the document and name it **4-ScreenImages**.
14. Print and then close **4-ScreenImages.docx**.
15. At a blank document, delete the custom color theme you created, as well as the custom font theme and the custom document theme.

Case Study

Part 1 — Data Files

You work for Jackson Photography and have been asked by the owner to create a new letterhead for the company. Open **JPLtrd.docx**, save the document as a template document **JPTemplate** in your WL2C4 folder, and then customize the text and image to create an attractive and professional-looking letterhead. Create a building block with the letterhead that is saved in **JPTemplate.dotx**. Delete the letterhead text and element(s) and then save and close the template.

Part 2

At a blank document, create and then save custom theme colors that match the letterhead you created for Jackson Photography in Part 1. Create and then save custom theme fonts that apply the Arial font to the headings and the Constantia font to the body text. Apply a custom theme effect of your choosing. Save the custom document theme in the Save Current Theme dialog box and name it with your initials followed by *JP*.

Part 3

Use File Explorer to open a blank document based on **JPTemplate.dotx**. Insert the Jackson Photography letterhead building block you created in Part 1, type the title Photography Services, and then insert a SmartArt graphic of your choosing that contains the following text:

- Wedding Photography
- Sports Portraits
- Senior Portraits
- Family Portraits
- Processing

Apply a heading style to the title *Photography Services*, apply the custom document theme to the document, and then save the document and name it **4-JPServices**. Print and then close **4-JPServices.docx**.

Part 4 — Data Files

Open **JPReport.docx** and then save it with the name **4-JPReport**. Format the report by applying or inserting the following in the document:

- Apply your custom document theme.
- Apply the Intense Quote style to the quote at the beginning and the quote at the end of the document.
- Insert a footer of your choosing.

Apply any other enhancements to improve the appearance of the document. Save **4-JPReport.docx**.

Part 5 — Data Files

With **4-JPReport.docx** open, insert at the end of the third paragraph in the section *Photography* a hyperlink that links to **KodakHistory.docx**. Using the Internet, research and locate at least one company that sells digital cameras. At the end of the document, insert text that tells the reader to click the hyperlink to link to that particular website and then insert the hyperlink to the site you found. Save, print, and then close **4-JPReport.docx**.

Word Level 2 | Unit 1 Chapter 4 | Customizing Themes, Creating Macros, and Navigating in a Document 31

Case Study requires analyzing a workplace scenario and then planning and executing a multipart project.

Students search the web and/or use the program's Help feature to locate additional information required to complete the Case Study.

Unit Performance Assessments Deliver Cross-Disciplinary, Comprehensive Evaluation

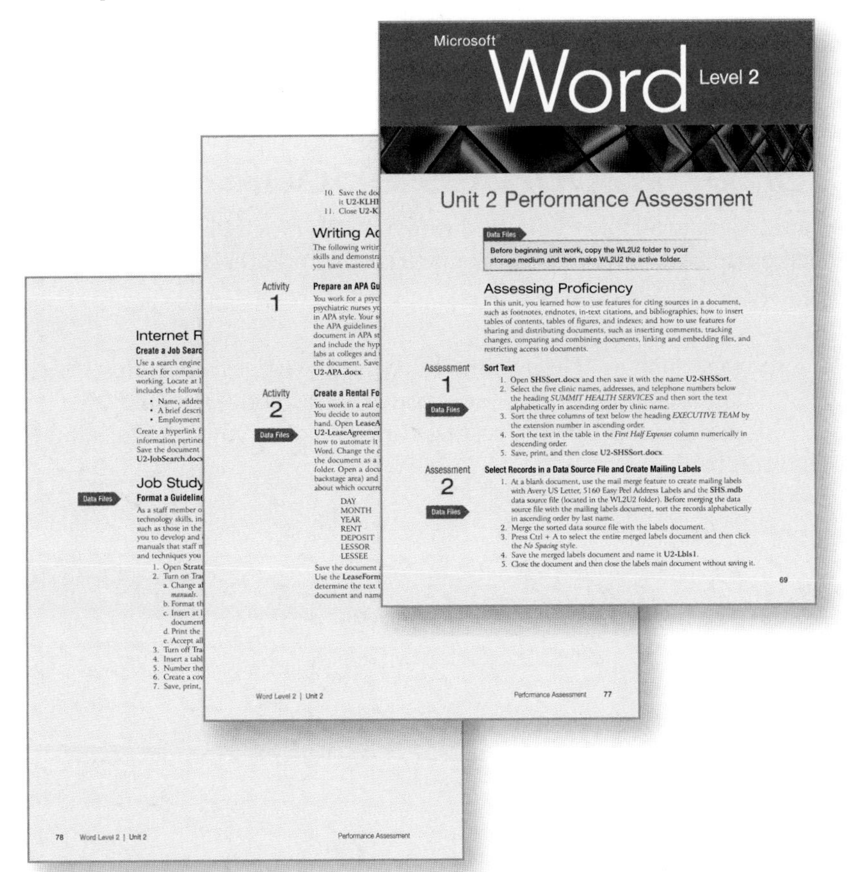

Microsoft Word Level 2

Unit 2 Performance Assessment

Data Files

Before beginning unit work, copy the WL2U2 folder to your storage medium and then make WL2U2 the active folder.

Assessing Proficiency

In this unit, you learned how to use features for citing sources in a document, such as footnotes, endnotes, in-text citations, and bibliographies; how to insert tables of contents, tables of figures, and indexes; and how to use features for sharing and distributing documents, such as inserting comments, tracking changes, comparing and combining documents, linking and embedding files, and restricting access to documents.

Assessment 1 — Data Files

Sort Text

1. Open **SHSSort.docx** and then save it with the name **U2-SHSSort**.
2. Select the five clinic names, addresses, and telephone numbers below the heading *SUMMIT HEALTH SERVICES* and then sort the text alphabetically in ascending order by clinic name.
3. Sort the three columns of text below the heading *EXECUTIVE TEAM* by the extension number in ascending order.
4. Sort the text in the table in the *First Half Expenses* column numerically in descending order.
5. Save, print, and then close **U2-SHSSort.docx**.

Assessment 2 — Data Files

Select Records in a Data Source File and Create Mailing Labels

1. At a blank document, use the mail merge feature to create mailing labels with Avery US Letter, 5160 Easy Peel Address Labels and the **SHS.mdb** data source file (located in the WL2U2 folder). Before merging the data source file with the mailing labels document, sort the records alphabetically in ascending order by last name.
2. Merge the sorted data source file with the labels document.
3. Press Ctrl + A to select the entire merged labels document and then click the *No Spacing* style.
4. Save the merged labels document and name it **U2-Lbls1**.
5. Close the document and then close the labels main document without saving it.

69

Assessing Proficiency exercises check mastery of features.

Writing Activities involve applying application skills in a communication context.

Internet Research projects reinforce research and information processing skills.

Job Study at the end of Unit 2 presents a capstone assessment requiring critical thinking and problem solving.

SNAP Training and Assessment

SNAP is a web-based training and assessment program and learning management system (LMS) for learning Microsoft Office 2016. SNAP is comprised of rich content, a sophisticated grade book, and robust scheduling and analytics tools. SNAP courseware supports the *Benchmark Series* content and delivers live-in-the-application assessments for students to demonstrate their skills mastery. Interactive tutorials increase skills-focused moments with guided training and measured practice. SNAP provides automatic scoring and detailed feedback on the many activities, exercises, and quizzes to help identify areas where additional support is needed, evaluating student performance both at an individual and course level. The *Benchmark Series* SNAP course content is also available to export into any LMS system that supports LTI tools.

Paradigm Education Solutions provides technical support for SNAP through 24-7 chat at ParadigmCollege.com. In addition, an online User Guide and other SNAP training tools for using SNAP are available.

Student eBook

The student ebook, available through SNAP or online at Paradigm.bookshelf.emcp.com, provides access to the *Benchmark Series* content from any device (desktop, tablet, and smartphone) anywhere, through a live Internet connection. The versatile ebook platform features dynamic navigation tools including a linked table of contents and the ability to jump to specific pages, search for terms, bookmark, highlight, and take notes. The ebook offers live links to the interactive content and resources that support the print textbook, including the student data files, Precheck and Recheck quizzes, and interactive tutorials. The *Workbook* pages of the ebook provide access to presentations with audio support and to end-of-chapter Concept Check, Skills Assessment, Visual Benchmark, Case Study, and end-of-unit Performance Assessment activities.

Instructor eResources eBook

All instructor resources are available digitally through a web-based ebook at Paradigm.bookshelf.emcp.com. The instructor materials include these items:

- Planning resources, such as lesson plans, teaching hints, and sample course syllabi
- Presentation resources, such as PowerPoint slide shows with lecture notes
- Assessment resources, including live and annotated PDF model answers for chapter work and workbook activities, rubrics for evaluating student work, and chapter-based exam banks

SNAP
Personalized. Powerful. Proven.
Welcome to a better way to teach Microsoft® Office.
SNAP 2016's Microsoft Office training and assessments give students real-world experience by working directly in the application. You have a suite of powerful tools at your fingertips, granting you instant access to performance metrics and reporting tools so you can focus on teaching.
Work live in Microsoft applications
One integrated system
Automatic grading
Instant performance insights
SNAP
Call 800-535-6865 or visit snap2016.com to schedule a demo.

Microsoft®

Word Level 2

Unit 1

Formatting and Customizing Documents

Microsoft®

Word

CHAPTER 1

Customizing Paragraphs and Pages

Performance Objectives

Upon successful completion of Chapter 1, you will be able to:

1 Apply custom numbering and bulleting formatting to text
2 Define and insert custom bullets
3 Define and insert multilevel list numbering
4 Insert, format, and customize images and text boxes
5 Group and ungroup objects
6 Edit points and wrap points in a shape
7 Link and unlink text boxes
8 Insert headers and footers in documents
9 Format, edit, and remove headers and footers
10 Insert and print sections
11 Control widows/orphans and keep text together on a page

Precheck

Check your current skills to help focus your study.

Word contains a variety of options for formatting text in paragraphs and applying page formatting. In this chapter, you will learn how to insert custom numbers and bullets, define new numbering formats, define picture and symbol bullets, apply multilevel numbering to text, and define a new multilevel list. You will also learn about customizing objects, inserting and editing headers and footers, printing specific sections of a document, and controlling text flow on pages.

Data Files

Before beginning chapter work, copy the WL2C1 folder to your storage medium and then make WL2C1 the active folder.

SNAP

If you are a SNAP user, launch the Precheck and Tutorials from your Assignments page.

Project 1 **Apply Number Formatting to an Agenda** **2 Parts**

You will open an agenda document, apply formatting that includes number formatting, and then define and apply custom numbering.

Preview Finished Project

Inserting Custom Numbers and Bullets

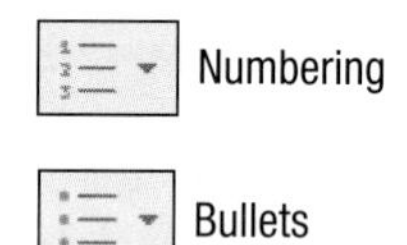

Number paragraphs or insert bullets before paragraphs using buttons in the Paragraph group on the Home tab. Use the Numbering button to insert numbers before specific paragraphs and use the Bullets button to insert bullets. To insert custom numbering or bullets, click the button arrow and then choose from the drop-down gallery that displays.

Inserting Custom Numbers

Insert numbers as text is typed or select text and then apply a numbering format. Type *1.* and then press the spacebar and Word indents the number approximately 0.25 inch. Type text after the number and then press the Enter key and Word indents all the lines in the paragraph 0.5 inch from the left margin (called a *hanging indent*). At the beginning of the next paragraph, Word inserts the number 2 followed by a period 0.25 inch from the left margin. Continue typing items and Word numbers successive paragraphs in the list. To number existing paragraphs of text, select the paragraphs and then click the Numbering button in the Paragraph group on the Home tab.

Click the Numbering button in the Paragraph group and arabic numbers (1., 2., 3., etc.) are inserted in the document. This default numbering can be changed by clicking the Numbering button arrow and then clicking an option at the Numbering drop-down gallery.

Hint If the automatic numbering or bulleting feature is on, press Shift + Enter to insert a line break without inserting a number or bullet.

To change list levels, click the Numbering button arrow, point to the *Change List Level* option at the bottom of the drop-down gallery, and then click a list level at the side menu. Set the numbering value with options at the Set Numbering Value dialog box, shown in Figure 1.1. Display this dialog box by clicking the Numbering button arrow and then clicking the *Set Numbering Value* option at the bottom of the drop-down gallery.

Figure 1.1 Set Numbering Value Dialog Box

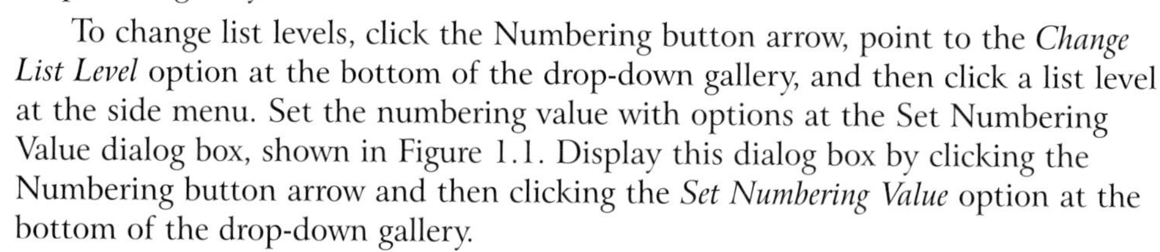

Project 1a Inserting Custom Numbers

Part 1 of 2

1. Open **FDAgenda.docx** and then save it with the name **1-FDAgenda**.
2. Restart the list numbering at 1 by completing the following steps:
   a. Select the numbered paragraphs.
   b. Click the Numbering button arrow in the Paragraph group on the Home tab and then click *Set Numbering Value* at the drop-down gallery.
   c. At the Set Numbering Value dialog box, select the number in the *Set value to* measurement box, type 1, and then press the Enter key.

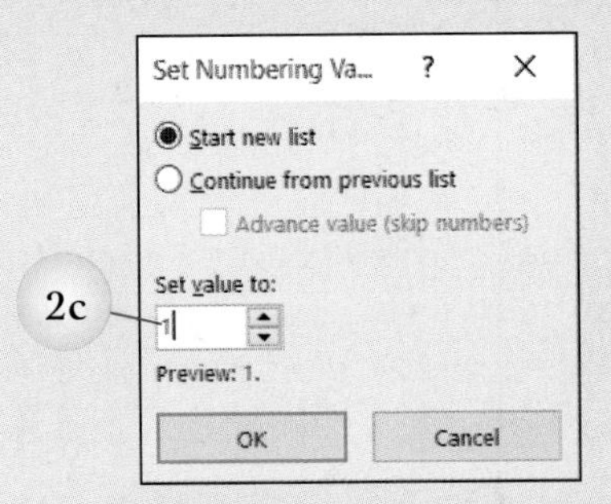

3. Change the paragraph numbers to letters by completing the following steps:
   a. With the numbered paragraphs selected, click the Numbering button arrow.
   b. At the Numbering drop-down gallery, click the option that uses capital letters (second column, second row in the *Numbering Library* section [this location may vary]).

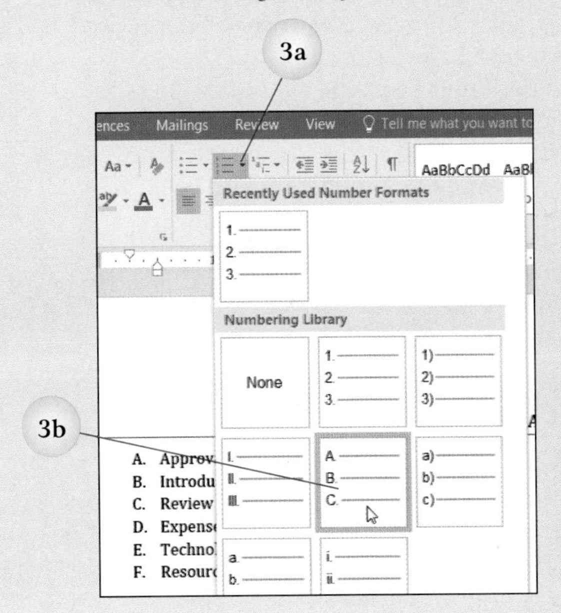

4. Add text by positioning the insertion point immediately right of the text *Introductions*, pressing the Enter key, and then typing Organizational Overview.

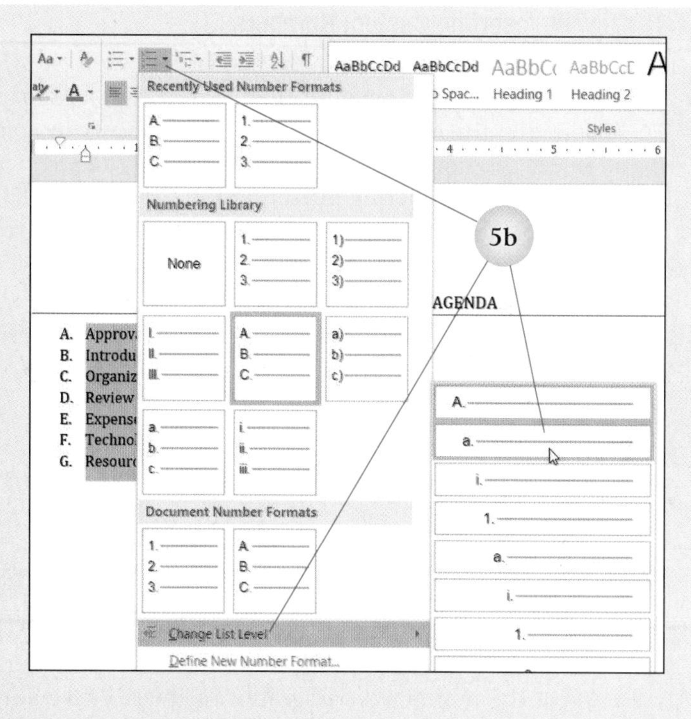

5. Demote the lettered list by completing the following steps:
   a. Select the lettered paragraphs.
   b. Click the Numbering button arrow, point to the *Change List Level* option, and then click the *a.* option at the side menu (*Level 2*).
6. With the paragraphs still selected, promote the list by clicking the Decrease Indent button in the Paragraph group on the Home tab. (The lowercase letters change back to capital letters.)
7. Move the insertion point to the end of the document and then type The meeting will stop for lunch, which is catered and will be held in the main conference center from 12:15 to 1:30 p.m.
8. Press the Enter key and then click the Numbering button.
9. Click the AutoCorrect Options button next to the *A.* inserted in the document and then click *Continue Numbering* at the drop-down list. (This changes the letter from *A.* to *H.*)

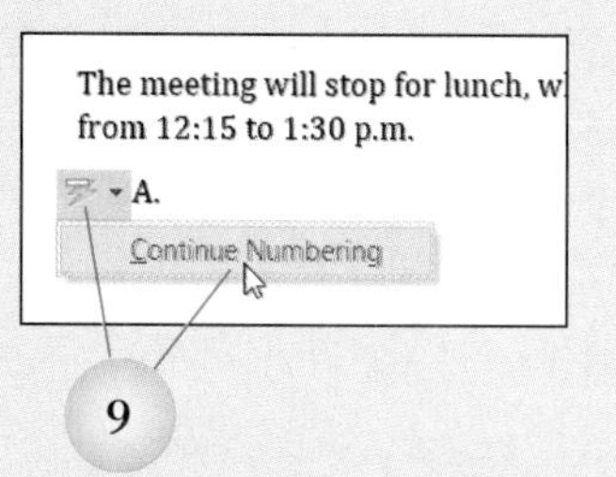

10. Type Future Goals, press the Enter key, type Proposals, press the Enter key, and then type Adjournment.
11. Press the Enter key and *K.* is inserted in the document. Turn off the list formatting by clicking the Numbering button arrow and then clicking the *None* option at the drop-down gallery.

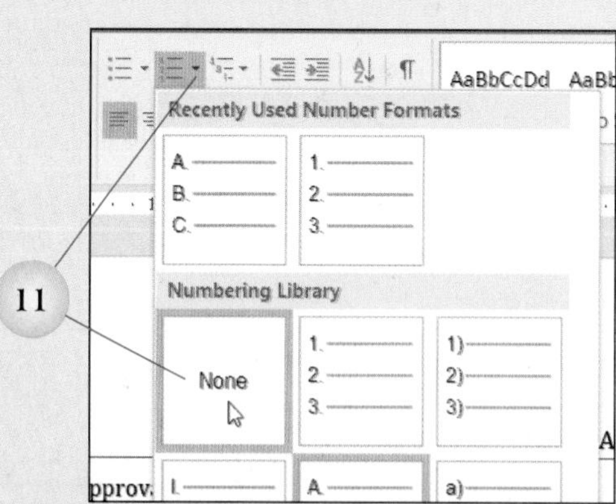

12. Save and then print **1-FDAgenda.docx**.
13. Select and then delete the paragraph of text in the middle of the list (the paragraph that begins *The meeting will stop*). (All the lettered items should be listed consecutively and the same amount of space should appear between them.)
14. Save **1-FDAgenda.docx**.

Check Your Work

Tutorial

Creating Custom Numbering

Quick Steps

Define New Number Format

1. Click Numbering button arrow.
2. Click *Define New Number Format.*
3. Specify format.
4. Click OK.

Creating Custom Numbering

Along with default and custom numbers, custom numbering formats can be created with options at the Define New Number Format dialog box, shown in Figure 1.2. Display this dialog box by clicking the Numbering button arrow and then clicking *Define New Number Format* at the drop-down gallery. Use options at the dialog box to specify the number style, font, and alignment. Preview the formatting in the *Preview* section.

Any number format created at the Define New Number Format dialog box is automatically included in the *Numbering Library* section of the Numbering button drop-down list. Remove a number format from the drop-down list by right-clicking the format and then clicking *Remove* at the shortcut menu.

Figure 1.2 Define New Number Format Dialog Box

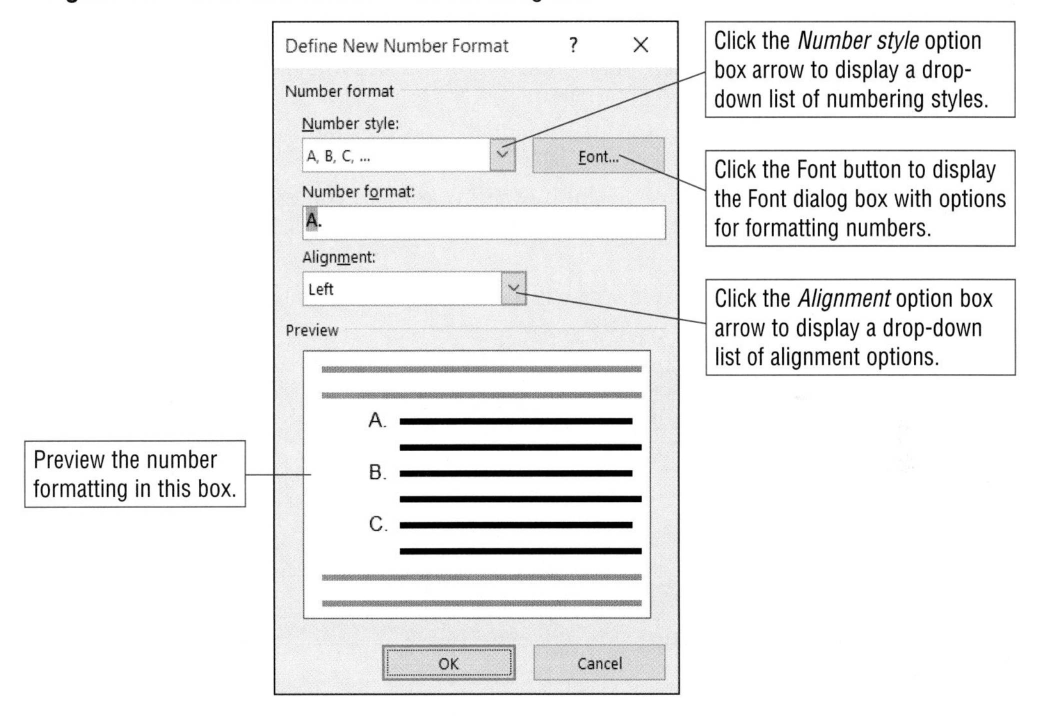

Project 1b Defining a Numbering Format

Part 2 of 2

1. With **1-FDAgenda.docx** open, define a new numbering format by completing the following steps:
   a. With the insertion point positioned anywhere in the numbered paragraphs, click the Numbering button arrow in the Paragraph group on the Home tab.
   b. Click *Define New Number Format* at the drop-down list.
   c. At the Define New Number Format dialog box, click the *Number style* option box arrow and then click the *I, II, III, ...* option.
   d. Click the Font button at the right side of the *Number style* list box.

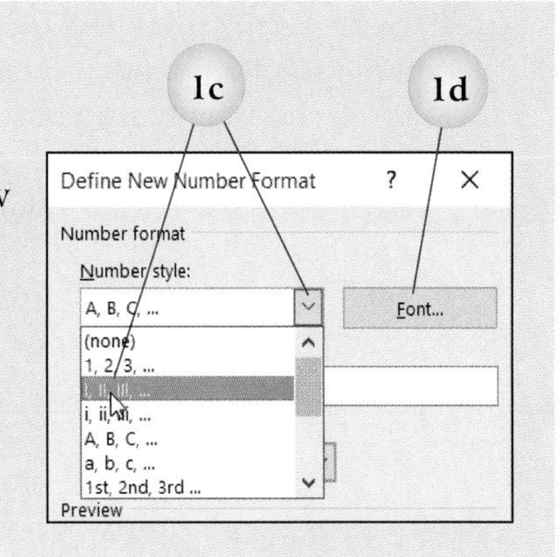

e. At the Font dialog box, scroll down the *Font* list box and then click *Calibri*.
f. Click *Bold* in the *Font style* list box.

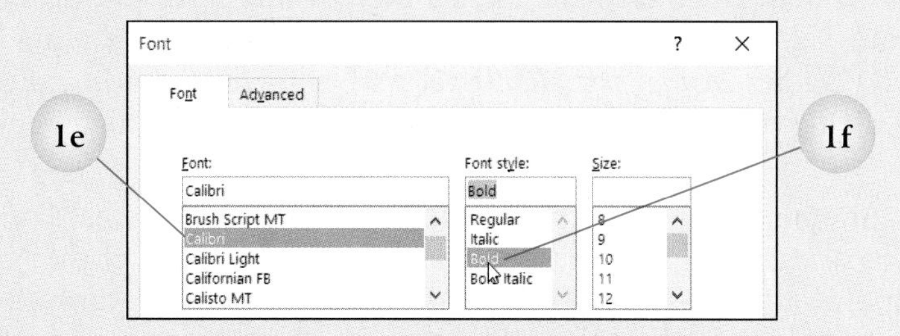

g. Click OK to close the Font dialog box.
h. Click the *Alignment* option box arrow and then click *Right* at the drop-down list.
i. Click OK to close the Define New Number Format dialog box. (This applies the new formatting to the numbered paragraphs in the document.)

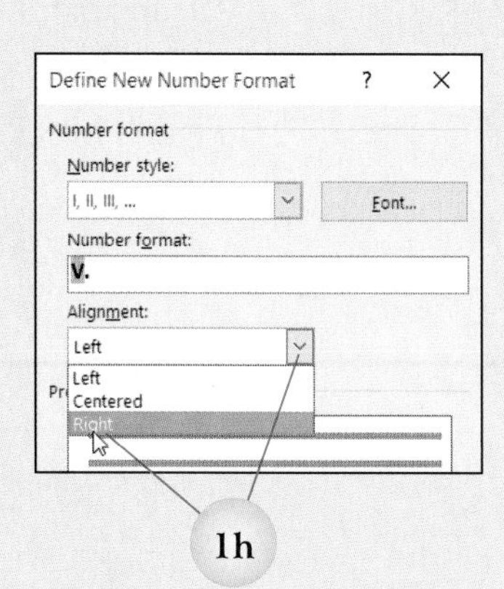

2. Insert a file into the current document by completing the following steps:
   a. Press Ctrl + End to move the insertion point to the end of the document and then press the Enter key two times.
   b. Click the Insert tab.
   c. Click the Object button arrow in the Text group and then click *Text from File* at the drop-down list.

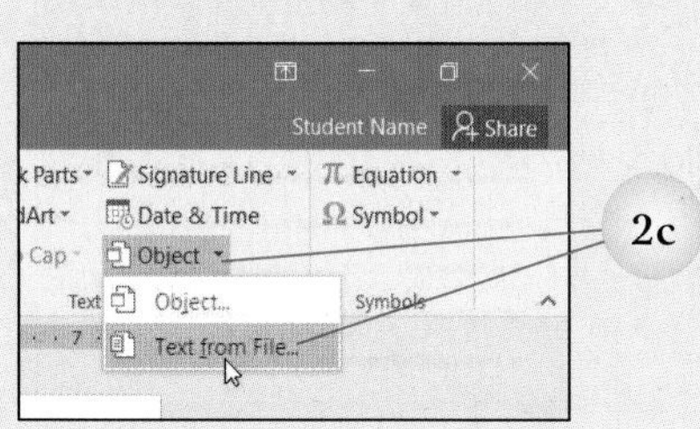

   d. At the Insert File dialog box, navigate to the WL2C1 folder and then double-click ***PDAgenda.docx***.
3. Select the text below the title *PRODUCTION DEPARTMENT AGENDA*, click the Home tab, click the Numbering button arrow, and then click the roman numeral style created in Step 1.
4. Remove from the Numbering Library the numbering format you created by completing the following steps:
   a. Click the Numbering button arrow.
   b. In the *Numbering Library* section, right-click the roman numeral numbering format that you created.
   c. Click *Remove* at the shortcut menu.
5. Save, print, and then close **1-FDAgenda.docx**.

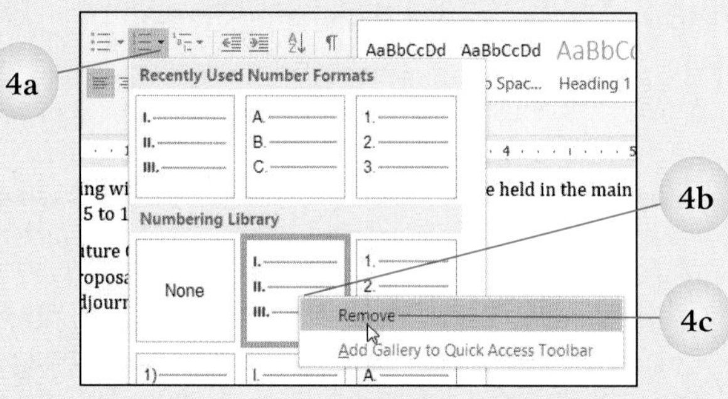

Check Your Work

Project 2 Apply Custom Bullets to a Travel Document

1 Part

You will open a travel document and then define and insert custom picture and symbol bullets.

Preview Finished Project

Tutorial

Creating Custom Bullets

Quick Steps

Define a Custom Bullet

1. Click Bullets button arrow.
2. Click *Define New Bullet* at drop-down gallery.
3. Click Symbol button or Picture button.
4. Click symbol or picture.
5. Click OK.
6. Click OK.

Hint Create a picture bullet to add visual interest to a document.

Creating Custom Bullets

Click the Bullets button in the Paragraph group and a round bullet is inserted in the document. Insert custom bullets by clicking the Bullets button arrow and then clicking a bullet type at the drop-down gallery. This drop-down gallery displays the most recently used bullets along with an option for defining a new bullet.

Click the *Define New Bullet* option and the Define New Bullet dialog box displays, as shown in Figure 1.3. Use options at the dialog box to choose a symbol or picture bullet, change the font size of the bullet, and specify the alignment of the bullet. When creating a custom bullet, consider matching the theme or mood of the document to maintain a consistent look or creating a picture bullet to add visual interest.

A bullet created at the Define New Bullet dialog box is automatically included in the *Bullet Library* section of the Bullets button drop-down gallery. Remove a custom bullet from the drop-down gallery by right-clicking the bullet and then clicking *Remove* at the shortcut menu.

As with the level of a numbered list, the level of a bulleted list can be changed. To do this, click the item or select the items to be changed, click the Bullets button arrow, and then point to *Change List Level*. At the side menu of bullet options that displays, click a bullet. To insert a line break in the list while the automatic bullets feature is on without inserting a bullet, press Shift + Enter. (A line break can also be inserted in a numbered list without inserting a number by pressing Shift + Enter.)

Figure 1.3 Define New Bullet Dialog Box

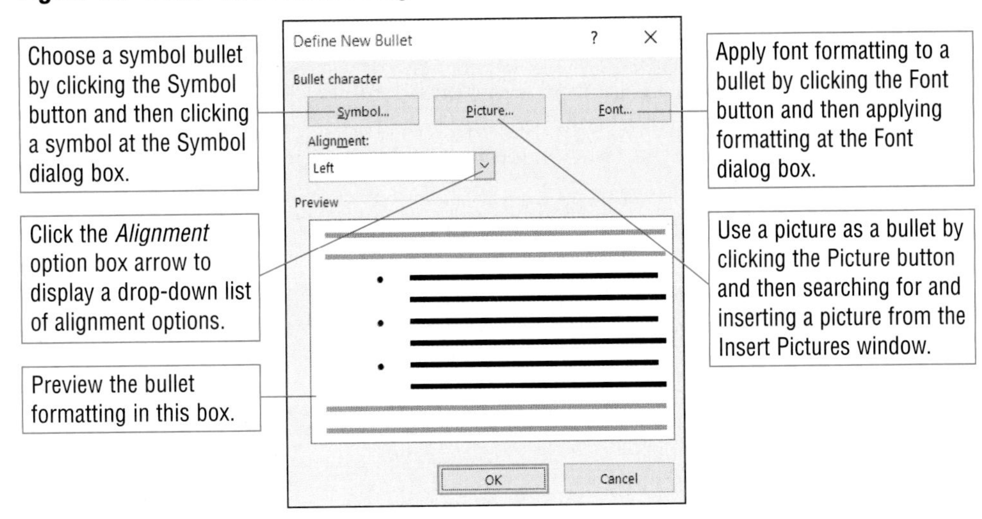

Choose a symbol bullet by clicking the Symbol button and then clicking a symbol at the Symbol dialog box.
Click the *Alignment* option box arrow to display a drop-down list of alignment options.
Preview the bullet formatting in this box.
Define New Bullet
Bullet character
Symbol...
Picture...
Font...
Alignment:
Left
Preview
OK
Cancel
Apply font formatting to a bullet by clicking the Font button and then applying formatting at the Font dialog box.
Use a picture as a bullet by clicking the Picture button and then searching for and inserting a picture from the Insert Pictures window.

Project 2 Defining and Inserting Custom Bullets

Part 1 of 1

1. Open **TTSHawaii.docx** and then save it with the name **1-TTSHawaii.**
2. Define and insert a picture bullet by completing the following steps:
   a. Select the four paragraphs of text below the heading *Rainy Day Activities*.
   b. Click the Bullets button arrow in the Paragraph group on the Home tab and then click *Define New Bullet* at the drop-down gallery.
   c. At the Define New Bullet dialog box, click the Picture button.
   d. At the Insert Picture dialog box, click the *Browse* option, navigate to the WL2C1 folder on your storage medium, and then double-click the ***Flower.png*** file.
   e. Click OK to close the Define New Bullet dialog box. (The new bullet is applied to the selected paragraphs.)

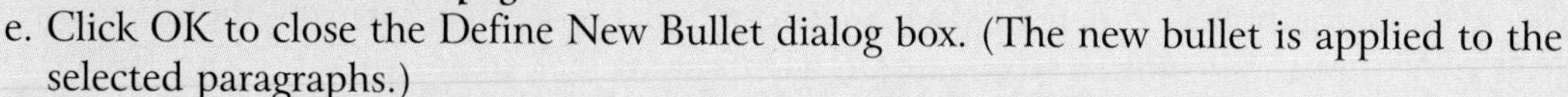

3. Define and insert a symbol bullet by completing the following steps:

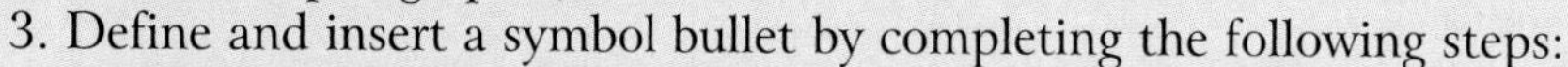

   a. Select the six paragraphs below the heading *Kauai Sights*.
   b. Click the Bullets button arrow and then click *Define New Bullet* at the drop-down gallery.
   c. At the Define New Bullet dialog box, click the Symbol button.
   d. At the Symbol dialog box, click the *Font* option box arrow, scroll down the drop-down list, and then click *Wingdings*.
   e. Click the flower symbol shown at the right.

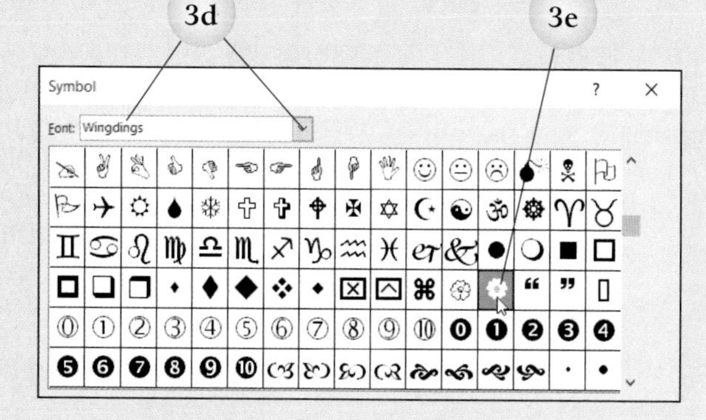

   f. Click OK to close the Symbol dialog box.
   g. At the Define New Bullet dialog box, click the Font button.
   h. At the Font dialog box, click *11* in the *Size* list box.
   i. Click the *Font color* option box arrow and then click the *Light Blue, Background 2, Darker 25%* color option (third column, third row in the *Theme Colors* section).
   j. Click OK to close the Font dialog box and then click OK to close the Define New Bullet dialog box.
4. Remove the two bullets you defined from the *Bullet Library* section by completing the following steps:
   a. Click the Bullets button arrow.
   b. Right-click the flower picture bullet in the *Bullet Library* section and then click *Remove* at the shortcut menu.
   c. Click the Bullets button arrow.
   d. Right-click the flower symbol bullet in the *Bullet Library* section and then click *Remove* at the shortcut menu.
5. Save, print, and then close **1-TTSHawaii.docx**.

Check Your Work

Project 3 Apply Multilevel List Numbering to a Job Search Document

2 Parts

You will open a document containing a list of job search terms, apply multilevel list numbering to the text, and then define and apply a new multilevel list numbering style.

Preview Finished Project

Tutorial

Applying Multilevel List Numbering

Quick Steps

Insert Multilevel List Numbering

1. Click Multilevel List button.
2. Click style at drop-down gallery.

Applying Multilevel List Numbering

Use the Multilevel List button in the Paragraph group on the Home tab to specify the type of numbering for paragraphs of text at the left margin, first tab, second tab, and so on. To apply predesigned multilevel numbering to text in a document, click the Multilevel List button and then click a numbering style at the drop-down gallery.

Some options at the Multilevel List button drop-down gallery display with *Heading 1*, *Heading 2*, and so on after the numbers. Click one of these options and Word inserts the numbering and applies the heading styles to the text.

Project 3a Inserting Multilevel List Numbering

Part 1 of 2

1. Open **JSList.docx** and then save it with the name **1-JSList(3a)**.
2. Select the paragraphs of text below the title and then apply multilevel list numbering by completing the following steps:
   a. Click the Multilevel List button in the Paragraph group on the Home tab.
   b. At the drop-down gallery, click the middle option in the top row of the *List Library* section.

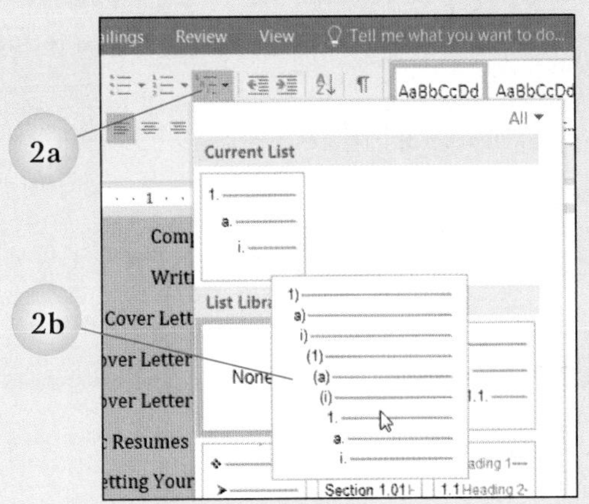

   c. Deselect the text.
3. Save, print, and then close **1-JSList(3a).docx**.

Check Your Work

Tutorial

Creating a Custom Multilevel List Option

Quick Steps

Define a Multilevel List

1. Click Multilevel List button.
2. Click *Define New Multilevel List.*
3. Choose level, number format, and/or position.
4. Click OK.

Hint When defining a multilevel list style, you can mix numbers and bullets in the same list.

Creating a Custom Multilevel List

The Multilevel List button drop-down gallery contains predesigned level numbering options. If the gallery does not contain the type of numbering required, custom numbering can be created. To do this, click the Multilevel List button and then click *Define New Multilevel List*. This displays the Define new Multilevel list dialog box, shown in Figure 1.4. At this dialog box, click a level in the *Click level to modify* list box and then specify the number format, style, position, and alignment.

Typing a Multilevel List

Select text and then apply a multilevel list or apply the list and then type the text. When typing the text, press the Tab key to move to the next level or press Shift + Tab to move to the previous level.

Figure 1.4 Define New Multilevel List Dialog Box

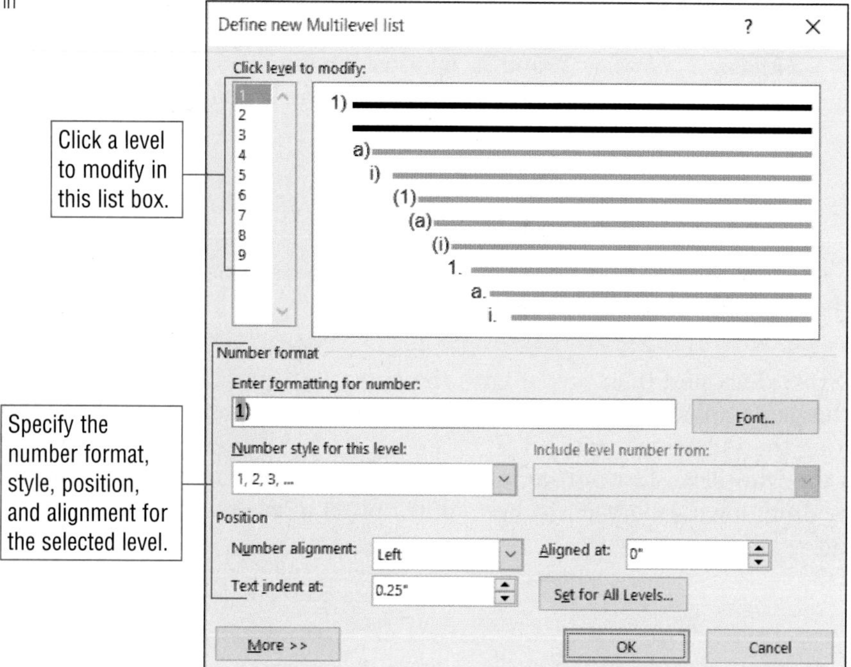

Project 3b Defining and Applying a New Multilevel List

1. Open **JSList.docx** and then save it with the name **1-JSList(3b)**.
2. Select the paragraphs of text below the title.
3. Click the Multilevel List button in the Paragraph group on the Home tab.
4. Click the *Define New Multilevel List* option at the drop-down gallery.
5. At the Define new Multilevel list dialog box, make sure *1* is selected in the *Click level to modify* list box.
6. Click the *Number style for this level* option box arrow and then click *A, B, C, ...* at the drop-down list.
7. Click in the *Enter formatting for number* text box, delete any text that displays after *A*, and then type a period (.). (The entry in the text box should now display as *A.*)
8. Click the *Aligned at* measurement box up arrow until *0.3"* displays in the measurement box.
9. Click the *Text indent at* measurement box up arrow until *0.6"* displays in the measurement box.
10. Click *2* in the *Click level to modify* list box.
11. Click the *Number style for this level* option box arrow and then click *1, 2, 3, ...* at the drop-down list.
12. Click in the *Enter formatting for number* text box, delete any text that displays after the *1*, and then type a period (.).
13. Click the *Aligned at* measurement box up arrow until *0.6"* displays in the measurement box.
14. Click the *Text indent at* measurement box up arrow until *0.9"* displays in the measurement box.

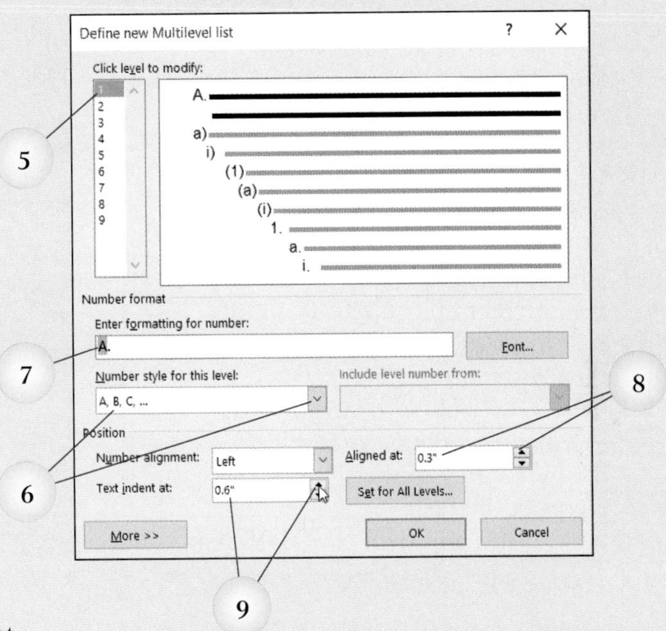

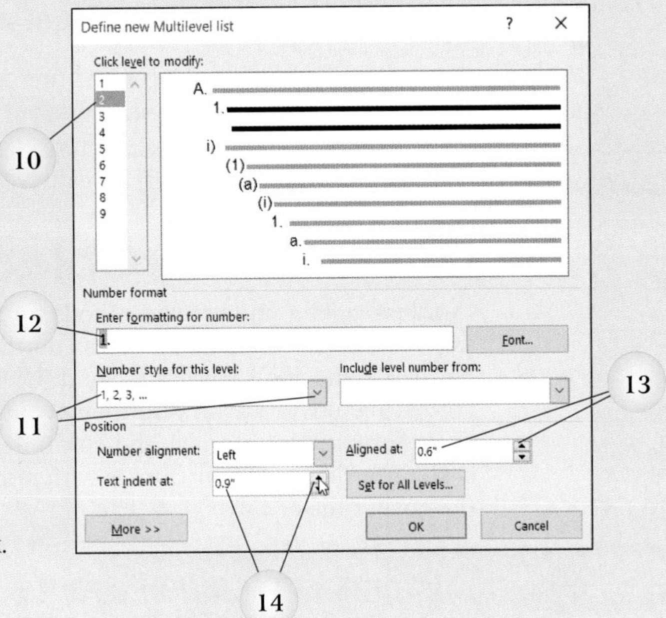

15. Click *3* in the *Click level to modify* list box.
16. Click the *Number style for this level* option box arrow and then click *a, b, c, …* at the drop-down list.
17. Make sure that *a)* displays in the *Enter formatting for number* text box. (If not, delete any text that displays after the *a* and then type a right parenthesis.)
18. Click the *Aligned at* measurement box up arrow until *0.9"* displays in the measurement box.
19. Click the *Text indent at* measurement box up arrow until *1.2"* displays in the measurement box.
20. Click OK to close the dialog box. (This applies the new multilevel list numbering to the selected text.)
21. Deselect the text.
22. Save, print, and then close **1-JSList(3b).docx**.

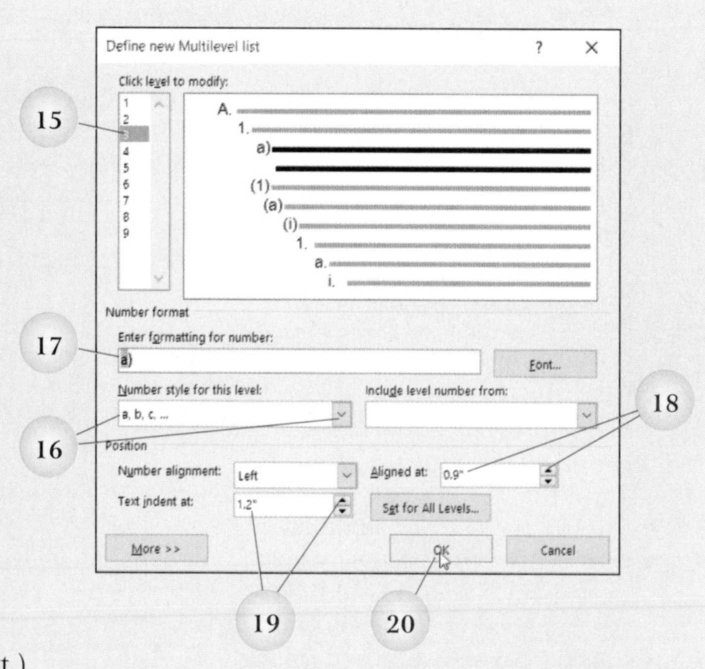

Check Your Work

Project 4 Insert Images and a Text Box in a Travel Document — 3 Parts

You will open a travel document on Maui, insert and customize a clip art image and photograph, and then insert and customize a text box.

Preview Finished Project

Customizing Objects

Word provides a number of methods for formatting and customizing objects, such as pictures, clip art images, shapes and text boxes. Format images with buttons on the Picture Tools Format tab and further customize images with options at the Format Picture task pane and the Layout dialog box. Use buttons on the Drawing Tools Format tab to format and customize shapes and text boxes and further customize shapes and text boxes with options at the Format Shape task pane and the Layout dialog box.

Customizing Image Layout

Tutorial

Formatting an Image at the Layout Dialog Box

Customize the layout of images with options at the Layout dialog box. Display the Layout dialog box by clicking the Size group dialog box launcher on the Picture Tools Format tab. The Layout dialog box contains three tabs. Click the Position tab and the dialog box displays as shown in Figure 1.5.

Figure 1.5 Layout Dialog Box with Position Tab Selected

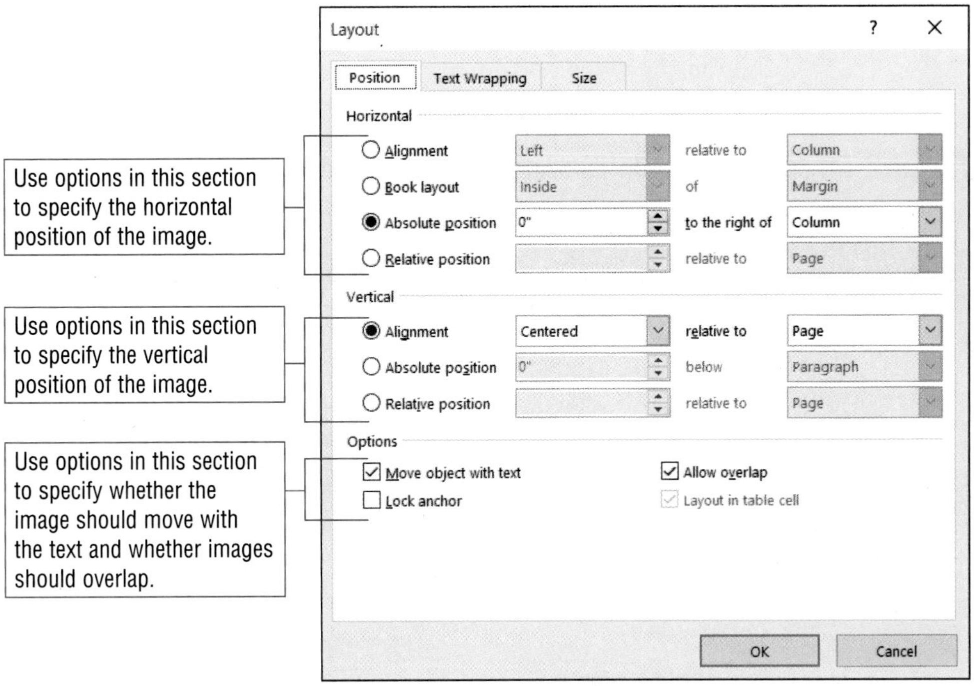

Use options in this section to specify the horizontal position of the image.

Use options in this section to specify the vertical position of the image.

Use options in this section to specify whether the image should move with the text and whether images should overlap.

Layout

Position | Text Wrapping | Size

Horizontal

Alignment: Left, relative to: Column

Book layout: Inside, of: Margin

Absolute position: 0", to the right of: Column

Relative position, relative to: Page

Vertical

Alignment: Centered, relative to: Page

Absolute position: 0", below: Paragraph

Relative position, relative to: Page

Options

Move object with text

Allow overlap

Lock anchor

Layout in table cell

OK | Cancel

Use options at the Layout dialog box with the Position tab selected to specify horizontal and vertical layout options. In the *Horizontal* section, choose the *Alignment* option to specify left, center, or right alignment relative to the margin, page, column, or character. Choose the *Book layout* option to align the image with the inside or outside margin of the page. Use the *Absolute position* option to align the image horizontally with the specified amount of space between the left edge of the image and the left edge of the page, column, left margin, or character. In the *Vertical* section of the dialog box, use the *Alignment* option to align the image at the top, bottom, center, inside, or outside relative to the page, margin, or line. In the *Options* section, attach (anchor) the image to a paragraph so that the image and paragraph move together. Choose the *Move object with text* option to move the image up or down on the page with the paragraph it is anchored to. Keep the image anchored in the same place on the page by choosing the *Lock anchor* option. Choose the *Allow overlap* option to overlap images with the same wrapping style.

Use options at the Layout dialog box with the Text Wrapping tab selected to specify the wrapping style for the image. Specify which sides of the image the text is to wrap around and the amounts of space between the text and the top, bottom, left, and right edges of the image.

Click the Size tab at the Layout dialog box to display options for specifying the height and width of the image relative to the margin, page, top margin, bottom margin, inside margin, or outside margin. Use the *Rotation* measurement box to rotate the image by degrees and use options in the *Scale* section to change the percentage of the height and width scales. By default, the *Lock aspect ratio* check box contains a check mark, which means that if a change is made to the height measurement of an image, the width measurement is automatically changed to maintain the proportional relationship between the height and width. Change the width measurement and the height measurement is automatically changed.

To change the height measurement of an image without changing the width or to change the width measurement without changing the height, remove the check mark from the *Lock aspect ratio* check box. To reset the image size, click the Reset button in the lower right corner of the dialog box.

Project 4a Inserting and Customizing the Layout of an Image

Part 1 of 3

1. Open **TTSMaui.docx** and then save it with the name **1-TTSMaui**.
2. Insert an image by completing the following steps:
   a. Click the Insert tab and then click the Pictures button in the Illustrations group.
   b. At the Insert Picture dialog box, navigate to the WL2C1 folder on your storage medium and then double-click ***HawaiiBanner.png***.
3. Select the current measurement in the *Shape Height* measurement box in the Size group on the Picture Tools Format tab, type 2, and then press the Enter key.

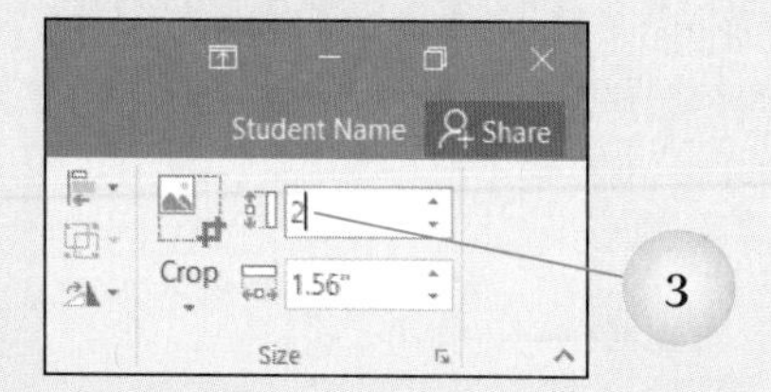

4. Click the *Beveled Matte, White* style in the Picture Styles group (second style from the left).

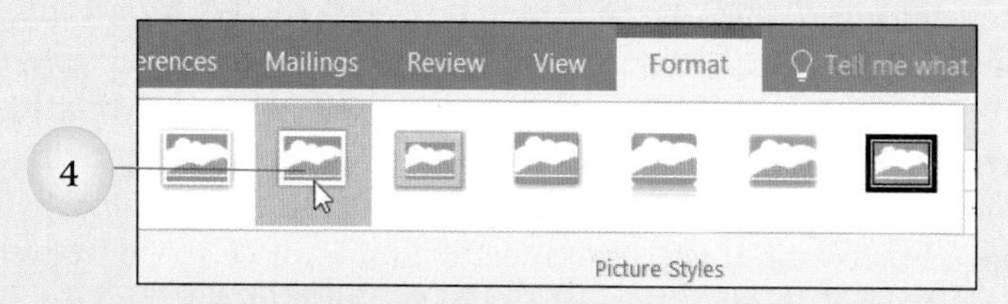

5. Click the Corrections button in the Adjust group and then click the *Brightness: −20% Contrast: +20%* option (second column, fourth row in the *Brightness/Contrast* section).
6. After looking at the image, you decide to reset it. Do this by clicking the Reset Picture button arrow in the Adjust group and then clicking *Reset Picture & Size* at the drop-down list.

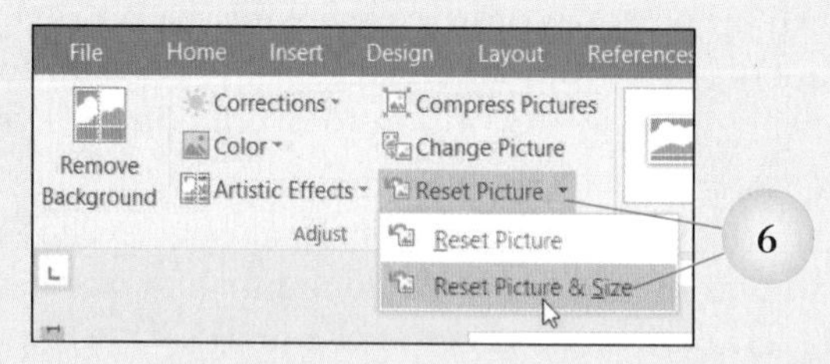

7. Select the current measurement in the *Shape Height* measurement box, type 1.3, and then press the Enter key.
8. Click the Wrap Text button in the Arrange group and then click *In Front of Text* at the drop-down gallery.

9. Position the image precisely on the page by completing the following steps:
   a. With the image selected, click the Size group dialog box launcher.
   b. At the Layout dialog box, click the Position tab.
   c. Make sure the *Absolute position* option in the *Horizontal* section is selected.
   d. Press the Tab key two times and then type 6.2 in the *Absolute position* measurement box.
   e. Click the *to the right of* option box arrow and then click *Page* at the drop-down list.
   f. Click the *Absolute position* option in the *Vertical* section.
   g. Select the current measurement in the box to the right of the *Absolute position* option and then type 2.
   h. Click the *below* option box arrow and then click *Page* at the drop-down list.
   i. Click OK to close the Layout dialog box. 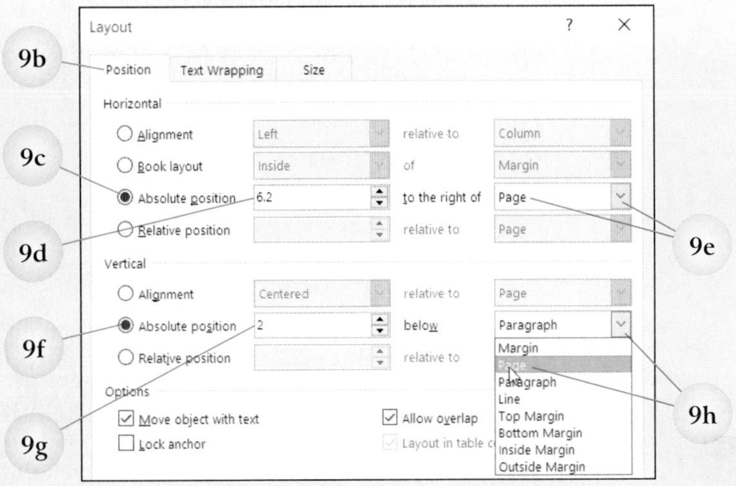
10. Click the *Drop Shadow Rectangle* style in the Picture Styles group (fourth style from the left).
11. Click the Color button in the Adjust group and then click the *Blue, Accent color 1 Light* option (second column, third row in the *Recolor* section).
12. Compress the image by clicking the Compress Pictures button in the Adjust group and then clicking OK at the Compress Pictures dialog box.
13. Click outside the image to deselect it.
14. Save **1-TTSMaui.docx**.

Check Your Work

Tutorial

Formatting an Image at the Format Picture Task Pane

Applying Formatting at the Format Picture Task Pane

Options for formatting an image are available at the Format Picture task pane, shown in Figure 1.6. Display this task pane by clicking the Picture Styles group task pane launcher on the Picture Tools Format tab.

The options in the Format Picture task pane vary depending on the icon selected. The formatting options may need to be expanded within the icons. For example, click *Shadow* in the task pane with the Effects icon selected to display options for applying shadow effects to an image. Many of the options available at the Format Picture task pane are also available on the Picture Tools Format tab. The task pane is a central location for formatting options and also includes some additional advanced formatting options.

Figure 1.6 Format Picture Task Pane

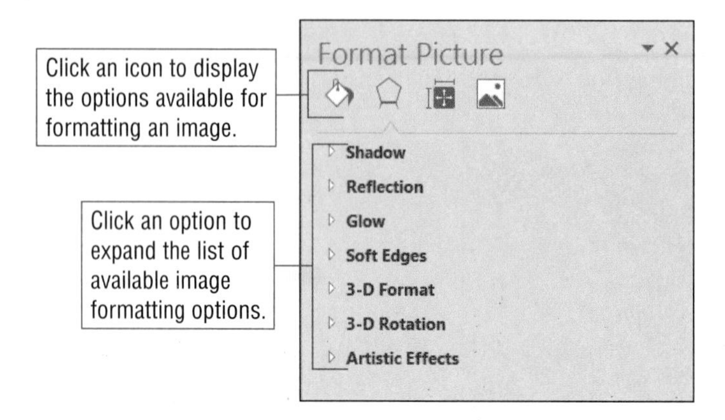

Applying Artistic Effects to Images

Apply an artistic effect to a selected image with the Artistic Effects button in the Adjust group on the Picture Tools Format tab. Click this button and a drop-down gallery displays with effect options. Hover the mouse over an option in the drop-down gallery to see the effect applied to the selected image. An artistic effect can also be applied to an image with options at the Format Picture task pane with the Effects icon selected.

Project 4b Inserting and Customizing a Photograph — Part 2 of 3

1. With **1-TTSMaui.docx** open, press Ctrl + End to move the insertion point to the end of the document and then insert a photograph by completing the following steps:
   a. Click the Insert tab and then click the Pictures button in the Illustrations group.
   b. At the Insert Picture dialog box, navigate to the WL2C1 folder on your storage medium and then double-click ***Surfing.png***.
2. With the surfing photograph selected, click the Picture Effects button in the Picture Styles group, point to *Bevel*, and then click the *Circle* option (first column, first row in the *Bevel* section).
3. Click the Artistic Effects button in the Adjust group and then click the *Cutout* option (first column, bottom row).
4. After looking at the formatting, you decide to remove it from the image by clicking the Reset Picture button in the Adjust group.
5. Select the current measurement in the *Shape Height* measurement box, type 1.4, and then press the Enter key.

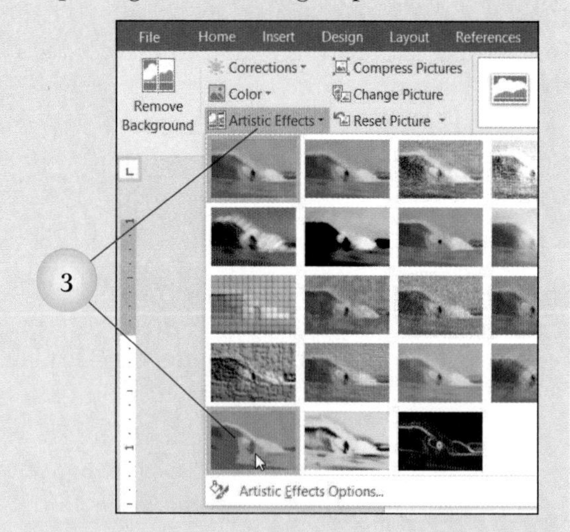

6. Format the photograph by completing the following steps:
   a. Click the Picture Styles group task pane launcher.
   b. At the Format Picture task pane, click *Reflection* to expand the reflection options in the task pane.
   c. Click the Presets button and then click the *Tight Reflection, touching* option (first column, first row in the *Reflection Variations* section).
   d. Click *Artistic Effects* in the task pane to expand the artistic effect options.
   e. Click the Artistic Effects button and then click the *Paint Brush* option (third column, second row).
   f. Close the task pane by clicking the Close button in the upper right corner of the task pane.

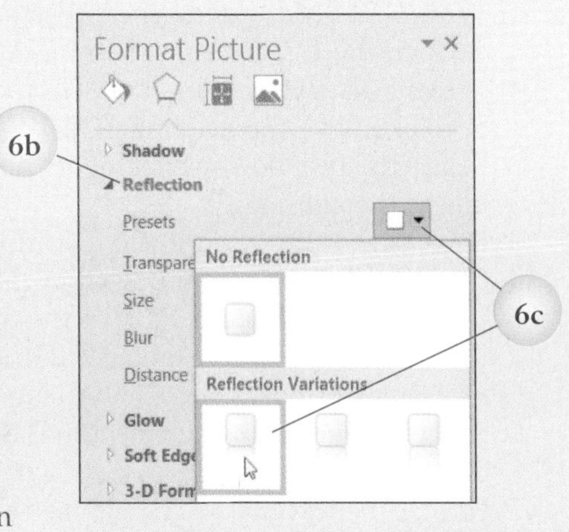

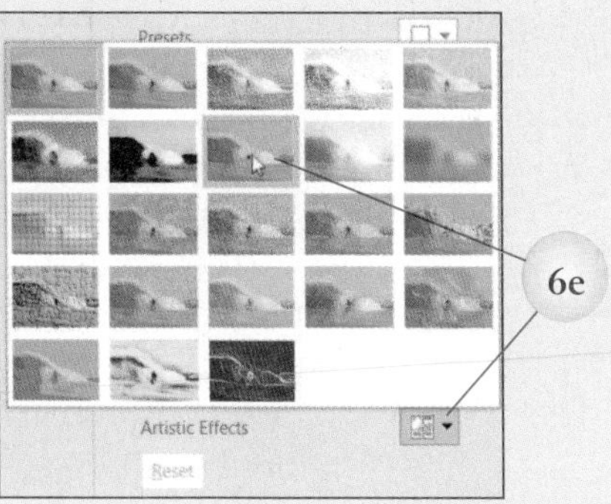

7. Click the Wrap Text button in the Arrange group on the Picture Tools Format tab and then click *Tight* at the drop-down list.
8. Position the photograph precisely on the page by completing the following steps:
   a. With the photograph selected, click the Position button in the Arrange group and then click *More Layout Options* at the bottom of the drop-down gallery.
   b. At the Layout dialog box with the Position tab selected, select the current measurement in the *Absolute position* measurement box in the *Horizontal* section and then type 5.3.
   c. Click the *to the right of* option box arrow and then click *Page* at the drop-down list.
   d. Select the current measurement in the *Absolute position* measurement box in the *Vertical* section and then type 6.6.
   e. Click the *below* option box arrow and then click *Page* at the drop-down list.
   f. Click OK to close the Layout dialog box.
9. Click outside the photograph to deselect it.
10. Save **1-TTSMaui.docx**.

Check Your Work

Customizing and Formatting Objects

When an object such as a text box or shape is inserted in a document, the Drawing Tools Format tab is active. Use options on this tab to format and customize a text box or shape or use options at the Format Shape task pane.

Customizing a Text Box Display the Format Shape task pane by clicking the Shape Styles group task pane launcher. The task pane displays with three icons: Fill & Line, Effects, and Layout & Properties. The Format Shape task pane can also be displa· d by clicking the WordArt Styles group task pane launcher. The Format Shap· sk pane displays with different icons than the Format Shape task pane that dis s when the Shape Styles group task pane launcher is clicked. Click the Wc ·t Styles group task pane launcher and the task pane displays with *Text Opti* ·lected and with three icons: Text Fill & Outline, Text Effects, and Layout · ·perties.

Project 4c Inserting and Customizing a Text Box

Part 3 of 3

1. With **1-TTSMaui.docx** open, insert a text box by completing the following steps:
   a. Click the Insert tab, click the Text Box button in the Text group, and then click the *Draw Text Box* option at the drop-down list.
   b. Click above the heading *MAUI SITES* and then type Hawaii, the Aloha State.
2. Select the text box by clicking its border. (This changes the text box border from a dashed line to a solid line.)
3. Press Ctrl + E to center the text in the text box.
4. Click the Text Direction button in the Text group and then click *Rotate all text 270°* at the drop-down list.
5. Select the current measurement in the *Shape Height* measurement box, type 6, and then press the Enter key.
6. Select the current measurement in the *Shape Width* measurement box, type 0.8, and then press the Enter key.
7. Format the text box by completing the following steps:
   a. Click the Shape Styles group task pane launcher.
   b. At the Format Shape task pane with the Fill & Line icon selected, click *Fill* to expand the options.
   c. Click the Fill Color button (displays to the right of the *Color* option) and then click the *Blue, Accent 1, Lighter 80%* option (fifth column, second row).
   d. Click the Effects icon and then click *Shadow* to expand the options.
   e. Click the Presets button and then click the *Offset Bottom* option (second column, first row in the *Outer* section).
   f. Scroll down the task pane and then click *Glow* to display the glow options.
   g. Click the Presets button in the *Glow* section and then click the *Blue, 5 pt glow, Accent color 1* option (first column, first row in the *Glow Variations* section).

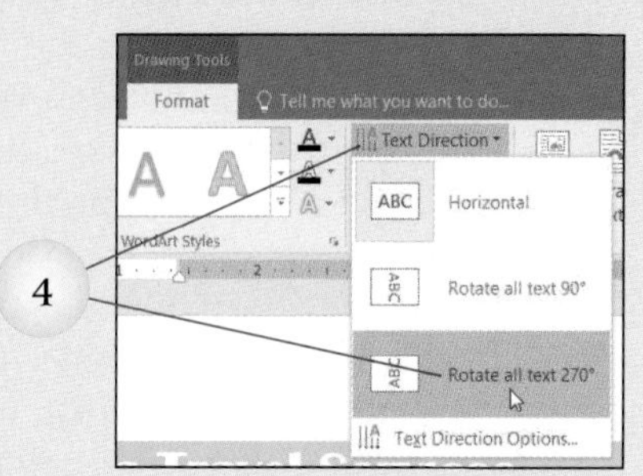

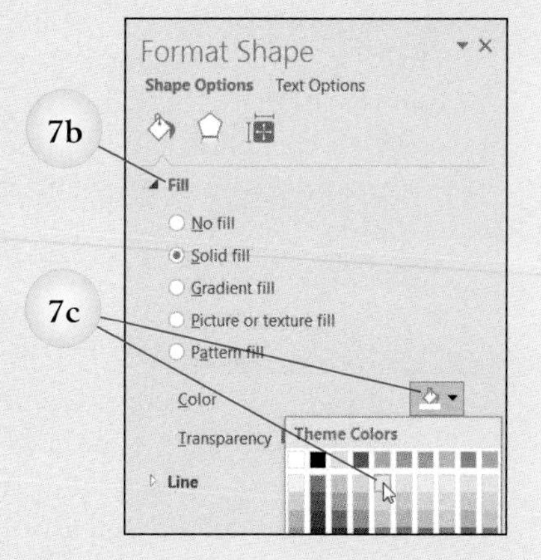

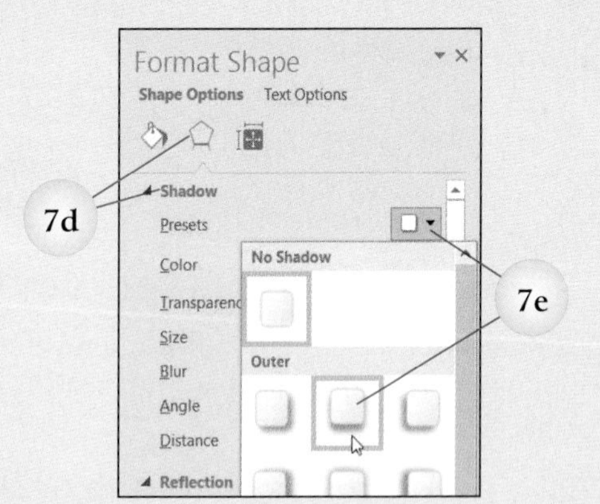

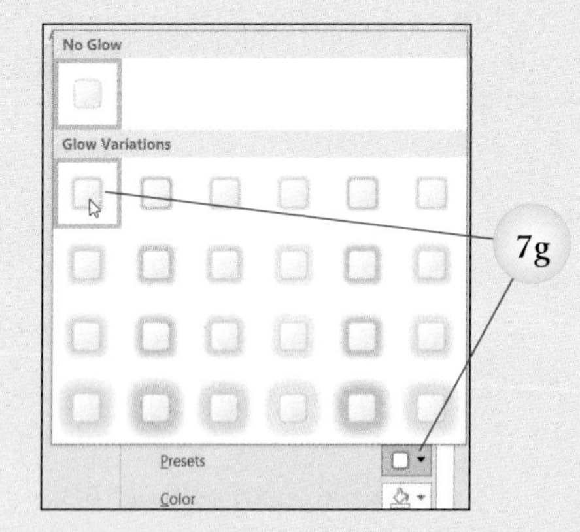

   h. Close the Format Shape task pane by clicking the Close button in the upper right corner of the task pane.
8. Click the More WordArt Styles button in the WordArt Styles group and then click the *Fill - Blue, Accent 5, Outline - Background 1, Hard Shadow - Accent 5* option (third column, third row).

9. Position the text box precisely on the page by completing the following steps:
   a. With the text box selected, click the Size group dialog box launcher.
   b. At the Layout dialog box, click the Position tab.
   c. Select the current measurement in the *Absolute position* measurement box in the *Horizontal* section and then type 1.
   d. Click the *to the right of* option box arrow and then click *Page* at the drop-down list.
   e. Select the current measurement in the *Absolute position* measurement box in the *Vertical* section and then type 2.7.
   f. Click the *below* option box arrow and then click *Page* at the drop-down list.
   g. Click OK to close the Layout dialog box.
10. Click the Home tab, click the *Font Size* option arrow, and then click *36* at the drop-down gallery.
11. Click outside the text box to deselect it.
12. Save **1-TTSMaui.docx**.

Check Your Work

Project 5 Customize Shapes and an Image in a Financial Document and Link and Unlink Text Boxes

4 Parts

You will open a financial document, format, group, customize, ungroup, and edit points of a shape. You will also edit wrap points around an image and link and unlink text boxes.

Preview Finished Project

Customizing Shapes Like a text box, a shape can be customized with buttons and options on the Drawing Tools Format tab or with options at the Format Shape task pane. Customize or format one shape or select multiple shapes and then customize and apply formatting to all of the selected shapes. Display the Format Shape task pane for a shape by clicking the Shape Styles group task pane launcher. When a shape is selected, the WordArt Styles group task pane launcher is dimmed and unavailable.

Tutorial

Grouping and Ungrouping Objects

Quick Steps

Group Objects

1. Select objects.
2. Click Picture Tools Format tab (or Drawing Tools Format tab).
3. Click Group button.
4. Click *Group*.

Hint Group multiple objects to work with them as if they are a single object.

Grouping and Ungrouping Objects Objects in a document such as an image, text box, or shape can be grouped so that the objects in the group can be sized, moved, or formatted as one object. To group objects, select the objects, click the Picture Tools Format tab (or Drawing Tools Format tab), click the Group button in the Arrange group, and then click *Group* at the drop-down list. With the objects grouped, move, size, or apply formatting to all of the objects in the group at once.

To select objects, click the first object, press and hold down the Shift key, click each remaining object to be included in the group, and then release the Shift key. Another method for grouping objects is to click the Select button in the Editing group on the Home tab, click the *Select Objects* option, and then use the mouse to draw a border around all of the objects. Turn off selecting objects by clicking the Select button and then clicking the *Select Objects* option.

Hint To group objects, a text wrapping other than *In Line with Text* must be applied to each object.

Hint A group can be created within a group.

Grouped objects can be sized, moved, and formatting as one object. However, an object within a group of objects can be sized, moved, or formatted individually. To do this, click the specific object and then make the changes to the individual object.

To ungroup grouped objects, click the group to select it, and then click the Picture Tools Format tab (or Drawing Tools Format tab). Click the Group button in the Arrange group and then click the *Ungroup* option at the drop-down list.

Project 5a Customizing and Formatting Shapes

Part 1 of 4

1. Open **Leland.docx** and then save it with the name **1-Leland**.
2. Rotate the middle arrow shape by completing the following steps:
   a. Scroll down the document and then click the middle arrow shape to select it (on the first page).
   b. Click the Drawing Tools Format tab.
   c. Click the Rotate button and then click *Flip Horizontal* at the drop-down list.

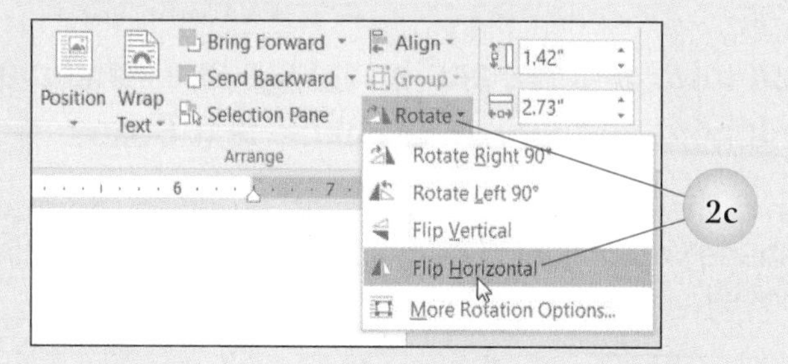

3. Align and format the arrow shapes by completing the following steps:
   a. With the middle arrow shape selected, press and hold down the Shift key.
   b. Click the top arrow shape, click the bottom arrow shape, and then release the Shift key.
   c. With all three arrow shapes selected, click the Align button and then click *Align Left* at the drop-down list.
   d. Click the Shape Styles group task pane launcher.
   e. At the Format Shape task pane with the Fill & Line icon selected, click *Fill* to display the fill options.
   f. Click the *Gradient fill* option.
   g. Click the Preset gradients button and then click the *Top spotlight - Accent 2* option (second column, second row).

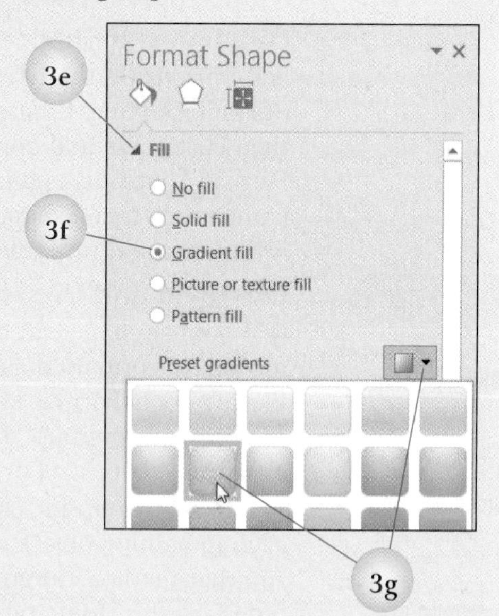

h. Scroll down the task pane and then click *Line* to display the line options.
i. If necessary, scroll down the task pane and then click the *No line* option.
j. Click the Effects icon (at the top of the task pane).
k. Click *Shadow* to display shadow options.
l. Click the Presets button and then click the *Inside Diagonal Top Right* option (third column, first row in the *Inner* section).
m. Close the Format Shape task pane.

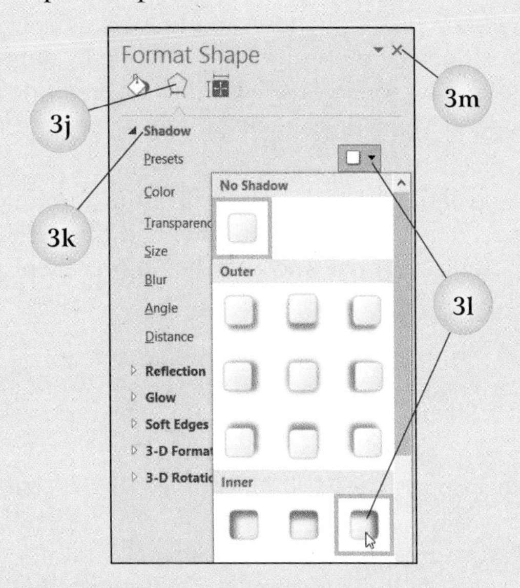

4. With the three arrow shapes still selected, group the shapes, size and move the group, and then ungroup the shapes by completing the following steps:
   a. Click the Group button and then click *Group* at the drop-down list.

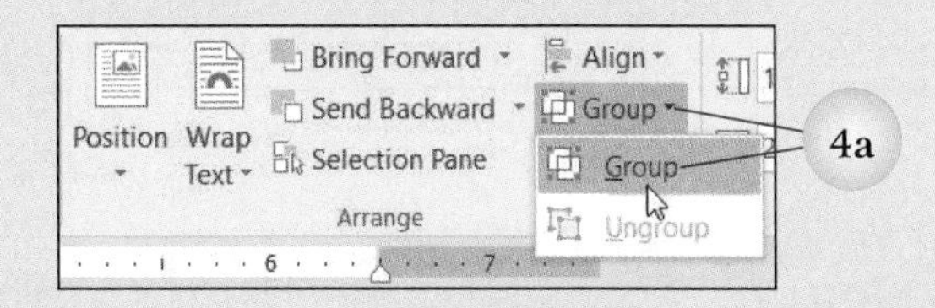

   b. Click in the *Shape Height* measurement box and then type 6.
   c. Click in the *Shape Width* measurement box, type 3.7, and then press the Enter key.
   d. Click the Position button in the Arrange group and then click the *Position in Bottom Center with Square Text Wrapping* option (second column, third row in the *With Text Wrapping* section).
   e. Click the Group button and then click *Ungroup* at the drop-down list.
   f. Click outside the arrow shapes to deselect the shapes.
5. Delete the bottom arrow shape by clicking the shape and then pressing the Delete key.
6. Save **1-Leland.docx**.

Check Your Work

Quick Steps

Display Editing Points

1. Select shape.
2. Click Drawing Tools Format tab.
3. Click Edit Shape button.
4. Click *Edit Points.*

Hint When the mouse pointer is positioned over an editing point, it displays as a box surrounded by four triangles; when positioned over a red line, it displays as a box inside a cross.

Edit Shape

Editing Points in a Shape Sizing handles are small, white circles that display around a selected shape. Depending on the shape, small, yellow circles might also display. Use the yellow circles to change the width or height of a specific element of the shape.

Another method for customizing specific elements is to display and then use edit points. Display edit points by selecting the shape, clicking the Edit Shape button in the Insert Shapes group on the Drawing Tools Format tab, and then clicking the *Edit Points* option. Edit points display as small, black squares at the intersecting points in the shape. A red line also displays between edit points in the shape. Position the mouse pointer on an edit point and the pointer displays as a box surrounded by four triangles. Click and hold down the left mouse button, drag to change the specific element in the shape, and then release the mouse button.

Create a custom editing point by pressing and holding down the Ctrl key, clicking a specific location on a red line, and then releasing the Ctrl key. Position the mouse pointer on a red line and the pointer displays as a box inside a cross.

Project 5b Editing Points in a Shape

Part 2 of 4

1. With **1-Leland.docx** open, press Ctrl + End to move the insertion point to the end of the document (page 2).
2. Click the shape on the second page to select the shape.
3. With the shape selected, edit points by completing the following steps:
   a. Position the mouse pointer on the top yellow circle, click and hold down the left mouse button, drag to the right approximately one-half inch (use the horizontal ruler as a guide and drag to approximately the 2.5-inch mark on the ruler), and then release the mouse button.

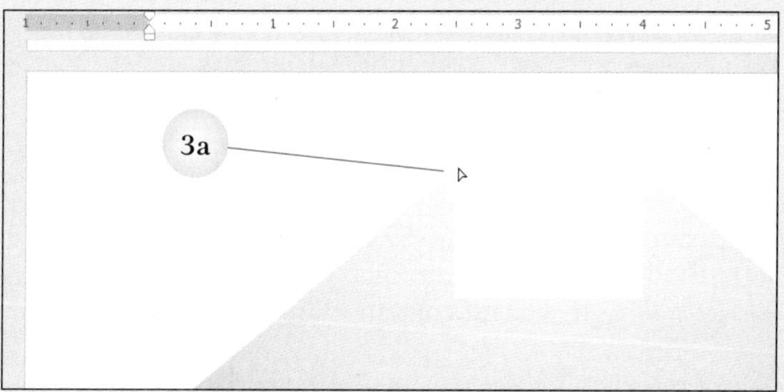

   b. Click the Drawing Tools Format tab, click the Edit Shape button in the Insert Shapes group, and then click *Edit Points* at the drop-down list.

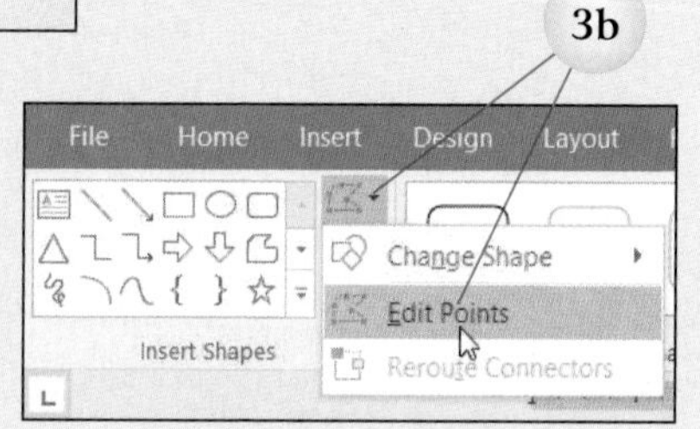

c. Position the mouse pointer on the edit point that displays at the tip of the arrow at the right side of the shape. Click and hold down the left mouse button, drag to the left approximately one inch (use the horizontal ruler as a guide), and then release the mouse button. (The shape will move when you release the mouse button.)

d. Position the mouse pointer on the edit point that displays at the tip of the arrow at the left side of the shape. Click and hold down the left mouse button, drag to the right approximately one inch (use the horizontal ruler as a guide), and then release the mouse button. (The shape will move when you release the mouse button.)

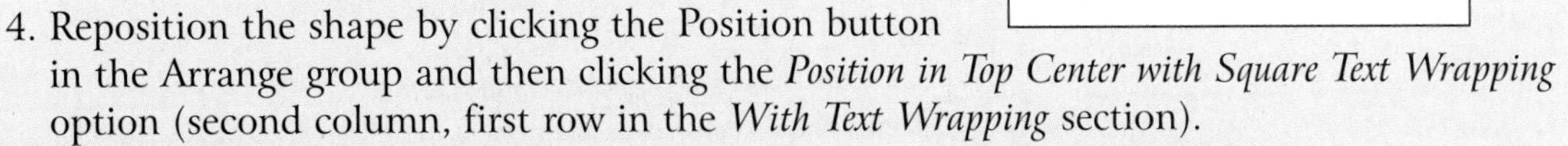

4. Reposition the shape by clicking the Position button in the Arrange group and then clicking the *Position in Top Center with Square Text Wrapping* option (second column, first row in the *With Text Wrapping* section).
5. Insert and format text in the shape by completing the following steps:
   a. With the shape selected, type Free seminar!, press the Enter key, and then type 1-888-555-4588.
   b. Select the text you just typed.
   c. Click the Text Fill button arrow in the WordArt Styles group and then click the *Orange, Accent 2, Darker 50%* color option (sixth column, bottom row in the *Theme Colors* section).
   d. Click the Home tab and then click the Bold button in the Font group.
   e. Click the *Font Size* option box arrow and then click *24* at the drop-down gallery.
6. Press Ctrl + Home to move the insertion point to the beginning of the document.
7. Save **1-Leland.docx**.

Check Your Work

Quick Steps

Display Wrap Points for Object

1. Select object.
2. Click Picture Tools Format tab (or Drawing Tools Format tab).
3. Click Wrap Text button.
4. Click *Edit Wrap Points.*

Hint Remove a wrap point by pressing and holding down the Ctrl key, clicking the wrap point, and then releasing the Ctrl key.

Editing Wrap Points in a Shape When an object such as an image or shape is inserted in a document, a series of wrap points are defined around the object. These wrap points display in a manner similar to the editing points that display around an object. The difference between editing points and wrap points is that editing points change the shape of specific elements in an object while wrap points wrap text closer or farther away from an object.

To display wrap points in a shape, select the shape, click the Drawing Tools Format tab, click the Wrap Text button in the Arrange group, and then click the *Edit Wrap Points* option. Display wrap points for an image in a similar manner except click the Wrap Text button on the Picture Tools Format tab. Use wrap points to change how text or other data wraps around an object by dragging specific wrap points.

When wrap points are displayed in an object, red lines display between wrap points. Create a custom wrap point by clicking and holding down the mouse pointer on a location on a red line and then dragging to a specific position.

Project 5c Editing Wrap Points in a Shape

Part 3 of 4

1. With **1-Leland.docx** open, click the border of the banner shape that displays in the paragraph of text below the title.
2. Edit wrap points in the shape by completing the following steps:
   a. Click the Drawing Tools Format tab.
   b. Click the Wrap Text button and then click *Edit Wrap Points* at the drop-down list.
   c. Drag the wrap point at the left side of the shape into the shape as shown below.

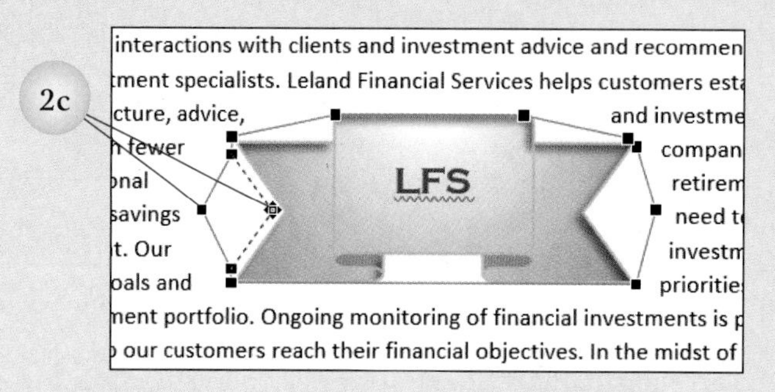

   d. Drag the wrap point at the right side of the shape into the shape as shown below.

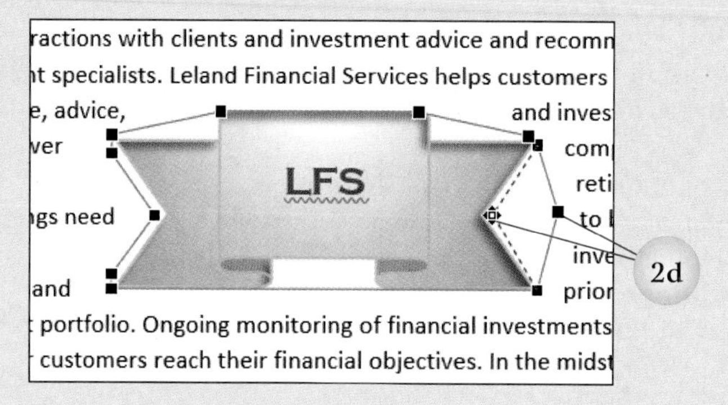

3. Click outside the shape to remove the wrap points.
4. Save **1-Leland.docx**.

Check Your Work

Tutorial

Linking and Unlinking Text Boxes

Create Link

Break Link

Quick Steps

Link Text Boxes
1. Select text box.
2. Click Drawing Tools Format tab.
3. Click Create Link button.
4. Click in another text box.

Inserting a Text Box on a Shape In addition to typing text directly in a shape, a text box can be drawn on a shape. When a text box is drawn on a shape, it is actually added as a layer on top of the shape. To format or move the text box with the shape, select or group the shape with the text box.

Linking and Unlinking Text Boxes Text in text boxes can flow from one text box to another by linking the text boxes. To do this, draw the text boxes, and then click in the first text box. Click the Create Link button in the Text group on the Drawing Tools Format tab and the mouse pointer displays with a pouring jug icon attached. Click an empty text box to link it with the selected text box. Type text in the first text box and the text will flow to the linked text box.

More than two text boxes can be linked. To link several text boxes, click the first text box, click the Create Link button on the Drawing Tools Format tab, and then click in the second text box. Select the second text box, click the Create Link button, and then click the third text box. Continue in this manner until all desired text boxes are linked.

Hint Link text boxes to flow text in columns across multiple pages.

To break a link between two boxes, select the first text box in the link and then click the Break Link button in the Text group. When a link is broken, all of the text is placed in the first text box.

Project 5d Linking and Unlinking Text Boxes

Part 4 of 4

1. With **1-Leland.docx** open, scroll down the document to display the first arrow shape on the first page.
2. Insert, size, and format a text box by completing the following steps:
   a. Click the Insert tab.
   b. Click the Text Box button in the Text group and then click *Draw Text Box* at the drop-down list.
   c. Click in the document near the first shape.
   d. With the text box selected, click in the *Shape Height* measurement box and then type 0.73.
   e. Click in the *Shape Width* measurement box and then type 2.
   f. Click the Shape Fill button arrow and then click *No Fill* at the drop-down list.
   g. Drag the text box so it is positioned on the first arrow (see image below).

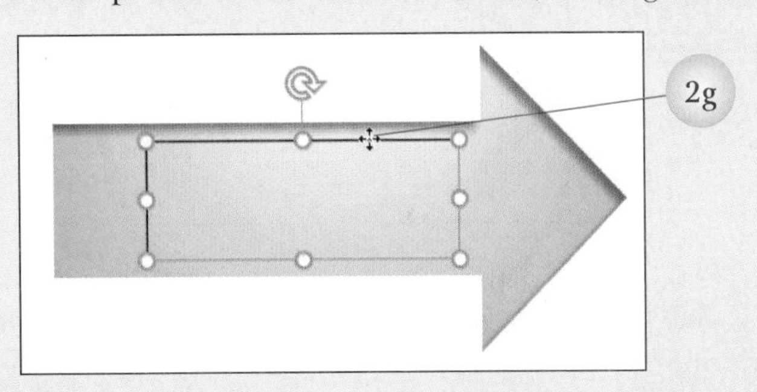

   h. Copy the text box to the second arrow shape by pressing and holding down the Ctrl key, clicking the text box border and holding down the left mouse button, dragging the copy of the text box so it is positioned on top of the second arrow shape, and then releasing the mouse button and the Ctrl key.
3. Link the text boxes by completing the following steps:
   a. Click the border of the text box on the first arrow shape to select the text box.
   b. Click the Create Link button in the Text group on the Drawing Tools Format tab.
   c. Click in the text box on the second arrow shape.
4. Insert text in the text box on the first arrow shape by completing the following steps:
   a. Click in the text box in the first arrow shape.
   b. Click the Home tab, change the font size to 12 points, apply the Orange, Accent 2, Darker 50% font color (sixth column, bottom row in the *Theme Colors* section), and apply bold formatting.

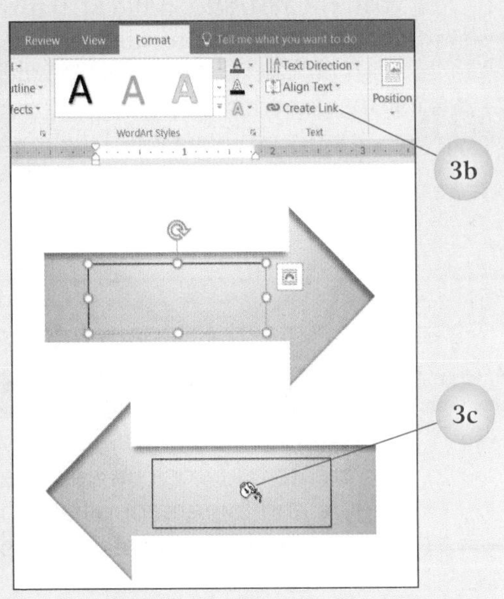

c. Click the Center button in the Paragraph group.
d. Click the Line and Paragraph Spacing button in the Paragraph group and then click *Remove Space After Paragraph*.
e. Click the Line and Paragraph Spacing button and then click *1.0*.
f. Type Let Leland Financial Services help you plan for retirement and provide you with information to determine your financial direction. (The text will flow to the text box on the second arrow.)

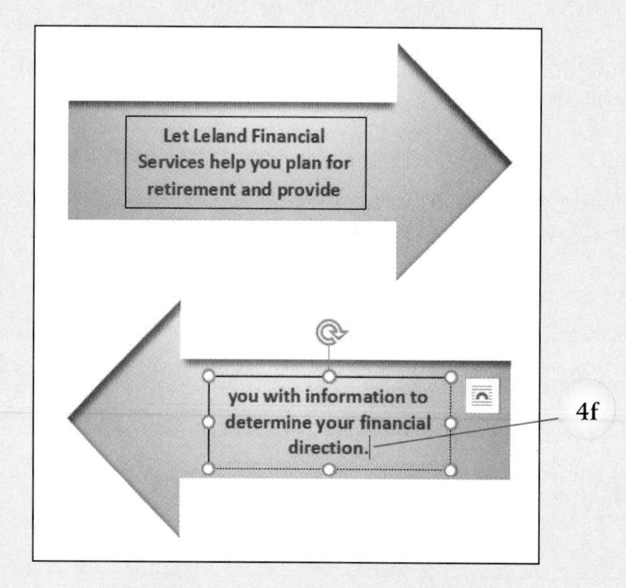

5. Break the link between the text boxes by completing the following steps:
   a. Select the text box in the first arrow shape by clicking the text box border.
   b. Click the Drawing Tools Format tab.
   c. Click the Break Link button in the Text group (previously the Create Link button).
6. Relink the text boxes by clicking the Create Link button and then clicking in the text box on the second arrow shape.
7. Remove the outline around the two text boxes by completing the following steps:
   a. With the text box on the first arrow shape selected, press and hold down the Shift key and then click the text box border of the second arrow shape.
   b. With both text boxes selected, click the Shape Outline button and then click *No Outline* at the drop-down list.
8. Save, print, and then close **1-Leland.docx**.

Check Your Work

Project 6 Insert Headers and Footers in a Computer Software Report — 8 Parts

You will open a report on productivity and graphics and multimedia software and then create and position headers and footers in the document. You will also create headers and footers for different pages in a document, divide a document into sections, and then create footers for specific sections.

Preview Finished Project

Tutorial

Creating a Custom Header and Footer

Hint One method for formatting a header or footer is to select the header or footer text and then use the options on the Mini toolbar.

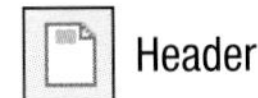
Header

Footer

Inserting Headers and Footers

Text that appears in the top margin of a page is called a *header* and text that appears in the bottom margin of a page is called a *footer*. Headers and footers are commonly used in manuscripts, textbooks, reports, and other publications to display the page numbers and section or chapter titles. For example, see the footer at the bottom of this page.

Insert a predesigned header by clicking the Insert tab and then clicking the Header button. This displays a drop-down list of header choices. Click the predesigned header and the formatted header is inserted in the document. Complete similar steps to insert a predesigned footer.

If the predesigned headers and footers do not meet specific needs, create a custom header or footer. To create a custom header, click the Insert tab, click the Header button in the Header & Footer group, and then click *Edit Header* at the drop-down list. This displays a Header pane in the document along with the Header & Footer Tools Design tab, as shown in Figure 1.7. Use options on this tab to insert elements such as page numbers, pictures, and images; to navigate to other headers or footers in the document; and to position headers and footers on different pages in a document.

Figure 1.7 Header & Footer Tools Design Tab

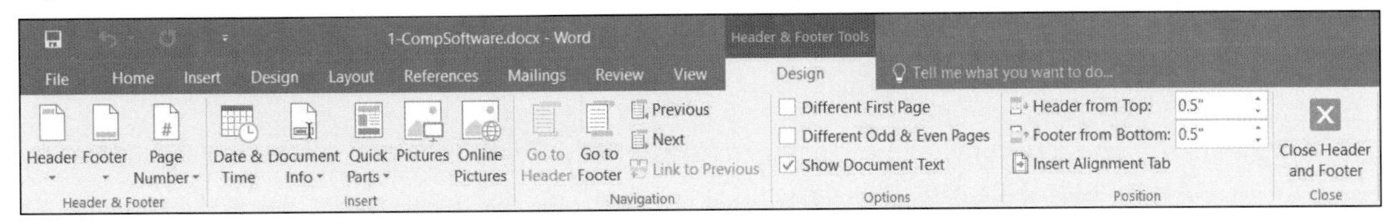

Inserting Elements in Headers and Footers

Use buttons in the Insert group on the Header & Footer Tools Design tab to insert elements into the header or footer, such as the date and time, Quick Parts, pictures, and images.

Click the Date & Time button in the Insert group and the Date and Time dialog box displays. This is the same dialog box that displays when the Date & Time button in the Text group on the Insert tab is clicked. Choose a date and time option in the *Available formats* list box of the dialog box and then click OK.

Click the Document Info button to display a drop-down list of document information fields that can be inserted into the document. Hover the mouse pointer over the *Document Property* option in the Document Info button drop-down list to display a side menu of document properties such as *Author*, *Comments*, and *Company* that can be inserted in the header or footer.

The Quick Parts button in the Insert group on the Header & Footer Tools Design tab displays the same options at the drop-down list as the Quick Parts button on the Insert tab. Click the Pictures button to display the Insert Picture dialog box and insert an image from the computer's hard drive or removable drive. Click the Online Pictures button and the Insert Pictures window displays with options for searching for and then downloading an image into the header or footer.

Project 6a Inserting Elements in a Header and Footer

Part 1 of 8

1. Open **CompSoftware.docx** and then save it with the name **1-CompSoftware**.
2. Insert a header by completing the following steps:
   a. Click the Insert tab.
   b. Click the Header button in the Header & Footer group and then click *Edit Header* at the drop-down list.
   c. With the insertion point positioned in the Header pane, click the Pictures button in the Insert group on the Header & Footer Tools Design tab.

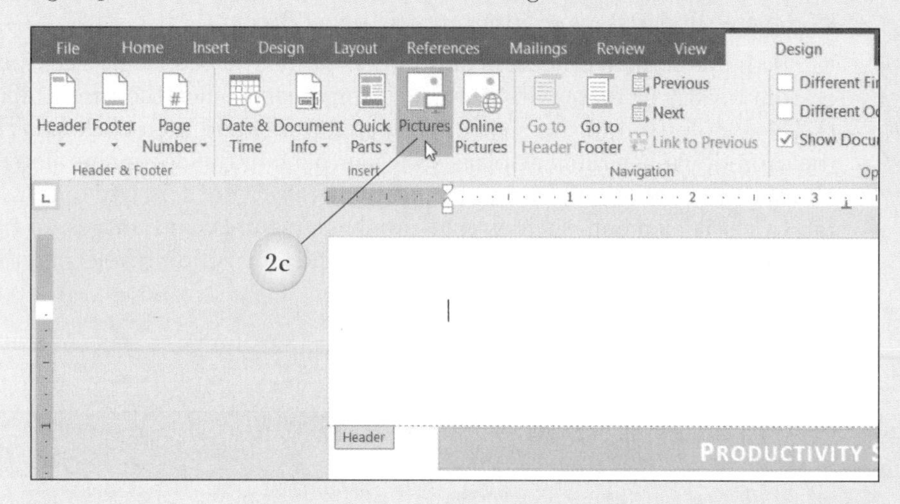

   d. At the Insert Picture dialog box, navigate to the WL2C1 folder on your storage medium and then double-click ***Worldwide.jpg***.
   e. With the image selected, click in the *Shape Height* measurement box, type 0.4, and then press the Enter key.
   f. Click the Wrap Text button in the Arrange group and then click *Behind Text* at the drop-down list.
   g. Drag the image up approximately one-third of an inch.
   h. Click outside the image to deselect it.
   i. Press the Tab key two times. (This moves the insertion point to the right margin.)
   j. Click the Header & Footer Tools Design tab and then click the Date & Time button in the Insert group.
   k. At the Date and Time dialog box, click the twelfth option from the top (the option that displays the date in numbers and the time) and then click OK to close the dialog box.
   l. Select the date and time text and then click the Home tab. Click the Bold button in the Font group, click the *Font Size* option box arrow, and then click *9* at the drop-down gallery.
   m. Double-click in the document to make the document active and dim the header.
3. Save **1-CompSoftware.docx**.

Check Your Work

Positioning Headers and Footers

Word inserts a header 0.5 inch from the top of the page and a footer 0.5 inch from the bottom of the page. These default positions can be changed with buttons in the Position group on the Header & Footer Tools Design tab. Use the *Header from Top* and the *Footer from Bottom* measurement boxes to adjust the position of the header and the footer, respectively, on the page.

By default, headers and footers contain two tab settings. A center tab is set at 3.25 inches and a right tab is set at 6.5 inches. If the document contains default left and right margin settings of 1 inch, the center tab set at 3.25 inches is the center of the document and the right tab set at 6.5 inches is at the right margin. If the default margins are changed, the default center tab may need to be changed before inserting header or footer text at the center tab. Position tabs with the Insert Alignment Tab button in the Position group. Click this button and the Alignment Tab dialog box displays. Use options at this dialog box to change tab alignment and set tabs with leaders.

Project 6b Positioning Headers and Footers

Part 2 of 8

1. With **1-CompSoftware.docx** open, change the margins by completing the following steps:
   a. Click the Layout tab, click the Margins button in the Page Setup group, and then click the *Custom Margins* option at the bottom of the drop-down list.
   b. At the Page Setup dialog box with the Margins tab selected, select the measurement in the *Left* measurement box and then type 1.25.
   c. Select the measurement in the *Right* measurement box and then type 1.25.
   d. Click OK to close the dialog box.
2. Create a footer by completing the following steps:
   a. Click the Insert tab.
   b. Click the Footer button in the Header & Footer group and then click *Edit Footer* at the drop-down list.
   c. With the insertion point positioned in the Footer pane, type your first and last names at the left margin.
   d. Press the Tab key. (This moves the insertion point to the center tab position.)
   e. Click the Page Number button in the Header & Footer group, point to *Current Position*, and then click *Accent Bar 2* at the drop-down list.

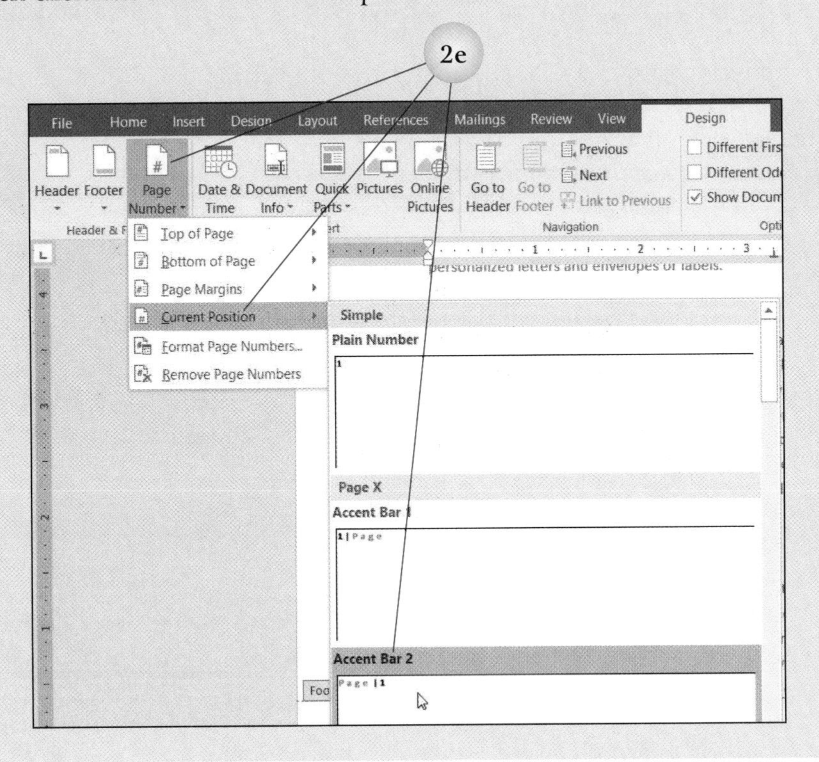

f. Press the Tab key.
g. Click the Document Info button in the Insert group and then click *File Name* at the drop-down list.

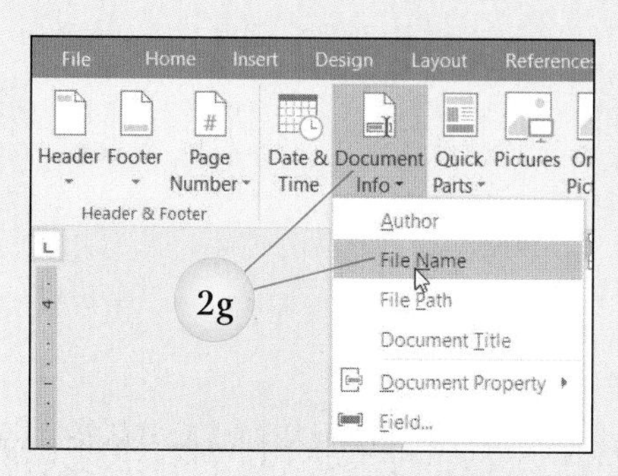

h. You notice that the center tab and right tab are slightly off, because the left and right margins in the document are set at 1.25 inches instead of 1 inch. To align the tabs correctly, drag the center tab marker to the 3-inch mark on the horizontal ruler and drag the right tab marker to the 6-inch mark on the horizontal ruler.

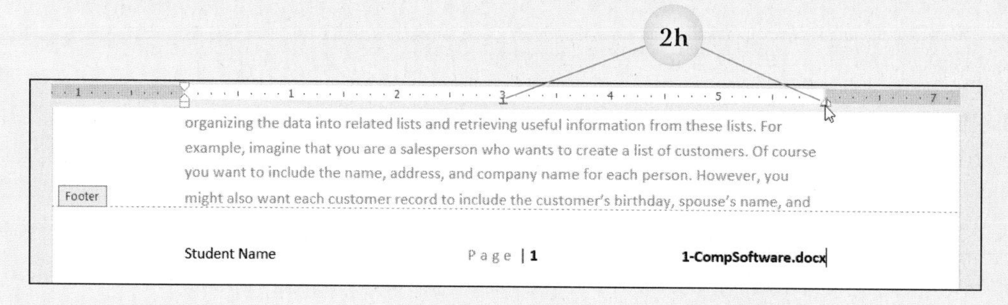

i. Select all the footer text and then change the font to 9-point Calibri and apply bold formatting.

3. Change the position of the header and footer by completing the following steps:
   a. With the Header & Footer Tools Design tab active, click the *Header from Top* measurement box up arrow until *0.8"* displays.
   b. Click in the *Footer from Bottom* measurement box, type 0.6, and then press the Enter key.
   c. Click the Close Header and Footer button.

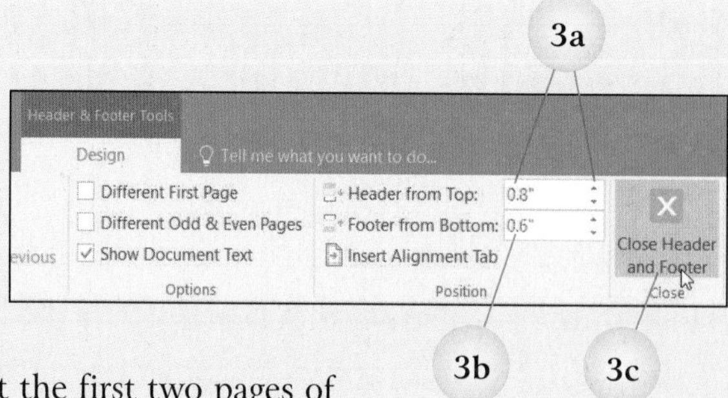

4. Save and then print the first two pages of **1-CompSoftware.docx**.

Check Your Work

Tutorial

Creating a Different First Page Header and Footer

Quick Steps

Create a Different First Page Header or Footer

1. Click Insert tab.
2. Click Header or Footer button.
3. Click *Edit Header* or *Edit Footer* at drop-down list.
4. Click *Different First Page* check box.
5. Insert elements and/or text.
6. Click Next button.
7. Insert elements and/or text.

Creating a Different First Page Header or Footer

A header and/or footer inserted in a document will display and print on every page in the document by default. However, different headers and footers can be created within one document. For example, a unique header or footer can be created for the first page of a document and a different header or footer can be created for the subsequent pages.

To create a different first page header, click the Insert tab, click the Header button, and then click *Edit Header* at the drop-down list. Click the *Different First Page* check box to insert a check mark and the First Page Header pane displays with the insertion point inside it. Insert elements or type text to create the first page header and then click the Next button in the Navigation group. This displays the Header pane with the insertion point positioned inside it. Insert elements and/or type text to create the header. Complete similar steps to create a different first page footer.

In some situations, the first page header or footer should be blank. This is particularly useful if a document contains a title page and the header or footer should not print on it.

Project 6c Creating a Header That Prints on All Pages Except the First Page

Part 3 of 8

1. With **1-CompSoftware.docx** open, press Ctrl + A to select the entire document and then press Ctrl + 2 to change to double-line spacing.
2. Remove the header and footer by completing the following steps:
   a. Click the Insert tab.
   b. Click the Header button in the Header & Footer group and then click *Remove Header* at the drop-down list.
   c. Click the Footer button in the Header & Footer group and then click *Remove Footer* at the drop-down list.
3. Press Ctrl + Home and then create a header that prints on all pages except the first page by completing the following steps:
   a. With the Insert tab active, click the Header button in the Header & Footer group.
   b. Click *Edit Header* at the drop-down list.
   c. Click the *Different First Page* check box in the Options group on the Header & Footer Tools Design tab to insert a check mark.
   d. With the insertion point positioned in the First Page Header pane, click the Next button in the Navigation group. (This tells Word that the first page header should be blank.)
   e. With the insertion point positioned in the Header pane, click the Page Number button in the Header & Footer group, point to *Top of Page*, and then click *Accent Bar 2* at the drop-down gallery.
   f. Click the Close Header and Footer button.
4. Scroll through the document and notice that the header appears on the second, third, fourth, and fifth pages.
5. Save and then print the first two pages of **1-CompSoftware.docx**.

Check Your Work

Tutorial

Creating Odd Page and Even Page Headers and Footers

Quick Steps

Create Odd and Even Page Headers or Footers

1. Click Insert tab.
2. Click Header or Footer button.
3. Click *Edit Header* or *Edit Footer.*
4. Click *Different Odd & Even Pages* check box.
5. Insert elements and/or text.

Creating Odd and Even Page Headers or Footers

If a document will be read in book form, consider inserting odd and even page headers or footers. When presenting pages in a document in book form with facing pages, the outside margins are the left side of the left page and the right side of the right page. Also, when a document has facing pages, the right-hand page is generally numbered with an odd number and the left-hand page is generally numbered with an even number.

Create even and odd headers or footers to insert this type of page numbering. Use the *Different Odd & Even Pages* check box in the Options group on the Header & Footer Tools Design tab to create odd and even headers and/or footers.

Project 6d Creating Odd and Even Page Footers

Part 4 of 8

1. With **1-CompSoftware.docx** open, remove the header from the document by completing the following steps:
   a. Click the Insert tab.
   b. Click the Header button in the Header & Footer group and then click *Edit Header* at the drop-down list.
   c. Click the *Different First Page* check box in the Options group on the Header & Footer Tools Design tab to remove the check mark.
   d. Click the Header button in the Header & Footer group and then click *Remove Header* at the drop-down list. (This displays the insertion point in an empty Header pane.)
2. Create one footer that prints on odd pages and another that prints on even pages by completing the following steps:
   a. Click the Go to Footer button in the Navigation group on the Header & Footer Tools Design tab.
   b. Click the *Different Odd & Even Pages* check box in the Options group to insert a check mark. (This displays the Odd Page Footer pane with the insertion point inside it.)
   c. Click the Page Number button in the Header & Footer group, point to *Bottom of Page*, and then click *Plain Number 3* at the drop-down list.

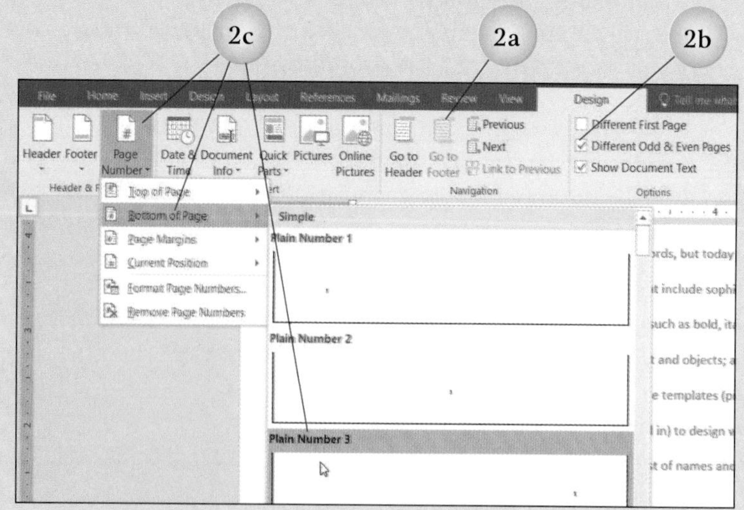

   d. Click the Next button in the Navigation group. (This displays the Even Page Footer pane with the insertion point inside it.)

e. Click the Page Number button in the Header & Footer group, point to *Current Position*, and then click *Plain Number* at the drop-down list.
f. Click the Close Header and Footer button.
3. Scroll through the document and notice the page numbers at the right sides of the odd page footers and the page numbers at the left sides of the even page footers.
4. Save and then print the first two pages of **1-CompSoftware.docx**.

Check Your Work

Creating Headers and Footers for Different Sections

Quick Steps

Create Headers or Footers for Different Sections
1. Insert section break.
2. Click Insert tab.
3. Click Header or Footer button.
4. Click *Edit Header* or *Edit Footer*.
5. Click Link to Previous button to deactivate.
6. Insert elements and/or text.
7. Click Next button.
8. Insert elements and/or text.

A document can be divided into sections and then different formatting can be applied to each section. Insert a section break to divide the document into sections. A section break can be inserted that begins a new page or a section break can be inserted that allows the sections to be formatted differently but does not begin a new page. A section break can also be inserted that starts a new section on the next even-numbered page or the next odd-numbered page.

To insert different headers and/or footers on pages in a document, divide the document into sections. For example, if a document contains several chapters, each chapter can be a separate section and a different header and footer can be created for each section. When dividing a document into sections by chapter, insert section breaks that also begin new pages.

Breaking a Section Link

Link to Previous

When a header or footer is created for a specific section in a document, it can be created for all the previous and following sections or only the following sections. By default, each section in a document is linked to the other sections. To print a header or footer only on the pages within a section and not the previous section, deactivate the Link to Previous button. This tells Word not to print the header or footer on previous sections. Word will, however, print the header or footer on following sections. To specify that the header or footer should not print on following sections, create a blank header or footer at the next section. When creating a header or footer for a specific section in a document, preview the document to determine if the header or footer appears on the correct pages.

Project 6e Creating Footers for Different Sections and Breaking a Section Link — Part 5 of 8

1. With **1-CompSoftware.docx** open, remove the odd and even page footers by completing the following steps:
   a. Click the Insert tab.
   b. Click the Footer button in the Header & Footer group and then click *Edit Footer* at the drop-down list.
   c. Click the *Different Odd & Even Pages* check box in the Options group on the Header & Footer Tools Design tab to remove the check mark.
   d. Click the Footer button in the Header & Footer group and then click *Remove Footer* at the drop-down list.
   e. Click the Close Header and Footer button.

2. Remove the page break before the second title in the document by completing the following steps:
   a. Move the insertion point immediately right of the period that ends the paragraph in the section *PRESENTATION SOFTWARE* (near the top of page 3).
   b. Press the Delete key two times. (The title *GRAPHICS AND MULTIMEDIA SOFTWARE* should now display below the paragraph on the third page.)
3. Insert an odd page section break (a section break that starts a section on the next odd page) by completing the following steps:
   a. Position the insertion point at the beginning of the title *GRAPHICS AND MULTIMEDIA SOFTWARE*.
   b. Click the Layout tab, click the Breaks button in the Page Setup group, and then click *Odd Page* at the drop-down list.
4. Create section titles and footers with page numbers for the two sections by completing the following steps:
   a. Position the insertion point at the beginning of the document.
   b. Click the Insert tab.
   c. Click the Footer button in the Header & Footer group and then click *Edit Footer* at the drop-down list.
   d. At the Footer -Section 1- pane, type Section 1 Productivity Software and then press the Tab key two times. (This moves the insertion point to the right margin.)
   e. Type Page and then press the spacebar.
   f. Click the Page Number button in the Header & Footer group, point to *Current Position*, and then click *Plain Number* at the side menu.
   g. Click the Next button in the Navigation group.
   h. Click the Link to Previous button to deactivate it. (This removes the message *Same as Previous* from the top right side of the footer pane.)

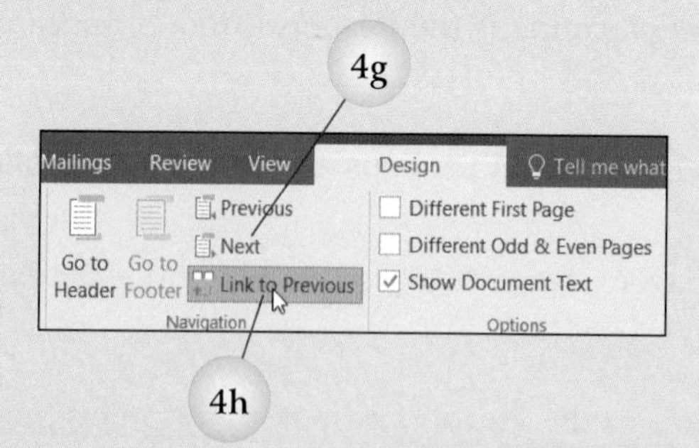

   i. Change the text *Section 1 Productivity Software* to *Section 2 Graphics and Multimedia Software* in the footer.
   j. Click the Close Header and Footer button.
5. Scroll through the document and notice the page numbering in the sections.
6. Save **1-CompSoftware.docx**.

Check Your Work

Tutorial

Customizing Page Numbers

Customizing Page Numbers

By default, Word inserts arabic numbers (1, 2, 3, and so on) and numbers pages sequentially beginning with 1. These default settings can be customized with options at the Page Number Format dialog box shown in Figure 1.8. To display this dialog box, click the Insert tab, click the Page Number button in the Header & Footer group, and then click *Format Page Numbers* at the drop-down list. Another method for displaying the dialog box is to click the Page Number button in the Header & Footer group on the Header & Footer Tools Design tab and then click the *Format Page Numbers* option.

Use the *Number format* option at the Page Number Format dialog box to change from arabic numbers to arabic numbers preceded and followed by hyphens, lowercase letters, uppercase letters, lowercase roman numerals, or uppercase roman numerals. By default, page numbering begins with 1 and continues sequentially from 1 through all the pages and sections in a document. Change the beginning page number with the *Start at* option by clicking the *Start at* option and then typing the beginning page number in the measurement box. The number in the *Start at* measurement box can also be changed by clicking the measurement box up or down arrow.

If section breaks are inserted in a document and then a header and footer is inserted with page numbering for each section, the page numbering is sequential throughout the document. The document used in Project 6f has a section break but the pages are numbered sequentially. If the page numbering in a section should start with a new number, use the *Start at* option at the Page Number Format dialog box.

Figure 1.8 Customizing Page Numbering

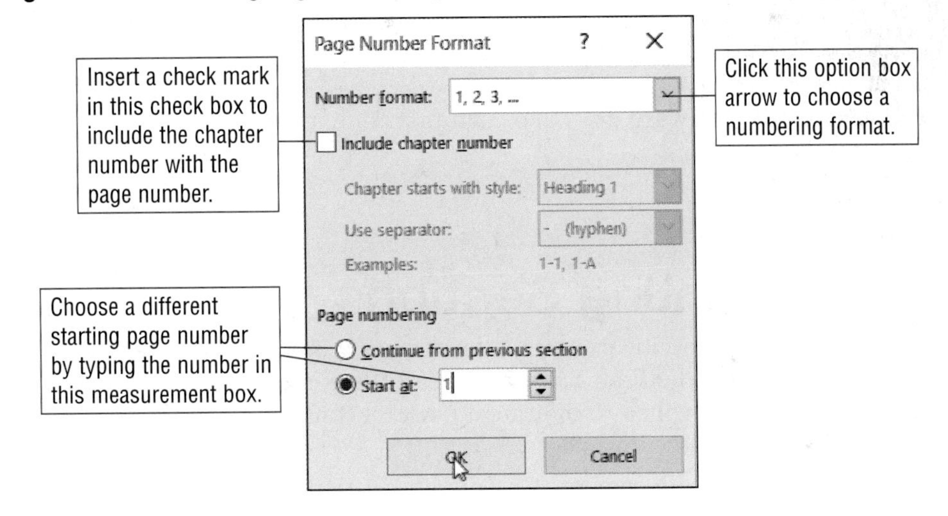

Project 6f Customizing Page Numbering

Part 6 of 8

1. With **1-CompSoftware.docx** open, change page numbering to lowercase roman numerals and change the starting page number by completing the following steps:
   a. Press Ctrl + Home.
   b. Click the Insert tab.
   c. Click the Page Number button in the Header & Footer group and then click *Format Page Numbers* at the drop-down list.
   d. At the Page Number Format dialog box, click the *Number format* option box arrow and then click *i, ii, iii, ...* at the drop-down list.
   e. Click the *Start at* option and then type 4.
   f. Click OK to close the dialog box.
2. Scroll through the document and notice the lowercase roman numeral page numbers (beginning with *iv*) that display at the right margin at the bottom of the pages.
3. Scroll to the bottom of the page containing the title *GRAPHICS AND MULTIMEDIA SOFTWARE* and notice that the page numbers did not change. (This is because the sections were unlinked.)
4. Position the insertion point in the first paragraph of text below the title *GRAPHICS AND MULTIMEDIA SOFTWARE* and then change page numbering by completing the following steps:
   a. Click the Page Number button in the Header & Footer group and then click *Format Page Numbers* at the drop-down list.
   b. At the Page Number Format dialog box, click the *Number format* option box arrow and then click *i, ii, iii, ...* at the drop-down list.
   c. Click the *Start at* option and then type 7.
   d. Click OK to close the dialog box.
5. Save **1-CompSoftware.docx** and then print only the first page.

Page Number Format ? ×
Number format: i, ii, iii, ...
Include chapter number
Chapter starts with style: Heading 1
Use separator: - (hyphen)
Examples: 1-1, 1-A
Page numbering
Continue from previous section
Start at: 4
OK Cancel
1d
1e
1f

Check Your Work

Tutorial

Printing Sections

Printing Sections

Print specific pages in a document by inserting page numbers in the *Pages* text box at the Print backstage area. When entering page numbers in this text box, use a hyphen to indicate a range of consecutive pages or a comma to specify nonconsecutive pages.

In a document that contains sections, use the *Pages* text box at the Print backstage area to specify the section and pages within the section to be printed. For example, if a document is divided into three sections, print only section 2 by typing *s2* in the *Pages* text box. If a document contains six sections, print sections 3 through 5 by typing *s3-s5* in the *Pages* text box. Specific pages within or between sections can also be identified for printing. For example, to print pages 2 through 5 of section 4, type *p2s4-p5s4*; to print from page 3 of section 1 through page 5 of section 4, type *p3s1-p5s4*; to print page 1 of section 3, page 4 of section 5, and page 6 of section 8, type *p1s3,p4s5,p6s8*.

Quick Steps

Print a Section
1. Click File tab.
2. Click *Print* option.
3. Click in *Pages* text box.
4. Type s followed by section number.
5. Click Print button.

Project 6g Changing Section Numbering and Printing Section Pages

Part 7 of 8

1. With **1-CompSoftware.docx** open, change the starting page number for section 2 to *1* by completing the following steps:
   a. Click the Insert tab, click the Footer button in the Header & Footer group, and then click *Edit Footer* at the drop-down list.
   b. At the Footer -Section 1- footer pane, click the Page Number button in the Header & Footer group and then click the *Format Page Numbers* option at the drop-down list.
   c. Click the *Number format* option box arrow and then click the *1, 2, 3, ...* option at the drop-down list.
   d. Select the current number in the *Start at* measurement box and then type 1.
   e. Click OK to close the dialog box.
   f. Display the section 2 footer by clicking the Next button in the Navigation group on the Header & Footer Tools Design tab.
   g. At the Footer -Section 2- footer pane, click the Page Number button in the Header & Footer group and then click the *Format Page Numbers* option at the drop-down list.
   h. At the Page Number Format dialog box, click the *Number format* option box arrow and then click the *1, 2, 3, ...* option at the drop-down list.
   i. Select the current number in the *Start at* measurement box and then type 1.
   j. Click OK to close the dialog box.
   k. Click the Close Header and Footer button.
2. Print only page 1 of section 1 and page 1 of section 2 by completing the following steps:
   a. Click the File tab and then click the *Print* option.
   b. At the Print backstage area, click in the *Pages* text box in the *Settings* category and then type p1s1,p1s2.
   c. Click the Print button.

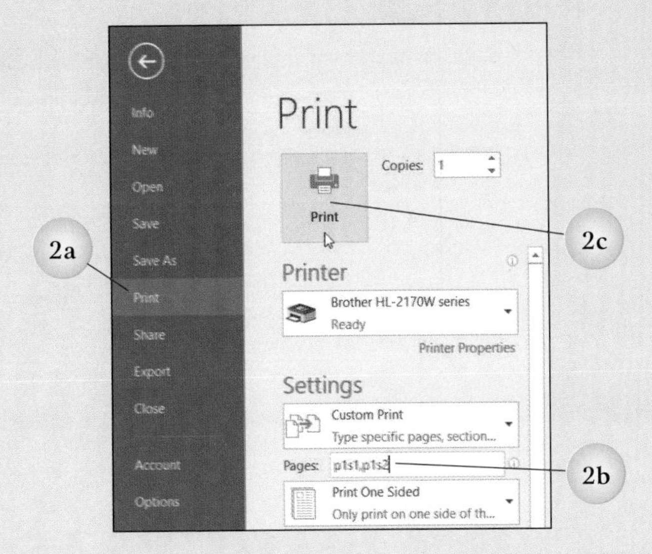

3. Save **1-CompSoftware.docx**.

Check Your Work

Tutorial

Keeping Text Together

Quick Steps

Keep Text Together

1. Click Paragraph group dialog box launcher.
2. Click Line and Page Breaks tab.
3. Click *Keep with next, Keep lines together,* and/or *Page break before.*
4. Click OK.

Hint Text formatted with *Keep with next* option applied to it is identified with a ■ nonprinting character in the left margin.

Keeping Text Together

In a multipage document, Word automatically inserts soft page breaks, which are page breaks that adjust when data is added or deleted from the document. However, a soft page break may occur in an undesirable location. For example, a soft page break may cause a heading to display at the bottom of a page while the text related to the heading displays at the top of the next page. A soft page break may also create a widow or orphan. A widow is the last line of text in a paragraph that appears by itself at the top of a page and an orphan is the first line of text in a paragraph that appears by itself at the bottom of a page.

Use options at the Paragraph dialog box with the Line and Page Breaks tab selected, as shown in Figure 1.9, to control widows and orphans and keep a paragraph, group of paragraphs, or group of lines together. Display this dialog box by clicking the Paragraph group dialog box launcher on the Home tab and then clicking the Line and Page Breaks tab at the dialog box.

By default, the *Widow/Orphan control* option is active and Word tries to avoid creating widows and orphans when inserting soft page breaks. The other three options in the *Pagination* section of the dialog box are not active by default. Use the *Keep with next* option to keep a line together with the next line. This is useful for keeping a heading together with the first line of text below it. To keep a group of selected lines together, use the *Keep lines together* option. Use the *Page break before* option to insert a page break before selected text.

Figure 1.9 Paragraph Dialog Box with Line and Page Breaks Tab Selected

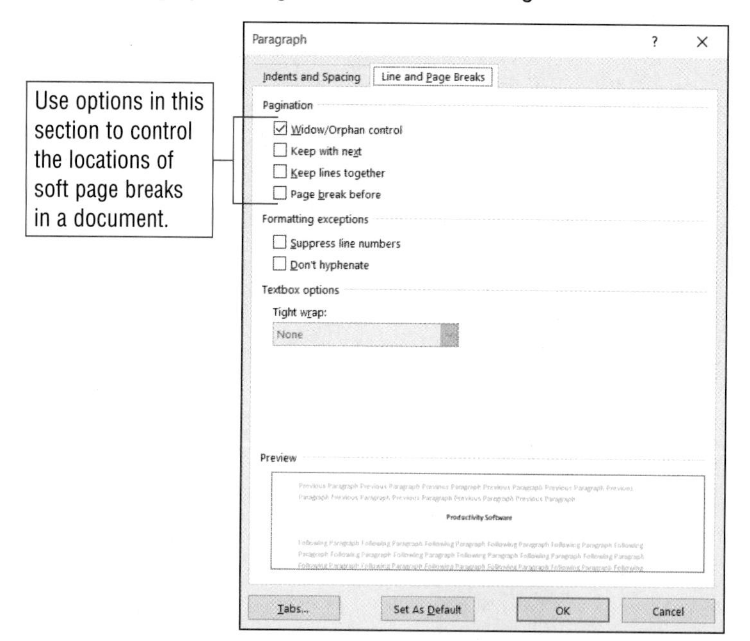

Project 6h Keeping Text Together

Part 8 of 8

1. With **1-CompSoftware.docx** open, scroll through the document and notice that the heading *SPREADSHEET SOFTWARE* displays at the bottom of page 1 and the paragraph that follows the heading displays at the top of page 2. Keep the heading and paragraph together by completing the following steps:
   a. Position the insertion point on any character in the heading *SPREADSHEET SOFTWARE*.
   b. Make sure the Home tab is active and then click the Paragraph group dialog box launcher.
   c. At the Paragraph dialog box, click the Line and Page Breaks tab.
   d. Click the *Keep with next* check box to insert a check mark.
   e. Click OK to close the dialog box.

2. Scroll through the document and notice the heading *MULTIMEDIA SOFTWARE* near the end of the document. Insert a soft page break at the beginning of the heading by completing the following steps:
   a. Move the insertion point to the beginning of the heading *MULTIMEDIA SOFTWARE*.
   b. Click the Paragraph group dialog box launcher.
   c. At the Paragraph dialog box with the Line and Page Breaks tab selected, click the *Page break before* check box to insert a check mark.
   d. Click OK to close the dialog box.
3. Save, print, and then close **1-CompSoftware.docx**.

Check Your Work

Chapter Summary

- Use the Bullets button to insert bullets before specific paragraphs of text and use the Numbering button to insert numbers.
- Insert custom numbers by clicking the Numbering button arrow and then clicking an option at the drop-down gallery.
- Define custom numbering formatting with options at the Define New Number Format dialog box. Display this dialog box by clicking the Numbering button arrow and then clicking *Define New Number Format* at the drop-down gallery.
- Insert custom bullets by clicking the Bullets button arrow and then clicking an option at the drop-down gallery.
- Define custom bullets with options at the Define New Bullet dialog box. Display this dialog box by clicking the Bullets button arrow and then clicking *Define New Bullet* at the drop-down gallery.
- Apply numbering to multilevel paragraphs of text by clicking the Multilevel List button in the Paragraph group on the Home tab.
- Define custom multilevel list numbering with options at the Define New Multilevel List dialog box. Display this dialog box by clicking the Multilevel List button and then clicking *Define New Multilevel List* at the drop-down gallery.
- When typing a multilevel list, press the Tab key to move to the next level and press Shift + Tab to move to the previous level.

- Customize the layout of images with options at the Layout dialog box. Display this dialog box by clicking the Size group dialog box launcher on the Picture Tools Format tab.
- The Layout dialog box contains three tabs. Click the Position tab to specify the position of an image in the document, click the Text Wrapping tab to specify a wrapping style for an image, and click the Size tab to display options for specifying the height and width of an image.
- Format an image with options at the Format Picture task pane. Display this task pane by clicking the Picture Styles group task pane launcher.
- Apply artistic effects to an image with the Artistic Effects button in the Adjust group on the Picture Tools Format tab or with options at the Format Picture task pane with the Effects icon selected.
- Use the yellow circles that display around certain selected shapes to change the width and height of a specific element in a shape.
- Use edit points to customize specific elements in a shape. Display edit points around a shape by clicking the Edit Shape button in the Insert Shapes group on the Drawing Tools Format tab, and then clicking *Edit Points*.
- Display wrap points around an object by clicking the Wrap Text button on the Picture Tools Format tab or Drawing Tools Format tab and then clicking *Edit Wrap Points*. Use wrap points to wrap text closer or father away from an object.
- Link text boxes with the Create Link button in the Text group on the Drawing Tools Format tab. Break a link with the Break Link button in the Text group.
- Text that appears at the top of every page is called a *header*; text that appears at the bottom of every page is called a *footer*.
- Insert predesigned headers and footers in a document or create custom headers and footers.
- To create a custom header, click the Header button in the Header & Footer group on the Insert tab and then click *Edit Header*. At the Header pane, insert elements or text. Complete similar steps to create a custom footer.
- Use buttons in the Insert group on the Header & Footer Tools Design tab to insert elements such as the date and time, Quick Parts, pictures, and images into a header or footer.
- Word inserts headers and footers 0.5 inch from the top and bottom of the page, respectively. Reposition a header or footer with buttons in the Position group on the Header & Footer Tools Design tab.
- A unique header or footer can be created on the first page; a header or footer can be omitted on the first page; different headers or footers can be created for odd and even pages; and different headers or footers can be created for sections in a document. Use options in the Options group on the Header & Footer Tools Design tab to specify the type of header or footer to be created.
- Insert page numbers in a document in a header or footer or with options from the Page Number button drop-down list in the Header & Footer group on the Insert tab.
- Remove page numbers with the *Remove Page Numbers* option from the Page Number button drop-down list.
- Format page numbers with options at the Page Number Format dialog box.

- To print specific sections or pages within a section, use the *Pages* text box at the Print backstage area. When specifying sections and pages, use the letter *s* before a section number and the letter *p* before a page number.
- Word attempts to avoid creating widows and orphans when inserting soft page breaks. Turn on or off the widow/orphan control feature at the Paragraph dialog box with the Line and Page Breaks tab selected. This dialog box also contains options for keeping a paragraph, group of paragraphs, or group of lines together.

Commands Review

FEATURE	RIBBON TAB, GROUP	BUTTON, OPTION
bulleting	Home, Paragraph	
create footer	Insert, Header & Footer	, *Edit Footer*
create header	Insert, Header & Footer	, *Edit Header*
Define New Bullet dialog box	Home, Paragraph	, *Define New Bullet*
Define New Multilevel List dialog box	Home, Paragraph	, *Define New Multilevel List*
Define New Number Format dialog box	Home, Paragraph	, *Define New Number Format*
edit points	Drawing Tools Format, Insert Shapes	, *Edit Points*
footer	Insert, Header & Footer	
header	Insert, Header & Footer	
multilevel list	Home, Paragraph	
numbering	Home, Paragraph	
Paragraph dialog box	Home, Paragraph	
text box	Insert, Text	
wrap points	Picture Tools Format, Arrange OR Drawing Tools Format, Arrange	, *Edit Wrap Points*

Workbook

Chapter study tools and assessment activities are available in the *Workbook* ebook. These resources are designed to help you further develop and demonstrate mastery of the skills learned in this chapter.

Microsoft®

Word

CHAPTER 2

Proofing Documents and Creating Charts

Performance Objectives

Upon successful completion of Chapter 2, you will be able to:

1. Complete a spelling check and a grammar check on the text in a document
2. Display readability statistics
3. Create a custom dictionary and change the default dictionary
4. Display synonyms and antonyms for specific words using the thesaurus
5. Display document word, paragraph, and character counts
6. Insert line numbers
7. Use the Smart Lookup feature
8. Use the translation feature to translate words from English to other languages
9. Insert and format charts

Precheck

Check your current skills to help focus your study.

Microsoft Word includes proofing tools to help you create well-written, error-free documents. These tools include a spelling checker, grammar checker, and thesaurus. Word also provides tools for translating words from English to other languages, as well as a Mini Translator that will translate specific words in a document. In this chapter, you will learn how to use these proofing tools and how to create a custom dictionary. You will also learn how to present text visually in a chart and apply formatting to the chart.

Data Files

Before beginning chapter work, copy the WL2C2 folder to your storage medium and then make WL2C2 the active folder.

SNAP

If you are a SNAP user, launch the Precheck and Tutorials from your Assignments page.

Project 1 **Check Spelling and Grammar in an Investment Plan Document** **1 Part**

You will open an investment plan document and then complete a spelling and grammar check on it.

Preview Finished Project

Checking the Spelling and Grammar

Word provides proofing tools to help create professional, polished documents. Two of these tools are the spelling checker and grammar checker.

The spelling checker works by finding misspelled words and offering replacement words. It also finds duplicate words and words with irregular capitalization. When checking a document, the spelling checker compares the words in the document with the words in its dictionary. If the spelling checker finds a match, it passes over the word. If the spelling checker does not find a match, it stops. The spelling checker stops when it discovers the following types of errors and unfamiliar words:

- a misspelled word (when it does not match another word in the dictionary)
- typographical errors (such as transposed letters)
- double occurrences of a word (such as *the the*)
- irregular capitalization
- some proper names
- jargon and some technical terms

Quick Steps

Check Spelling and Grammar

1. Click Review tab.
2. Click Spelling & Grammar button.
   OR
   Press F7.
3. Change or ignore errors.
4. Click OK.

The grammar checker searches a document for errors in grammar, punctuation, and word usage. Using the spelling checker and grammar checker can help create well-written documents but does not replace the need for proofreading.

Begin a spelling and grammar check by clicking the Review tab and then clicking the Spelling & Grammar button or pressing the F7 function key. If Word detects a possible spelling error, it selects the text containing the error and displays the Spelling task pane, similar to the one shown in Figure 2.1. Possible corrections for the word display in the Spelling task pane list box along with buttons for changing or ignoring the spelling error, as described in Table 2.1. The Spelling task pane also displays a definition of the selected word in the task pane list box.

Figure 2.1 Spelling Task Pane with Error Selected

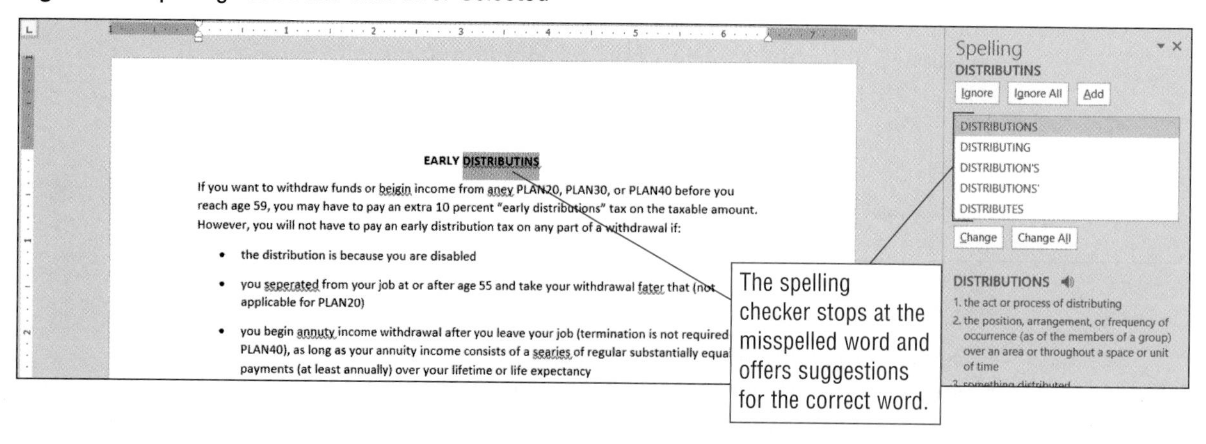

Table 2.1 Spelling Task Pane and Grammar Task Pane Buttons

Button	Function
Ignore	during spell checking, skips that occurrence of the word; during grammar checking, leaves the currently selected text as written
Ignore All	during spell checking, skips that occurrence of the word and all other occurrences of it
Add	adds the selected word to the main spelling check dictionary
Delete	deletes the currently selected word
Change	replaces the selected word with the selected word in the task pane list box
Change All	replaces the selected word and all other occurrences of it with the selected word in the task pane list box

Hint Complete a spelling and grammar check on part of a document by first selecting the text and then clicking the Spelling & Grammar button.

If Word detects a grammar error, it selects the word(s) or the sentence containing the error and displays possible corrections in the Grammar task pane. Depending on the error selected, some of the buttons described in Table 2.1 may display in the Grammar task pane. A description of the grammar rule, with suggestions on how to correct an error, may display in the lower half of the Grammar task pane. Choose to ignore or change errors found by the grammar checker by clicking the Change, Change All, Ignore, or Ignore All button.

Editing During a Spelling and Grammar Check

When checking the spelling and grammar in a document, edits or corrections can be made in the document. Do this by clicking in the document outside the task pane, making the changes or edits, and then clicking the Resume button in the task pane.

Tutorial

Customizing Spelling and Grammar Checking

Customizing Spell Checking

Customize the spelling checker with options at the Word Options dialog box with the *Proofing* option selected, as shown in Figure 2.2. Display this dialog box by clicking the File tab and then clicking *Options*. At the Word Options dialog box, click *Proofing* in the left panel. Use options at this dialog box to specify what the spelling checker should review or ignore.

A custom dictionary can be created for use when spell checking a document. Click the Custom Dictionaries button in the Word Options dialog box to display the Custom Dictionaries dialog box with options for creating a new dictionary or editing an existing dictionary.

Figure 2.2 Word Options Dialog Box with *Proofing* Selected

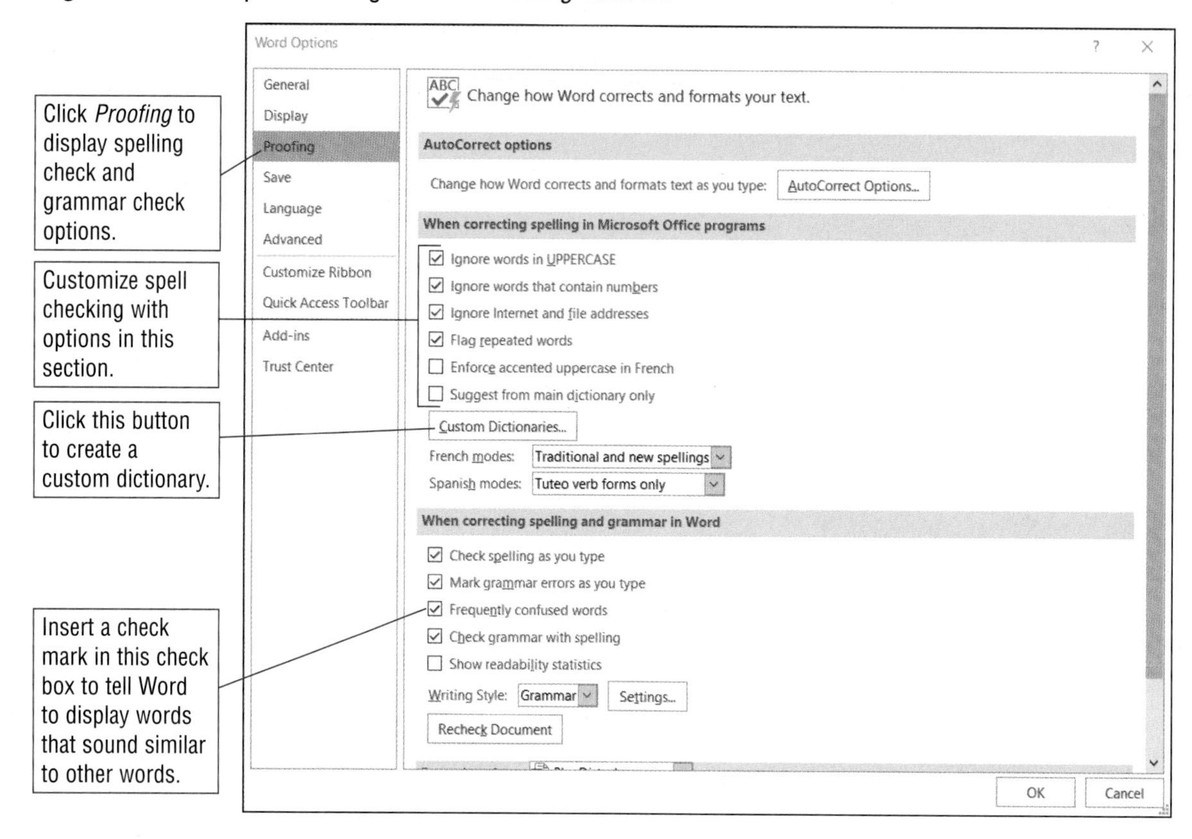

Project 1 Spell Checking a Document with Uppercase Words and Numbers

Part 1 of 1

1. Open **PlanDists.docx** and then save it with the name **2-PlanDists**.
2. Change a spell checking option by completing the following steps:
   a. Click the File tab.
   b. Click *Options*.
   c. At the Word Options dialog box, click the *Proofing* option in the left panel.
   d. Click the *Ignore words in UPPERCASE* check box to remove the check mark.
   e. Click OK to close the dialog box.
3. Complete a spelling check on the document by completing the following steps:
   a. Click the Review tab.
   b. Click the Spelling & Grammar button in the Proofing group.

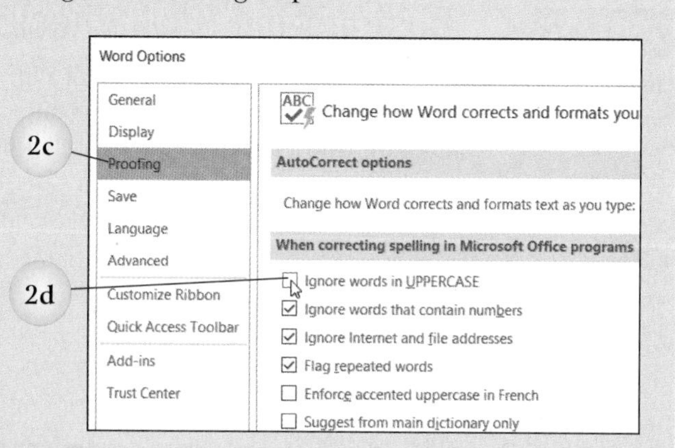

c. The spelling checker selects the word *DISTRIBUTINS* and displays the Spelling task pane. The proper spelling, *DISTRIBUTIONS*, is selected in the Spelling task pane list box and a defintion of *DISTRIBUTIONS* displays below the list box. Click the Change button (or Change All button).

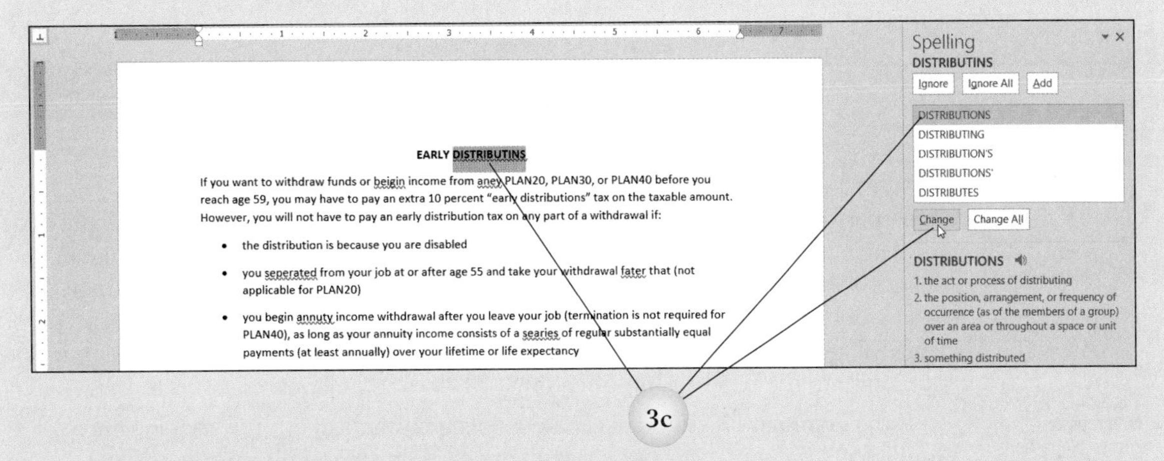

d. The spelling checker selects the word *beigin*. The proper spelling of the word is selected in the task pane list box, so click the Change button.

e. The spelling checker selects the word *aney*. The proper spelling of the word is selected in the task pane list box, so click the Change button.

f. The spelling checker selects *seperated*. The proper spelling is selected in the task pane list box, so click the Change button.

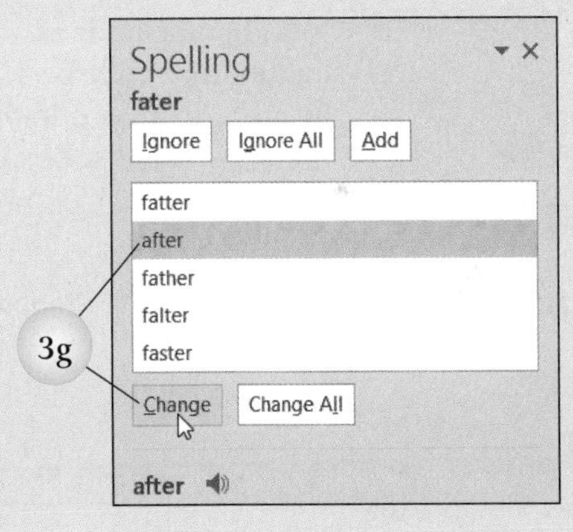

g. The spelling checker selects *fater*. The proper spelling *after* is not selected in the task pane list box but it is one of the words suggested. Click *after* in the task pane list box and then click the Change button.

h. The spelling checker selects *annuty*. The proper spelling is selected in the task pane list box, so click the Change button.

i. The spelling checker selects *searies*. The proper spelling is selected in the task pane list box, so click the Change button.

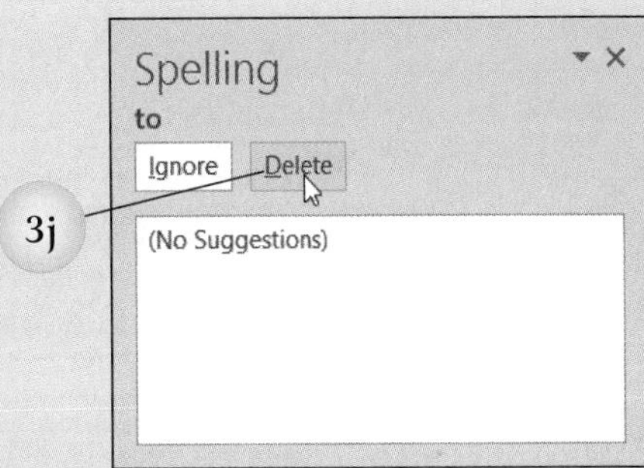

j. The spelling checker selects *to*. (This is a double word occurrence.) Click the Delete button to delete the second occurrence of *to*.

k. The spelling checker selects *Haverson*. This is a proper name, so click the Ignore button.

l. When the message displays that the spelling and grammar check is complete, click OK.

4. Complete steps similar to those in Step 2 to insert a check mark in the *Ignore words in UPPERCASE* check box.
5. Save, print, and then close **2-PlanDists.docx**.

Check Your Work

Project 2 Check the Grammar in a Medical Document — 2 Parts

You will check the grammar in a medical document, change the grammar settings, and then check the grammar again. You will also display readability statistics for the document.

Preview Finished Project

Checking the Grammar

When performing a spelling check and grammar check, Word stops and highlights text that may contain grammatical errors and displays the Grammar task pane, similar to the one shown in Figure 2.3. Like the spelling checker, the grammar checker does not find every error in a document and may stop at correct sentences. Using the grammar checker can help create well-written documents but using it does not eliminate the need for proofreading.

Hint Read grammar suggestions carefully. Some may not be valid in a specific context and a problem identified by the grammar checker may not actually be an issue.

If the grammar checker detects a possible grammatical error in the document, Word selects the sentence containing the possible error and inserts a possible correction in the Grammar task pane list box. The Grammar task pane may also display information on the grammar rule that may have been broken and offer possible methods for correcting the error. Choose to ignore or change a possible error found by the grammar checker by clicking the Change, Change All, Ignore, or Ignore All button.

The Spelling task pane and the Grammar task pane include a pronunciation feature that will speak the word currently selected in the task pane list box. To hear the word pronounced, click the speaker icon to the right of the word below the task pane list box. For this feature to work, the computer speakers must be turned on.

Figure 2.3 Grammar Task Pane with Grammar Error Selected

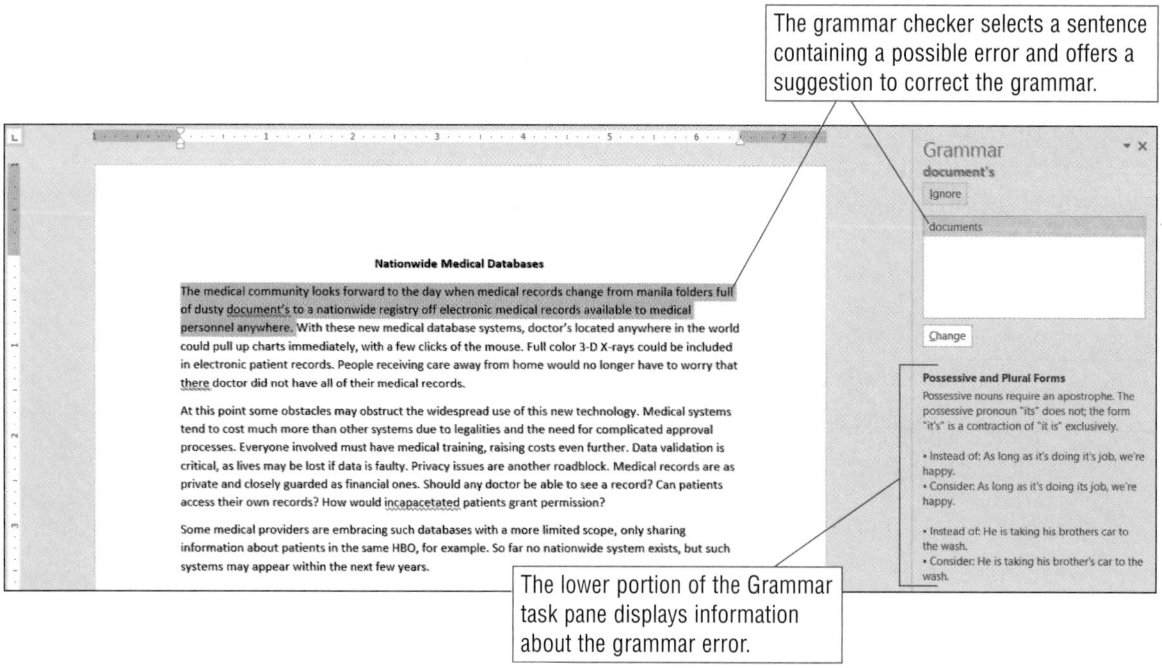

The grammar checker selects a sentence containing a possible error and offers a suggestion to correct the grammar.

Nationwide Medical Databases

The medical community looks forward to the day when medical records change from manila folders full of dusty document's to a nationwide registry off electronic medical records available to medical personnel anywhere. With these new medical database systems, doctor's located anywhere in the world could pull up charts immediately, with a few clicks of the mouse. Full color 3-D X-rays could be included in electronic patient records. People receiving care away from home would no longer have to worry that there doctor did not have all of their medical records.

At this point some obstacles may obstruct the widespread use of this new technology. Medical systems tend to cost much more than other systems due to legalities and the need for complicated approval processes. Everyone involved must have medical training, raising costs even further. Data validation is critical, as lives may be lost if data is faulty. Privacy issues are another roadblock. Medical records are as private and closely guarded as financial ones. Should any doctor be able to see a record? Can patients access their own records? How would incapacetated patients grant permission?

Some medical providers are embracing such databases with a more limited scope, only sharing information about patients in the same HBO, for example. So far no nationwide system exists, but such systems may appear within the next few years.

Grammar
document's
Ignore
documents
Change

Possessive and Plural Forms
Possessive nouns require an apostrophe. The possessive pronoun "its" does not; the form "it's" is a contraction of "it is" exclusively.

- Instead of: As long as it's doing it's job, we're happy.
- Consider: As long as it's doing its job, we're happy.

- Instead of: He is taking his brothers car to the wash.
- Consider: He is taking his brother's car to the wash.

The lower portion of the Grammar task pane displays information about the grammar error.

Project 2a Checking Grammar

Part 1 of 2

1. Open **MedData.docx** and then save it with the name **2-MedData**.
2. Check the grammar in the document by completing the following steps:
   a. Click the Review tab.
   b. Click the Spelling & Grammar button in the Proofing group.
   c. The grammar checker selects the first sentence in the first paragraph and displays *documents* in the list box. Read the information on possessive and plural forms below the list box in the task pane.
   d. Click the Change button to change *document's* to *documents*.
   e. The grammar checker selects *there* in the document and displays *their* in the list box. Read the definitions of *there* and *their* in the task pane.
   f. Click the Change button.
   g. The spelling checker selects the word *incapacetated* and displays the proper spelling in the task pane list box. Listen to the pronunciation of the word *incapacitated* by clicking the speaker icon at the right of the word *incapacitated* below the list box. (Your computer speakers must be turned on to hear the pronunciation.)
   h. With the proper spelling of *incapacitated* selected in the task pane list box, click the Change button.
   i. At the message telling you that the spelling and grammar check is complete, click OK.
3. Save **2-MedData.docx**.

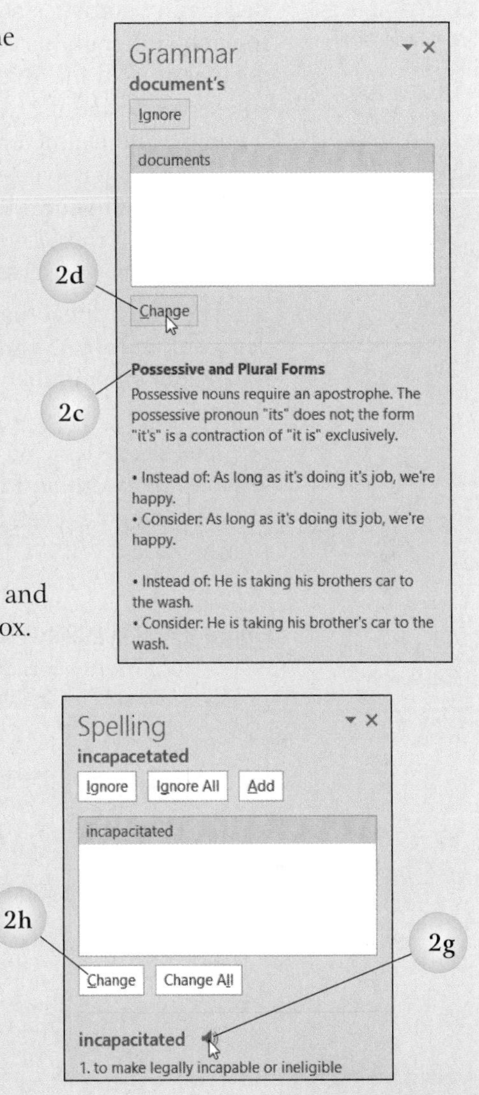

Check Your Work

Setting the Proofing Language

Language

Quick Steps

Choose Proofing Language

1. Click Review tab.
2. Click Language button.
3. Click *Set Proofing Language*.
4. Click language in list box.
5. Click OK.

Microsoft provides a number of dictionaries for proofing text in various languages. To change the language used for proofing a document, click the Review tab, click the Language button in the Language group, and then click *Set Proofing Language* at the drop-down list. At the Language dialog box, click a language in the *Mark selected text as* list box. To make the selected language the default, click the Set As Default button in the lower left corner of the dialog box. Click OK to close the Language dialog box.

Displaying Readability Statistics

Quick Steps

Show Readability Statistics

1. Click File tab.
2. Click *Options.*
3. Click *Proofing.*
4. Click *Show readability statistics* check box.
5. Click OK.
6. Complete spelling and grammar check.

Readability statistics about a document can be displayed when completing a spelling and grammar check of it. Figure 2.4 lists the readability statistics for the document used in Project 2b. The statistics include word, character, paragraph, and sentence counts; average number of sentences per paragraph, words per sentence, and characters per word; and readability information such as the percentage of passive sentences in the document, the Flesch Reading Ease score, and the Flesch-Kincaid Grade Level score. Control the display of readability statistics with the *Show readability statistics* check box in the Word Options dialog box with *Proofing* selected.

The Flesch Reading Ease score is based on the average number of syllables per word and the average number of words per sentence. The higher the score, the greater the number of people who will be able to understand the text in the document. Standard writing generally scores in the 60 to 70 range.

The Flesch-Kincaid Grade Level score is based on the average number of syllables per word and the average number of words per sentence. The score indicates a grade level. Standard writing is generally scored at the seventh or eighth grade level.

Figure 2.4 Readability Statistics Dialog Box

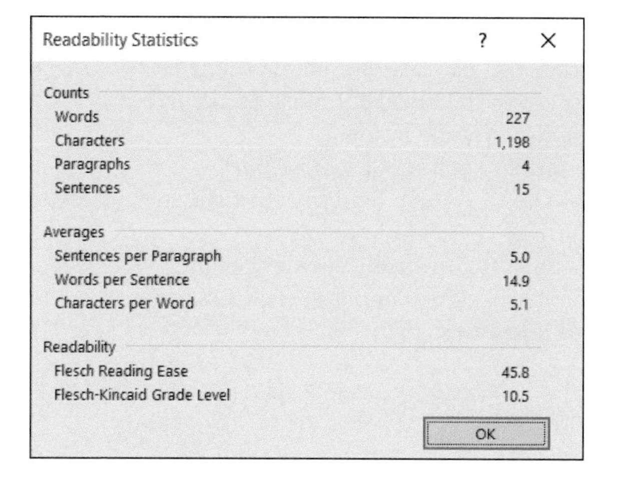

Project 2b **Displaying Readability Statistics** — Part 2 of 2

1. With **2-MedData.docx** open, display readability statistics about the document by completing the following steps:
   a. Click the File tab and then click *Options.*
   b. At the Word Options dialog box, click *Proofing* in the left panel.
   c. Click the *Show readability statistics* check box to insert a check mark.
   d. Click OK to close the Word Options dialog box.
   e. At the document, make sure the Review tab is selected and then click the Spelling & Grammar button.

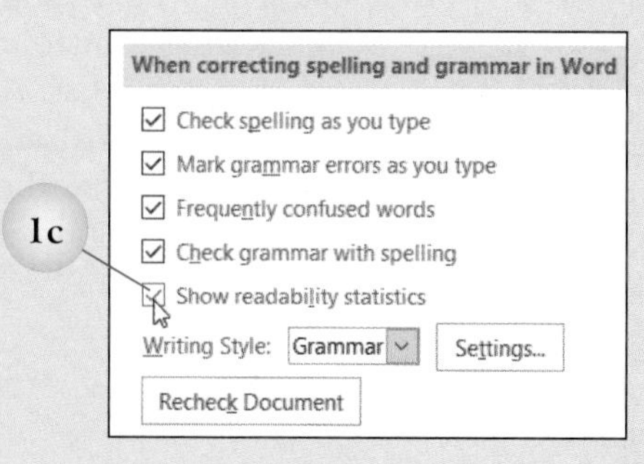

f. Look at the readability statistics that display in the Readability Statistics dialog box and then click OK to close the dialog box.
2. Stop the display of readability statistics after completing a spelling check by completing the following steps:
   a. Click the File tab and then click *Options*.
   b. At the Word Options dialog box, click *Proofing* in the left panel.
   c. Click the *Show readability statistics* check box to remove the check mark.
   d. Click OK to close the Word Options dialog box.
3. Save and then close **2-MedData.docx**.

Project 3 Check the Spelling in an Online Banking Document 4 Parts

You will open an online banking document, create a custom dictionary, add specific terms to the custom dictionary, and then complete a spelling check. You will also display word count, use the Thesaurus feature to replace a word with a synonym, insert line numbers, and display the Smart Lookup task pane and review information about selected text.

Preview Finished Project

Tutorial

Creating a Custom Dictionary

Quick Steps

Create a Custom Dictionary
1. Click File tab.
2. Click *Options*.
3. Click *Proofing*.
4. Click Custom Dictionaries button.
5. Click New button.
6. Type name for dictionary; press Enter.

Hint When you change the custom dictionary settings in one Microsoft Office program, the changes affect all the other programs in the suite.

Creating a Custom Dictionary

When completing a spelling check on a document, Word uses the main dictionary, named RoamingCustom.dic, to compare words. This main dictionary contains most common words but may not include specific proper names, medical terminology, technical terms, acronyms, or other text related to a specific field or business. If documents will be created with specific words, terms, or acronyms not found in the main dictionary, consider creating a custom dictionary. When completing a spelling check, the spelling checker will compare words in a document with the main dictionary as well as a custom dictionary.

To create a custom dictionary, display the Word Options dialog box with *Proofing* selected and then click the Custom Dictionaries button. This displays the Custom Dictionaries dialog box, as shown in Figure 2.5. To create a new dictionary, click the New button. At the Create Custom Dictionary dialog box, type a name for the dictionary in the *File name* text box and then press the Enter key. The new dictionary name displays in the *Dictionary List* list box in the Custom Dictionaries dialog box. More than one dictionary can be used when spell checking a document. Insert a check mark in the check box next to each dictionary to be used when spell checking.

Changing the Default Dictionary

At the Custom Dictionaries dialog box, the default dictionary displays in the *Dictionary List* list box followed by *(Default)*. Change this default by clicking the dictionary name in the list box and then clicking the Change Default button.

Removing a Dictionary

Quick Steps

Remove a Custom Dictionary
1. Click File tab.
2. Click *Options*.
3. Click *Proofing*.
4. Click Custom Dictionaries button.
5. Click custom dictionary name.
6. Click Remove button.
7. Click OK.

Remove a custom dictionary with the Remove button at the Custom Dictionaries dialog box. To do this, display the Custom Dictionaries dialog box, click the dictionary name in the *Dictionary List* list box, and then click the Remove button. No prompt will display confirming the deletion, so make sure the correct dictionary name is selected before clicking the Remove button.

Figure 2.5 Custom Dictionaries Dialog Box

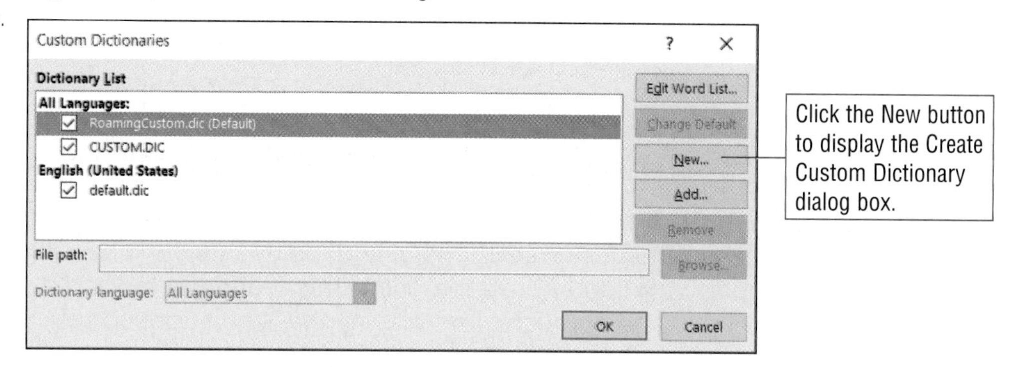

Project 3a **Creating a Custom Dictionary and Changing the Default Dictionary** **Part 1 of 4**

1. Open **BankBrazil.docx**, notice the wavy red lines indicating words not recognized by the spelling checker (words not in the main dictionary), and then close the document.
2. Create a custom dictionary, add words to the dictionary, and then change the default dictionary by completing the following steps:
   a. Click the File tab and then click *Options*.
   b. At the Word Options dialog box, click *Proofing* in the left panel.
   c. Click the Custom Dictionaries button.

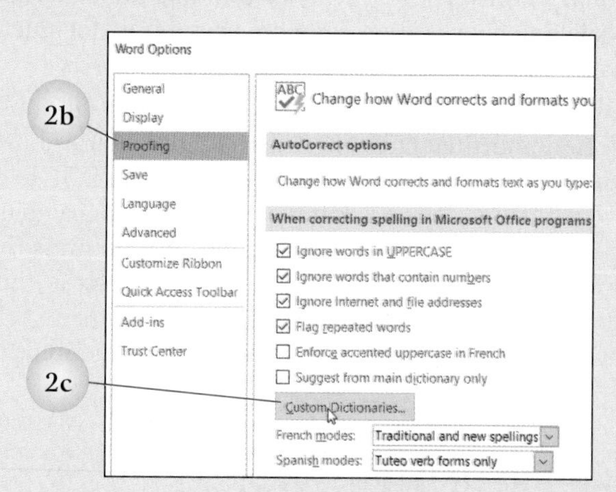

   d. At the Custom Dictionaries dialog box, click the New button.
   e. At the Create Custom Dictionary dialog box, type your first and last names (without a space between them) in the *File name* text box and then press the Enter key.

f. At the Custom Dictionaries dialog box, add a word to your dictionary by completing the following steps:
   1) Click the name of your dictionary in the *Dictionary List* list box.
   2) Click the Edit Word List button.
   3) At the dialog box for your custom dictionary, type Abreu in the *Word(s)* text box.
   4) Click the Add button.

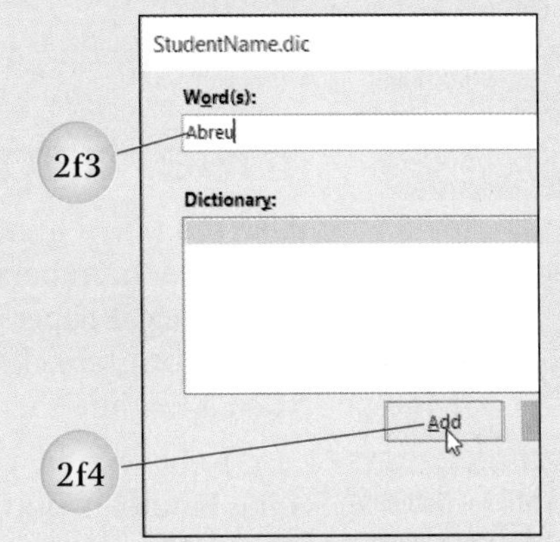

g. Complete steps similar to those in Steps 2f3 and 2f4 to add the following words:

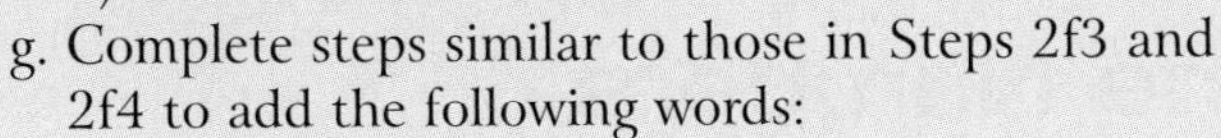

Banco
Itau
Bradesco
Unibanco
Monteiro
Lipschultz

h. When you have added all the words, click OK to close the dialog box.
i. At the Custom Dictionaries dialog box with the name of your dictionary selected in the *Dictionary List* list box, click the Change Default button. (Notice that the word *(Default)* displays after your custom dictionary.)

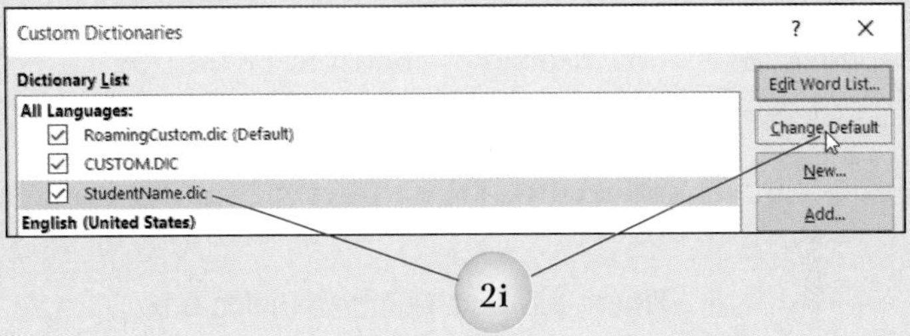

j. Click OK to close the Custom Dictionaries dialog box.
k. Click OK to close the Word Options dialog box.

3. Open **BankBrazil.docx** and then save it with the name **2-BankBrazil**.
4. Complete a spelling and grammar check on the document and correct misspelled words. (The spelling checker will not stop at the words you added to your custom dictionary.)
5. Save and then print **2-BankBrazil.docx**.
6. Change the default dictionary and then remove your custom dictionary by completing the following steps:
   a. Click the File tab and then click *Options*.
   b. At the Word Options dialog box, click *Proofing* in the left panel.
   c. Click the Custom Dictionaries button.
   d. At the Custom Dictionaries dialog box, click *RoamingCustom.dic* in the *Dictionary List* list box.
   e. Click the Change Default button. (This changes the default back to the RoamingCustom.dic dictionary.)
   f. Click the name of your dictionary in the *Dictionary List* list box.
   g. Click the Remove button.
   h. Click OK to close the Custom Dictionaries dialog box.
   i. Click OK to close the Word Options dialog box.

Check Your Work

Tutorial

Displaying Word Count

Quick Steps

Display the Word Count Dialog Box

Click word count section of Status bar.
OR
1. Click Review tab.
2. Click Word Count button.

 Word Count

Displaying the Word Count

Words are counted as they are typed in a document and the total number of words in a document is displayed on the Status bar. To display more information—such as the numbers of pages, paragraphs, and lines—display the Word Count dialog box. Display the Word Count dialog box by clicking the word count section of the Status bar or by clicking the Review tab and then clicking the Word Count button in the Proofing group.

Count words in a portion of the document, rather than the entire document, by selecting the portion of text and then displaying the Word Count dialog box. To determine the total word count of several sections throughout a document, select the first section, press and hold down the Ctrl key, and then select the other sections.

Tutorial

Inserting Line Numbers

 Line Numbers

Quick Steps

Insert Line Numbers

1. Click Layout tab.
2. Click Line Numbers button.
3. Click line number option.

Inserting Line Numbers

Use the Line Numbers button in the Page Setup group on the Layout tab to insert line numbers in a document. Numbering lines has practical applications for certain legal papers and reference purposes. To number lines in a document, click the Layout tab, click the Line Numbers button in the Page Setup group, and then click a line number option at the drop-down list.

To have more control over inserting line numbers in a document, click the Line Numbers button and then click *Line Numbering Options* at the drop-down list. At the Page Setup dialog box with the Layout tab selected, click the Line Numbering button at the bottom of the dialog box and the Line Numbers dialog box displays as shown in Figure 2.6. Use options at this dialog box to insert line numbering and to specify the starting number, the location line numbers are printed, the interval between printed line numbers, and whether line numbers are consecutive or start over at the beginning of each page.

Figure 2.6 Line Numbers Dialog Box

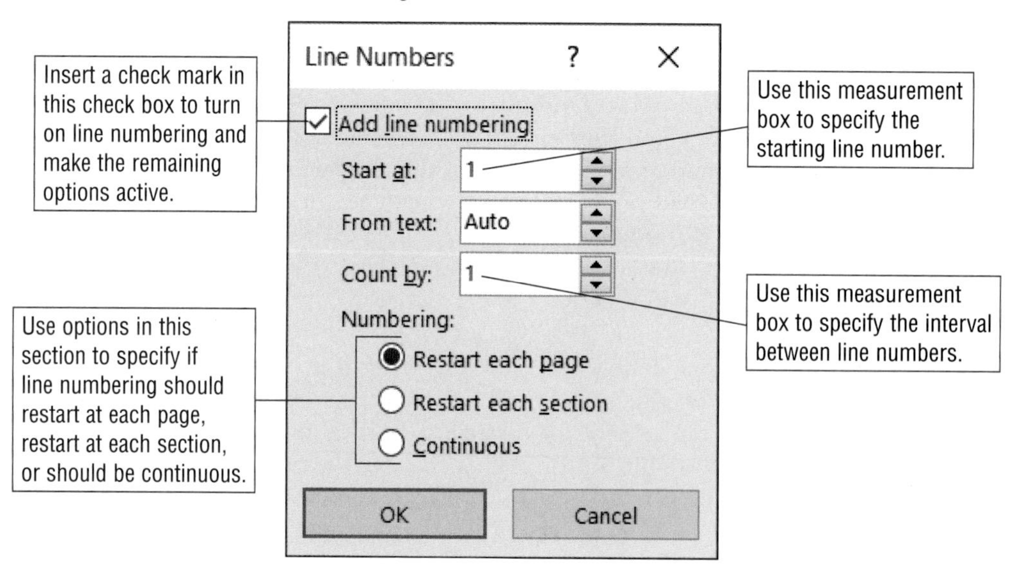

Tutorial

Using the Thesaurus

Thesaurus

Quick Steps

Use the Thesaurus

1. Click Review tab.
2. Click Thesaurus button.
3. Type word in search text box.
4. Press Enter.

Using the Thesaurus

Word offers a Thesaurus feature for finding synonyms, antonyms, and related words for a particular word. Synonyms are words that have the same or nearly the same meaning. When the Thesaurus feature is used, antonyms may display for some words, which are words with opposite meanings.

To use the Thesaurus feature, click the Review tab and then click the Thesaurus button in the Proofing group or use the keyboard shortcut Shift + F7. At the Thesaurus task pane that displays, click in the search text box at the top of the task pane, type a word, and then press the Enter key or click the Start searching button (which contains a magnifying glass icon). A list of synonyms and antonyms for the typed word displays in the task pane list box. Another method for finding synonyms and antonyms is to select a word and then display the Thesaurus task pane. Figure 2.7 shows the Thesaurus task pane with synonyms and antonyms for the word *normally* displayed.

Depending on the word typed in the search text box, the words in the Thesaurus task pane list box may display followed by *(n.)* for *noun*, *(adj.)* for *adjective*, or *(adv.)* for *adverb*. Any antonyms that display at the end of the list of related synonyms will be followed by *(Antonym)*. If a dictionary is installed on the computer, a definition of the selected word will display below the task pane list box.

The Thesaurus feature provides synonyms for the selected word as well as a list of related synonyms. For example, in the Thesaurus task pane list box shown in Figure 2.7, the main synonym *usually* displays for *normally* and is preceded by a collapse triangle (a right-and-down-pointing triangle). The collapse triangle indicates that the list of related synonyms is displayed. Click the collapse triangle

Figure 2.7 Thesaurus Task Pane

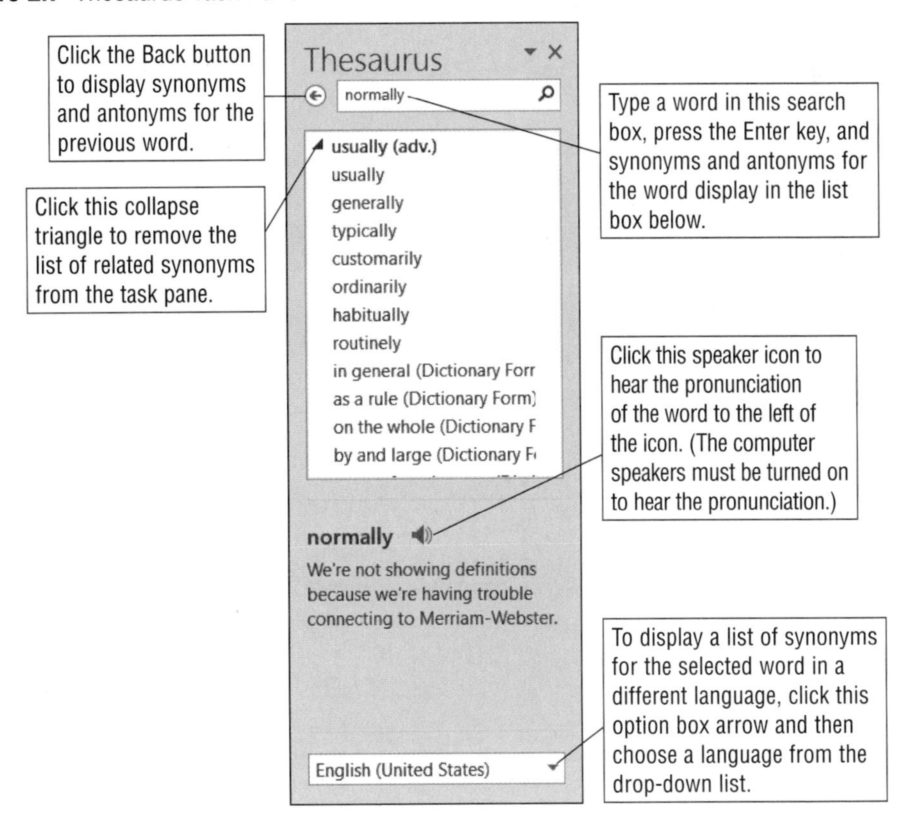

and the list of related synonyms is removed from the task pane list box and the collapse triangle changes to an expand triangle (a right-pointing triangle). Click a word in the Thesaurus task pane list box to see synonyms for it.

When reviewing synonyms and antonyms for words within a document, display the list of synonyms and antonyms for the previous word by clicking the Back button (left-pointing arrow) at the left side of the search text box. Click the down-pointing triangle at the left side of the Close button in the upper right corner of the task pane and a drop-down list displays with options for moving, sizing, and closing the task pane.

To replace a selected word in the document with a synonym in the Thesaurus task pane, hover the mouse pointer over the synonym in the task pane list box until a down arrow displays. Click the down arrow and then click *Insert* at the drop-down list.

The Thesaurus task pane, like the Spelling task pane and Grammar task pane, includes a pronunciation feature that will speak the word currently selected in the task pane. To hear the word pronounced, click the speaker icon at the right side of the word below the task pane list box. (For this feature to work, the computer speakers must be turned on.)

The Thesaurus task pane also includes a language option for displaying synonyms of the selected word in a different language. To use this feature, click the option box arrow at the bottom of the task pane and then click a language at the drop-down list.

Project 3b Displaying Word Count, Inserting Line Numbers, and Using the Thesaurus — Part 2 of 4

1. With **2-BankBrazil.docx** open, click the word count section of the Status bar.
2. After reading the statistics in the Word Count dialog box, click the Close button.
3. Display the Word Count dialog box by clicking the Review tab and then clicking the Word Count button in the Proofing group.
4. Click the Close button to close the Word Count dialog box.
5. Press Ctrl + A to select the entire document, click the Home tab, click the Line and Paragraph Spacing button in the Paragraph group, and then click *2.0* at the drop-down gallery.
6. Insert line numbering by completing the following steps:
   a. Click the Layout tab.
   b. Click the Line Numbers button in the Page Setup group and then click *Continuous* at the drop-down list.
   c. Scroll through the document and notice the line numbers that display at the left side of the document.
   d. With the document selected, click the Line Numbers button and then click the *Restart Each Page* option.
   e. Scroll through the document and notice that the line numbers start over again at the beginning of page 2.

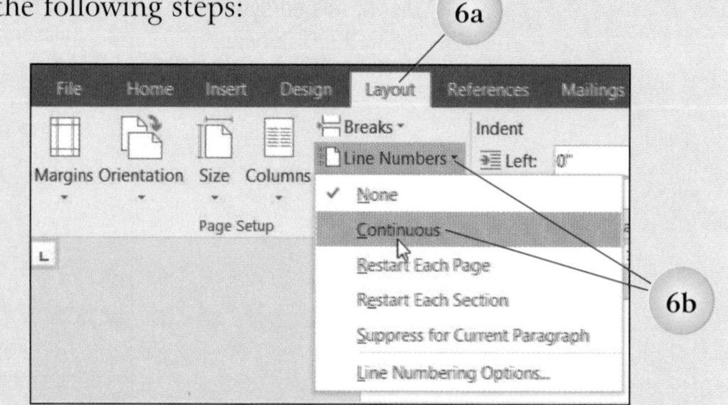

f. With the document selected, click the Line Numbers button and then click *Line Numbering Options* at the drop-down list.
g. At the Page Setup dialog box, click the Line Numbers button toward the bottom of the dialog box.
h. At the Line Numbers dialog box, select the current number in the *Start at* measurement box and then type 30.
i. Click the *Count by* measurement box up arrow. (This displays *2* in the measurement box.)
j. Click the *Continuous* option in the *Numbering* section.
k. Click OK to close the Line Numbers dialog box.

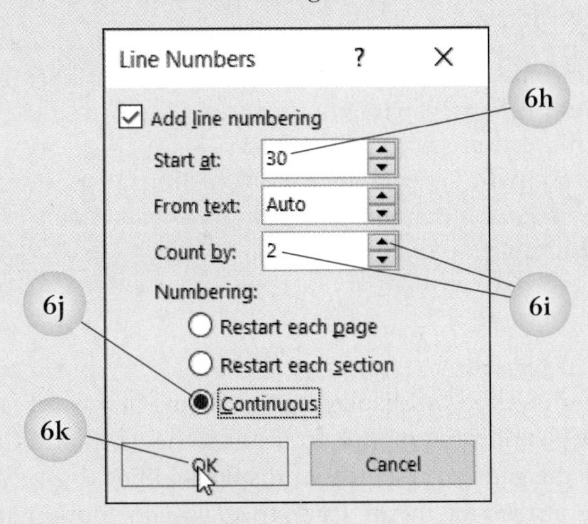

l. Click OK to close the Page Setup dialog box.
m. Scroll through the document and notice the line numbers that display at the left side of the document. The numbers start with *30* and increment by two.
n. Click the Line Numbers button and then click *None* at the drop-down list.

7. With the document selected, click the Home tab, click the Line and Paragraph Spacing button in the Paragraph group, and then click *1.0* at the drop-down gallery.
8. Use the Thesaurus feature to change the word *normally* in the first paragraph to *generally* by completing the following steps:
   a. Select the word *normally* in the first paragraph (first word in the seventh line of text).
   b. Click the Review tab.
   c. Click the Thesaurus button in the Proofing group.
   d. At the Thesaurus task pane, hover the mouse pointer over the synonym *generally*, click the down arrow at the right of the word, and then click *Insert* at the drop-down list.

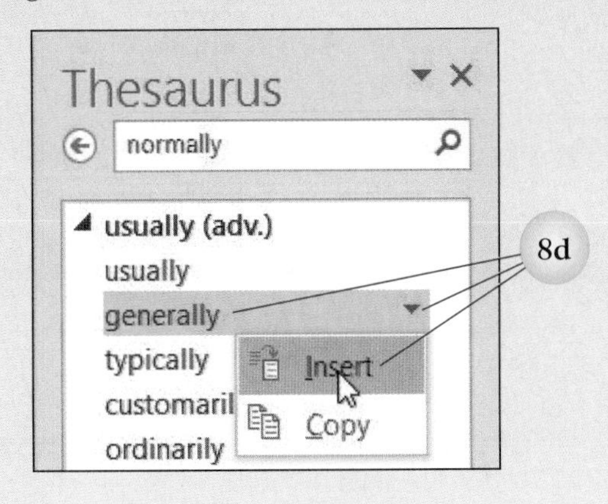

e. Click the word *generally* in the Thesaurus task pane.
f. If your computer speakers are turned on, listen to the pronunciation of the word *generally* by clicking the speaker icon next to the word below the task pane list box.

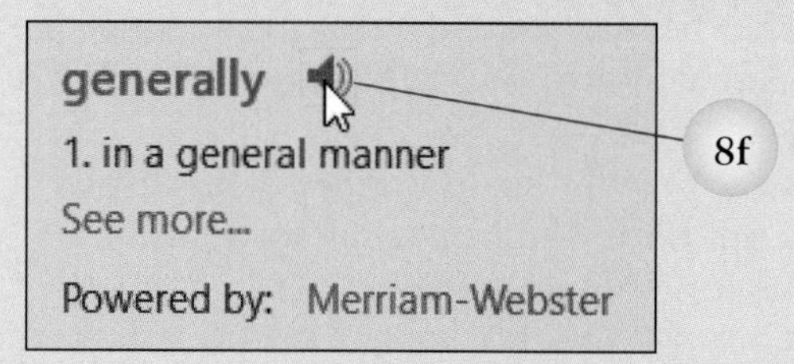

9. Follow similar steps to make the following changes using the Thesaurus feature:
   a. Change *acquaintances* in the first paragraph to *friends*.
   b. Change *combat* in the second paragraph to *battle*.
10. Close the Thesaurus task pane by clicking the Close button in the upper right corner of the task pane.
11. Save **2-BankBrazil.docx**.

Check Your Work

Another method for displaying synonyms of a word is to use a shortcut menu. To do this, position the mouse pointer on the word and then click the right mouse button. At the shortcut menu that displays, point to *Synonyms* and then click the a synonym at the side menu. Click the *Thesaurus* option at the bottom of the side menu to display synonyms and antonyms for the word in the Thesaurus task pane.

Project 3c Replacing Synonyms Using the Shortcut Menu

Part 3 of 4

1. With **2-BankBrazil.docx** open, position the mouse pointer on the word *vogue* in the second sentence of the third paragraph.
2. Click the right mouse button.
3. At the shortcut menu, point to *Synonyms* and then click *fashion* at the side menu.
4. Save **2-BankBrazil.docx**.

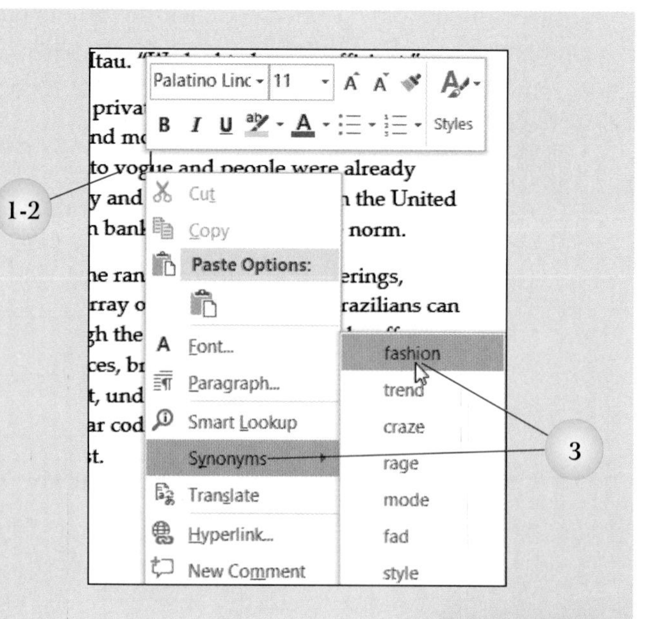

Check Your Work

Tutorial

Using Smart Lookup

Using Smart Lookup

The Smart Lookup feature provides information on selected text from a variety of sources on the web, such as Wikipedia, Bing, and the Oxford Dictionary. To use the Smart Lookup feature, select text and then click the Smart Lookup button in the Insights group on the Review tab. This opens the Smart Lookup task pane at the right side of the screen.

The Smart Lookup task pane contains the *Explore* and *Define* options. With the *Explore* option selected, the task pane displays information about the selected text from sources on the web, as shown in Figure 2.8. Click the *Define* option and a definition from the Oxford Dictionary website displays for the selected text, as shown in Figure 2.9.

The Smart Lookup task pane, like the Spelling, Grammar, and Thesaurus task panes, includes a pronunciation feature that will speak the word displayed in the task pane. To hear the word pronounced, click the speaker icon in the task pane. For this feature to work, the computer speakers must be turned on.

The Smart Lookup feature can also be accessed through the Tell Me feature. To use Tell Me for Smart Lookup, click in the *Tell Me* text box, type text or a function, and then click the *Smart Lookup* option at the drop-down list.

Figure 2.8 Smart Lookup Task Pane with the *Explore* Option Selected

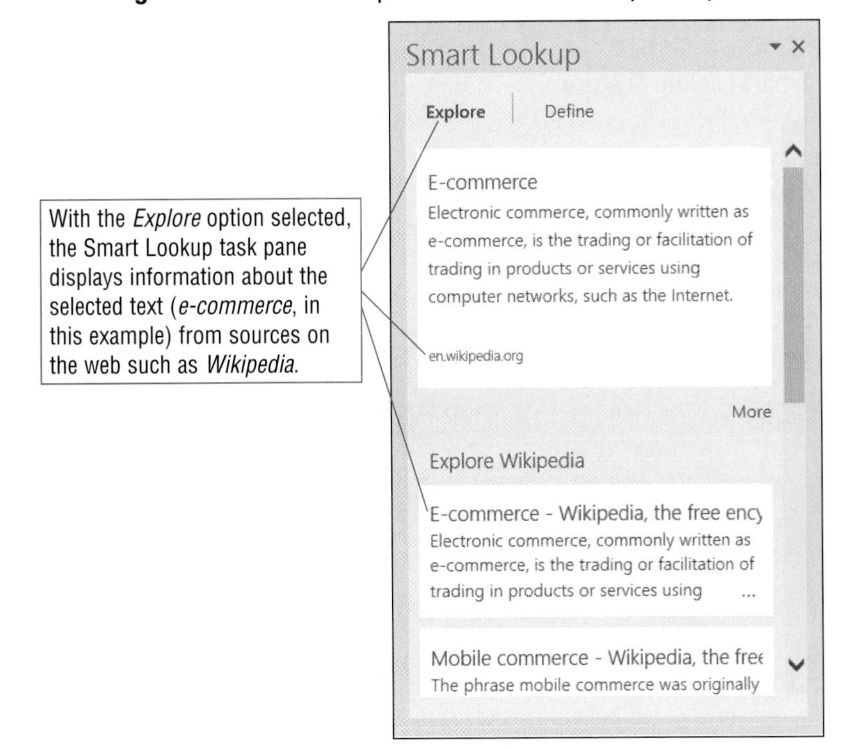

Figure 2.9 Smart Lookup Task Pane with the *Details* Option Selected

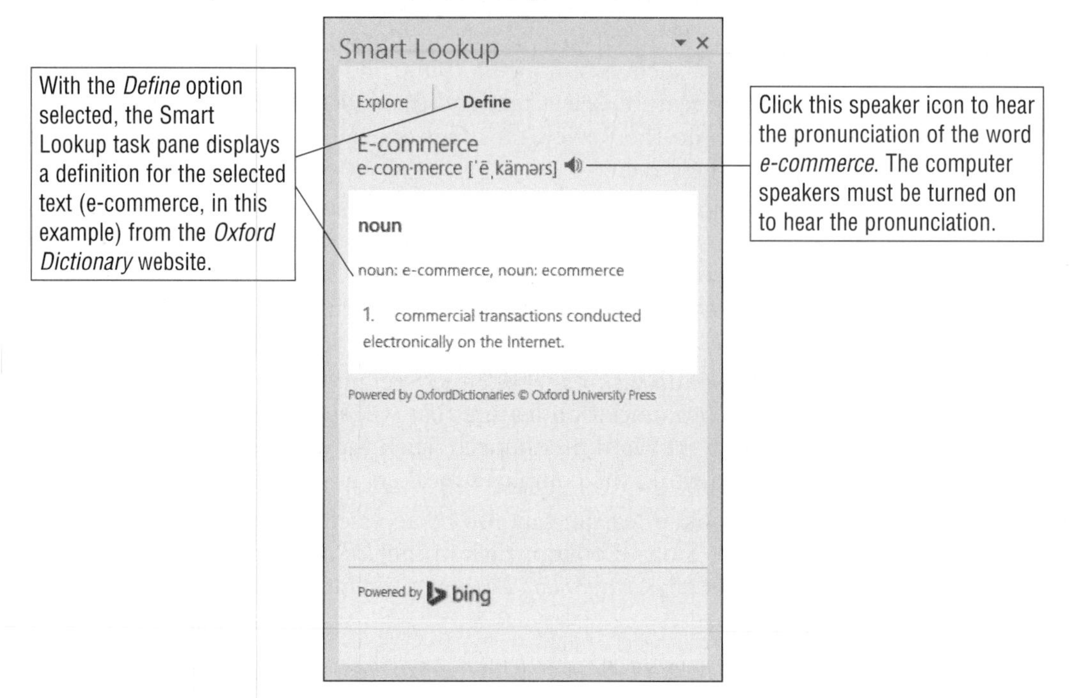

Project 3d Using the Smart Lookup Feature

Part 4 of 4

1. With **2-BankBrazil.docx** open, display information about and definitions for words by completing the following steps:
   a. Select the word *e-commerce* in the third sentence of the first paragraph.
   b. Click the Review tab, if necessary, and then click the Smart Lookup button in the Insights group.
   c. Look at the information about e-commerce in the Smart Lookup task pane with the *Explore* option selected.
   d. Click the *Define* option.
   e. Read the definition in the task pane.
   f. If the computer speakers are turned on, click the speaker icon at the top of the task pane.
   g. Click the Close button in the upper right corner of the Smart Lookup task pane.
   h. Select the word *economy* in the second sentence of the second paragraph.
   i. Click the Smart Lookup button in the Insights group.
   j. Look at the information that displays in the Smart Lookup task pane and then click the *Define* option.
   k. Read the definition in the task pane.
   l. Click the Close button to close the Smart Lookup task pane.
2. Save, print, and then close **2-BankBrazil.com**.

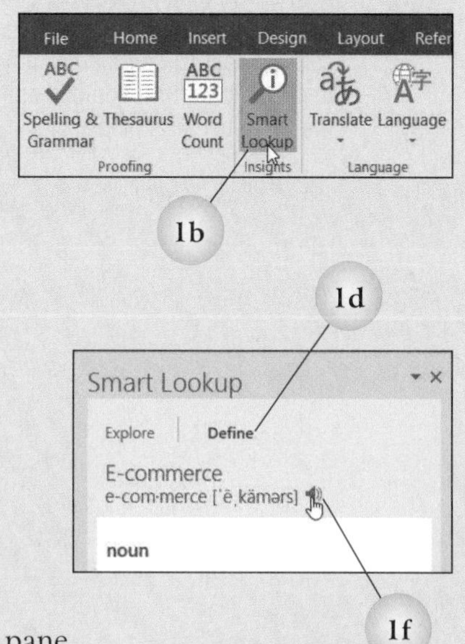

Check Your Work

Project 4 Translate Text in a Computer Document and Translation Document

1 Part

You will use the translation feature to translate text from English to Spanish and English to French.

Preview Finished Project

Tutorial

Translating Text to and from Different Languages

 Translate

Translating Text to and from Different Languages

Word provides several methods of translating text from one language into another. One method is provided at the Thesaurus task pane. The Translate button in the Language group on the Review tab provides additional translation methods. Click the Translate button and a drop-down list displays with options for translating the entire document or selected text and for turning on the Mini Translator.

Translating Text

Quick Steps

Translate an Entire Document
1. Open document.
2. Click Review tab.
3. Click Translate button.
4. Click *Translate Document*.
5. Click Yes button.

Translate Selected Text
1. Select text.
2. Click Review tab.
3. Click Translate button.
4. Click *Translate Selected Text*.
5. Click Yes button.

Hint Press and hold down the Alt key and then click anywhere in the document to display the Research task pane.

Click the first option, *Translate Document*, and a message displays indicating that the document will be sent over the Internet in a secured format to Microsoft or a third-party translation service provider. To continue to the translator, click the Yes button. The computer must be connected to the Internet for the document to be sent to Microsoft or a third-party translation service provider.

Click the second option, *Translate Selected Text*, and Microsoft Translator or a third-party translation service provider will translate the selected text in the document and insert the translation in the Research task pane. The Research task pane displays at the right side of the screen and includes options for translating text to and from different languages.

Click the third option, *Mini Translator*, to turn on this feature. With the Mini Translator turned on, point to a word or select a phrase in the document and the translation of the text displays in a box above the text. To turn off the Mini Translator, click the *Mini Translator* option at the Translate button drop-down list. When the Mini Translator is turned on, the icon positioned to the left of the *Mini Translator* option displays with a light-gray background.

Choosing a Translation Language

Quick Steps

Turn on Mini Translator
1. Click Review tab.
2. Click Translate button.
3. Click *Mini Translator*.

Click the fourth option in the Translate button drop-down list, *Choose Translation Language*, and the Translation Language Options dialog box displays, as shown in Figure 2.10. At this dialog box, specify the translate-from language and the translate-to language and also the translate-to language for the Mini Translator.

Figure 2.10 Translation Language Options Dialog Box

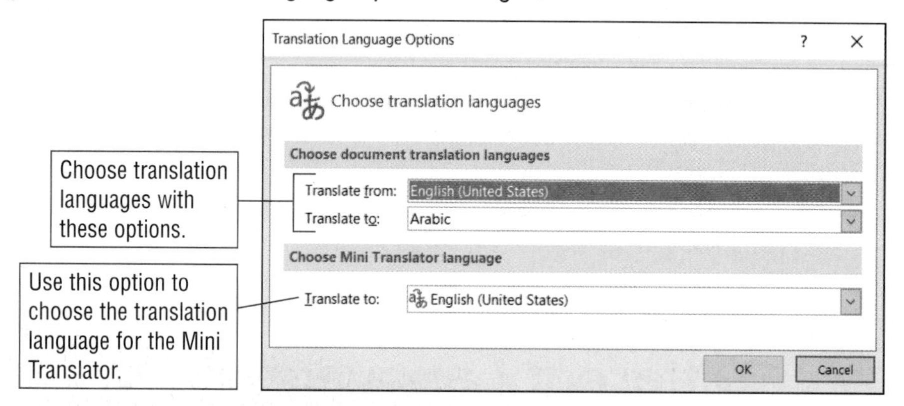

Preparing Documents for Translation

The translation features in Word are considered machine translations because a machine rather than a person is translating text from one language to another. While machine translation is useful for basic information, important or sensitive information should be translated by a person to ensure that the translation reflects the full meaning of the information.

When using Word's translation features, consider the following content standards and guidelines when translating information to reduce confusion or errors and optimize the translation:

1. Use standard, formal language
2. Use proper punctuation and grammar
3. Spell words correctly
4. Avoid abbreviations and acronyms
5. Avoid using slang, colloquialisms, and idioms
6. Avoid ambiguities and vague references
7. Write sentences that are direct and express only one idea
8. Use articles (such as *the*) in sentences whenever possible
9. Repeat the noun in a sentence instead of using a pronoun
10. Apply predesigned heading styles to headings in a document

Project 4 Translating Text

Part 1 of 1

Note: Check with your instructor before completing this project to make sure you have access to the Internet.

1. Open **ChapQuestions.docx** and then save it with the name **2-ChapQuestions**.
2. Change the translation language to Spanish by completing the following steps:
   a. Click the Review tab.
   b. Click the Translate button in the Language group and then click the *Choose Translation Language* option at the drop-down list.

c. At the Translation Language Options dialog box, make sure that *English (United States)* displays in the *Translate from* option box.

d. Click the *Translate to* option box arrow in the *Choose document translation languages* section and then click *Spanish (Spain)* at the drop-down list. (Skip this step if *Spanish (Spain)* is already selected.)

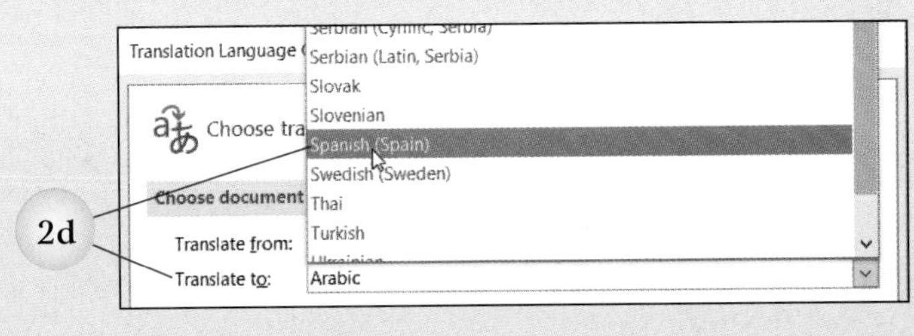

e. Click OK to close the dialog box.

3. Translate the entire document to Spanish by completing the following steps:
   a. Click the Translate button and then click the *Translate Document [English (United States) to Spanish (Spain)]* option.
   b. At the message indicating that the document will be sent over the Internet in a secured format to Microsoft or a third-party translation service provider, click the Yes button.

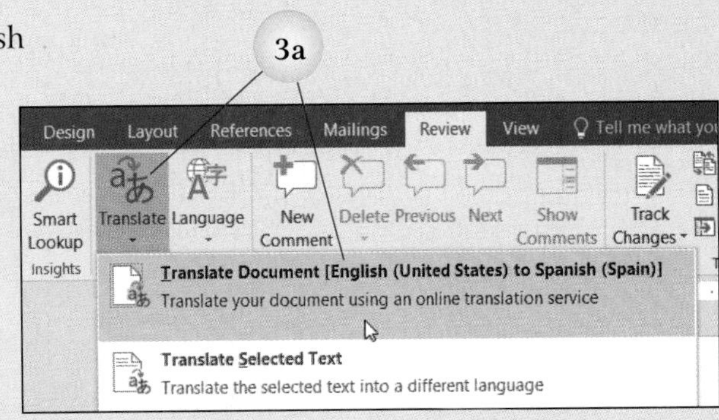

   c. In a few moments, the Microsoft Translator window will open (or a window from a third-party translation service provider).
   d. Select the translated text.
   e. Press Ctrl + C to copy the text.
   f. Close the Microsoft Translator window.
   g. At the **2-ChapQuestions.docx** document, press Ctrl + End to move the insertion point to the end of the document and then press Ctrl + V to insert the copied text.
4. Save, print, and then close **2-ChapQuestions.docx**.
5. Open **TranslateTerms.docx** and then save it with the name **2-TranslateTerms**.
6. Translate the word *Central* into Spanish by completing the following steps:
   a. Click the Review tab.
   b. Click the Translate button and then click the *Choose Translation Language* option at the drop-down list.
   c. At the Translation Language Options dialog box, click the *Translate to* option box arrow in the *Choose Mini Translator language* section and then click *Spanish (Spain)* at the drop-down list. (Skip this step if *Spanish (Spain)* is already selected.)
   d. Click OK to close the dialog box.
   e. Click the Translate button and then click *Mini Translator [Spanish (Spain)]* at the drop-down list.
   f. At the message that displays, click the Yes button.
   g. Hover the mouse pointer over the word *Central* in the table. (The Mini Translator displays dimmed above the word.) Move the mouse pointer to the Mini Translator and then look at the translation in the box above the term. Type one of the Spanish terms in the *Spanish* column.
   h. Complete steps similar to those in Step 6g to display Spanish translations for the remaining terms. For each term, type the corresponding Spanish term in the appropriate location in the table. Type the terms without any accents or special symbols.

7. Use the Mini Translator to translate terms into French by completing the following steps:
   a. Click the Translate button and then click the *Choose Translation Language* option at the drop-down list.
   b. At the Translation Language Options dialog box, click the *Translate to* option box arrow in the *Choose Mini Translator lanuguage* section and then click *French (France)* at the drop-down list.
   c. Click OK to close the dialog box.
   d. With the Mini Translator turned on, hover the mouse pointer over the word *Central* in the table. (The Mini Translator displays dimmed above the term.)
   e. Move the mouse pointer to the Mini Translator and then choose one of the French terms and type it in the *French* column.
   f. Complete steps similar to those in Steps 7d and 7e to display French translations for the remaining terms. For each term, type the corresponding French term in the appropriate location in the table. Type the terms without any accents or special symbols.
8. Turn off the Mini Translator by clicking the Translate button and then clicking *Mini Translator [French (France)]* at the drop-down list.
9. Save, print, and then close **2-TranslateTerms.docx**.

Check Your Work

Project 5 Create and Format a Column Chart and Pie Chart — 5 Parts

You will use the Chart feature to create and format a column chart and then create and format a pie chart.

Preview Finished Project

Tutorial

Creating a Chart

 Chart

Quick Steps

Insert a Chart

1. Click Insert tab.
2. Click Chart button.
3. Enter data in Excel worksheet.
4. Close Excel.

Hint You can copy a chart from Excel to Word and embed it as static data or link it to the worksheet.

Creating a Chart

A chart is a visual presentation of data. In Word, a variety of charts can be created, including bar and column charts, pie charts, area charts, and many more. To create a chart, click the Insert tab and then click the Chart button in the Illustrations group. This displays the Insert Chart dialog box, as shown in Figure 2.11. At this dialog box, choose the chart type in the list at the left side, click the chart style, and then click OK.

Click OK at the Insert Chart dialog box and a chart is inserted in the document and Excel opens with sample data, as shown in Figure 2.12. Type specific data in the Excel worksheet cells over the existing data. As data is typed in the Excel worksheet, it appears in the chart in the Word document. To type data in the Excel worksheet, click in a cell and type the data; then press the Tab key to make the next cell active, press Shift + Tab to make the previous cell active, or press the Enter key to make the cell below active.

The sample worksheet contains a data range of four columns and five rows and the cells in the data range display with a light fill color. Excel uses the data in the range to create the chart in the document. The sample worksheet is not limited to four columns and five rows. Simply type data in cells outside the data range and Excel expands the data range and incorporates the new data in the chart. This occurs because the table AutoExpansion feature is turned on by

Figure 2.11 Insert Chart Dialog Box

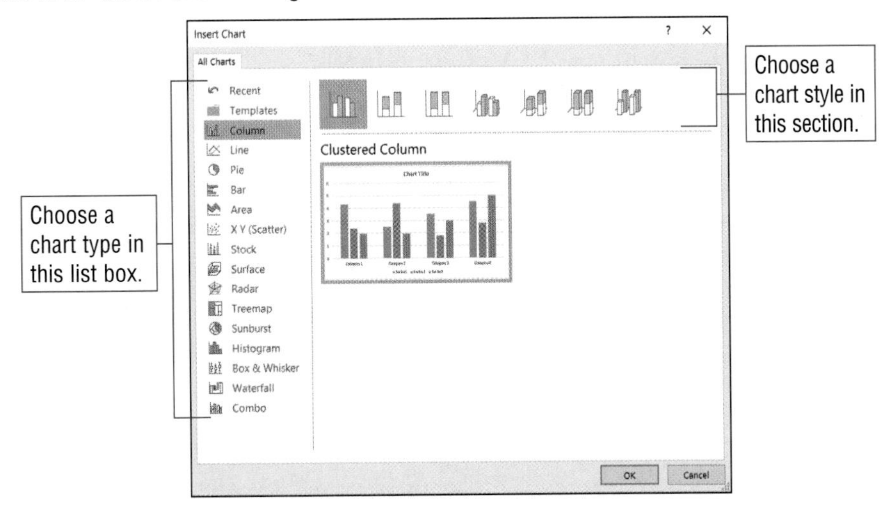

Figure 2.12 Sample Chart

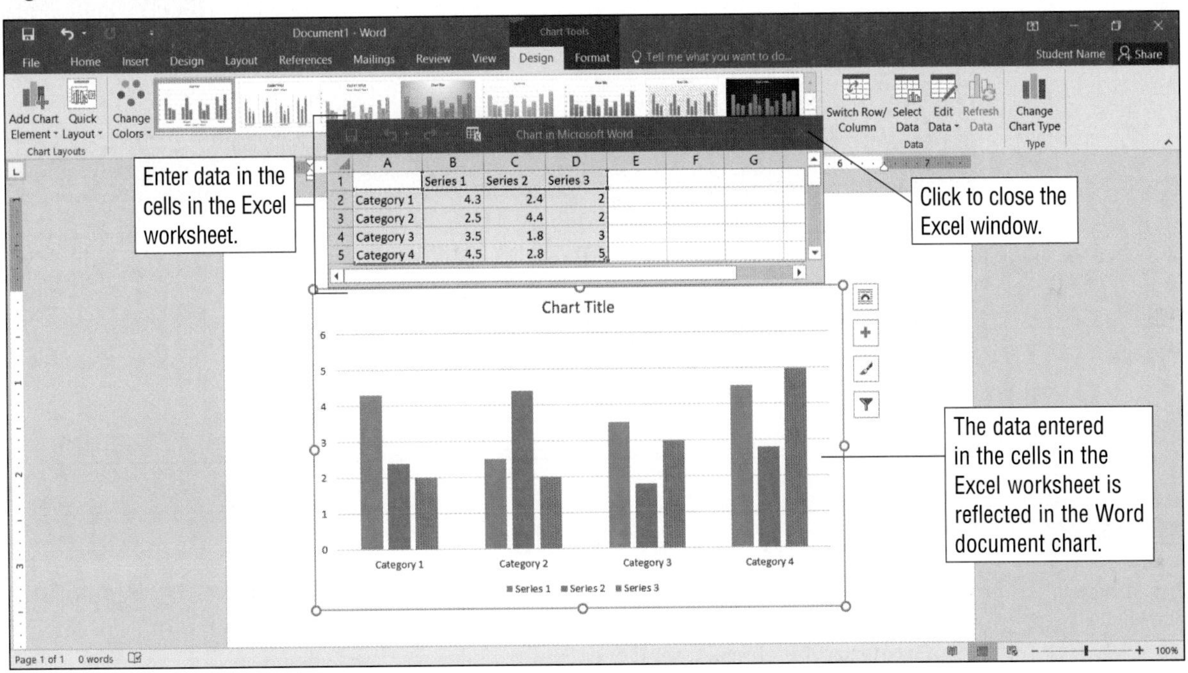

default. If data is typed in a cell outside the data range, an AutoCorrect Options button displays in the lower right corner of the cell. Use this button to turn off AutoExpansion.

If data is not typed in all four columns and five rows, decrease the size of the data range. To do this, position the mouse pointer on the small, square, blue icon in the lower right corner of cell E5 until the pointer displays as a diagonally pointing two-headed arrow and then drag up to decrease the number of rows in the range and/or drag left to decrease the number of columns.

When all the data is typed in the worksheet, click the Close button in the upper right corner of the Excel window. This closes the Excel window, expands the Word document window, and displays the chart in the document.

Project 5a Creating a Column Chart

Part 1 of 5

1. At a blank document, click the Insert tab and then click the Chart button in the Illustrations group.
2. At the Insert Chart dialog box, click OK.
3. Type Sales 2016 in cell B1 in the Excel worksheet.
4. Press the Tab key and then type Sales 2017 in cell C1.
5. Press the Tab key and then type Sales 2018 in cell D1.
6. Press the Tab key. (This makes cell A2 active.)
7. Continue typing the remaining data in cells, as indicated in Figure 2.13. After typing the last entry, click in cell A1.
8. Click the Close button in the upper right corner of the Excel window.
9. Save the document and name it **2-Charts**.

Chart

	A	B	C
1		Sales 2016	Series 2
2	Category 1	4.3	2.4
3	Category 2	2.5	4.4
4	Category 3	3.5	1.8
5	Category 4	4.5	2.8

3

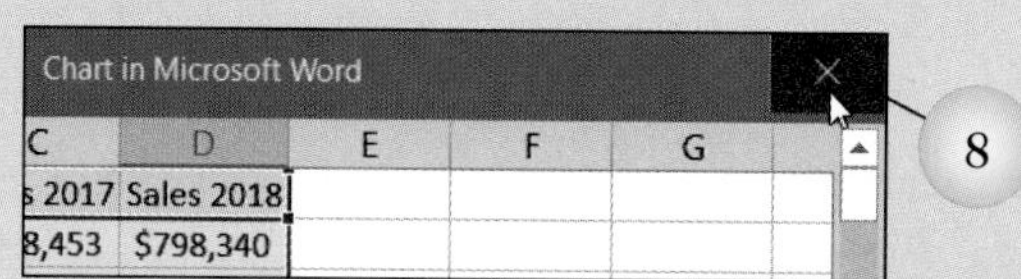

Check Your Work

Figure 2.13 Project 5a

Chart in Microsoft Word

	A	B	C	D	E	F	G
1		Sales 2016	Sales 2017	Sales 2018			
2	Northeast	$729,300	$698,453	$798,340			
3	Southeast	$320,455	$278,250	$333,230			
4	Northwest	$610,340	$700,100	$525,425			
5	Southwest	$522,340	$500,340	$625,900			

Tutorial

Formatting with Chart Buttons

Formatting with Chart Buttons

When a chart is inserted in a document, four buttons display at the right side of the chart border, as shown in Figure 2.14. These buttons contain options for applying formatting to the chart.

Click the top button, Layout Options, and a side menu displays with text wrapping options. Click the next button, Chart Elements, and a side menu displays with chart elements, such as axis title, chart title, data labels, data table, gridlines, and legend. Elements with check marks inserted in the check boxes are included in the chart. To include other elements, insert check marks in the check boxes for them.

Click the Chart Styles button at the right side of the chart and a side menu gallery of styles displays. Scroll down the gallery and hover the mouse over an option and the style formatting is applied to the chart. In addition to providing options for chart styles, the Chart Styles button side menu gallery provides options for chart colors. Click the Chart Styles button, click the Color tab to the right of the Style tab, and then click a color option at the color palette that displays. Hover the mouse over a color option to view how the color change affects the elements in the chart.

Figure 2.14 Chart Buttons

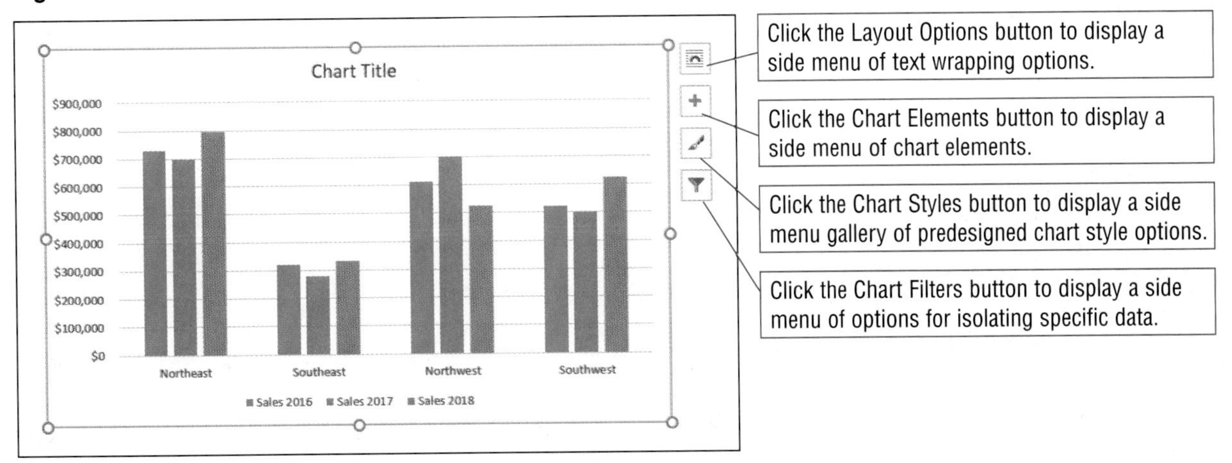

Hint Use a pie chart if the data series you want to plot has seven categories or less and the categories represent parts of a whole.

Use the bottom button, Chart Filters, to isolate specific data in the chart. Click the button and a side menu displays. Specify the series or categories to display in the chart. To do this, remove check marks from those elements that should not appear in the chart. After removing any check marks, click the Apply button in the lower left corner of the side menu. Click the Names tab at the Chart Filters button side menu and options display for turning on and off the display of column and row names.

Project 5b Formatting with Chart Buttons

Part 2 of 5

1. With **2-Charts.docx** open, make sure the chart is selected.
2. Click the Layout Options button that displays outside the upper right side of the chart and then click the *Square* option in the side menu (first option in the *With Text Wrapping* section).
3. Remove and add chart elements by completing the following steps:
   a. Click the Chart Elements button that displays below the Layout Options button outside the upper right side of the chart.
   b. At the side menu, click the *Chart Title* check box to remove the check mark.
   c. Click the *Data Table* check box to insert a check mark.

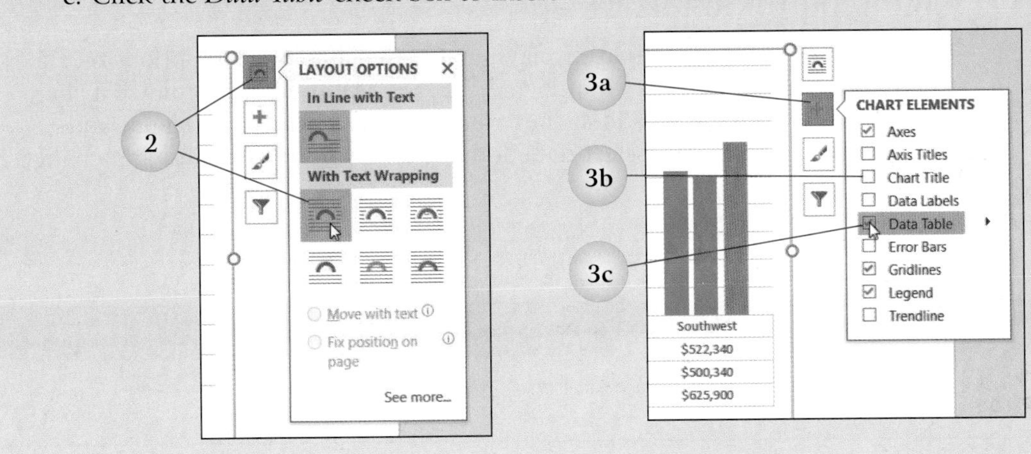

4. Apply a different chart style by completing the following steps:
   a. Click the Chart Styles button below the Chart Elements button.
   b. At the side menu gallery, click the *Style 3* option (third option in the gallery).
   c. Click the Color tab at the top of the side menu and then click the *Color 4* option at the drop-down gallery (fourth row in the *Colorful* section).
   d. Click the Chart Styles button to close the side menu.

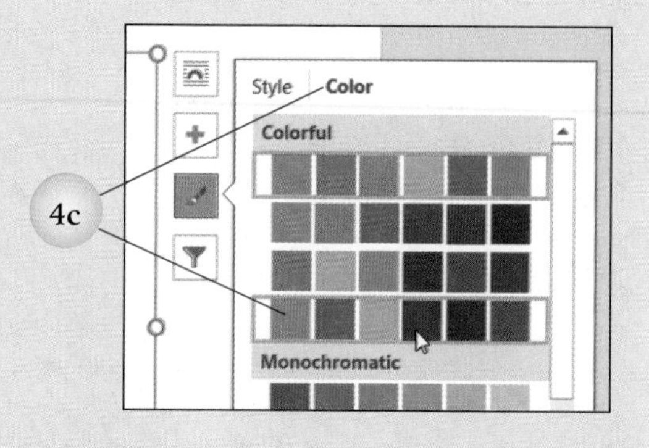

5. Display only Northeast and Southeast sales by completing the following steps:
   a. Click the Chart Filters button that displays below the Chart Styles button.
   b. Click the *Northwest* check box in the *Categories* section to remove the check mark.
   c. Click the *Southwest* check box in the *Categories* section to remove the check mark.
   d. Click the Apply button in the lower left corner of the side menu.
   e. Click the Chart Filters button to close the side menu.
   f. After viewing only Northeast and Southeast sales, redisplay the other regions by clicking the Chart Filters button, clicking the *Northwest* and *Southwest* check boxes, and then clicking the Apply button.
   g. Click the Chart Filters button to close the side menu.
6. Save **2-Charts.docx**.

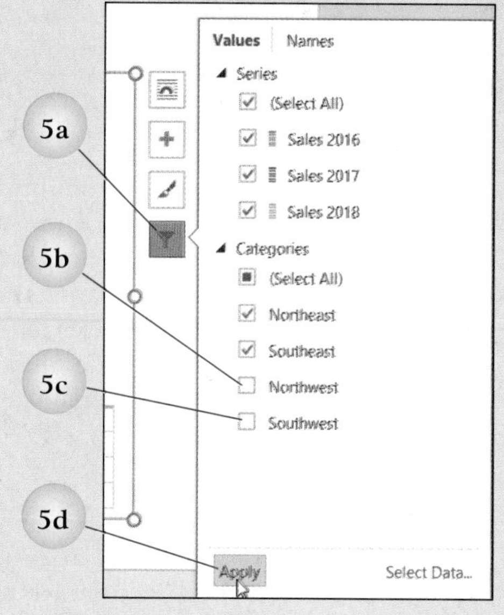

Check Your Work

Tutorial

Changing the Chart Design

Changing the Chart Design

In addition to the buttons that display outside the chart border, options on the Chart Tools Design tab, shown in Figure 2.15, can be used to customize a chart. Use options on this tab to add a chart element, change the chart layout and colors, apply a chart style, select data and switch rows and columns, and change the chart type.

Figure 2.15 Chart Tools Design Tab

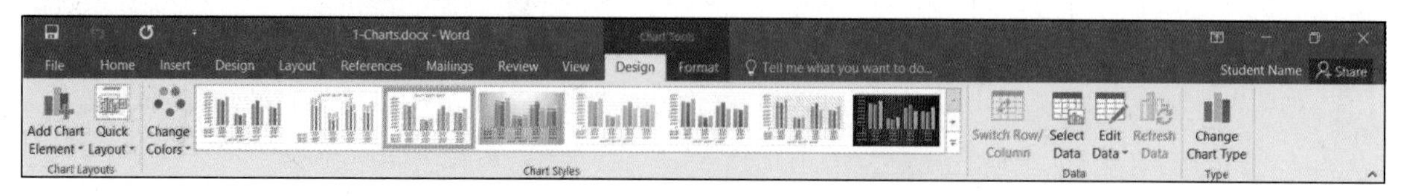

Project 5c Changing the Chart Design

Part 3 of 5

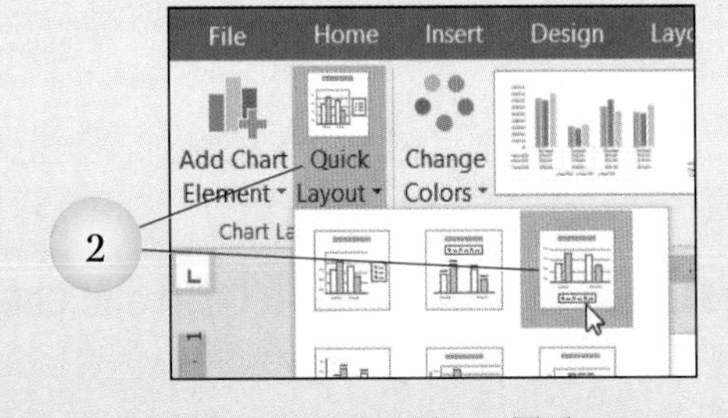

1. With **2-Charts.docx** open, make sure the chart is selected and the Chart Tools Design tab is active.
2. Change to a different layout by clicking the Quick Layout button in the Chart Layouts group and then clicking the *Layout 3* option (third column, first row in the drop-down gallery).
3. Click the *Style 7* chart style in the Chart Styles group (seventh option from the left).
4. Click the Add Chart Element button in the Chart Layouts group, point to *Chart Title* at the drop-down list, and then click *Centered Overlay* at the side menu.

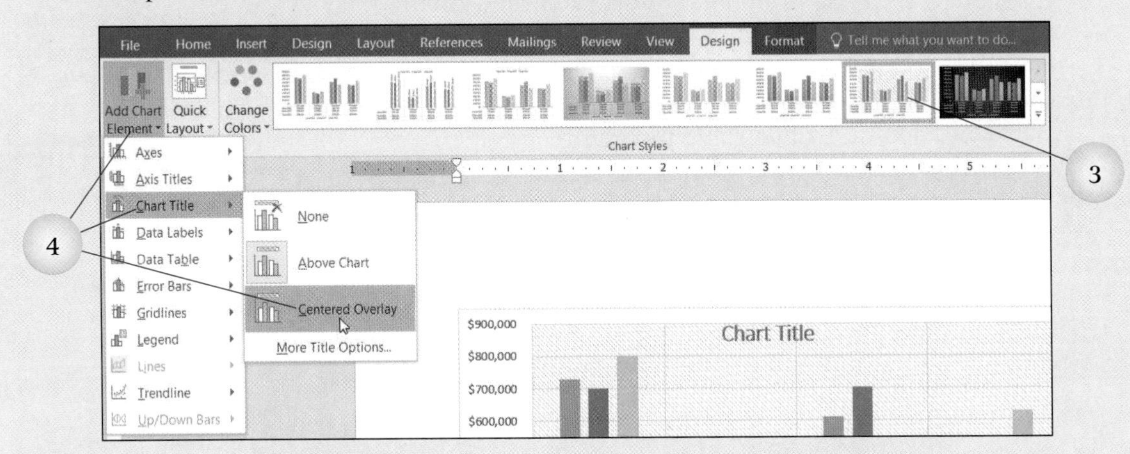

5. Select the words *Chart Title* and then type Regional Sales.
6. Click the chart border to deselect the chart title.
7. Edit the data by completing the following steps:
   a. Click the Edit Data button in the Data group.
   b. Click in cell C3 in the Excel worksheet.
   c. Type 375250. (Typing this text replaces the original amount, *$278,250*.)
   d. Click in cell C5, type 550300, and then press the Tab key.
   e. Click the Close button in the upper right corner of the Excel window.
8. Save **2-Charts.docx**.

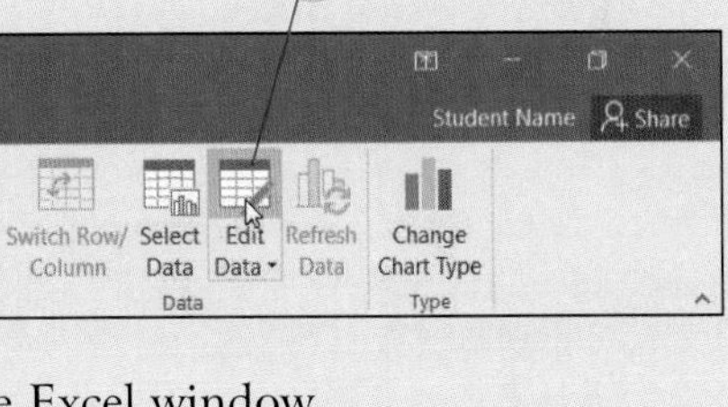

Check Your Work

Tutorial

Changing Chart Formatting

Changing Chart Formatting

Use buttons on the Chart Tools Format tab, shown in Figure 2.16, to format and customize a chart and chart elements. To format or modify a specific element in a chart, select the element. Do this by clicking the element or by clicking the *Chart Elements* option box in the Current Selection group and then clicking the element at the drop-down list. Use other options on the Chart Tools Format tab to apply a shape style and WordArt style and arrange and size the chart or chart element.

Figure 2.16 Chart Tools Format Tab

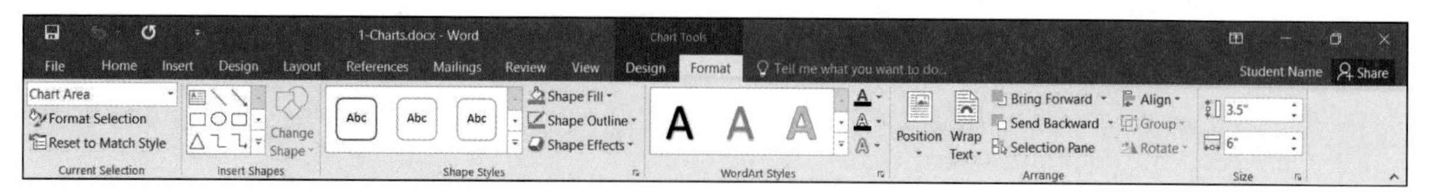

Project 5d Formatting a Chart and Chart Elements

Part 4 of 5

1. With **2-Charts.docx** open and the chart selected, click the Chart Tools Format tab.
2. Apply a shape style to the chart title by completing the following steps:
   a. Click the *Chart Elements* option box arrow in the Current Selection group and then click *Chart Title* at the drop-down list.
   b. Click the *Colored Outline - Blue, Accent 1* style option (second option in the Shape Styles group).
3. Change the color of the Sales 2018 series by completing the followings steps:
   a. Click the *Chart Elements* option box arrow in the Current Selection group and then click *Series "Sales 2018"* at the drop-down list.
   b. Click the Shape Fill button arrow in the Shape Styles group and then click the *Dark Red* option (first color option in the *Standard Colors* section).

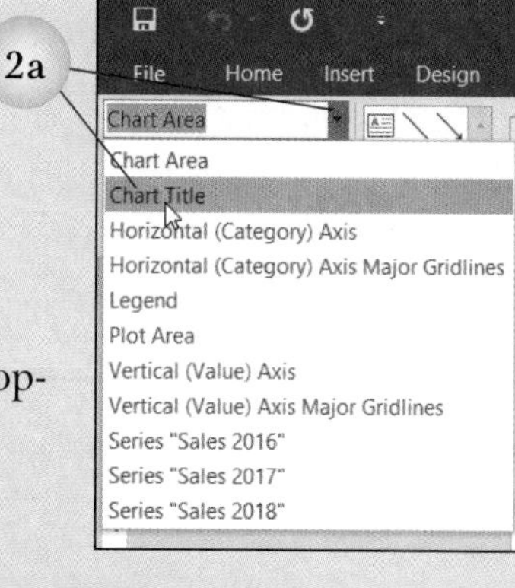

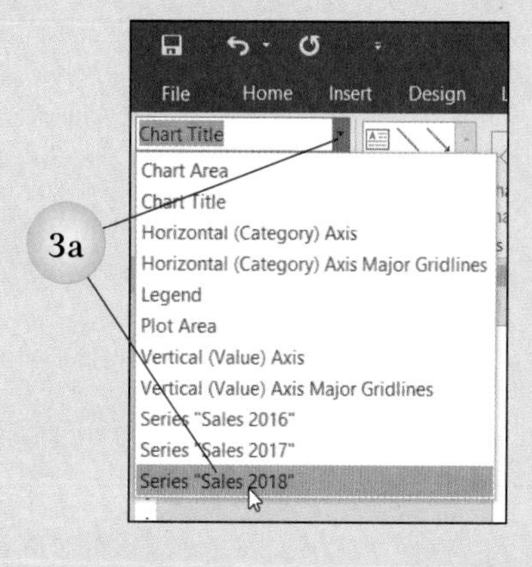

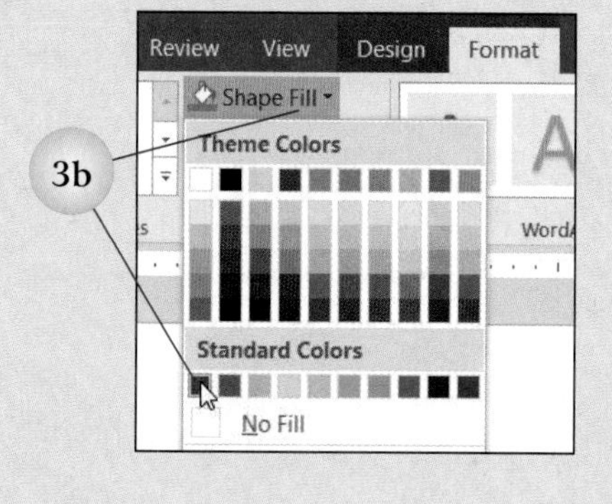

4. Apply a WordArt style to all the text in the chart by completing the following steps:
   a. Click the *Chart Elements* option box arrow.
   b. Click *Chart Area* at the drop-down list.
   c. Click the first WordArt style in the WordArt Styles group (*Fill - Black, Text 1, Shadow*).

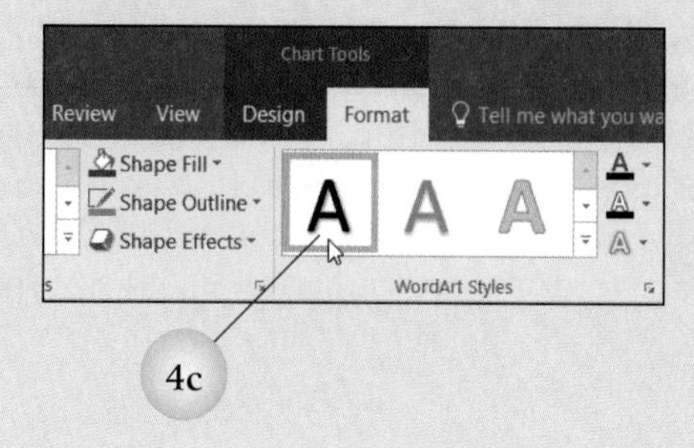

5. Change the size of the chart by completing the following steps:
   a. Click in the *Shape Height* measurement box and then type 3.
   b. Click in the *Shape Width* measurement box, type 5.5, and then press the Enter key.
6. With the chart selected (not a chart element), change its position by clicking the Position button in the Arrange group and then clicking the *Position in Top Center with Square Text Wrapping* option (second column, first row in the *With Text Wrapping* section).
7. Save and then print **2-Charts.docx**.

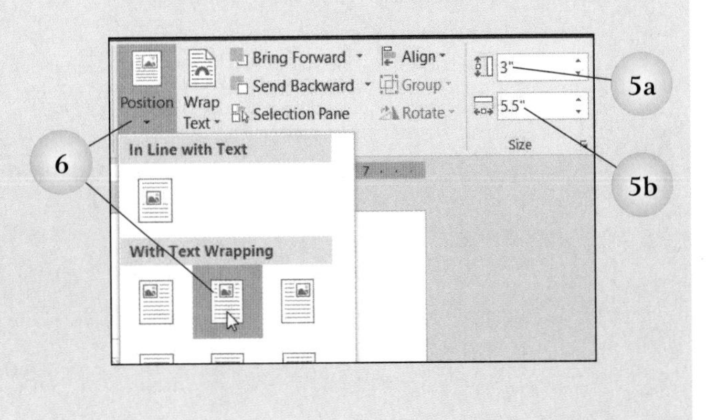

Check Your Work

Formatting a Chart with Task Pane Options

Format Selection

Additional formatting options are available at various task panes. Display a task pane by clicking the Format Selection button in the Current Selection group on the Chart Tools Format tab or a group task pane launcher. The Shape Styles and WordArt Styles groups on the Chart Tools Format tab contain task pane launchers. Which task pane opens at the right side of the screen depends on which chart or chart element is selected.

Project 5e Creating and Formatting a Pie Chart

Part 5 of 5

1. With **2-Charts.docx** open, press Ctrl + End (which deselects the chart) and then press the Enter key 12 times to move the insertion point below the chart.
2. Click the Insert tab and then click the Chart button in the Illustrations group.
3. At the Insert Chart dialog box, click *Pie* in the left panel and then click OK.
4. Type the data in the Excel worksheet cells as shown in Figure 2.17. After typing the last entry, click in cell A1.
5. Click the Close button in the upper right corner of the Excel window.
6. Click in the title *Percentage* and then type Investments.
7. Add data labels to the pie chart by completing the following steps:
   a. Click the Add Chart Element button in the Chart Layouts group on the Chart Tools Design tab.
   b. Point to *Data Labels* at the drop-down list and then click *Inside End* at the side menu.
8. Click on the chart border to select the chart (not a chart element).
9. Click the Chart Tools Format tab.

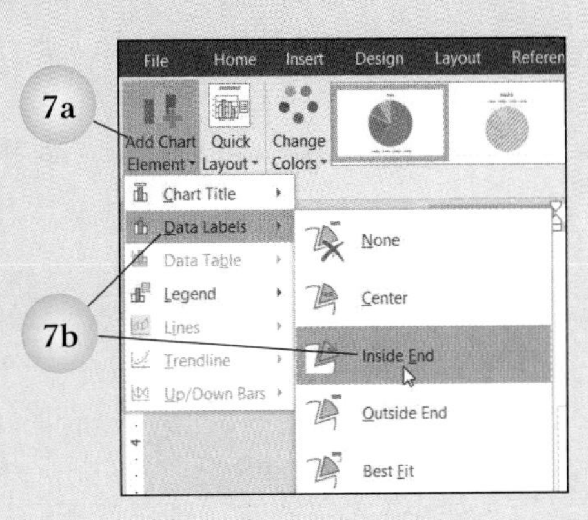

10. Apply formatting to the chart with options at the Format Chart Area task pane by completing the following steps:
    a. With the chart selected, click the Shape Styles group task pane launcher.
    b. At the Format Chart Area task pane with the Fill & Line icon selected, click *Fill*. (This expands the options below *Fill*.)
    c. Click the *Gradient fill* option.
    d. Click the Effects icon at the top of the task pane.
    e. Click *Shadow* to expand the shadow options.
    f. Click the Presets button.
    g. Click the *Offset Bottom* option (second column, first row in the *Outer* section).

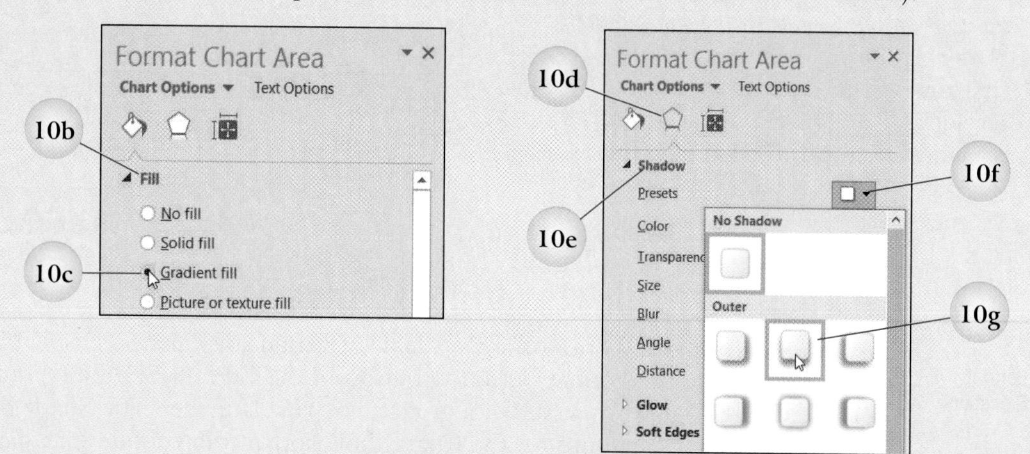

    h. Click the Text Options tab at the top of the task pane.
    i. Click *Text Outline* to expand the options.
    j. Click the *Solid line* option.
    k. Click the Color button and then click the *Blue, Accent 1, Darker 50%* option (fifth column, last row in the *Theme Colors* section).

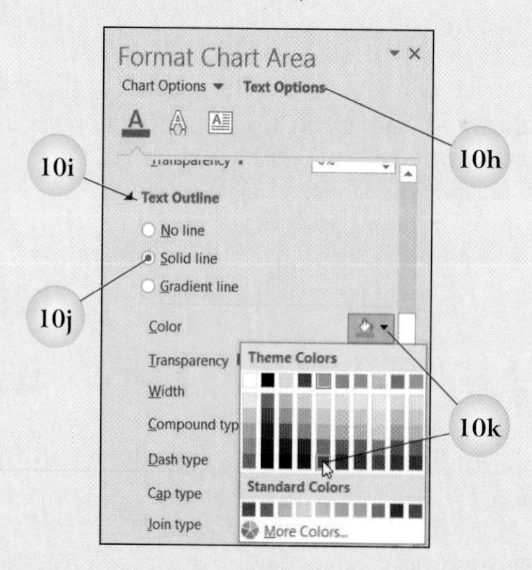

11. Format the pie chart by completing the following steps:
    a. Click in any piece of the pie. (This selects all the pieces of the pie. Notice that the name of the task pane has changed to *Format Data Series*.)

b. Click the Effects icon at the top of the task pane.
c. Click *3-D Format* to expand the options.
d. Click the Top bevel button and then click the *Soft Round* option at the drop-down gallery (second column, second row in the *Bevel* section).
e. Close the task pane by clicking the Close button in the upper right corner.

12. Click the chart border to select the chart (not a chart element).
13. Change the size of the chart by completing the following steps:
    a. Click in the *Shape Height* measurement box and then type 3.
    b. Click in the *Shape Width* measurement box, type 5.5, and then press the Enter key.
14. Change the position of the chart by clicking the Position button in the Arrange group and then clicking the *Position in Bottom Center with Square Text Wrapping* option (second column, third row in the *With Text Wrapping* section).
15. Save, print, and then close **2-Charts.docx**.

Check Your Work

Figure 2.17 Project 5

	A	B
1	Assets	Percentage
2	Loans	34%
3	Bonds	22%
4	Mutuals	20%
5	Stocks	17%
6	Other	7%
7		

Chapter Summary

- The spelling checker matches the words in the document with the words in its dictionary. If a match is not found, the word is selected and possible corrections are suggested.
- When checking the spelling and grammar in a document, changes can be made by clicking in the document outside the task pane, making the changes, and then clicking the Resume button in the task pane to continue checking.
- Customize spell checking options at the Word Options dialog box with *Proofing* selected in the left panel.
- Use the grammar checker to search a document for correct grammar, punctuation, and word usage.
- To display readability statistics for a document, insert a check mark in the *Show readability statistics* check box in the Word Options dialog box with *Proofing* selected and then complete a spelling and grammar check.
- Word uses the RoamingCustom.dic dictionary when spell checking a document. A custom dictionary can be added at the Custom Dictionaries dialog box. Display this dialog box by clicking the Custom Dictionaries button at the Word Options dialog box with *Proofing* selected.

- The Word Count dialog box displays the numbers of pages, words, characters, paragraphs, and lines in a document. Display this dialog box by clicking the word count section of the Status bar or by clicking the Word Count button in the Proofing group on the Review tab.
- Number lines in a document with options at the Line Numbers button drop-down list or the Line Numbers dialog box.
- Use the Thesaurus feature to find synonyms and antonyms for words in a document. Display synonyms and antonyms at the Thesaurus task pane or by right-clicking a word and then pointing to *Synonyms* at the shortcut menu.
- The Smart Lookup feature provides information on selected text from a variety of sources on the web, such as Wikipedia, Bing, and the Oxford Dictionary. To use the Smart Lookup feature, select text and then click the Smart Lookup button in the Insights group on the Review tab. This displays the Smart Lookup task pane at the right side of the screen.
- Use the Translate button in the Language group on the Review tab to translate a document, a selected section of text, or a word from one language to another.
- To present data visually, create a chart with the Chart button on the Insert tab. Choose a chart type at the Insert Chart dialog box. Enter chart data in an Excel worksheet.
- Four buttons display at the right side of a selected chart. Use the Layout Options button to apply text wrapping, the Chart Elements button to add or remove chart elements, the Chart Styles button to apply a predesigned chart style, and the Chart Filters button to isolate specific data in the chart.
- Modify a chart design with options and buttons on the Chart Tools Design tab.
- The cells in an Excel worksheet used to create a chart are linked to the chart in the document. To edit the chart data, click the Edit Data button on the Chart Tools Design tab and then make changes to the data in the Excel worksheet.
- Customize the format of a chart and chart elements with options and buttons on the Chart Tools Format tab. Select the chart or a specific chart element and then apply a style to a shape, apply a WordArt style to the text, and arrange and size the chart.
- Apply formatting to a chart with options in task panes. Display a task pane by clicking the Format Selection button on the Chart Tools Format tab or a group task pane launcher. The options in the task pane vary depending on the chart or chart element selected.

Commands Review

FEATURE	RIBBON TAB, GROUP	BUTTON, OPTION	KEYBOARD SHORTCUT
Insert Chart dialog box	Insert, Illustrations		
line numbers	Layout, Page Setup		
Mini Translator	Review, Language	, *Mini Translator*	
Smart Lookup task pane	Review, Insights		
spelling and grammar checker	Review, Proofing		F7
Thesaurus task pane	Review, Proofing		Shift + F7
translate selected text	Review, Language	, *Translate Selected Text*	
translate text in document	Review, Language	, *Translate Document*	
Translation Language Options dialog box	Review, Language	, *Choose Translation Language*	
Word Count dialog box	Review, Proofing		

Workbook

Chapter study tools and assessment activities are available in the ***Workbook*** ebook. These resources are designed to help you further develop and demonstrate mastery of the skills learned in this chapter.

Microsoft®

Word

CHAPTER 3

Automating and Customizing Formatting

Performance Objectives

Upon successful completion of Chapter 3, you will be able to:

1 Specify AutoCorrect exceptions
2 Add and delete AutoCorrect text
3 Use the AutoCorrect Options button
4 Customize AutoFormatting
5 Insert and sort building blocks
6 Create, edit, modify, and delete custom building blocks
7 Insert document property placeholders from Quick Parts
8 Insert and update fields from Quick Parts
9 Customize the Quick Access Toolbar
10 Customize the ribbon
11 Export Quick Access Toolbar and ribbon customizations

Precheck

Check your current skills to help focus your study.

Microsoft Word offers a number of features to help you customize documents and streamline the formatting of documents. In this chapter, you will learn how to customize the AutoCorrect feature and use the AutoCorrect Options button. You will also learn how to build a document using building blocks; create, save, and edit your own building blocks; and customize the Quick Access Toolbar and the ribbon.

Data Files

Before beginning chapter work, copy the WL2C3 folder to your storage medium and then make WL2C3 the active folder.

SNAP

If you are a SNAP user, launch the Precheck and Tutorials from your Assignments page.

Project 1 Create a Travel Document Using AutoCorrect

4 Parts

You will create several AutoCorrect entries, open a letterhead document, and then use the AutoCorrect entries to type text in the document.

Preview Finished Project

Tutorial

Customizing AutoCorrect

Quick Steps

Display the AutoCorrect Exceptions Dialog Box

1. Click File tab.
2. Click *Options*.
3. Click *Proofing*.
4. Click AutoCorrect Options button.
5. Click AutoCorrect tab.
6. Click Exceptions button.

Customizing AutoCorrect

Word's AutoCorrect feature corrects certain text automatically as it is typed. The types of corrections that can be made are specified with options at the AutoCorrect dialog box with the AutoCorrect tab selected, as shown in Figure 3.1.

Display this dialog box by clicking the File tab, clicking *Options*, clicking *Proofing*, clicking the AutoCorrect Options button, and then clicking the AutoCorrect tab. At the dialog box, turn AutoCorrect features on or off by inserting or removing check marks from the check boxes. In addition, specify AutoCorrect exceptions, replace frequently misspelled words with the correctly spelled words, add frequently used words, and specify keys to quickly insert the words in a document.

Specifying AutoCorrect Exceptions

The check box options at the AutoCorrect dialog box with the AutoCorrect tab selected identify the types of corrections made by AutoCorrect. Specify which corrections should not be made with options at the AutoCorrect Exceptions dialog box, shown in Figure 3.2. Display this dialog box by clicking the Exceptions button at the AutoCorrect dialog box with the AutoCorrect tab selected.

Figure 3.1 AutoCorrect Dialog Box with AutoCorrect Tab Selected

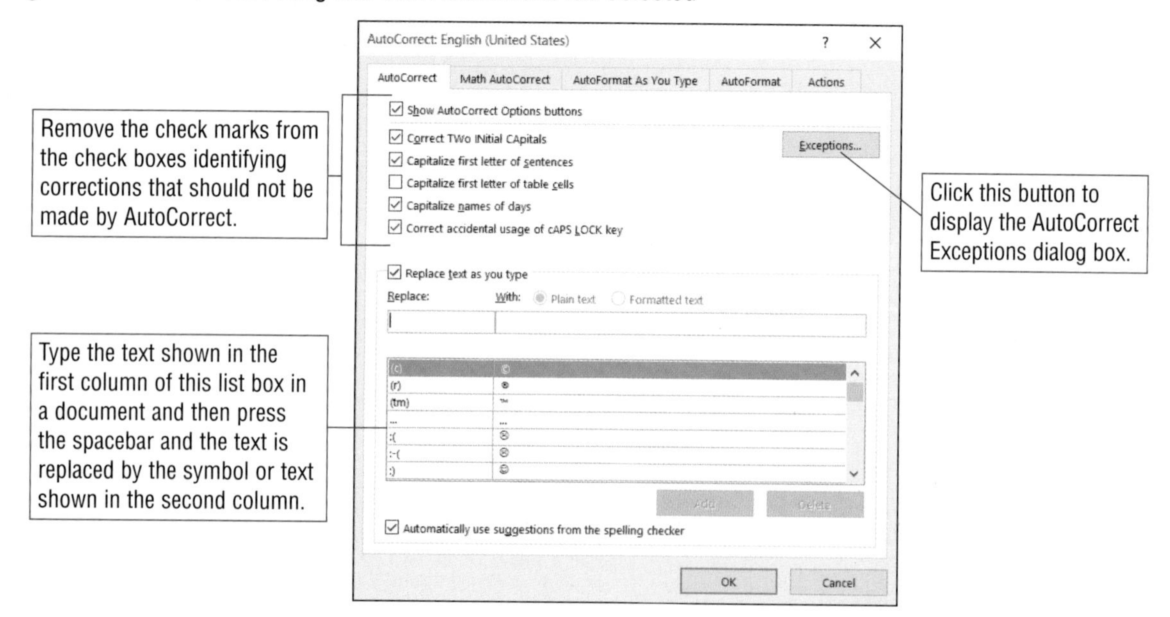

Figure 3.2 AutoCorrect Exceptions Dialog Box

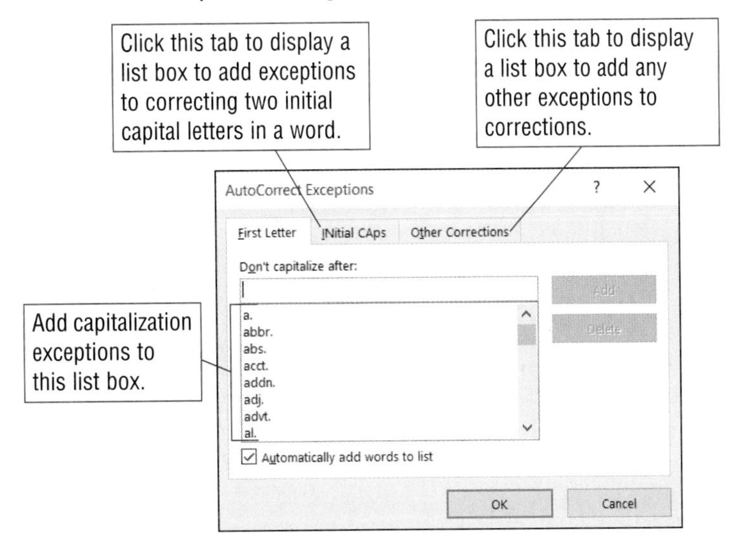
Click this tab to display a list box to add exceptions to correcting two initial capital letters in a word.
Click this tab to display a list box to add any other exceptions to corrections.
Add capitalization exceptions to this list box.
AutoCorrect Exceptions
First Letter
INitial CAps
Other Corrections
Don't capitalize after:
Add
Delete
a.
abbr.
abs.
acct.
addn.
adj.
advt.
al.
Automatically add words to list
OK
Cancel

AutoCorrect usually capitalizes a word that comes after an abbreviation ending in a period, since a period usually ends a sentence. Exceptions to this general practice display in the AutoCorrect Exceptions dialog box with the First Letter tab selected. Many exceptions already display in the dialog box but additional exceptions can be added by typing each exception in the *Don't capitalize after* text box and then clicking the Add button.

By default, AutoCorrect corrects the use of two initial capital letters in a word. If AutoCorrect should not correct these instances, display the AutoCorrect Exceptions dialog box with the INitial CAps tab selected and then type the exception text in the *Don't correct* text box. At the AutoCorrect Exceptions dialog box with the Other Corrections tab selected, type the text that should not be corrected in the *Don't correct* text box. Delete an exception from the dialog box with any of the tabs selected by clicking the text in the list box and then clicking the Delete button.

Tutorial

Adding and Deleting an AutoCorrect Entry

Quick Steps

Add a Word to AutoCorrect

1. Click File tab.
2. Click *Options*.
3. Click *Proofing*.
4. Click AutoCorrect Options button.
5. Click AutoCorrect tab.
6. Type misspelled or abbreviated word.
7. Press Tab.
8. Type correctly spelled or complete word.
9. Click Add button.
10. Click OK.

Adding and Deleting an AutoCorrect Entry

Commonly misspelled words and/or typographical errors can be added to AutoCorrect. For example, if a user consistently types *relavent* instead of *relevant*, *relavent* can be added to AutoCorrect with the direction to correct it to *relevant*. The AutoCorrect dialog box also contains a few symbols that can be inserted in a document. For example, type *(c)* and AutoCorrect changes the text to © (copyright symbol). Type *(r)* and AutoCorrect changes the text to ® (registered trademark symbol). The symbols display at the beginning of the AutoCorrect dialog box list box.

An abbreviation can be added to AutoCorrect that will insert the entire word (or words) in the document when it is typed. For example, in Project 1a, the abbreviation *fav* will be added to AutoCorrect and *Family Adventure Vacations* will be inserted when *fav* is typed followed by a press of the spacebar. The capitalization of the abbreviation can also be controlled. For example, in Project 1a, the abbreviation *Na* will be added to AutoCorrect and *Namibia* will be inserted when *Na* is typed and *NAMIBIA* will be inserted when *NA* is typed.

AutoCorrect text can be deleted from the AutoCorrect dialog box. To do this, display the AutoCorrect dialog box with the AutoCorrect tab selected, click the word or words in the list box, and then click the Delete button.

Project 1a Adding Text and Specifying Exceptions to AutoCorrect

Part 1 of 4

1. At a blank document, click the File tab and then click *Options*.
2. At the Word Options dialog box, click *Proofing* in the left panel.
3. Click the AutoCorrect Options button in the *AutoCorrect options* section.
4. At the AutoCorrect dialog box with the AutoCorrect tab selected, add an exception to AutoCorrect by completing the following steps:
   a. Click the Exceptions button.
   b. At the AutoCorrect Exceptions dialog box, click the INitial CAps tab.
   c. Click in the *Don't correct* text box, type STudent, and then click the Add button.
   d. Click in the *Don't correct* text box, type STyle, and then click the Add button.
   e. Click OK.
5. At the AutoCorrect dialog box with the AutoCorrect tab selected, click in the *Replace* text box and then type fav.
6. Press the Tab key (which moves the insertion point to the *With* text box) and then type Family Adventure Vacations.
7. Click the Add button. (This adds *fav* and *Family Adventure Vacations* to AutoCorrect and also selects *fav* in the *Replace* text box.)

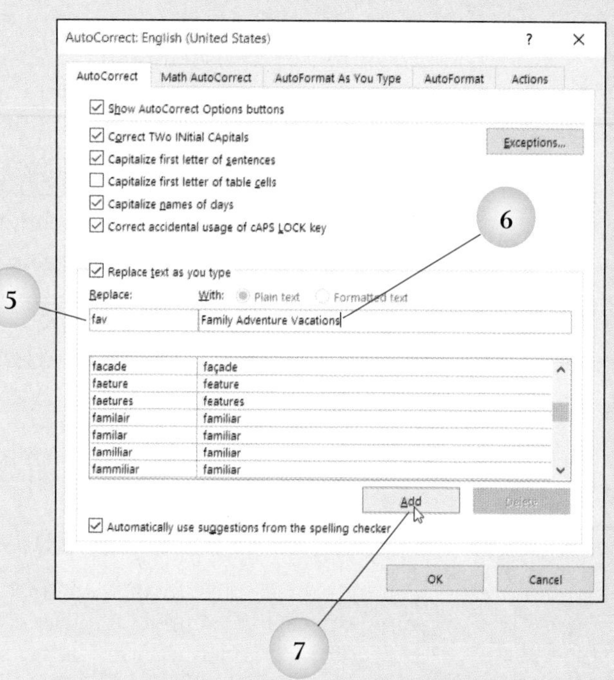

8. Type Na in the *Replace* text box. (The text *fav* is automatically removed when the typing of *Na* begins.)
9. Press the Tab key and then type Namibia.
10. Click the Add button.
11. With the insertion point positioned in the *Replace* text box, type vf.
12. Press the Tab key and then type Victoria Falls.
13. Click the Add button.
14. With the insertion point positioned in the *Replace* text box, type tts.
15. Press the Tab key and then type Terra Travel Services.
16. Click the Add button.
17. Click OK to close the AutoCorrect dialog box and then click OK to close the Word Options dialog box.
18. Open **TTSLtrhd.docx** and then save it with the name **3-TTSAfrica**.
19. Type the text shown in Figure 3.3. Type the text exactly as shown (including applying bold formatting and centering *fav* at the beginning of the document). AutoCorrect will correct the words as they are typed.
20. Save **3-TTSAfrica.docx**.

Check Your Work

Figure 3.3 Project 1a

> **fav**
>
> Na and vf Adventure
>
> tts is partnering with fav to provide adventurous and thrilling family vacations. Our first joint adventure is a holiday trip to Na. Na is one of the most fascinating holiday destinations in Africa and offers comfortable facilities, great food, cultural interaction, abundant wildlife, and a wide variety of activities to interest people of all ages.
>
> During the 12-day trip, you and your family will travel across Na through national parks, enjoying the beautiful and exotic scenery and watching wildlife in natural habitats. You will cruise along the Kwando and Chobe rivers and spend time at the Okapuka Lodge located near Windhoek, the capital of Na.
>
> If you or your family member is a college student, contact one of our college travel adventure consultants to learn more about the newest Student Travel package titled "STudent STyle" that offers a variety of student discounts, rebates, and free travel accessories for qualifying participants.
>
> tts and fav are offering a 15 percent discount if you sign up for this once-in-a-lifetime trip to Na. This exciting adventure is limited to twenty people, so don't wait to sign up.

Tutorial

Undoing an AutoCorrect Correction

AutoCorrect Options

Using the AutoCorrect Options Button

After AutoCorrect corrects a portion of text, hover the mouse pointer near the text and a small blue box displays below it. Move the mouse pointer to this blue box and the AutoCorrect Options button displays. Click this button to display a drop-down list with the options to change the text back to the original version, stop automatically correcting the specific text, and display the AutoCorrect dialog box.

If the AutoCorrect Options button does not display, turn on the feature. To do this, display the AutoCorrect dialog box with the AutoCorrect tab selected, click the *Show AutoCorrect Options buttons* check box to insert a check mark, and then click OK to close the dialog box.

Project 1b Using the AutoCorrect Options Button

Part 2 of 4

1. With **3-TTSAfrica.docx** open, select and then delete the last paragraph.
2. With the insertion point positioned on the blank line below the last paragraph of text (you may need to press the Enter key), type the following text. (AutoCorrect will automatically change *Ameria* to *America*, which you will change in the next step.) Through the sponsorship of Ameria Resorts, we are able to offer you a 15 percent discount for groups of twelve or more people.
3. Change the spelling of *America* back to *Ameria* by completing the following steps:
   a. Position the mouse pointer over *America* until a blue box displays below it.
   b. Position the mouse pointer on the blue box until the AutoCorrect Options button displays.

c. Click the AutoCorrect Options button and then click the *Change back to "Ameria"* option.

4. Save and then print **3-TTSAfrica.docx**.

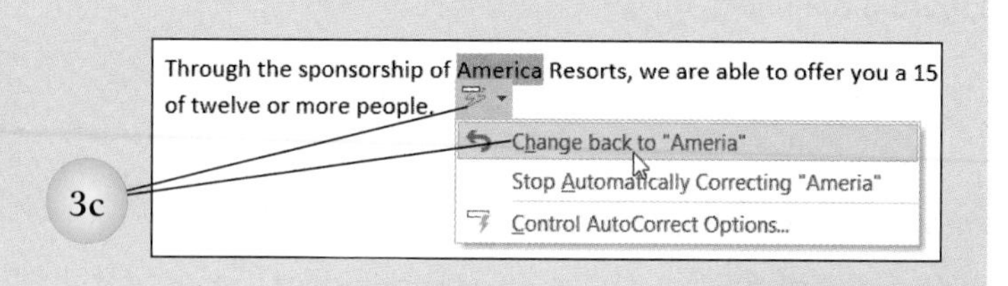

Check Your Work

Inserting Symbols Automatically

AutoCorrect recognizes and replaces symbols as well as text. Several symbols included in AutoCorrect display in the AutoCorrect dialog box and are listed first in the *Replace* text box. Table 3.1 lists these symbols along with the characters to insert them. Along with the symbols provided by Word, other symbols can be inserted in the AutoCorrect dialog box with the AutoCorrect button in the Symbol dialog box. To insert a symbol in the AutoCorrect dialog box, click the Insert tab, click the Symbol button in the Symbols group, and then click *More Symbols* at the drop-down list. At the Symbol dialog box, click the specific symbol and then click the AutoCorrect button that displays in the lower left corner of the dialog box. This displays the AutoCorrect dialog box with the symbol inserted in the *With* text box and the insertion point positioned in the *Replace* text box. Type the text that will insert the symbol, click the Add button, and then click OK to close the AutoCorrect dialog box. Click the Close button to close the Symbol dialog box.

Table 3.1 AutoCorrect Symbols Available at the AutoCorrect Dialog Box

Type	To Insert
(c)	©
(r)	®
(tm)	™
...	. . .
:) or :-)	☺
:| or :-|	😐
:(or :-(	☹
-->	→
<--	←
==>	➔
<==	🡸
<=>	⇔

Project 1c Inserting Symbols Using AutoCorrect

1. With **3-TTSAfrica.docx** open, move the insertion point so it is positioned immediately right of the last *s* in *Resorts* (located in the last paragraph) and then type (r). (This inserts the registered trademark symbol.)
2. Move the insertion point immediately left of the *1* in *15* and then type ==>. (This inserts the ➔symbol.)
3. Move the insertion point immediately right of the *t* in *discount* and then type <==. (This inserts the 🡐 symbol.)
4. Insert the pound (£) currency unit symbol in AutoCorrect by completing the following steps:
   a. Click the Insert tab.
   b. Click the Symbol button and then click *More Symbols* at the drop-down list.
   c. At the Symbol dialog box, make sure that *(normal text)* displays in the *Font* option box. If it does not, click the *Font* option box arrow and then click *(normal text)* at the drop-down list (first option in the list).
   d. Scroll through the list of symbols and then click the pound (£) currency unit symbol (located in approximately the sixth or seventh row; character code *00A3*).
   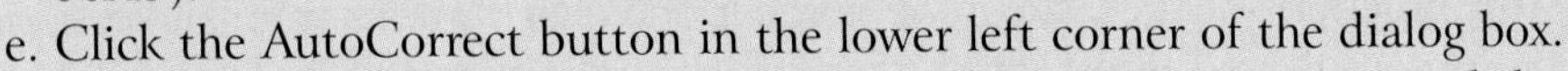
   e. Click the AutoCorrect button in the lower left corner of the dialog box.
   f. At the AutoCorrect dialog box, type pcu in the *Replace* text box and then click the Add button.
   g. Click OK to close the AutoCorrect dialog box.

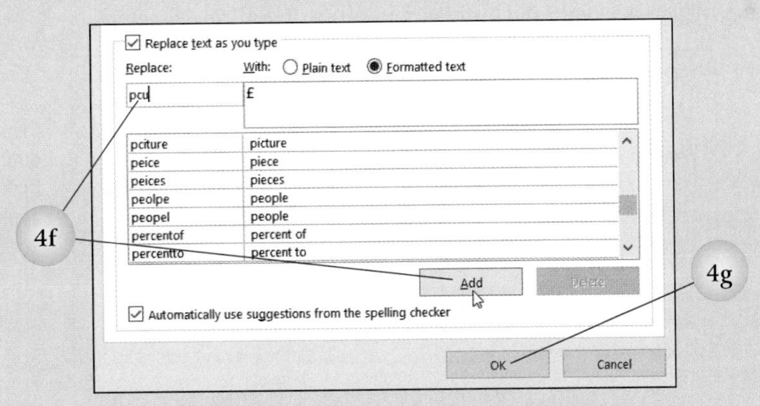

   h. Click the Close button to close the Symbol dialog box.
5. Press Ctrl + End to move the insertion point to the end of the document and then press the Enter key.
6. Type the text shown in Figure 3.4. (Press Shift + Enter or the Enter key as indicated in the figure.) Create the pound currency unit symbol by typing pcu and then pressing the spacebar. Press the Backspace key once and then type 1,999. (Complete similar steps when typing *£1,599 (UK)*.)
7. Save **3-TTSAfrica.docx**.

Check Your Work

Figure 3.4 Project 1c

Individual price: *(press Shift+ Enter)*
$3,299 (US) *(press Shift+ Enter)*
£1,999 (UK) *(press Enter)*

Individual price for groups of twenty or more: *(press Shift+ Enter)*
$3,999 (US) *(press Shift+ Enter)*
£1,599 (UK)

Tutorial

Customizing AutoFormatting

Customizing AutoFormatting

When typing text, Word provides options to automatically apply some formatting, such as changing a fraction to a fraction character (1/2 to ½), changing numbers to ordinals (1st to 1st), changing an Internet or network path to a hyperlink (www.emcp.net to www.emcp.net), and applying bullets or numbers to text. The autoformatting options display in the AutoCorrect dialog box with the AutoFormat As You Type tab selected, as shown in Figure 3.5.

Display this dialog box by clicking the File tab and then clicking *Options*. At the Word Options dialog box, click *Proofing* in the left panel and then click the AutoCorrect Options button. At the AutoCorrect dialog box, click the AutoFormat As You Type tab. At the dialog box, remove the check marks from those options to be turned off and insert check marks for those options to be formatted automatically.

Figure 3.5 AutoCorrect Dialog Box with the AutoFormat As You Type Tab Selected

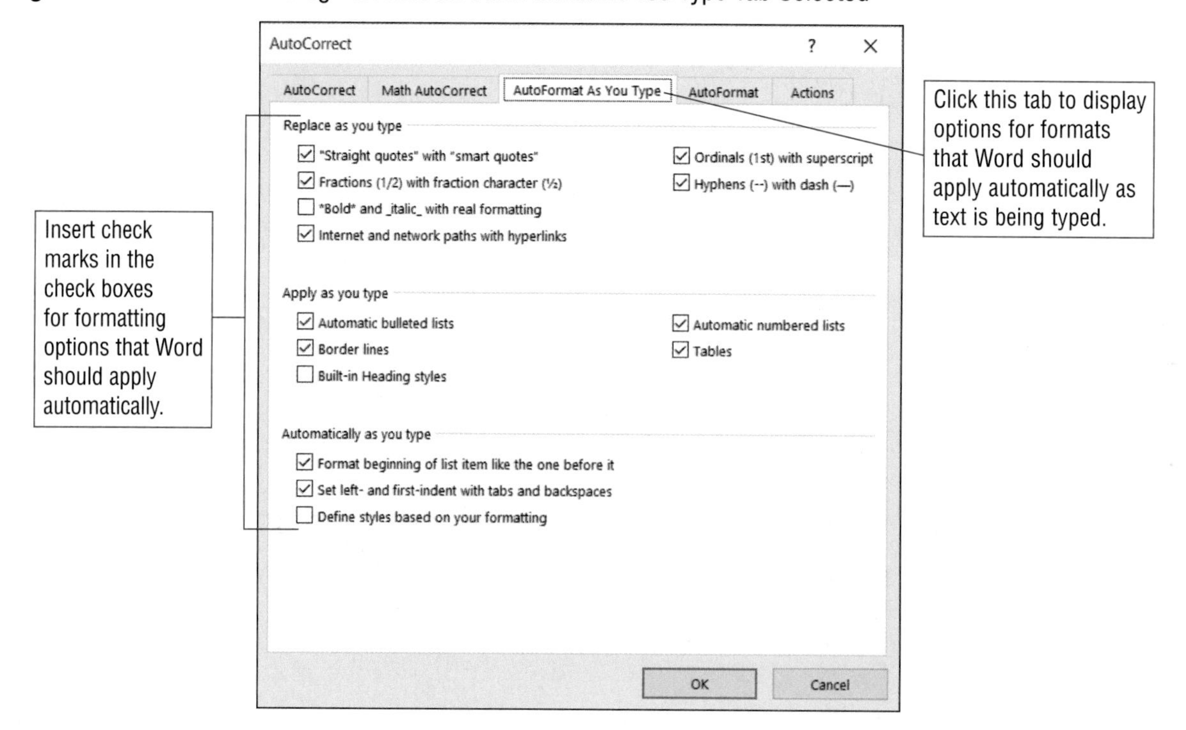

Project 1d Changing AutoFormatting and Deleting AutoCorrect Text

1. Make sure **3-TTSAfrica.docx** is open.
2. Suppose that you need to add a couple of web addresses to a document and do not want the addresses automatically formatted as hyperlinks (since you are sending the document as hard copy rather than electronically). Turn off the autoformatting of web addresses by completing the following steps:
   a. Click the File tab and then click *Options*.
   b. At the Word Options dialog box, click *Proofing* in the left panel.
   c. Click the AutoCorrect Options button.
   d. At the AutoCorrect dialog box, click the AutoFormat As You Type tab.
   e. Click the *Internet and network paths with hyperlinks* check box to remove the check mark.

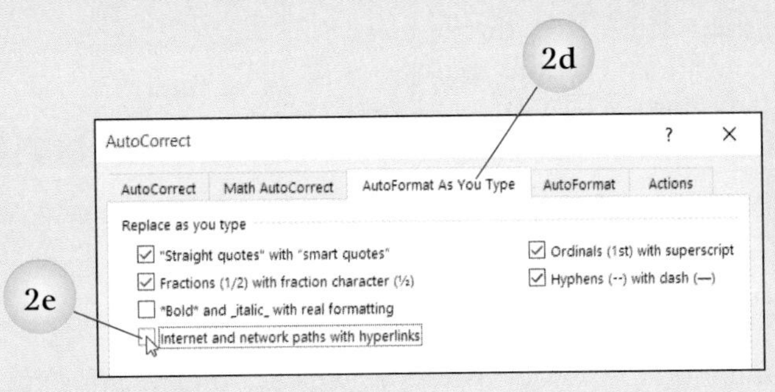

   f. Click OK to close the AutoCorrect dialog box.
   g. Click OK to close the Word Options dialog box.
3. Press Ctrl + End to move the insertion point to the end of the document, press the Enter key, and then type the text shown in Figure 3.6.
4. Turn on the autoformatting of web addresses that was turned off in Step 2 by completing Steps 2a through 2g (except in Step 2e, insert the check mark rather than remove it).
5. Delete *fav* from AutoCorrect by completing the following steps:
   a. Click the File tab and then click *Options*.
   b. At the Word Options dialog box, click *Proofing* in the left panel.
   c. Click the AutoCorrect Options button.
   d. At the AutoCorrect dialog box, click the AutoCorrect tab.
   e. Click in the *Replace* text box and then type fav. (This selects the entry in the list box.)
   f. Click the Delete button.
6. Complete steps similar to those in Steps 5e-5f to delete the *Na*, *tts*, and *vf* AutoCorrect entries.

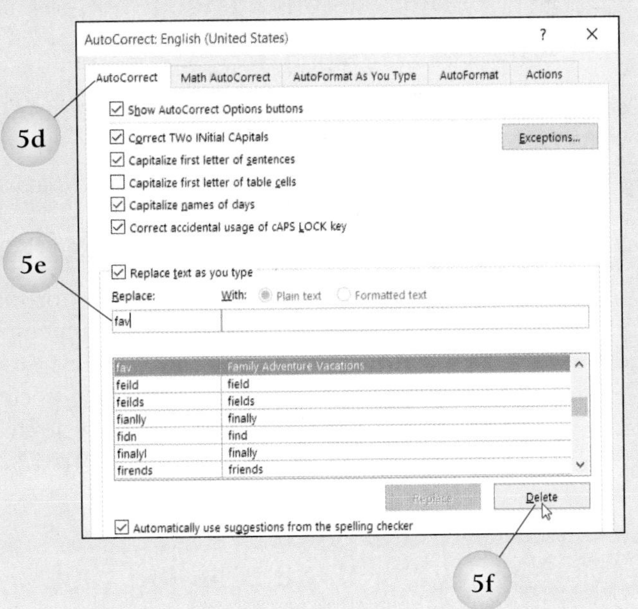

7. Delete the exceptions added to the AutoCorrect Exceptions dialog box by completing the following steps:
   a. At the AutoCorrect dialog box with the AutoCorrect tab selected, click the Exceptions button.
   b. At the AutoCorrect Exceptions dialog box, if necessary, click the INitial CAps tab.
   c. Click *STudent* in the list box and then click the Delete button.
   d. Click *STyle* in the list box and then click the Delete button.
   e. Click OK to close the AutoCorrect Exceptions dialog box.
8. Click OK to close the AutoCorrect dialog box.
9. Click OK to close the Word Options dialog box.
10. Save, print, and then close **3-TTSAfrica.docx**.

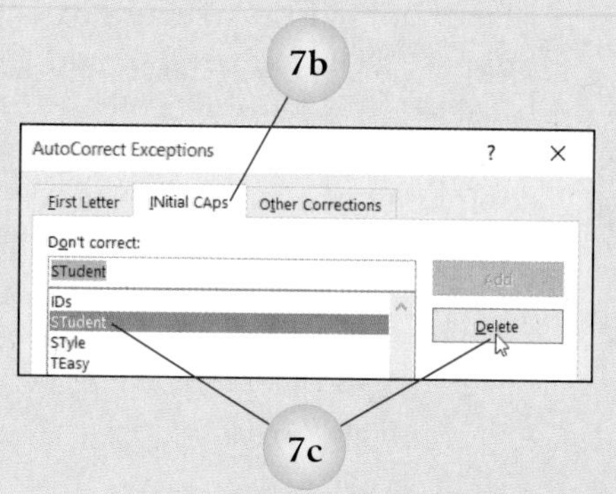

Check Your Work

Figure 3.6 Project 1d

For additional information on the Na adventure, as well as other exciting vacation specials, please visit our website at www.emcp.net/terratravel or visit www.emcp.net/famadv.

Project 2 Build a Document with Predesigned and Custom Building Blocks — 1 Part

You will open a report document and then add elements to it by inserting predesigned building blocks.

Preview Finished Project

Managing Building Blocks

Word includes a variety of tools for inserting data such as text, fields, objects, and other items to help build a document. To view some of the tools available, click the Quick Parts button in the Text group on the Insert tab. This displays a drop-down list of choices for inserting document properties, fields, and building blocks. Building blocks are tools for developing a document. Word provides a number of building blocks that can be inserted in a document or custom building blocks can be created.

Tutorial

Inserting and Sorting Building Blocks

Inserting a Building Block

To insert a building block into a document, click the Insert tab, click the Quick Parts button in the Text group, and then click *Building Blocks Organizer* at the drop-down list. This displays the Building Blocks Organizer dialog box, shown in

Quick Steps

Insert a Building Block

1. Click Insert tab.
2. Click Quick Parts button.
3. Click *Building Blocks Organizer.*
4. Click building block.
5. Click Insert button.
6. Click Close.

Figure 3.7. The dialog box displays columns of information about the building blocks. The columns in the dialog box display information about the building block, including its name, the gallery that contains it, the template in which it is stored, its behavior, and a brief description of it.

The Building Blocks Organizer dialog box is a central location for viewing all the predesigned building blocks available in Word. Some of the building blocks were used in previous chapters when a predesigned header or footer, cover page, page number, or watermark were inserted in a document. Other galleries in the Building Blocks Organizer dialog box contain predesigned building blocks such as bibliographies, equations, tables of contents, tables, and text boxes. The Building Blocks Organizer dialog box provides a convenient location for viewing and inserting building blocks.

Sorting Building Blocks

Quick Steps

Sort Building Blocks

1. Click Insert tab.
2. Click Quick Parts button.
3. Click *Building Blocks Organizer.*
4. Click column heading.

The Building Blocks Organizer dialog box displays the building blocks in the list box sorted by the *Gallery* column. The building blocks can be sorted by another column by clicking that column heading. For example, to sort the building blocks alphabetically by name, click the *Name* column heading.

Figure 3.7 Building Blocks Organizer Dialog Box

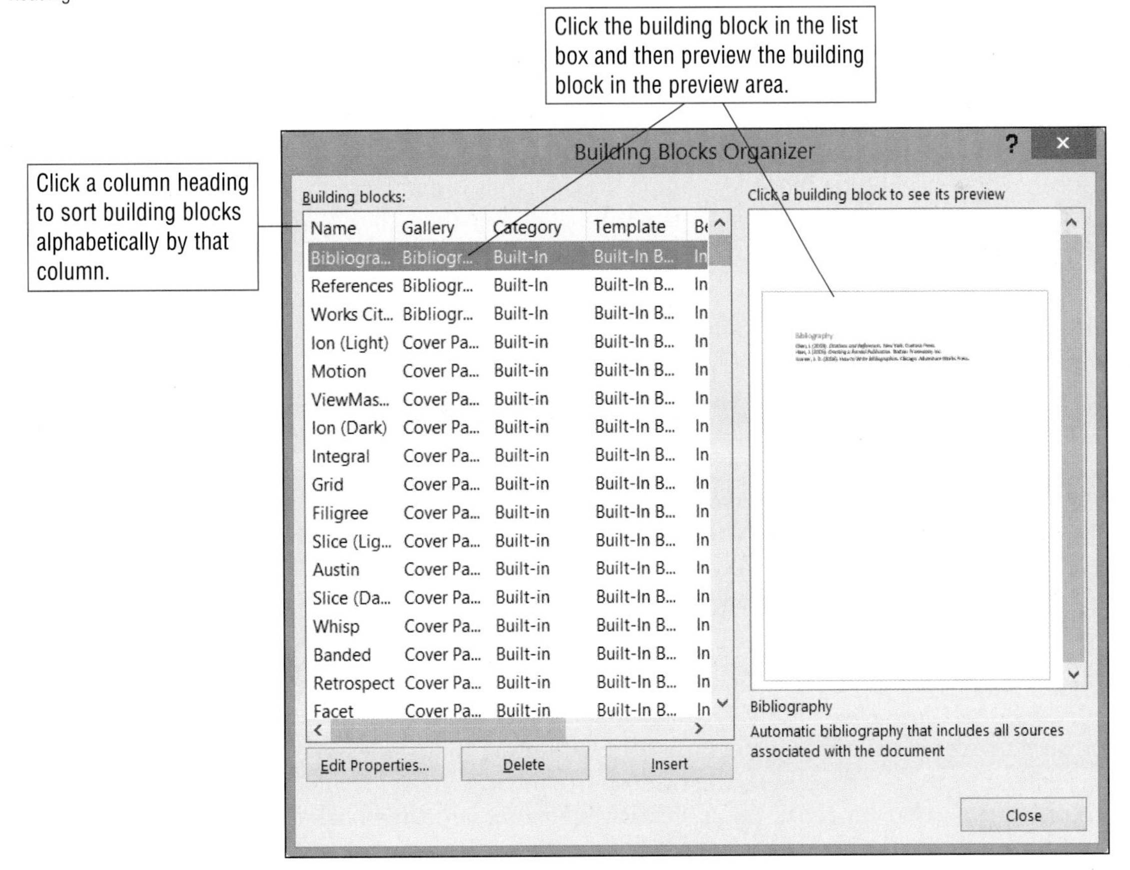

Project 2 Inserting Predesigned Building Blocks

Part 1 of 1

1. Open **CompViruses.docx** and then save it with the name **3-CompViruses**.
2. Sort the building blocks and then insert a table of contents building block by completing the following steps:
   a. Press Ctrl + Home to move the insertion point to the beginning of the document, press Ctrl + Enter to insert a page break, and then press Ctrl + Home again.
   b. Click the Insert tab, click the Quick Parts button in the Text group, and then click *Building Blocks Organizer* at the drop-down list.

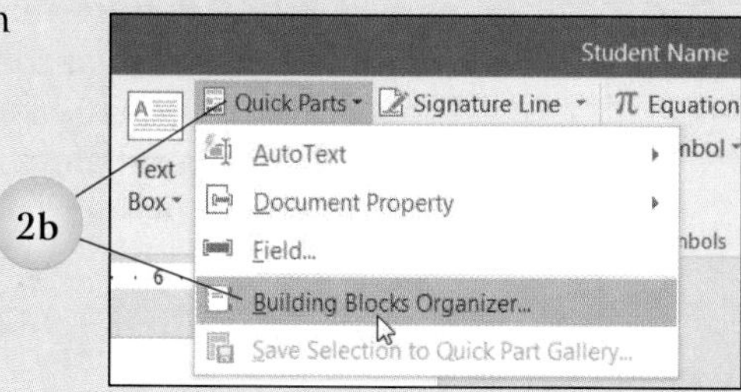

   c. At the Building Blocks Organizer dialog box, notice the arrangement of building blocks in the list box. (The building blocks are most likely organized alphabetically by the *Gallery* column.)
   d. Click the *Name* column heading. (This sorts the building blocks alphabetically by name. However, some blank building blocks may display at the beginning of the list box.)

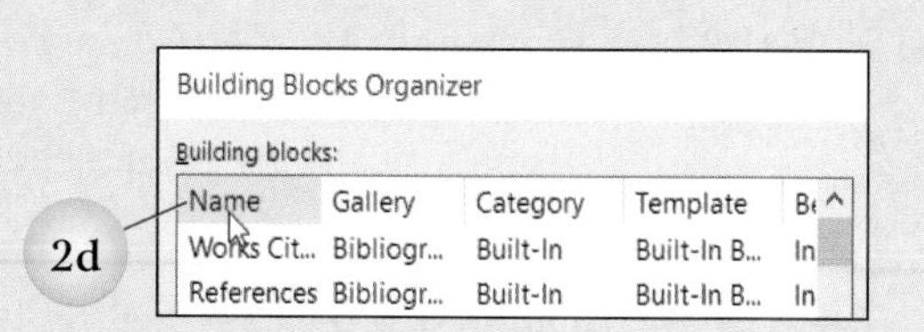

   e. Scroll down the list box and then click *Automatic Table 1*. (You may see only a portion of the name. Click the name and the full name as well as a description display in the dialog box below the preview of the table of contents building block.)
   f. Click the Insert button at the bottom of the dialog box. (This inserts a contents page at the beginning of the document and creates a table of contents that includes the headings with styles applied.)
3. Insert a footer building block by completing the following steps:
   a. Click the Quick Parts button on the Insert tab and then click *Building Blocks Organizer*.
   b. Scroll down the Building Blocks Organizer list box, click the *Sempahore* footer, and then click the Insert button.

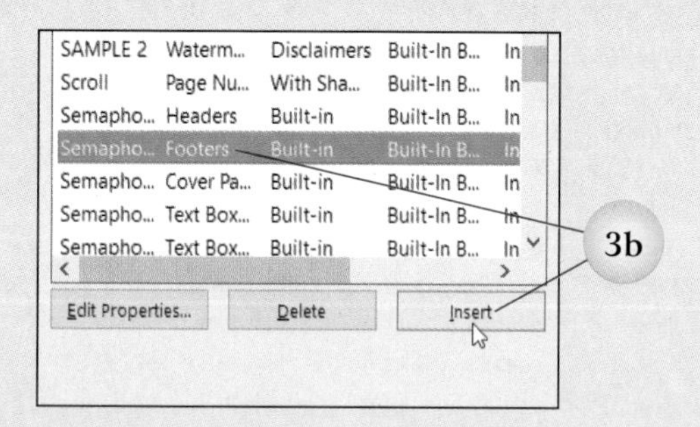

   c. Decrease the *Footer from Bottom* measurement to 0.3 inch (in the Position group on the Header & Footer Tools Design tab).
   d. Click the Close Header and Footer button.
4. Insert a cover page building block by completing the following steps:
   a. Press Ctrl + Home to move the insertion point to the beginning of the document.
   b. Click the Insert tab, click the Quick Parts button, and then click *Building Blocks Organizer*.
   c. Scroll down the Building Blocks Organizer list box, click the *Semaphore* cover page, and then click the Insert button.
   d. Click the *[DATE]* placeholder and then type today's date.

e. Click the *[DOCUMENT TITLE]* placeholder and then type Northland Security Systems. (The text will be converted to all uppercase letters.)
f. Click the *[DOCUMENT SUBTITLE]* placeholder and then type Computer Viruses and Security Strategies.
g. Select the name above the *[COMPANY NAME]* placeholder and then type your first and last names.

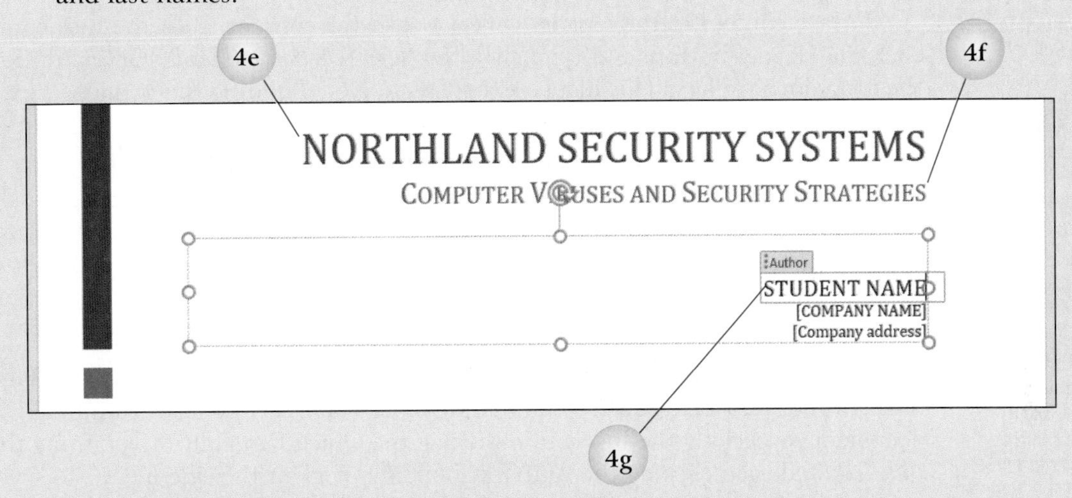

h. Select and then delete the *[COMPANY NAME]* placeholder.
i. Select and then delete the *[Company address]* placeholder.

5. Scroll through the document and look at each page. The semaphore footer and cover page building blocks that were inserted have similar formatting and are part of the Semaphore group. Using building blocks from the same group provides consistency in the document and gives it a polished and professional appearance.
6. Save, print, and then close **3-CompViruses.docx**.

Check Your Work

Project 3 Create a Letter Document Using Custom Building Blocks — 3 Parts

You will create custom building blocks and then use them to prepare a business letter.

Preview Finished Project

Tutorial

Saving Content as a Building Block

Saving Content as a Building Block

Consider saving data that is typed and formatted on a regular basis as a building block. Saving commonly created data as a building block saves time and reduces errors that might occur each time the data is typed or formatting is applied. The data can be saved as a building block in a specific gallery, such as the Text Box, Header, or Footer gallery, or saved to the AutoText gallery or Quick Part gallery.

Quick Steps

Save Content to a Text Box Gallery
1. Select content.
2. Click Insert tab.
3. Click Text Box button.
4. Click *Save Selection to Text Box Gallery.*

Save Content to a Header Gallery
1. Select content.
2. Click Insert tab.
3. Click Header button.
4. Click *Save Selection to Header Gallery.*

Save Content to a Footer Gallery
1. Select content.
2. Click Insert tab.
3. Click Footer button.
4. Click *Save Selection to Footer Gallery.*

Save Content to the AutoText Gallery
1. Select content.
2. Click Insert tab.
3. Click Quick Parts button.
4. Point to *AutoText.*
5. Click *Save Selection to AutoText Gallery.*

Saving Content to a Specific Gallery To save content in a specific gallery, use the button for the gallery. For example, to save a text box in the Text Box gallery, use the Text Box button. To do this, select the text box, click the Insert tab, click the Text Box button, and then click the *Save Selection to Text Box Gallery* option at the drop-down gallery. At the Create New Building Block dialog box as shown in Figure 3.8, type a name for the text box building block, type a description of it, and then click OK.

To save content in the Header gallery, select the content, click the Insert tab, click the Header button, and then click the *Save Selection to Header Gallery* option at the drop-down gallery. This displays the Create New Building Block dialog box, as shown in Figure 3.8 (except *Headers* displays in the *Gallery* option box). Complete similar steps to save content to the Footer gallery and Cover Page gallery.

When data is saved as a building block, it is available in the Building Blocks Organizer dialog box. If content is saved as a building block in a specific gallery, the building block is available at both the Building Blocks Organizer dialog box and the gallery. For example, if a building block is saved in the Footer gallery, it is available when the Footer button on the Insert tab is clicked.

Saving Content to the AutoText Gallery Content can be saved as a building block in the AutoText gallery. The building block can easily be inserted into a document by clicking the Insert tab, clicking the Quick Parts button, pointing to *AutoText*, and then clicking the AutoText building block at the side menu. To save content in the AutoText gallery, type and format the content and then select it. Click the Insert tab, click the Quick Parts button, point to *AutoText*, and then click the *Save Selection to AutoText Gallery* option at the side menu or use the keyboard shortcut Alt + F3. At the Create New Building Block dialog box, type a name for the building block, type a description of it, and then click OK.

Quick Steps

Save Content to the Quick Part Gallery
1. Select content.
2. Click Insert tab.
3. Click Quick Parts button.
4. Click *Save Selection to Quick Part Gallery.*

Saving Content to the Quick Part Gallery Not only can content be saved in the AutoText gallery, but selected content can also be saved in the Quick Part gallery. To do this, select the content, click the Insert tab, click the Quick Parts button, and then click the *Save Selection to Quick Part Gallery* option at the drop-down gallery. This displays the Create New Building Block dialog box with *Quick Parts* specified in the *Gallery* option box and *Building Blocks.dotx* specified in the *Save in* option box. Type a name for the building block, type a description of it, and then click OK.

Hint When selecting content to save as a building block, turn on the display of nonprinting characters by clicking the Show/Hide ¶ button in the Paragraph group on the Home tab.

Figure 3.8 Create New Building Block Dialog Box

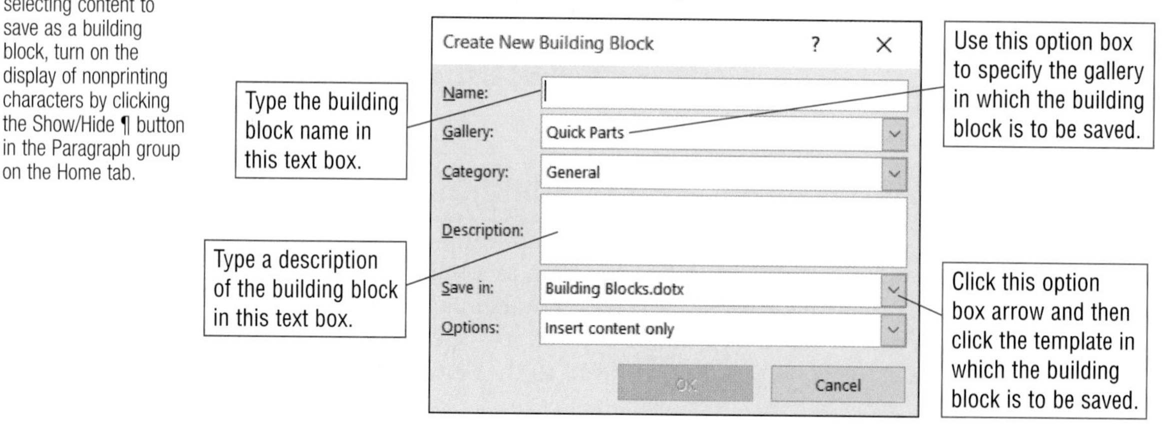

Quick Steps
Save a Template
1. Click File tab.
2. Click *Save As* option.
3. Click *Browse* option.
4. Click *Save as type* option.
5. Click *Word Template (*.dotx)*.
6. Type a name for the template.
7. Click Save button.

Quick Steps
Open a Document Based on a Template
1. Click File tab.
2. Click *New* option.
3. Click *PERSONAL* option.
4. Click template thumbnail.

OR

1. Click File Explorer icon on taskbar.
2. Navigate to folder containing template.
3. Double-click template.

Saving Building Blocks in a Specific Template By default, building block content is saved in one of two templates, either Building Blocks.dotx or Normal.dotm. The template location depends on the gallery selected at the Create New Building Block dialog box. A building block saved in either of these templates is available each time a document is opened in Word. In a public environment, such as a school, saving to one of these templates may not be possible. To create a new personal template, display the Save As dialog box and then change the *Save as type* option to *Word Template (*.dotx)*. Choosing this option automatically selects the Custom Office Templates folder. Type a name for the template, click the Save button, and the template is saved in the Custom Office Templates folder.

To open a document based on a personal template, click the File tab and then click the *New* option. At the New backstage area, click the *PERSONAL* option that displays below the search text box. This displays thumbnails of the templates saved in the Custom Office Templates folder. Click the thumbnail of a specific template and a blank document opens based on the selected template.

Another option for opening a document based on a template is to save a template to a location other than the Custom Office Templates folder, such as the WL2C3 folder on your storage medium, and then use File Explorer to open a document based on the template. To do this, click the File Explorer icon on the taskbar, navigate to the folder containing the template, and then double-click the template. Instead of the template opening, a blank document opens that is based on the template.

To specify the template in which a building block is to be saved, click the *Save in* option box arrow in the Create New Building Block dialog box and then click the specific template. A document must be opened based on a personal template for the template name to display in the drop-down list.

Project 3a Saving a Template and Saving Content to the Text Box, Footer, AutoText, and Quick Part Galleries

Part 1 of 3

1. Press Ctrl + N to display a blank document and then save the document as a template by completing the following steps:
   a. Press the F12 function key to display the Save As dialog box.
   b. At the Save As dialog box, type FAVTemplate in the *File name* text box.
   c. Click the *Save as type* option box and then click *Word Template (*.dotx)* at the drop-down list.
   d. Navigate to the WL2C3 folder on your storage medium.
   e. Click the Save button.
2. Close **FAVTemplate.dotx**.
3. Open a document based on the template by completing the following steps:
   a. Click the File Explorer icon on the taskbar. (The taskbar displays along the bottom of the screen.)
   b. Navigate to the WL2C3 folder on your storage medium.
   c. Double-click ***FAVTemplate.dotx***.
4. Insert **FAVContent.docx** into the current document. (Do this with the Object button arrow on the Insert tab. This document is located in your WL2C3 folder.)

5. Save the text box as a building block in the Text Box gallery by completing the following steps:
   a. Select the text box by clicking in it and then clicking its border.
   b. With the Insert tab active, click the Text Box button, and then click *Save Selection to Text Box Gallery* at the drop-down list.

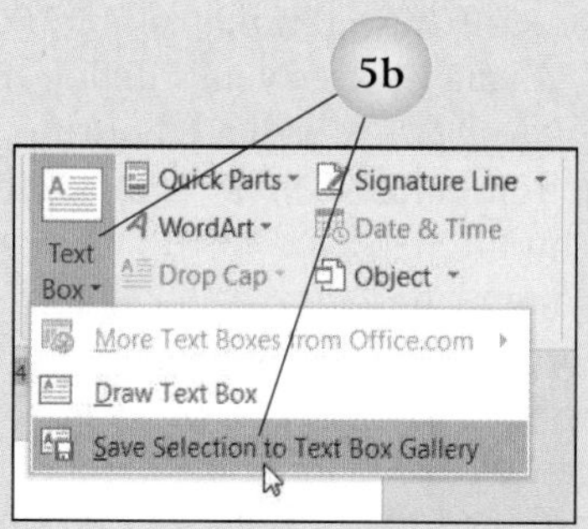

   c. At the Create New Building Block dialog box, type FAVTextBox in the *Name* text box.
   d. Click the *Save in* option box arrow and then click *FAVTemplate.dotx* at the drop-down list.
   e. Click OK to close the Create New Building Block dialog box.

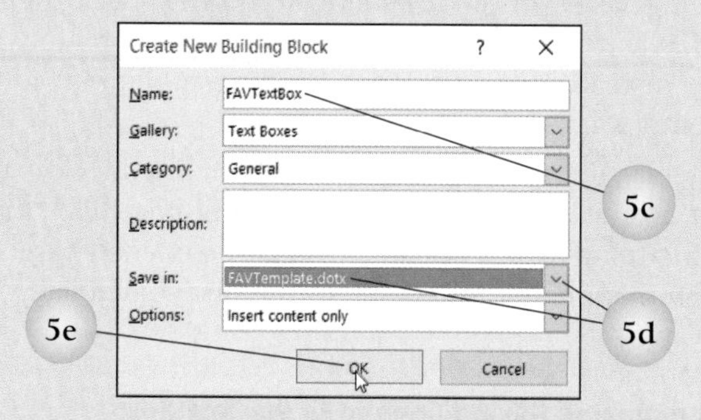

6. Save content as a building block in the Footer gallery by completing the following steps:
   a. Select the text *"Making your vacation dreams a reality"* below the text box. (Be sure to select the paragraph mark at the end of the text. If necessary, click the Show/Hide ¶ button in the Paragraph group on the Home tab to display the paragraph mark.)
   b. Click the Footer button in the Header & Footer group on the Insert tab and then click *Save Selection to Footer Gallery* at the drop-down list.
   c. At the Create New Building Block dialog box, type FAVFooter in the *Name* text box.
   d. Click the *Save in* option box and then click *FAVTemplate.dotx* at the drop-down list.
   e. Click OK to close the Create New Building Block dialog box.

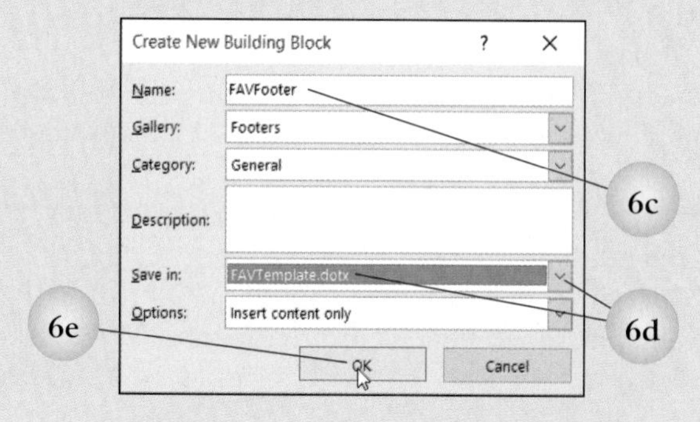

7. Save the company name *Pacific Sky Cruise Lines* and the address below it as a building block in the AutoText gallery by completing the following steps:
   a. Select the company name and address (the two lines below the company name). (Be sure to include the paragraph mark at the end of the last line of the address).
   b. Click the Quick Parts button in the Text group on the Insert tab, point to *AutoText*, and then click *Save Selection to AutoText Gallery* at the side menu.

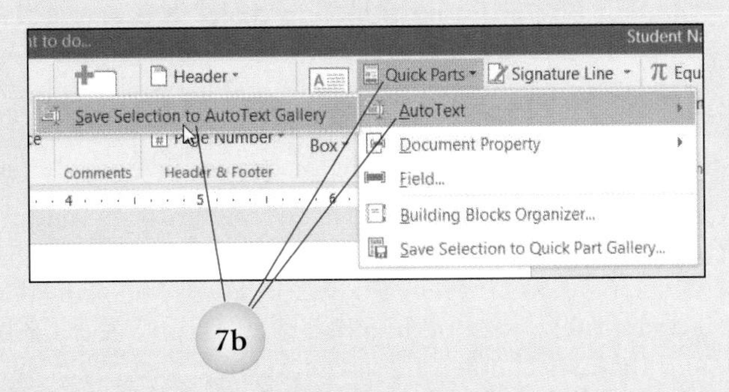

   c. At the Create New Building Block dialog box, type PacificSky in the *Name* text box.
   d. Click the *Save in* option box arrow and then click *FAVTemplate.dotx* at the drop-down list.
   e. Click OK to close the dialog box.
8. Type your name and company title and then save the text as a building block in the AutoText gallery by completing the following steps:
   a. Move the insertion point to a blank line one double space below the address for Pacific Sky Cruise Lines.
   b. Type your first and last names and then press the spacebar.
   c. Press the Down Arrow key to move the insertion point to the next line and then type Travel Consultant. (Do not press the Enter key.)
   d. Select your first and last names and the title *Travel Consultant*. (Include the paragraph mark at the end of the title.)
   e. Press Alt + F3.
   f. At the Create New Building Block dialog box, type Title in the *Name* text box.
   g. Click the *Save in* option box arrow and then click *FAVTemplate.dotx* at the drop-down list.
   h. Click OK to close the dialog box.
9. Save the letterhead as a building block in the Quick Part gallery by completing the following steps:
   a. Select the letterhead text (the company name *FAMILY ADVENTURE VACATIONS*, the address below the name, and the paragraph mark at the end of the address and telephone number).
   b. Click the Quick Parts button in the Text group on the Insert tab and then click *Save Selection to Quick Part Gallery* at the drop-down list.
   c. At the Create New Building Block dialog box, type FAV in the *Name* text box and change the *Save in* option to *FAVTemplate.dotx*.
   d. Click OK to close the dialog box.
10. Close the document without saving it.
11. At the message that displays indicating that you have modified styles, building blocks, or other content stored in FAVTemplate.dotx and asking if you want to save changes to the template, click the Save button.

Tutorial

Editing Building Block Properties

Editing Building Block Properties

Changes can be made to the properties of a building block with options at the Modify Building Block dialog box. This dialog box contains the same options as the Create New Building Block dialog box.

Display the Modify Building Block dialog box by opening the Building Blocks Organizer dialog box, clicking the specific building block in the list box, and then clicking the Edit Properties button. This dialog box can also be displayed for a building block in the Quick Parts button drop-down gallery. To do this, click the Quick Parts button, right-click the building block in the drop-down gallery, and then click *Edit Properties* at the shortcut menu. Make changes to the Modify Building Block dialog box and then click OK. At the confirmation message, click Yes.

The dialog box can also be displayed for a custom building block in a button drop-down gallery by clicking the button, right-clicking the custom building block, and then clicking the *Edit Properties* option at the shortcut menu. For example, to modify a custom text box building block, click the Insert tab, click the Text Box button, and then scroll down the drop-down gallery to display the custom text box building block. Right-click the custom text box building block and then click *Edit Properties* at the shortcut menu.

Quick Steps

Edit a Building Block

1. Click Insert tab.
2. Click Quick Parts button.
3. Click *Building Blocks Organizer*.
4. Click building block.
5. Click Edit Properties button.
6. Make changes.
7. Click OK.

OR

1. Click button.
2. Right-click custom building block.
3. Click *Edit Properties*.
4. Make changes.
5. Click OK.

Project 3b Editing Building Block Properties

Part 2 of 3

1. Open a blank document based on your template **FAVTemplate.dotx** by completing the following steps:
   a. Click the File Explorer icon on the taskbar.
   b. Navigate to the WL2C3 folder on your storage medium.
   c. Double-click ***FAVTemplate.dotx***.
2. Edit the PacificSky building block by completing the following steps:
   a. Click the Insert tab, click the Quick Parts button, and then click *Building Blocks Organizer* at the drop-down list.
   b. At the Building Blocks Organizer dialog box, click the *Gallery* heading to sort the building blocks by gallery. (This displays the *AutoText* galleries at the beginning of the list.)
   c. Using the horizontal scroll bar at the bottom of the *Building blocks* list box, scroll to the right and notice that the PacificSky building block does not contain a description.
   d. Click the *PacificSky* building block in the list box.
   e. Click the Edit Properties button at the bottom of the dialog box.

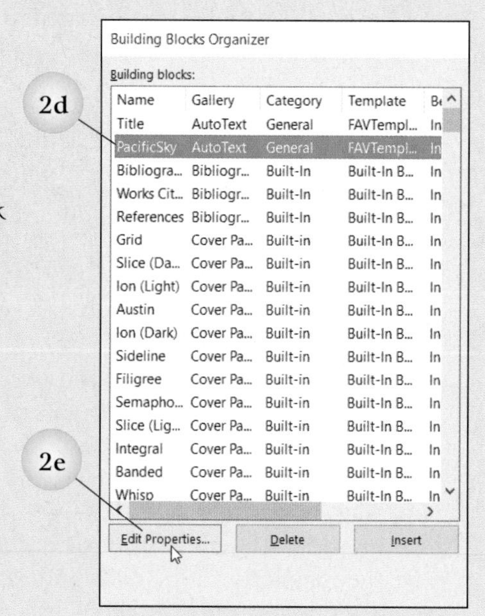

f. At the Modify Building Block dialog box, click in the *Name* text box and then type Address at the end of the name.
g. Click in the *Description* text box and then type Inserts the Pacific Sky name and address.
h. Click OK to close the dialog box.
i. At the message asking if you want to redefine the building block entry, click Yes.
j. Close the Building Blocks Organizer dialog box.
3. Edit the letterhead building block by completing the following steps:
a. Click the Quick Parts button in the Text group on the Insert tab, right-click the Family Adventure Vacations letterhead building block, and then click *Edit Properties* at the shortcut menu.
b. At the Modify Building Block dialog box, click in the *Name* text box and then type Letterhead at the end of the name.
c. Click in the *Description* text box and then type Inserts the Family Adventure Vacations letterhead including the company name and address.
d. Click OK to close the dialog box.
e. At the message asking if you want to redefine the building block entry, click Yes.
4. Close the document.
5. At the message that displays, click the Save button.

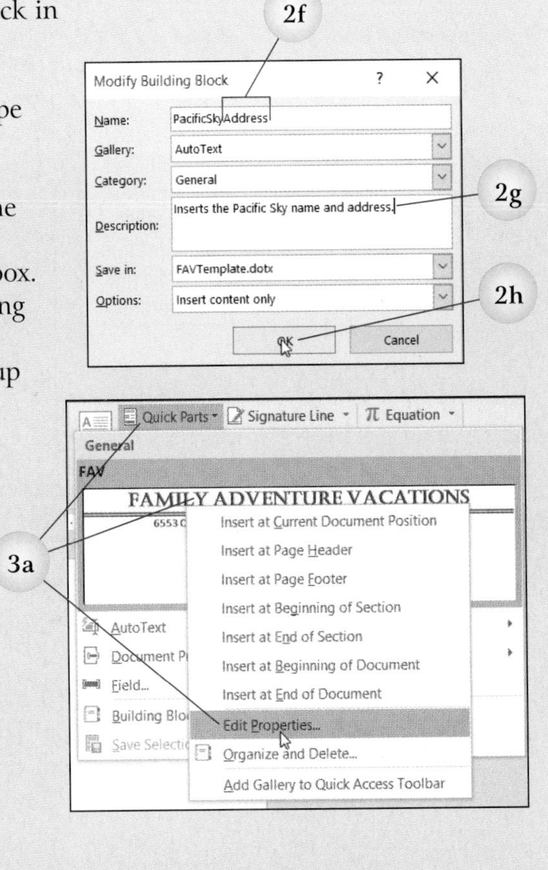

Tutorial

Inserting a Custom Building Block

Inserting a Custom Building Block

Any content saved as a building block can be inserted in a document using options at the Building Blocks Organizer dialog box. Some content can also be inserted using specific drop-down galleries. For example, insert a custom text box building block by clicking the Text Box button on the Insert tab and then clicking the text box at the drop-down gallery. Insert a custom header at the Header button drop-down gallery, a custom footer at the Footer button drop-down gallery, a custom cover page at the Cover Page button drop-down gallery, and so on.

Use the button drop-down gallery to specify where the custom building block content should be inserted in a document. To do this, display the button drop-down gallery, right-click the custom building block, and then click the location at the shortcut menu. For example, click the Insert tab, click the Quick Parts button, and then right-click the *FAVLetterhead* building block, and a shortcut menu displays, as shown in Figure 3.9.

Figure 3.9 Quick Parts Button Drop-Down Gallery Shortcut Menu

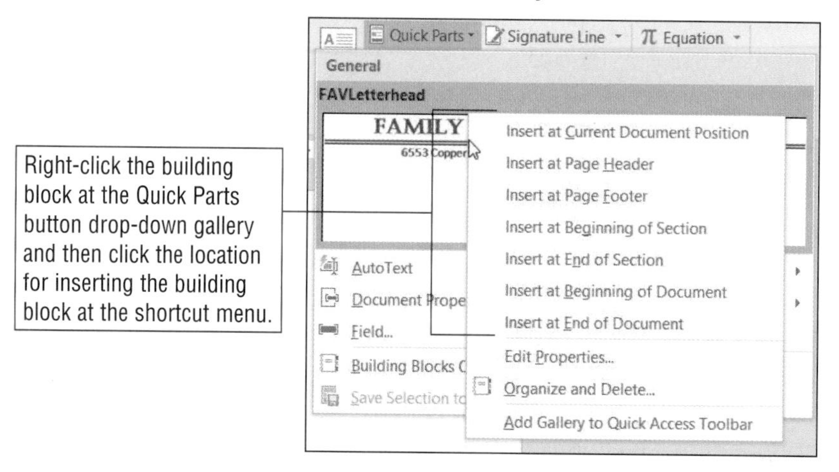

Project 3c Inserting Custom Building Blocks

Part 3 of 3

1. Open File Explorer, navigate to your WL2C3 folder, and then double-click ***FAVTemplate.dotx***.
2. At the blank document, click the *No Spacing* style in the Styles group on the Home tab and then change the font to Candara.
3. Insert the letterhead building block as a header by completing the following steps:
   a. Click the Insert tab.
   b. Click the Quick Parts button, right-click the *FAVLetterhead* building block, and then click the *Insert at Page Header* option at the shortcut menu.

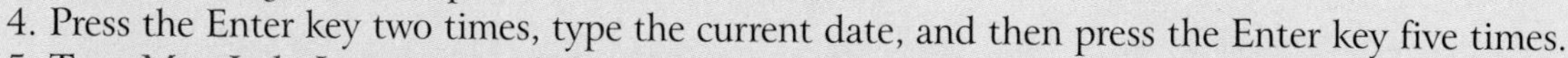

4. Press the Enter key two times, type the current date, and then press the Enter key five times.
5. Type Mrs. Jody Lancaster and then press the Enter key.
6. Insert the Pacific Sky Cruise Lines name and address building block by clicking the Quick Parts button, pointing to *AutoText*, and then clicking the *PacificSkyAddress* building block at the side menu.

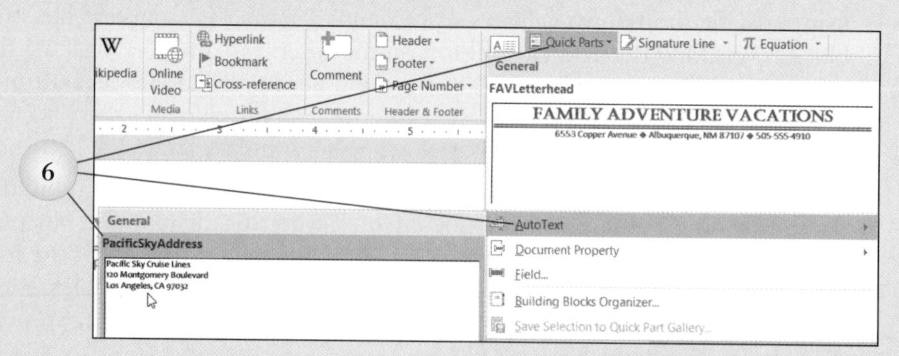

7. Press the Enter key and then insert a letter document by completing the following steps:
   a. Click the Object button arrow in the Text group on the Insert tab and then click *Text from File* at the drop-down list.
   b. At the Insert File dialog box, navigate to the WL2C3 folder on your storage medium and then double-click ***PSLetter01.docx***.

8. With the insertion point positioned one double space below the last paragraph of text in the body of the letter, type Sincerely, and then press the Enter key four times.
9. Insert your name and title building block by clicking the Quick Parts button, pointing to *AutoText*, and then clicking the *Title* building block at the side menu.
10. Press the Enter key and then type 3-PSLtr01.docx.
11. Press the Enter key five times and then insert the custom text box you saved as a building block by completing the following steps:
    a. Click the Text Box button in the Text group on the Insert tab.
    b. Scroll to the end of the drop-down gallery and then click the *FAVTextBox* building block. (Your custom text box will display in the *General* section of the drop-down gallery.)
    c. Click in the document to deselect the text box.
12. Insert the custom footer you created by completing the following steps:
    a. Click the Insert tab.
    b. Click the Footer button in the Header & Footer group.
    c. Scroll to the end of the drop-down gallery and then click the *FAVFooter* building block. (Your custom footer will display in the *General* section.)
    d. Close the footer pane by double-clicking in the document.
13. Save the completed letter and name it **3-PSLtr01**.
14. Print and then close **3-PSLtr01.docx**.

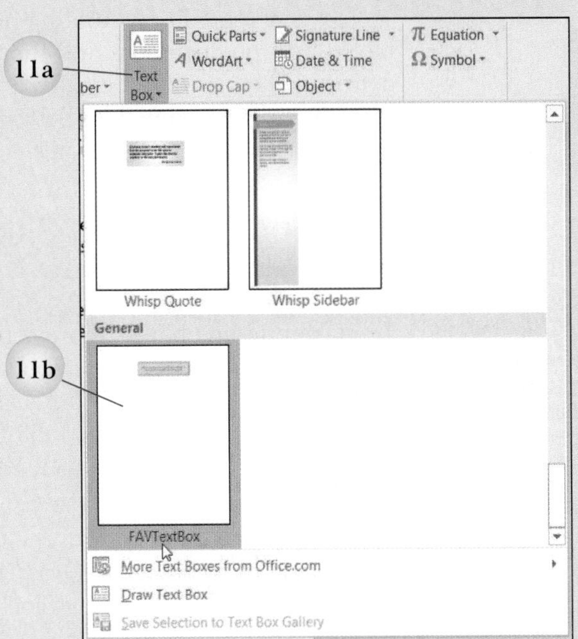

Check Your Work

Project 4 Create a Letter Document with Modified Building Blocks and Save Building Blocks to a Different Template

3 Parts

You will modify your custom building blocks and use them to prepare a business letter. You will also save building blocks to a different template, use the building blocks to format an announcement, and then delete your custom building blocks.

Preview Finished Project

Tutorial

Modifying and Deleting Building Blocks

Modifying a Custom Building Block

A building block can be inserted in a document, corrections or changes can be made to the building block, and then the building block can be saved with the same name or a different name. Save a building block with the same name when updating the building block to reflect any changes. Save the building block with a new name when using an existing building block as the foundation for creating a new building block.

To save a modified building block with the same name, insert the building block into the document and then make modifications. Select the building block data and then specify the gallery. At the Create New Building Block dialog box, type the original name and description and then click OK. At the confirmation message that displays, click Yes.

Inserting a Building Block Gallery as a Button on the Quick Access Toolbar

Quick Steps

Insert Building Block Gallery as a Button on Quick Access Toolbar

1. Click specific button.
2. Right-click building block.
3. Click *Add Gallery to Quick Access Toolbar*.

To make building blocks more accessible, insert a building block gallery as a button on the Quick Access Toolbar. To do this, right-click a building block and then click *Add Gallery to Quick Access Toolbar*. For example, to add the *Quick Part* gallery to the Quick Access Toolbar, click the Quick Parts button on the Insert tab, right-click a building block at the drop-down gallery, and then click *Add Gallery to Quick Access Toolbar*.

To remove a button from the Quick Access Toolbar, right-click the button and then click *Remove from Quick Access Toolbar* at the shortcut menu. Removing a button containing a building block gallery does not delete the building block.

Project 4a Modifying Building Blocks and Inserting Custom Building Blocks as Buttons on the Quick Access Toolbar

Part 1 of 3

1. Open File Explorer, navigate to your WL2C3 folder, and then double-click ***FAVTemplate.dotx***.
2. Modify your name and title building block to reflect a title change by completing the following steps:
   a. At the blank document, click the Insert tab, click the Quick Parts button in the Text group, point to *AutoText*, and then click the *Title* building block at the side menu.
   b. Edit your title so it displays as *Senior Travel Consultant*.
   c. Select your name and title, click the Quick Parts button, point to *AutoText*, and then click the *Save Selection to AutoText Gallery* option.
   d. At the Create New Building Block dialog box, type Title in the *Name* text box.
   e. Click the *Save in* option box arrow and then click *FAVTemplate.dotx* at the drop-down list.
   f. Click OK.
   g. At the message asking if you want to redefine the building block entry, click Yes.
   h. With your name and title selected, press the Delete key to remove them from the document.

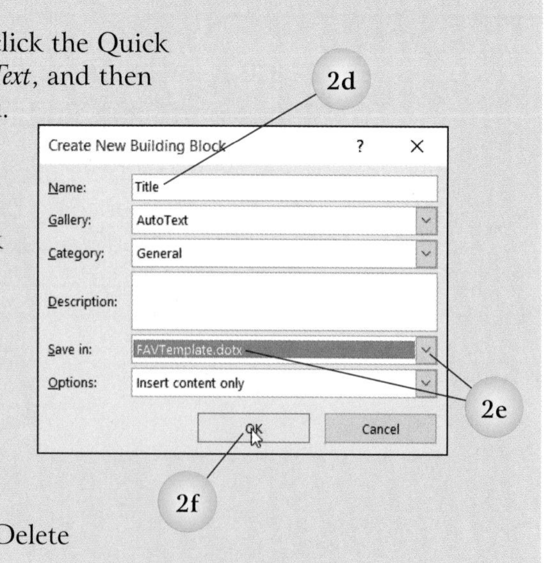

3. Since most of the correspondence you send to Pacific Sky Cruise Lines is addressed to Jody Lancaster, you decide to include her name at the beginning of the company name and address by completing the following steps:
   a. With the Insert tab active, click the Quick Parts button, point to *AutoText*, and then click the *PacificSkyAddress* building block at the side menu.
   b. Type Mrs. Jody Lancaster above the name of the cruise line.
   c. Select the name, company name, and address.
   d. Click the Quick Parts button, point to *AutoText*, and then click the *Save Selection to AutoText Gallery* option.
   e. At the Create New Building Block dialog box, type PacificSkyAddress (the original name) in the *Name* text box.

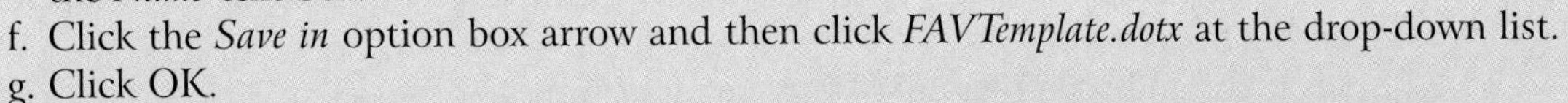

   f. Click the *Save in* option box arrow and then click *FAVTemplate.dotx* at the drop-down list.
   g. Click OK.
   h. At the message asking if you want to redefine the building block entry, click Yes.
4. Press Ctrl + End and then add the FAVFooter building block to the Quick Part gallery by completing the following steps:
   a. Click the Footer button on the Insert tab, scroll down the drop-down gallery, and then click the *FAVFooter* custom building block.
   b. Press the Backspace key to delete the extra space below the footer and then press Ctrl + A to select the footer.
   c. Click the Insert tab, click the Quick Parts button, and then click *Save Selection to Quick Part Gallery*.
   d. At the Create New Building Block dialog box, type FAVFooter in the *Name* text box.
   e. Click the *Save in* option box arrow and then click *FAVTemplate.dotx* at the drop-down list.
   f. Click OK to close the Create New Building Block dialog box. (You now have the footer saved in the Footer gallery and Quick Part gallery.)
   g. Double-click in the document.
5. Insert the Quick Part gallery as a button on the Quick Access Toolbar by completing the following steps:
   a. Click the Insert tab, click the Quick Parts button, and then right-click one of your custom building blocks.
   b. At the shortcut menu, click the *Add Gallery to Quick Access Toolbar* option. (Notice the Explore Quick Parts button that appears at the right side of the Quick Access Toolbar.)

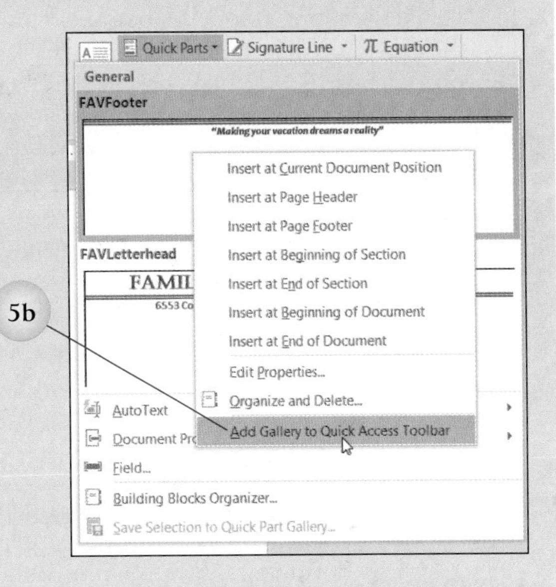

6. Insert the AutoText gallery as a button on the Quick Access Toolbar by completing the following steps:
   a. Click the Quick Parts button, point to *AutoText*, and then right-click one of your custom building blocks.
   b. At the shortcut menu, click the *Add Gallery to Quick Access Toolbar* option. (Notice the AutoText button that appears at the right side of the Quick Access Toolbar.)

7. Close the document without saving it. At the message that displays, click the Save button.
8. Create a business letter by completing the following steps:
   a. Use File Explorer to open a blank document based on **FAVTemplate.dotx** in the WL2C3 folder on your storage medium.
   b. Click the *No Spacing* style in the Styles group on the Home tab, and then change the font to Candara.
   c. Insert the FAVLetterhead building block as a page header.
   d. Press the Enter key two times, type today's date, and then press the Enter key four times.
   e. Insert the building block that includes Jody Lancaster's name as well as the cruise line name and address by clicking the AutoText button on the Quick Access Toolbar and then clicking the *PacificSkyAddress* building block at the drop-down list.
   f. Press the Enter key and then insert the file named **PSLetter02.docx** in the WL2C3 folder on your storage medium. ***Hint: Do this with the Object button arrow in the Text group on the Insert tab.***
   g. Type Sincerely, and then press the Enter key four times.
   h. Click the AutoText button on the Quick Access Toolbar and then click the *Title* building block.
   i. Press the Enter key and then type 3-PSLtr02.docx.
   j. Insert the footer building block by clicking the Explore Quick Parts button on the Quick Access Toolbar, right-clicking *FAVFooter*, and then clicking *Insert at Page Footer* at the shortcut menu.

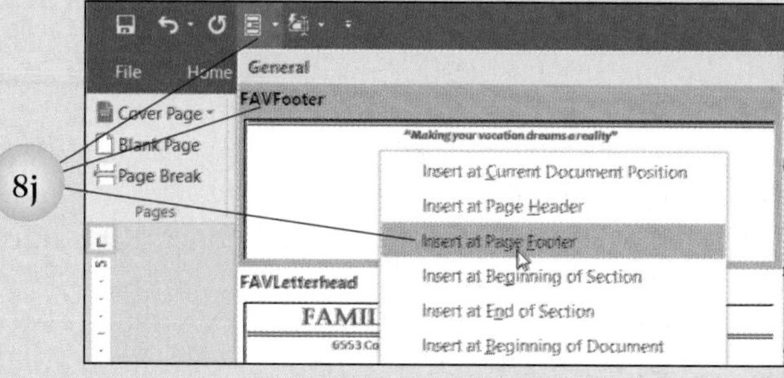

9. Save the completed letter and name it **3-PSLtr02**.
10. Print and then close **3-PSLtr02.docx**.
11. Use File Explorer to open a blank document based on your template **FAVTemplate.dotx**.
12. Click the AutoText button on the Quick Access Toolbar, press the Print Screen button on your keyboard, and then click in the document to remove the drop-down list.
13. At the blank document, click the Paste button. (This pastes the screen capture in your document.)
14. Print the document and then close it without saving it.
15. Remove the Explore Quick Parts button you added to the Quick Access Toolbar by right-clicking the Explore Quick Parts button and then clicking *Remove from Quick Access Toolbar* at the shortcut menu. Complete similar steps to remove the AutoText button from the Quick Access Toolbar. (The buttons will display dimmed if no documents are open.)

Check Your Work

Saving Building Blocks in a Different Template

Building blocks saved to a personal template are available only when a document is opened based on the template. To make building blocks available for all documents, save them in Building Block.dotx or Normal.dotm. Use the *Save in* option at the Create New Building Block or Modify Building Block dialog box to save building blocks to one of these two templates.

If an existing building block in a personal template is modified and saved in Normal.dotm or Building Block.dotx, the building block is no longer available in the personal template. It is available only in documents based on the default template Normal.dotm. To keep a building block in a personal template and also make it available for other documents, insert the building block content in the document, select the content, and then create a new building block.

Project 4b Saving Building Blocks in a Different Template

Part 2 of 3

1. Use File Explorer to open a blank document based on your template **FAVTemplate.dotx**.
2. Create a new FAVLetterhead building block and save it in Building Block.dotx so it is available for all documents by completing the following steps:
   a. Click the Insert tab.
   b. Click the Quick Parts button and then click the *FAVLetterhead* building block to insert the content in the document.
   c. Select the letterhead (company name, address, and telephone number including the paragraph mark at the end of the line containing the address and telephone number).
   d. Click the Quick Parts button on the Insert tab and then click *Save Selection to Quick Part Gallery* at the drop-down list.
   e. At the Create New Building Block dialog box, type XXX-FAVLetterhead. (Type your initials in place of the *XXX*.)
   f. Make sure *Building Blocks.dotx* displays in the *Save in* option box and then click OK. (The FAVLetterhead building block is still available in your template FAVTemplate.dotx and the new XXX-FAVLetterhead building block is available in all documents, including documents based on FAVTemplate.dotx.)

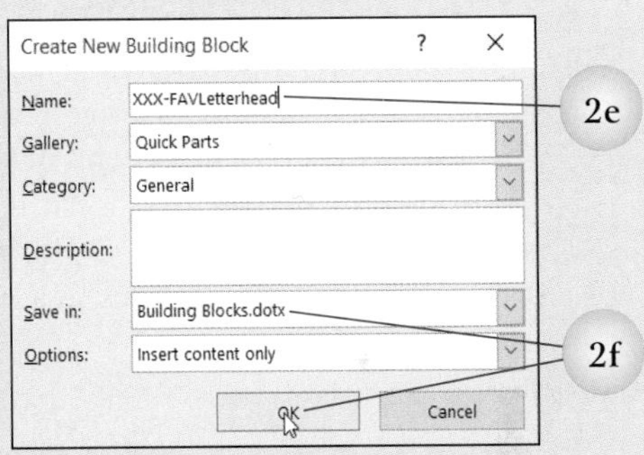

   g. Delete the selected letterhead text.
3. Create a new FAVFooter building block and then save it in Building Blocks.dotx so it is available for all documents by completing the following steps:
   a. Click the Quick Parts button on the Insert tab and then click the *FAVFooter* building block to insert the content in the document.
   b. Select the footer text *"Making your travel dreams a reality"* and make sure you select the paragraph mark at the end of the text.
   c. Click the Quick Parts button on the Insert tab and then click *Save Selection to Quick Part Gallery* at the drop-down list.
   d. At the Create New Building Block dialog box, type XXX-FAVFooter. (Type your initials in place of the *XXX*.)
   e. Make sure *Building Blocks.dotx* displays in the *Save in* option box and then click OK.
4. Close the document without saving it.
5. Open **FAVContent.docx**.
6. Create a new FAVTextBox building block and save it in Building Blocks.dotx so it is available for all documents by completing the following steps:
   a. Select the text box by clicking the text box and then clicking the text box border.
   b. Click the Insert tab, click the Text Box button, and then click *Save Selection to Text Box Gallery* at the drop-down list.
   c. At the Create New Building Block dialog box, type XXX-FAVTextBox. (Type your initials in place of the *XXX*.)
   d. Make sure *Building Blocks.dotx* displays in the *Save in* option box and then click OK.

7. Close **FAVContent.docx.**
8. Insert in a document the building blocks you created by completing the following steps:
   a. Open **PSAnnounce.docx** and then save it with the name **3-PSAnnounce**.
   b. Insert the XXX-FAVLetterhead building block by clicking the Insert tab, clicking the Quick Parts button, right-clicking *XXX-FAVLetterhead* (where your initials display in place of the *XXX*), and then clicking *Insert at Page Header* at the shortcut menu.

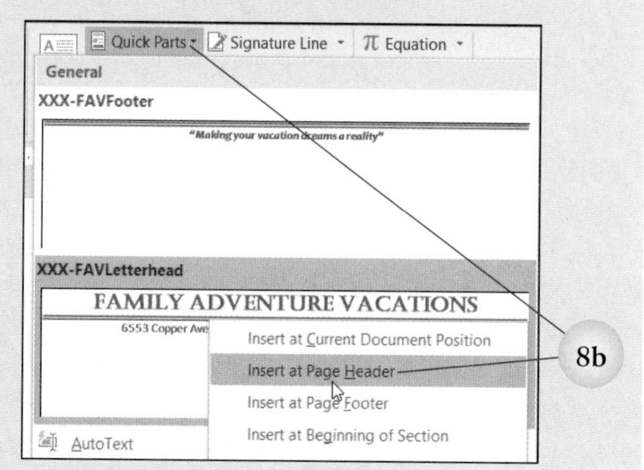

   c. Insert the XXX-FAVFooter building block by clicking the Quick Parts button, right-clicking *XXX-FAVFooter* (where your initials display in place of the *XXX*), and then clicking *Insert at Page Footer* at the shortcut menu.
   d. Press Ctrl + End to move the insertion point to the end of the document.
   e. Insert the XXX-FAVTextBox building block by clicking the Text Box button, scrolling down the drop-down gallery, and then clicking *XXX-FAVTextBox* (where your initials display in place of the *XXX*).
   f. Horizontally align the text box by clicking the Align button in the Arrange group on the Drawing Tools Format tab and then clicking *Distribute Horizontally* at the drop-down list.

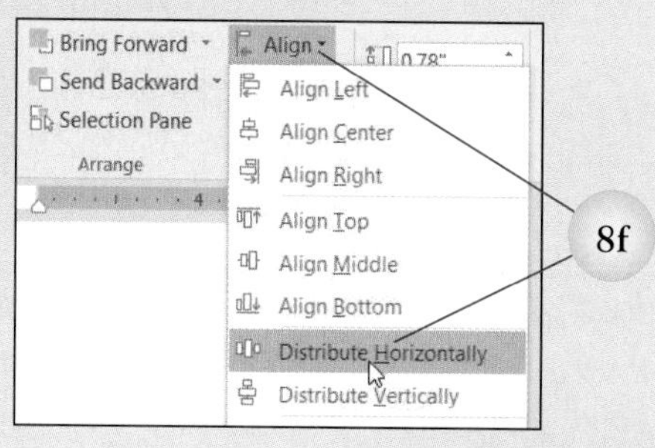

9. Save, print, and then close **3-PSAnnounce.docx**.
10. At the message that displays, click the Save button.

Check Your Work

Deleting a Building Block

Quick Steps

Delete a Building Block

1. Display Building Blocks Organizer dialog box.
2. Click building block.
3. Click Delete button.
4. Click Yes.

OR

1. Display button drop-down gallery.
2. Right-click building block.
3. Click *Organize and Delete* option.
4. Click Delete button.
5. Click Yes.

A custom building block that is no longer needed can be deleted by displaying the Building Blocks Organizer dialog box, clicking the building block, and then clicking the Delete button. At the confirmation message that displays, click Yes.

Another method for deleting a custom building block is to right-click the building block at the drop-down gallery and then click the *Organize and Delete* option at the shortcut menu. This displays the Building Blocks Organizer dialog box with the building block selected. Click the Delete button and then click Yes at the confirmation message box.

Project 4c Deleting Building Blocks

Part 3 of 3

1. At a blank document, delete the XXX-FAVLetterhead building block by completing the following steps:
   a. Click the Insert tab and then click the Quick Parts button in the Text group.
   b. Right-click the *XXX-FAVLetterhead* building block and then click *Organize and Delete* at the shortcut menu.

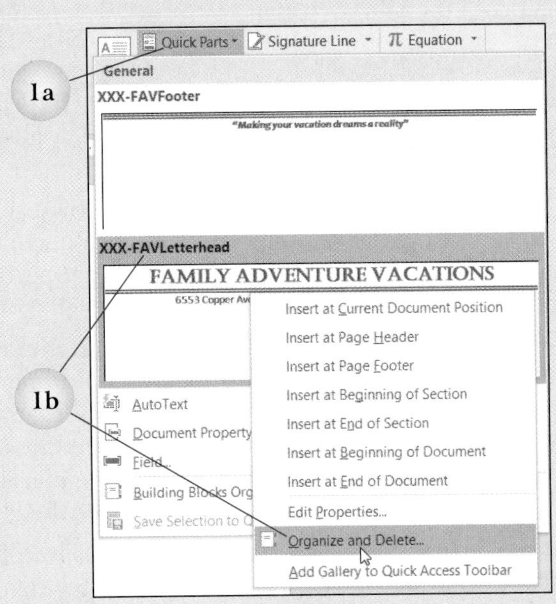

   c. At the Building Blocks Organizer dialog box with the building block selected, click the Delete button.
   d. At the message that displays asking if you are sure you want to delete the selected building block, click Yes.
   e. Close the Building Blocks Organizer dialog box.
2. Delete the XXX-FAVFooter building block by completing the following steps:
   a. Click the Quick Parts button, right-click the *XXX-FAVFooter* building block, and then click *Organize and Delete* at the shortcut menu.
   b. At the Building Blocks Organizer dialog box with the building block selected, click the Delete button.
   c. At the message asking if you are sure you want to delete the selected building block, click Yes.
   d. Close the Building Blocks Organizer dialog box.
3. Delete the *XXX-FAVTextBox* (in the Text Box gallery) by completing the following steps:
   a. Click the Text Box button in the Text group on the Insert tab.
   b. Scroll down the drop-down gallery to display your custom text box.
   c. Right-click your text box and then click *Organize and Delete* at the shortcut menu.
   d. At the Building Blocks Organizer dialog box with the building block selected, click the Delete button.
   e. At the message asking if you are sure you want to delete the selected building block, click Yes.
   f. Close the Building Blocks Organizer dialog box.
4. Close the document without saving it.

Project 5 **Insert Document Properties and Fields in a Testing Agreement Document** **2 Parts**

You will open a testing agreement document and then insert and update document properties and fields.

Preview Finished Project

Inserting a Document Property Placeholder

Click the Quick Parts button on the Insert tab and then point to *Document Property* at the drop-down list and a side menu displays with document property options. Click an option at this side menu and a document property placeholder is inserted in the document. Text can be typed in the placeholder.

If a document property placeholder is inserted in multiple locations in a document, updating one of the placeholders will automatically update all occurrences of that placeholder in the document. For example, in Project 5a, a Company document property placeholder is inserted in six locations in a document. The content of the first occurrence of the placeholder will be changed and the remaining placeholders will update to reflect the change.

Click the File tab and the Info backstage area displays containing information about the document. Document properties display at the right side of the Info backstage area, including information such as the document size, number of pages, title, and comments.

Project 5a Inserting Document Property Placeholders

Part 1 of 2

1. Open **TestAgrmnt.docx** and then save it with the name **3-TestAgrmnt**.
2. Select the first occurrence of *FP* in the document (in the first line of text after the title) and then insert a document property placeholder by completing the following steps:
   a. Click the Insert tab, click the Quick Parts button in the Text group, point to *Document Property*, and then click *Company* at the side menu.
   b. Type Frontier Productions in the company placeholder.
   c. Press the Right Arrow key to move the insertion point outside the company placeholder. 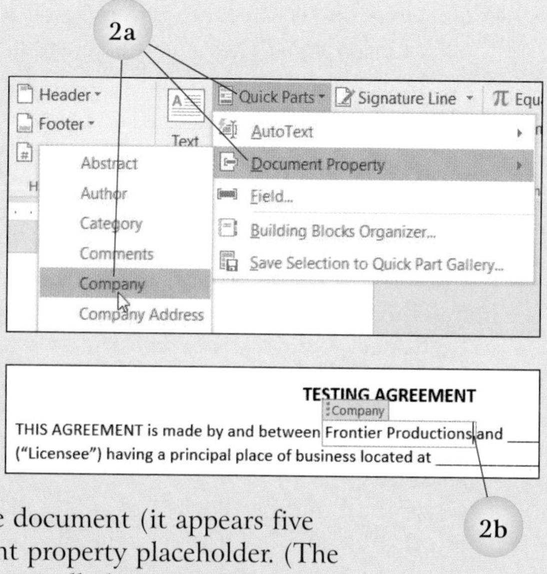
3. Select each remaining occurrence of *FP* in the document (it appears five more times) and insert the company document property placeholder. (The company name, *Frontier Productions,* will automatically be inserted in the placeholder.)

4. Press Ctrl + End to move the insertion point to the end of the document and then insert a comments document property placeholder by completing the following steps:
   a. Click the Quick Parts button, point to *Document Property*, and then click *Comments* at the side menu.
   b. Type First Draft in the comments placeholder.
   c. Press the Right Arrow key.
   d. Press Shift + Enter.
5. Click the File tab, make sure the *Info* option is selected, and then notice that the comment typed in the comments document property placeholder displays at the right side of the backstage area. Click the Back button to display the document.

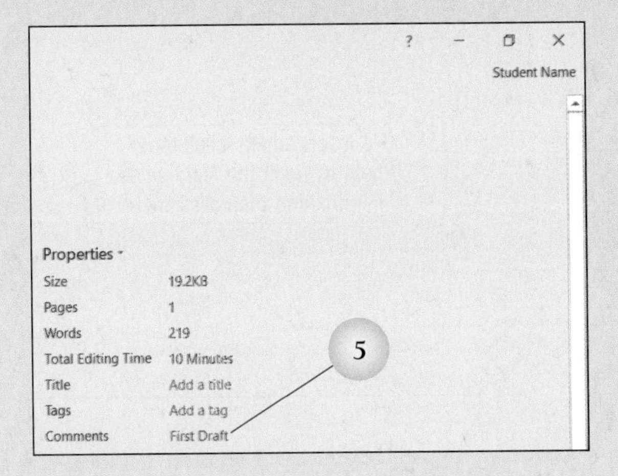

6. Save and then print **3-TestAgrmnt.docx**.
7. Click in the first occurrence of the company name *Frontier Productions* and then click the company placeholder tab. (This selects the company placeholder.)
8. Type Frontier Video Productions.
9. Press the Right Arrow key. (Notice that the other occurrences of the Company document property placeholder automatically updated to reflect the new name.)
10. Save **3-TestAgrmnt.docx**.

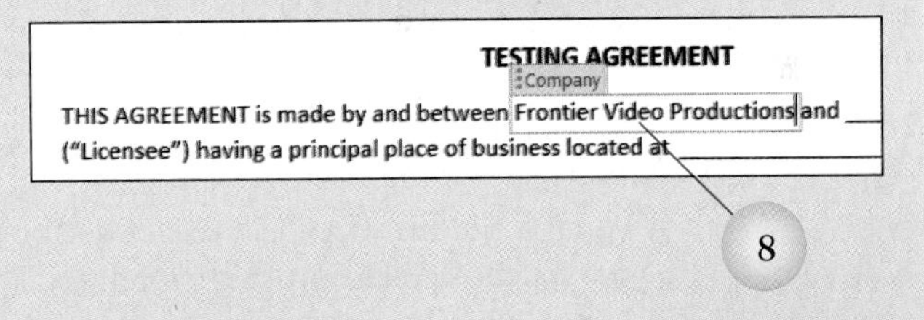

Check Your Work

Tutorial

Inserting and Updating Fields

Quick Steps

Insert a Field
1. Click Insert tab.
2. Click Quick Parts button.
3. Click *Field* at drop-down list.
4. Click field.
5. Click OK.

Inserting, Formatting, and Updating Fields

Fields are placeholders for data that varies. Word provides buttons for many of the types of fields that can be inserted in a document as well as options at the Field dialog box, shown in Figure 3.10. This dialog box contains a list of all available fields. Just as the Building Blocks Organizer dialog box is a central location for building blocks, the Field dialog box is a central location for fields.

To display the Field dialog box, click the Insert tab, click the Quick Parts button in the Text group, and then click *Field* at the drop-down list. At the Field dialog box, click a field in the *Field names* list box and then click OK.

Figure 3.10 Field Dialog Box

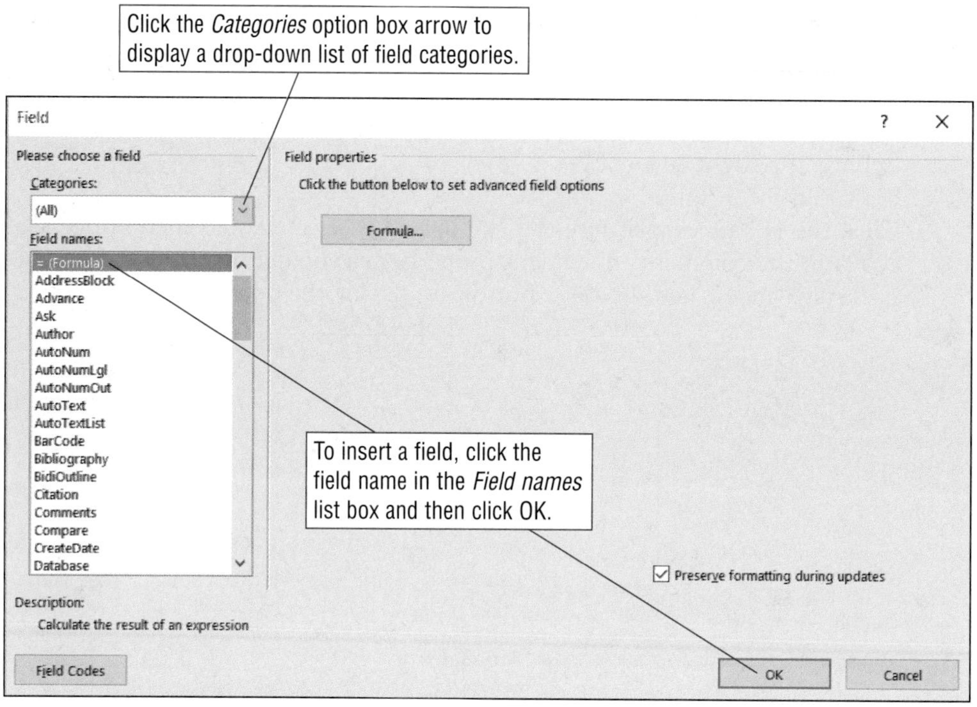

Click the *Categories* option box arrow to display a drop-down list of field categories.

Field ? X
Please choose a field
Categories:
(All)
Field names:
= (Formula)
AddressBlock
Advance
Ask
Author
AutoNum
AutoNumLgl
AutoNumOut
AutoText
AutoTextList
BarCode
Bibliography
BidiOutline
Citation
Comments
Compare
CreateDate
Database
Field properties
Click the button below to set advanced field options
Formula...
Preserve formatting during updates
Description:
Calculate the result of an expression
Field Codes
OK
Cancel

To insert a field, click the field name in the *Field names* list box and then click OK.

Choosing Field Categories

All available fields display in the *Field names* list box at the Field dialog box. Narrow the list of fields to a specific category by clicking the *Categories* option box arrow and then clicking a specific category at the drop-down list. For example, to display only date and time fields, click the *Date and Time* category at the drop-down list.

Creating Custom Field Formats

Click a field in the *Field names* list box and a description of the field displays below the list box. Field properties related to the selected field also display in the dialog box. A custom field format can be created for some fields. For example, click the *NumWords* field in the *Field names* list box and custom formatting options display in the *Format* list box and the *Numeric format* list box.

By default, the *Preserve formatting during updates* check box contains a check mark. With this option active, the custom formatting specified for a field will be preserved if the field is updated.

Updating Fields

Quick Steps

Update a Field

1. Click field.
2. Click Update tab.

OR

1. Click field.
2. Press F9.

OR

1. Right-click field.
2. Click *Update Field.*

Some fields, such as the date and time field, update automatically when a document is opened. Other fields can be updated manually. A field can be updated manually by clicking the field and then clicking the Update tab; by clicking the field and then pressing the F9 function key; and by right-clicking the field and then clicking *Update Field* at the shortcut menu. Update all fields in a document (except headers, footers, and text boxes) by pressing Ctrl + A to select the document and then pressing the F9 function key.

Project 5b Inserting and Formatting Fields

1. With **3-TestAgrmnt.docx** open, press Ctrl + End to move the insertion point to the end of the document.
2. Type Current date and time:, press the spacebar, and then insert a field that inserts the current date and time by clicking the following steps:
   a. Click the Insert tab.
   b. Click the Quick Parts button and then click *Field* at the drop-down list.
   c. At the Field dialog box, click the *Categories* option box arrow and then click *Date and Time* at the drop-down list. (This displays only fields in the Date and Time category in the *Field names* list box.)
   d. Click *Date* in the *Field names* list box.
   e. Click the twelfth option in the *Date formats* list box (the option that will insert the date in figures followed by the time [hours and minutes]).
   f. Click OK to close the dialog box.
3. Press Shift + Enter, type File name and path:, press the spacebar, and then insert a field for the current file name with custom field formatting by completing the following steps:
   a. With the Insert tab active, click the Quick Parts button and then click *Field* at the drop-down list.
   b. At the Field dialog box, click the *Categories* option box arrow and then click *Document Information* at the drop-down list.
   c. Click *FileName* in the *Field names* list box.
   d. Click the *Uppercase* option in the *Format* list box.
   e. Click the *Add path to filename* check box to insert a check mark.

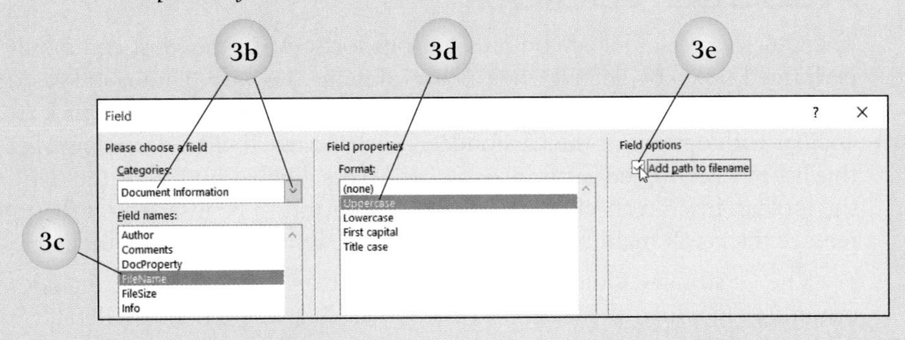

   f. Click OK to close the dialog box. (The current file name is inserted in the document in uppercase letters and includes the path to the file name.)
4. Insert a header and then insert a custom field in the header by completing the following steps:
   a. Click the Header button in the Header & Footer group and then click *Edit Header* at the drop-down list.
   b. In the header pane, press the Tab key two times. (This moves the insertion point to the right tab at the right margin.)

c. Click the Quick Parts button in the Insert group on the Header & Footer Tools Design tab and then click *Field* at the drop-down list.
d. At the Field dialog box, click the *Categories* option box arrow and then click *Date and Time* at the drop-down list.
e. Click in the *Date formats* text box and then type MMMM yyyy. (This tells Word to insert the month as text followed by the four-digit year.)
f. Click OK to close the dialog box.
g. Double-click in the document.

5. Update the time in the date and time field at the end of the document by clicking the date and time and then clicking the Update tab.
6. Save, print, and then close **3-TestAgrmnt.docx**.

Check Your Work

Project 6 **Customize the Quick Access Toolbar and Ribbon** **4 Parts**

You will open a document, customize the Quick Access Toolbar by inserting and removing buttons, customize the ribbon by inserting a new tab, and export ribbon and Quick Access Toolbar customizations.

Preview Finished Project

Tutorial

Customizing the Quick Access Toolbar

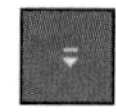
Customize Quick Access Toolbar

Quick Steps

Customize the Quick Access Toolbar

1. Click Customize Quick Access Toolbar button.
2. Insert check mark before each button to insert.
3. Remove check mark before each button to remove.

Customizing the Quick Access Toolbar

The Quick Access Toolbar contains buttons for some of the most commonly performed tasks. By default, the toolbar contains the Save, Undo, and Redo buttons. Some basic buttons can be easily inserted on or removed from the Quick Access Toolbar with options at the Customize Quick Access Toolbar drop-down list. Display this list by clicking the Customize Quick Access Toolbar button at the right side of the toolbar. Insert a check mark before each button to be inserted on the toolbar and remove the check mark from each button to be removed from the toolbar.

The Customize Quick Access Toolbar button drop-down list includes an option for moving the location of the Quick Access Toolbar. By default, the Quick Access Toolbar is positioned above the ribbon. To move the toolbar below the ribbon, click the *Show Below the Ribbon* option at the drop-down list.

Buttons or commands from a tab can be inserted on the Quick Access Toolbar. To do this, click the tab, right-click the button or command, and then click *Add to Quick Access Toolbar* at the shortcut menu.

Project 6a Customizing the Quick Access Toolbar

1. Open **InterfaceApps.docx** and then save it with the name **3-InterfaceApps**.
2. Insert the New button on the Quick Access Toolbar by clicking the Customize Quick Access Toolbar button at the right of the toolbar and then clicking *New* at the drop-down list.
3. Insert the Open button on the Quick Access Toolbar by clicking the Customize Quick Access Toolbar button and then clicking *Open* at the drop-down list.
4. Click the New button on the Quick Access Toolbar. (This displays a new blank document.)
5. Close the document.
6. Click the Open button on the Quick Access Toolbar to display the Open backstage area.
7. Press the Esc key to return to the document.
8. Move the Quick Access Toolbar by clicking the Customize Quick Access Toolbar button and then clicking *Show Below the Ribbon* at the drop-down list.
9. Move the Quick Access Toolbar back to the default position by clicking the Customize Quick Access Toolbar button and then clicking *Show Above the Ribbon* at the drop-down list.
10. Insert the Margins and the Themes buttons on the Quick Access Toolbar by completing the following steps:
    a. Click the Layout tab.
    b. Right-click the Margins button in the Page Setup group and then click *Add to Quick Access Toolbar* at the shortcut menu.

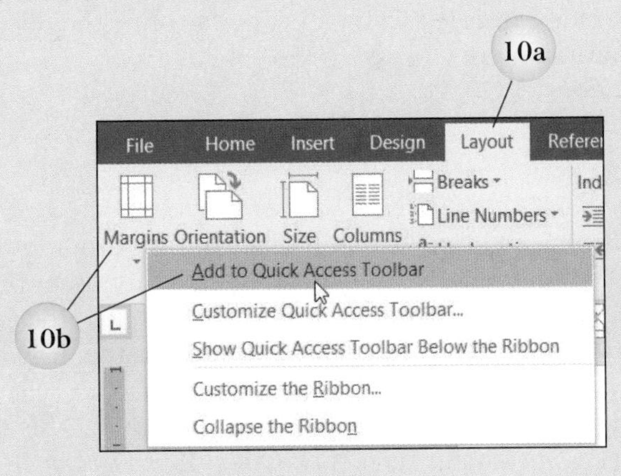

    c. Click the Design tab.
    d. Right-click the Themes button in the Themes group and then click *Add to Quick Access Toolbar* at the shortcut menu.
11. Change the top margin by completing the following steps:
    a. Click the Margins button on the Quick Access Toolbar and then click *Custom Margins* at the drop-down list.
    b. At the Page Setup dialog box, change the top margin to 1.5 inches and then click OK.
12. Change the theme by clicking the Themes button on the Quick Access Toolbar and then clicking *View* at the drop-down gallery.

13. Create a screenshot of the Quick Access Toolbar by completing the following steps:
    a. Click the New button on the Quick Access Toolbar. (This displays a new blank document.)
    b. Click the Insert tab, click the Screenshot button in the Illustrations group, and then click *Screen Clipping* at the drop-down list.

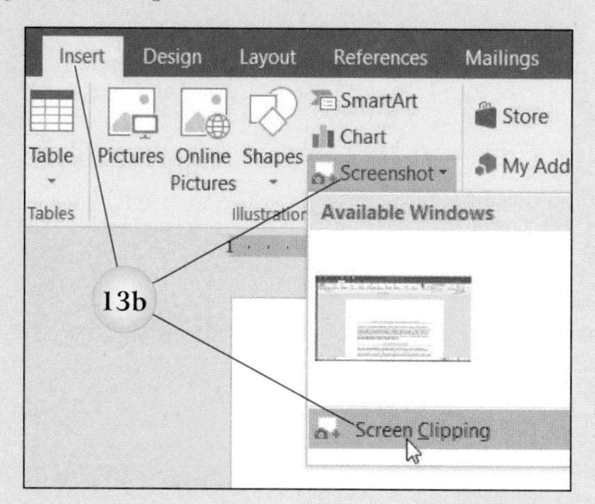

    c. In a few moments, **3-InterfaceApps.docx** displays in a dimmed manner. Using the mouse, drag down and to the right from the upper left corner of the screen to capture the Quick Access Toolbar and then release the mouse button.

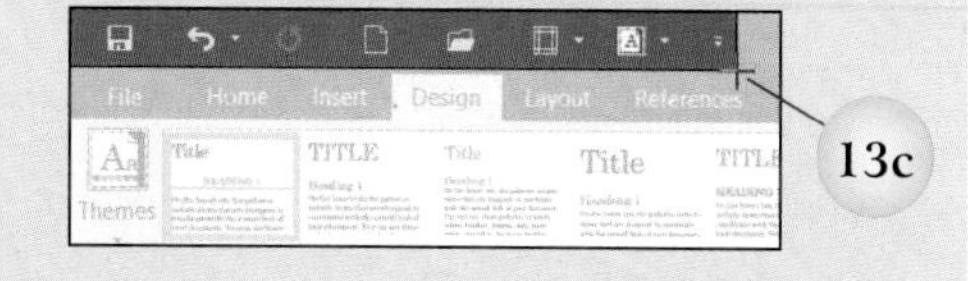

    d. With the screenshot image inserted in the document, print the document and then close the document without saving it.
14. Save **3-InterfaceApps.docx**.

Check Your Work

Quick Steps

Add Buttons to the Quick Access Toolbar from the Word Options Dialog Box

1. Click Customize Quick Access Toolbar button.
2. Click *More Commands* at drop-down list.
3. Click desired command in left list box.
4. Click Add button.
5. Click OK.

The Customize Quick Access Toolbar button drop-down list contains 11 of the most commonly used buttons. However, many other buttons can be inserted on the toolbar. To display the buttons available, click the Customize Quick Access Toolbar button and then click *More Commands* at the drop-down list. This displays the Word Options dialog box with *Quick Access Toolbar* selected in the left panel, as shown in Figure 3.11. Another method for displaying this dialog box is to click the File tab, click *Options*, and then click *Quick Access Toolbar* in the left panel of the Word Options dialog box.

To reset the Quick Access Toolbar to the default (Save, Undo, and Redo buttons), click the Reset button in the lower right corner of the dialog box and then click *Reset only Quick Access Toolbar* at the drop-down list. At the message that displays asking if the Quick Access Toolbar shared between all documents should be restored to its default contents, click Yes.

Figure 3.11 Word Options Dialog Box with *Quick Access Toolbar* Selected

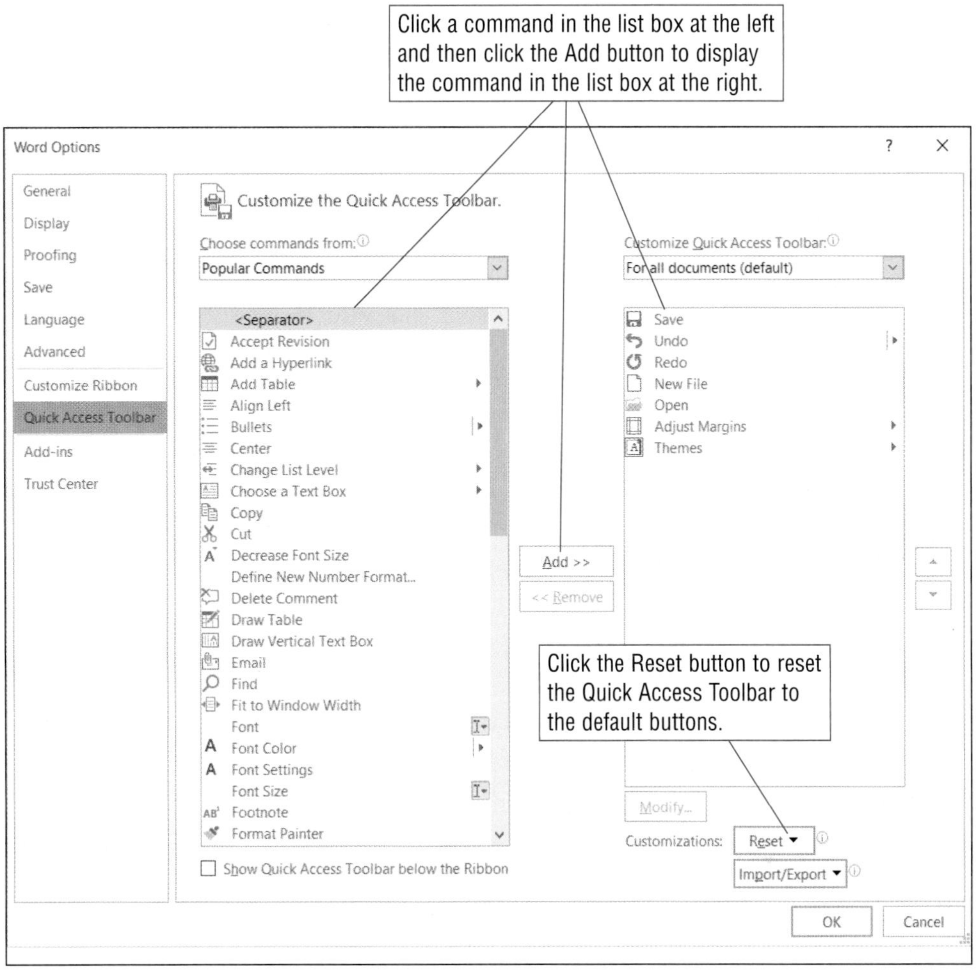

Click a command in the list box at the left and then click the Add button to display the command in the list box at the right.

Click the Reset button to reset the Quick Access Toolbar to the default buttons.

The Quick Access Toolbar can be customized for all documents or for a specific document. To customize the toolbar for the currently open document, display the Word Options dialog box with *Quick Access Toolbar* selected, click the *Customize Quick Access Toolbar* option box arrow, and then click the *For (document name)* option, where the name of the currently open document displays.

The *Choose commands from* option has a default setting of *Popular Commands*. At this setting, the list box below the option displays only a portion of all the commands available to insert as buttons on the Quick Access Toolbar. To display all the commands available, click the *Choose commands from* option box arrow and then click *All Commands*. The drop-down list also contains options for specifying commands that are not currently available on the ribbon, as well as commands on the File tab and various other tabs.

To insert a button on the Quick Access Toolbar, click the command in the list box at the left side of the dialog box and then click the Add button between the two list boxes. Continue inserting buttons and then click OK to close the dialog box.

Project 6b Inserting Buttons on and Removing Buttons from the Quick Access Toolbar Part 2 of 4

1. With **3-InterfaceApps.docx** open, reset the Quick Access Toolbar by completing the following steps:
   a. Click the Customize Quick Access Toolbar button at the right of the Quick Access Toolbar and then click *More Commands* at the drop-down list.
   b. At the Word Options dialog box, click the Reset button at the bottom of the dialog box and then click *Reset only Quick Access Toolbar* at the drop-down list.

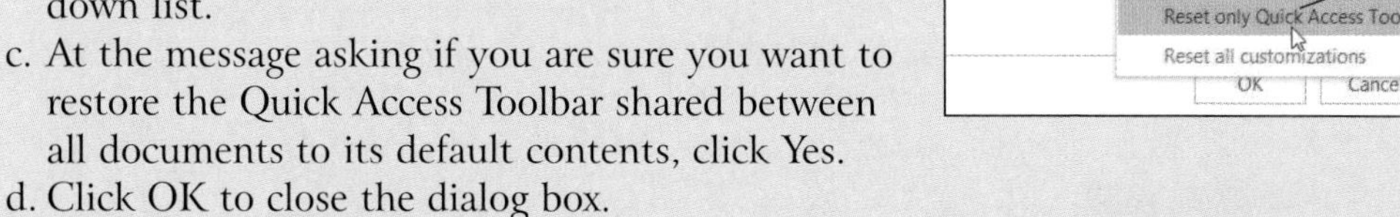

   c. At the message asking if you are sure you want to restore the Quick Access Toolbar shared between all documents to its default contents, click Yes.
   d. Click OK to close the dialog box.
2. Insert buttons on the Quick Access Toolbar for the currently open document by completing the following steps:
   a. Click the Customize Quick Access Toolbar button and then click *More Commands*.
   b. At the Word Options dialog box, click the *Customize Quick Access Toolbar* option box arrow and then click *For 3-InterfaceApps.docx* at the drop-down list.
   c. Click the *Choose commands from* option box arrow and then click *All Commands*.
   d. Scroll down the list box and then click the *Close File* command. (Commands are listed in alphabetical order.)
   e. Click the Add button between the two list boxes.

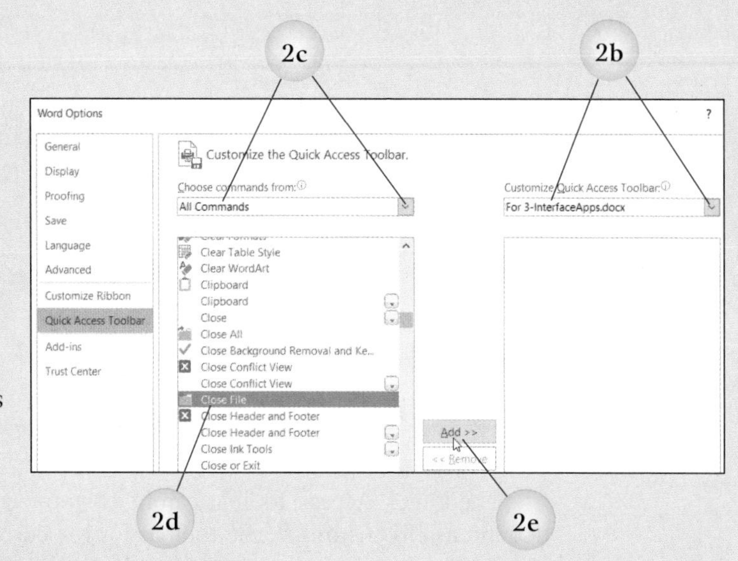

   f. Scroll up the list box and then click *Add a Footer*.
   g. Click the Add button.
   h. Click OK to close the dialog box.
   i. Check the Quick Access Toolbar and notice that the two buttons display along with the default buttons.
3. Insert a footer by completing the following steps:
   a. Click the Add a Footer button on the Quick Access Toolbar.
   b. Click *Integral* at the drop-down list.
   c. Select the name in the footer and then type your first and last names.
   d. Double-click in the document.
4. Save and then print **3-InterfaceApps.docx**.
5. Close the document by clicking the Close button on the Quick Access Toolbar.

Check Your Work

Tutorial

Customizing the Ribbon

Customizing the Ribbon

Just as the Quick Access Toolbar can be customized, the ribbon can be customized by creating a new tab and inserting groups with buttons on the tab. To customize the ribbon, click the File tab and then click *Options*. At the Word Options dialog box, click *Customize Ribbon* in the left panel and the dialog box displays as shown in Figure 3.12.

With options at the *Choose commands from* drop-down list, choose to display only popular commands, which is the default, or choose to display all commands, commands not on the ribbon, and all tabs or commands on the File tab, main tabs, tool tabs, and custom tabs and groups. The commands in the list box vary depending on the option selected at the *Choose commands from* option drop-down list. Click the *Customize the Ribbon* option box arrow and a drop-down list displays with options for customizing all tabs, only main tabs, or only tool tabs. By default, *Main Tabs* is selected.

Figure 3.12 Word Options Dialog Box with *Customize Ribbon* Selected

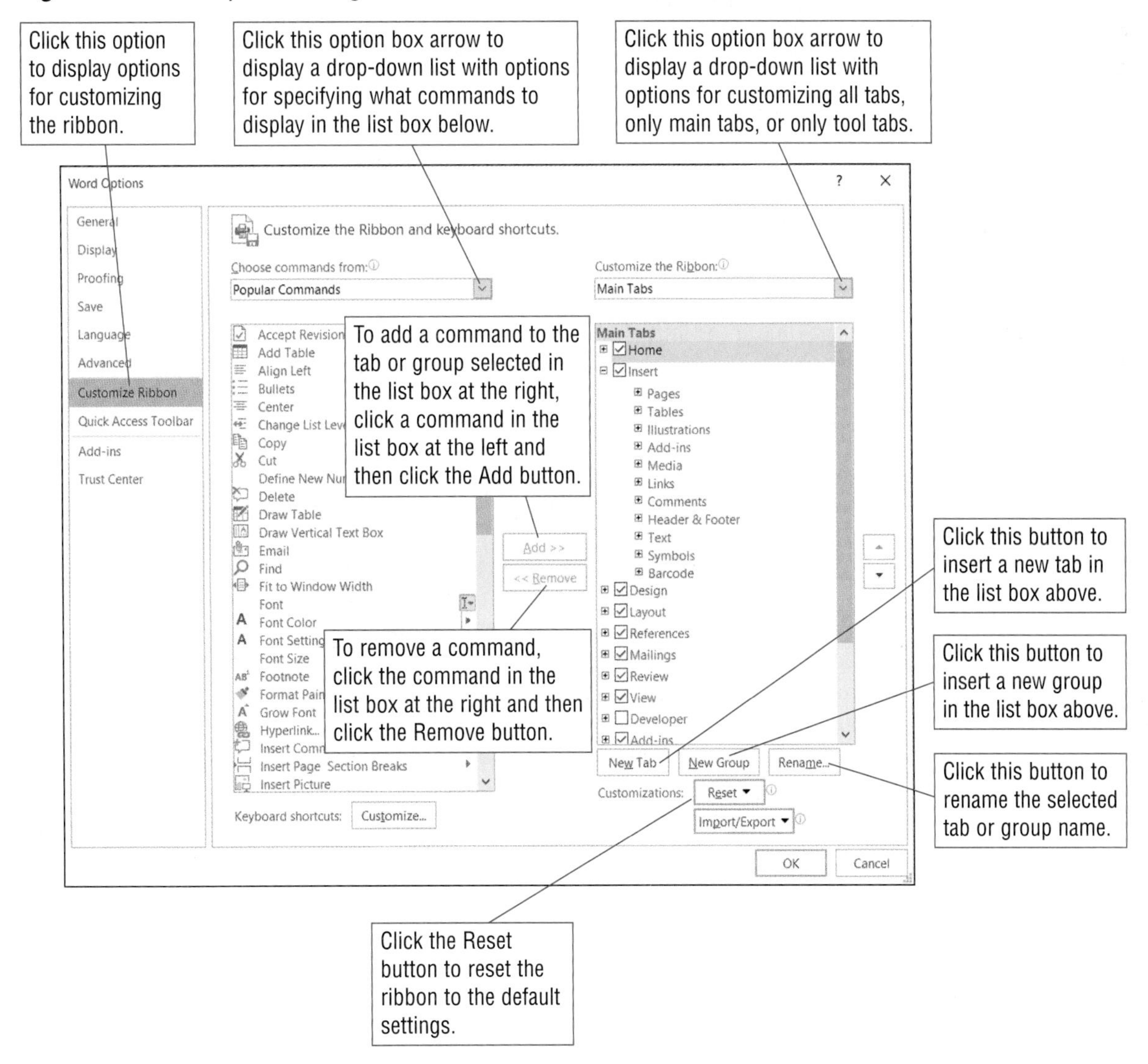
Click this option to display options for customizing the ribbon.
Click this option box arrow to display a drop-down list with options for specifying what commands to display in the list box below.
Click this option box arrow to display a drop-down list with options for customizing all tabs, only main tabs, or only tool tabs.
Word Options
General
Display
Proofing
Save
Language
Advanced
Customize Ribbon
Quick Access Toolbar
Add-ins
Trust Center
Customize the Ribbon and keyboard shortcuts.
Choose commands from:
Popular Commands
Customize the Ribbon:
Main Tabs
To add a command to the tab or group selected in the list box at the right, click a command in the list box at the left and then click the Add button.
To remove a command, click the command in the list box at the right and then click the Remove button.
Add >>
<< Remove
Main Tabs
Home
Insert
Pages
Tables
Illustrations
Add-ins
Media
Links
Comments
Header & Footer
Text
Symbols
Barcode
Design
Layout
References
Mailings
Review
View
Developer
Add-ins
New Tab
New Group
Rename...
Customizations:
Reset
Import/Export
Keyboard shortcuts:
Customize...
OK
Cancel
Click this button to insert a new tab in the list box above.
Click this button to insert a new group in the list box above.
Click this button to rename the selected tab or group name.
Click the Reset button to reset the ribbon to the default settings.

Creating a New Tab

Add a command to an existing tab or create a new tab and then add commands in groups on it. To create a new tab, click the tab name in the list box at the right side of the Word Options dialog box that will precede the new tab and then click the New Tab button below the list box. This inserts a new tab in the list box along with a new group below the new tab. Move the new tab up or down in the list box by clicking the new tab and then clicking the Move Up or Move Down button. Both buttons display to the right of the list box.

Renaming a Tab and Group

Rename a tab by clicking the tab in the list box and then clicking the Rename button below the list box at the right. At the Rename dialog box, type a new name for the tab and then click OK. The Rename dialog box also can be displayed by right-clicking the tab name and then clicking *Rename* at the shortcut menu.

Complete similar steps to rename a group. Click the group name and then click the Rename button (or right-click the group name and then click *Rename* at the shortcut menu) and a Rename dialog box displays containing a variety of symbols. Use the symbols to identify new buttons in the group, rather than the group name.

Adding Commands to a Tab Group

Add commands to a tab by clicking the group name on the tab, clicking the command in the list box at the left, and then clicking the Add button between the two list boxes. Remove commands in a similar manner. Click the command to be removed from the tab group and then click the Remove button between the two list boxes.

Removing a Tab and Group

Remove a tab by clicking the tab name in the list box at the right and then clicking the Remove button that displays between the two list boxes. Remove a group in a similar manner.

Resetting the Ribbon

If the ribbon has been customized by adding tabs and groups, all customizations can be removed by clicking the Reset button below the list box at the right side of the dialog box. Click the Reset button and a drop-down list displays with two options: *Reset only selected Ribbon tab* and *Reset all customizations*. Click the *Reset all customizations* option and a message displays asking if all ribbon and Quick Access Toolbar customizations for this program should be deleted. At this message, click Yes to reset all the customizations to the ribbon and the Quick Access Toolbar.

Project 6c Customizing the Ribbon

Part 3 of 4

1. Open **3-InterfaceApps.docx** and then add a new tab and group by completing the following steps:
   a. Click the File tab and then click *Options*.
   b. At the Word Options dialog box, click *Customize Ribbon* in the left panel.
   c. Click *View* in the list box at the right side of the dialog box. (Do not click the check box before *View*.)
   d. Click the New Tab button below the list box. (This inserts a new tab below *View*.)

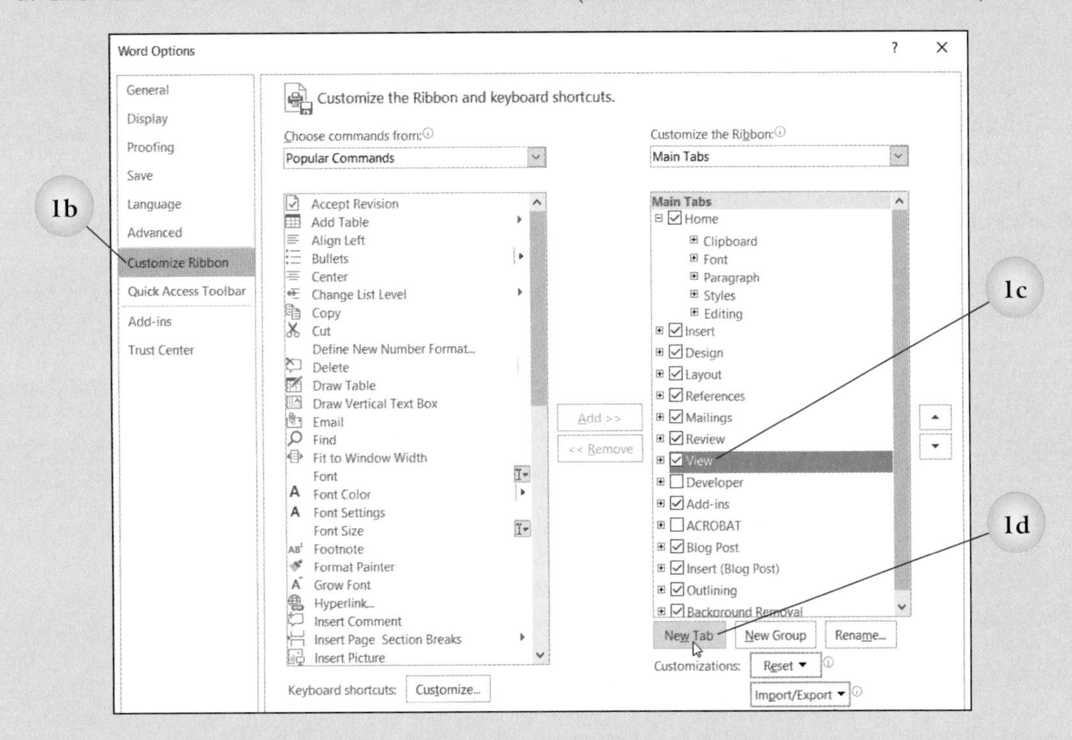

2. Rename the tab and group by completing the following steps:
   a. Click *New Tab (Custom)*. (Do not click the check box.)
   b. Click the Rename button below the list box.
   c. At the Rename dialog box, type your initials and then click OK.
   d. Click *New Group (Custom)* below your initials tab.
   e. Click the Rename button.
   f. At the Rename dialog box, type IP Movement and then click OK. (Use *IP* to stand for *insertion point*.)

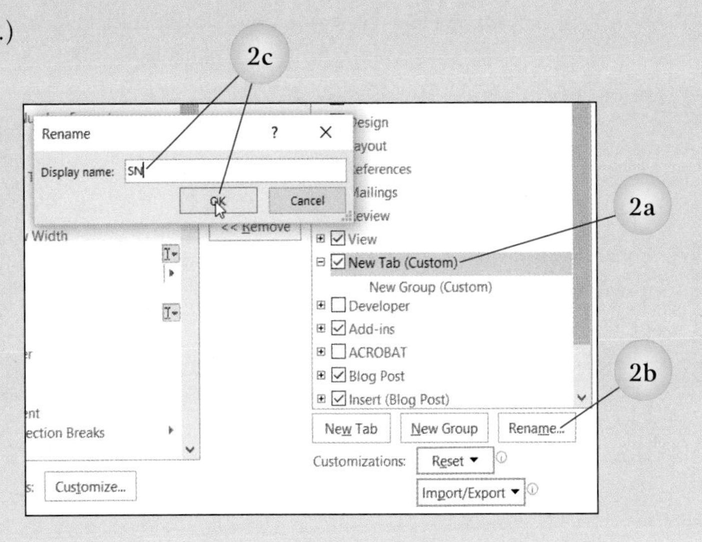

3. Add buttons to the IP Movement (Custom) group by completing the following steps:
   a. Click *IP Movement (Custom)* in the list box at the right side.
   b. Click the *Choose commands from* option box arrow and then click *Commands Not in the Ribbon* at the drop-down list.
   c. Scroll down the list box at the left side of the dialog box (which displays alphabetically), click the *End of Document* command, and then click the Add button. (This inserts the command below the *IP Movement (Custom)* group name.)
   d. With the *End of Line* command selected in the list box at the left side of the dialog box, click the Add button.
   e. Scroll down the list box at the left side of the dialog box, click the *Page Down* command, and then click the Add button.
   f. Click the *Page Up* command in the list box and then click the Add button.
   g. Scroll down the list box, click the *Start of Document* command, and then click the Add button.
   h. With the *Start of Line* command selected in the list box, click the Add button.
4. Click OK to close the Word Options dialog box.
5. Move the insertion point in the document by completing the following steps:
   a. Click the tab containing your initials.
   b. Click the End of Document button in the IP Movement group on the tab.
   c. Click the Start of Document button in the IP Movement group.
   d. Click the End of Line button.
   e. Click the Start of Line button.

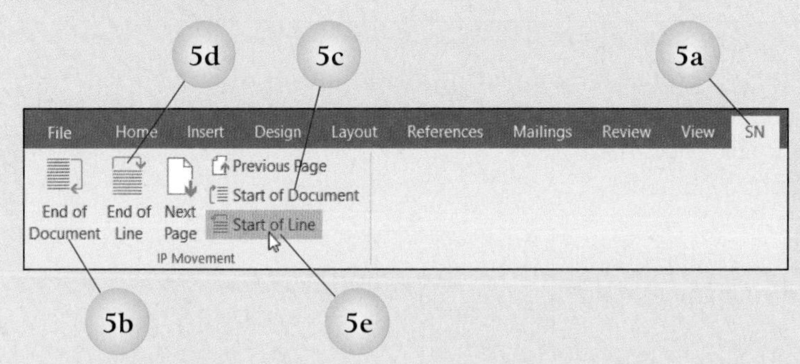

6. Create a screenshot of the ribbon with the tab containing your initials the active tab by completing the following steps:
   a. Make sure your tab is active and then press Ctrl + N to display a new blank document.
   b. Click the Insert tab, click the Screenshot button in the Illustrations group, and then click *Screen Clipping* at the drop-down list.

c. In a few moments, the **3-InterfaceApps.docx** document displays in a dimmed manner. Using the mouse, drag from the upper left corner of the screen down and to the right to capture the Quick Access Toolbar and the buttons on the tab containing your initials and then release the mouse button.
d. With the screenshot image inserted in the document, print the document and then close the document without saving it.

7. Reset the Quick Access Toolbar and ribbon by completing the following steps:
   a. Click the File tab and then click *Options*.
   b. At the Word Options dialog box, click *Customize Ribbon* in the left panel.
   c. Click the Reset button below the list box at the right side of the dialog box and then click *Reset all customizations* at the drop-down list.
   d. At the message asking if you want to delete all the ribbon and Quick Access Toolbar customizations, click Yes.
   e. Click OK to close the Word Options dialog box. (The buttons you added to the Quick Access Toolbar will display while this document is open.)

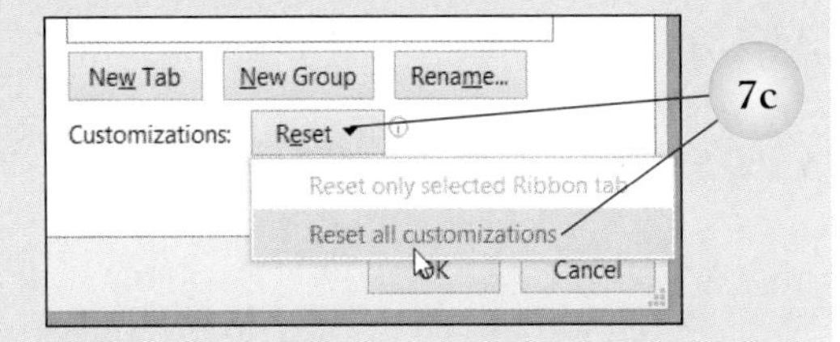

8. Save **3-InterfaceApps.docx**.

Check Your Work

Quick Steps

Export Customizations
1. Click File tab.
2. Click *Options*.
3. Click *Customize Ribbon*.
4. Click Import/Export button.
5. Click *Export all customizations*.
6. At File Save dialog box, navigate to folder.
7. Click in *File name* text box.
8. Type name.
9. Press Enter.

Import Customizations
1. Click File tab.
2. Click *Options*.
3. Click *Customize Ribbon* or *Quick Access Toolbar*.
4. Click Import/Export button.
5. Click *Import customization file*.
6. At File Open dialog box, navigate to folder.
7. Double-click file.
8. Click Yes.

Importing and Exporting Customizations

If the ribbon and/or Quick Access Toolbar are customized, the customizations can be exported to a file and then that file can be used on other computers. To export the customized ribbon and/or Quick Access Toolbar, display the Word Options dialog box with *Customize Ribbon* or *Quick Access Toolbar* selected in the left panel, click the Import/Export button that displays below the list box at the right side of the dialog box, and then click *Export all customizations* at the drop-down list. At the File Save dialog box that displays, navigate to the desired folder, type a name for the file in the *File name* text box, and then press the Enter key or click the Save button. By default, Word saves the file type as *Exported Office UI file (*.exportedUI)* with the *.exportedUI* file extension.

To import a ribbon and Quick Access Toolbar customization file, display the Word Options dialog box with *Customize Ribbon* or *Quick Access Toolbar* selected in the left panel, click the Import/Export button, and then click *Import customization file* at the drop-down list. At the File Open dialog box, navigate to the folder containing the customization file and then double-click the file. (The file name will display with the *.exportedUI* file extension.) At the message that displays asking if all existing ribbon and Quick Access Toolbar customizations for this program should be replaced, click Yes.

Project 6d Exporting Customizations

Part 4 of 4

1. With **3-InterfaceApps.docx** open, export your ribbon and Quick Access Toolbar customizations to a file by completing the following steps:
   a. Click the File tab and then click *Options*.
   b. Click *Customize Ribbon* in the left panel at the Word Options dialog box.
   c. Click the Import/Export button that displays below the list box at the right side of the dialog box and then click *Export all customizations* at the drop-down list.
   d. At the File Save dialog box, navigate to your WL2C3 folder.
   e. Click in the *File name* text box. (This selects the file name.)
   f. Type CustomRibbon&QAT and then press the Enter key.

Outlining
Background Removal
New Tab
New Group
Rename...
Customizations:
Reset
Import/Export
Import customization file
Export all customizations
1c

2. Reset the Quick Access Toolbar and ribbon by completing the following steps:
   a. Click the Reset button that displays below the list box at the right side of the dialog box and then click *Reset all customizations* at the drop-down list.
   b. At the message asking if you want to delete all ribbon and Quick Access Toolbar customizations, click Yes.
   c. Click OK to close the Word Options dialog box.
3. Save and then close **3-InterfaceApps.docx**.

Chapter Summary

- Words can be added to AutoCorrect during a spelling check and at the AutoCorrect dialog box. Display the AutoCorrect dialog box by clicking the File tab, clicking *Options*, clicking *Proofing*, and then clicking the AutoCorrect Options button.
- Display the AutoCorrect Exceptions dialog box by clicking the Exceptions button at the AutoCorrect dialog box with the AutoCorrect tab selected. Specify AutoCorrect exceptions at this dialog box.
- Use the AutoCorrect Options button, which displays when the mouse pointer is hovered over corrected text, to change corrected text back to the original spelling, stop automatically correcting specific text, or display the AutoCorrect dialog box.
- The AutoCorrect dialog box contains several symbols that can be inserted in a document by typing specific text or characters.
- A symbol can be inserted from the Symbol dialog box into the AutoCorrect dialog box. To do this, display the Symbol dialog box, click the specific symbol, and then click the AutoCorrect button.
- When typing text, control what Word formats automatically with options at the AutoCorrect dialog box with the AutoFormat As You Type tab selected.
- Word provides a number of predesigned building blocks that can be used to help build a document.
- Insert building blocks at the Building Blocks Organizer dialog box. Display the dialog box by clicking the Quick Parts button on the Insert tab and then clicking *Building Blocks Organizer* at the drop-down list. Sort building blocks in the dialog box by clicking the column heading.

- Content can be saved as building blocks to specific galleries, such as the Text Box, Header, Footer, and Cover Page galleries.
- Save content to the AutoText gallery by selecting the content, clicking the Insert tab, clicking the Quick Parts button, pointing to *AutoText*, and then clicking the *Save Selection to AutoText Gallery* option.
- Save content to the Quick Part gallery by selecting the content, clicking the Insert tab, clicking the Quick Parts button, and then clicking *Save Selection to Quick Part Gallery* at the drop-down gallery.
- By default, building block content is saved in one of two templates, either Building Block.dotx or Normal.dotm, depending on the gallery selected. Change where a building block is saved with the *Save in* option box at the Create New Building Block dialog box.
- Create and save a personal template to the Custom Office Templates folder by changing the *Save as type* option at the Save As dialog box to *Word Template (*.dotx)*, typing a name for the template, and then clicking the Save button.
- Open a personal template from the Custom Office Templates folder by displaying the New backstage area, clicking the *PERSONAL* option, and then clicking the personal template thumbnail.
- A personal template can be saved to a location other than the Custom Office Templates folder. To open a document based on a personal template that is saved in a location other than the Custom Office Templates folder, open File Explorer, navigate to the folder containing the personal template, and then double-click the template.
- Edit a building block with options at the Modify Building Block dialog box. Display this dialog box by displaying the Building Blocks Organizer dialog box, clicking the building block, and then clicking the Edit Properties button.
- Insert a custom building block from a gallery using a button by clicking the specific button (such as the Text Box, Header, Footer, or Cover Page button), scrolling down the drop-down gallery, and then clicking the custom building block near the end of the gallery.
- Insert a custom building block saved to the AutoText gallery by clicking the Insert tab, clicking the Quick Parts button, pointing to *AutoText*, and then clicking the building block at the side menu.
- Insert a custom building block saved to the Quick Part gallery by clicking the Insert tab, clicking the Quick Parts button, and then clicking the building block at the drop-down list.
- A building block gallery can be inserted as a button on the Quick Access Toolbar by clicking a button, such as the Quick Parts button, right-clicking a building block and then clicking *Add Gallery to Quick Access Toolbar* at the shortcut menu.
- Remove a button from the Quick Access Toolbar by right-clicking the button and then clicking *Remove from Quick Access Toolbar* at the shortcut menu.
- Delete a building block at the Building Blocks Organizer dialog box by clicking the building block, clicking the Delete button, and then clicking Yes at the confirmation question.
- Insert a document property placeholder by clicking the Insert tab, clicking the Quick Parts button, pointing to *Document Property*, and then clicking the document property placeholder at the side menu.

- Fields are placeholders for data and can be inserted with options at the Field dialog box, which is a central location for all the fields provided by Word. Display the Field dialog box by clicking the Quick Parts button on the Insert tab and then clicking *Field*.
- Some fields in a document update automatically when a document is opened. A field can also be updated manually by clicking the field and then clicking the Update tab, by pressing the F9 function key, or by right-clicking the field and then clicking *Update Field*.
- Customize the Quick Access Toolbar with options from the Customize Quick Access Toolbar button drop-down list and options at the Word Options dialog box with *Quick Access Toolbar* selected.
- Insert a button or command on the Quick Access Toolbar by right-clicking the button or command and then clicking *Add to Quick Access Toolbar* at the shortcut menu.
- Use options at the Word Options dialog box with *Quick Access Toolbar* selected to display all the options and buttons available for adding to the Quick Access Toolbar and to reset the Quick Access Toolbar. The Quick Access Toolbar can be customized for all documents or for a specific document.
- Use options at the Word Options dialog box with *Customize Ribbon* selected to add a new tab and group, rename a tab or group, add a command to a new group, remove a command from a tab group, and reset the ribbon.
- Export a file containing customizations to the ribbon and/or Quick Access Toolbar with the Import/Export button at the Word Options dialog box with *Customize Ribbon* or *Quick Access Toolbar* selected.

Commands Review

FEATURE	RIBBON TAB, GROUP/OPTION	BUTTON, OPTION	KEYBOARD SHORTCUT
AutoCorrect dialog box	File, *Options*	*Proofing*, AutoCorrect Options	
Building Blocks Organizer dialog box	Insert, Text	, *Building Blocks Organizer*	
Create New Building Block dialog box	Insert, Text	, *Save Selection to Quick Part Gallery*	Alt + F3
Document Property side menu	Insert, Text	, *Document Property*	
Field dialog box	Insert, Text	, *Field*	
Word Options dialog box	File, *Options*		

Workbook

Chapter study tools and assessment activities are available in the *Workbook* ebook. These resources are designed to help you further develop and demonstrate mastery of the skills learned in this chapter.

Microsoft®

Word

Customizing Themes, Creating Macros, and Navigating in a Document

CHAPTER 4

Performance Objectives

Upon successful completion of Chapter 4, you will be able to:

1. Create custom theme colors, theme fonts, and theme effects
2. Save a custom theme
3. Apply, edit, and delete custom themes
4. Reset the template theme
5. Apply styles and modify existing styles
6. Record, run, and delete macros
7. Assign a macro to a keyboard command
8. Navigate in a document using the Navigation pane, bookmarks, hyperlinks, and cross-references
9. Insert hyperlinks to a location in the same document, a different document, a file in another program, and an email address

Precheck

Check your current skills to help focus your study.

The Microsoft Office suite offers themes that provide consistent formatting and help create documents with a professional and polished look. Apply formatting with the themes provided by Office or create custom themes. Word provides a number of predesigned styles, grouped into style sets, for applying consistent formatting to text in documents. Word also allows you to build macros to automate the formatting of a document.

In this chapter, you will learn how to customize themes; how to modify an existing style; how to record and run macros; and how to insert hyperlinks, bookmarks, and cross-references to provide additional information for readers and to allow for more efficient navigation within a document.

Data Files

Before beginning chapter work, copy the WL2C4 folder to your storage medium and then make WL2C4 the active folder.

SNAP

If you are a SNAP user, launch the Precheck and Tutorials from your Assignments page.

Project 1 Apply Custom Themes to Company Documents — 5 Parts

You will create custom theme colors and theme fonts and then apply theme effects. You will save the changes as a custom theme, which you will apply to a company services document and a company security document.

Preview Finished Project

Customizing Themes

A document created in Word is based on the template Normal.dotm. This template provides a document with default layout, formatting, styles, and themes. The default template provides a number of built-in or predesigned themes. Some of these built-in themes have been used in previous chapters to apply colors, fonts, and effects to content in documents. The same built-in themes are available in Microsoft Word, Excel, Access, PowerPoint, and Outlook. Because the same themes are available across these applications, business files—such as documents, workbooks, databases, and presentations—can be branded with a consistent and professional appearance.

Hint Every document created in Word 2016 has a theme applied to it.

A theme is a combination of theme colors, theme fonts, and theme effects. Within a theme, any of these three elements can be changed with the additional buttons in the Document Formatting group on the Design tab. Apply one of the built-in themes or create a custom theme. A custom theme will display in the *Custom* section of the Themes drop-down gallery. To create a custom theme, change the theme colors, theme fonts, and/or theme effects.

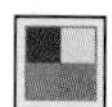
Colors

Fonts

The Themes, Colors, and Fonts buttons in the Document Formatting group on the Design tab display representations of the current theme. For example, the Themes button displays an uppercase and lowercase A with colored squares below it. When the theme colors are changed, the changes are reflected in the small colored squares on the Themes button and the four squares on the Colors button. If the theme fonts are changed, the letters on the Themes button and the Fonts button reflect the change.

Tutorial

Creating and Applying Custom Theme Colors

Creating Custom Theme Colors

Quick Steps

Create Custom Theme Colors

1. Click Design tab.
2. Click Colors button.
3. Click *Customize Colors.*
4. Type name for custom theme colors.
5. Change background, accent, and hyperlink colors.
6. Click Save button.

To create custom theme colors, click the Design tab, click the Colors button, and then click *Customize Colors* at the drop-down gallery. This displays the Create New Theme Colors dialog box, similar to the one shown in Figure 4.1. Type a name for the custom theme colors in the *Name* text box and then change colors. Theme colors contain four text and background colors, six accent colors, and two hyperlink colors, as shown in the *Theme colors* section of the dialog box. Change a color in the list box by clicking the color button at the right side of the color option and then clicking a color at the color palette.

After making all the changes to the colors, click the Save button. This saves the custom theme colors and also applies the color changes to the active document. Display the custom theme by clicking the Colors button. The custom theme will display at the top of the drop-down gallery in the *Custom* section.

Figure 4.1 Create New Theme Colors Dialog Box

Type a name for the custom theme in the *Name* text box.

Click the Reset button to reset the colors back to the defult.

Change a theme color by clicking the color button and then clicking a color at the drop-down palette.

Resetting Custom Theme Colors

If changes have been made to colors at the Create New Theme Colors dialog box, the colors can be reset to the default colors by clicking the Reset button in the lower left corner of the dialog box. Clicking this button restores the colors to the default Office theme colors.

Project 1a Creating Custom Theme Colors

Part 1 of 5

***Note:** If you are running Word 2016 on a computer connected to a network in a public environment, such as a school, you may need to complete all five parts of Project 1 during the same session. Network system software may delete your custom themes when you exit Word. Check with your instructor.*

1. At a blank document, click the Design tab.
2. Click the Colors button in the Document Formatting group and then click *Customize Colors* at the drop-down gallery.
3. At the Create New Theme Colors dialog box, click the color button to the right of the *Text/Background - Light 1* option and then click the *Dark Red* color (first option in the *Standard Colors* section).
4. Click the color button to the right of the *Accent 1* option and then click the *Yellow* color (fourth option in the *Standard Colors* section).

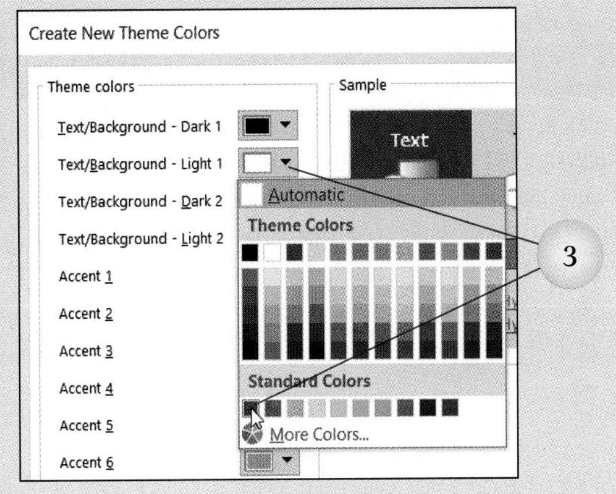

5. You decide that you do not like the colors you have chosen and want to start over. To do this, click the Reset button in the lower left corner of the dialog box.
6. Click the color button to the right of the *Text/Background - Dark 2* option and then click the *Blue* color (eighth option in the *Standard Colors* section).
7. Change the color for the *Accent 1* option by completing the following steps:
   a. Click the color button to the right of the *Accent 1* option.
   b. Click the *More Colors* option below the color palette.
   c. At the Colors dialog box, click the Standard tab.
   d. Click the dark green color, as shown below.
   e. Click OK to close the dialog box.

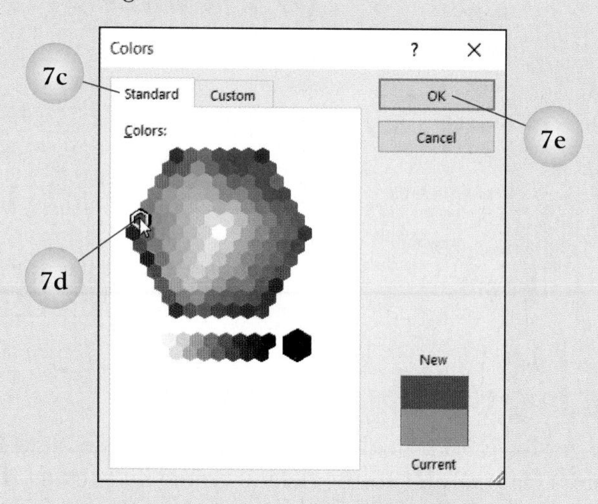

8. Save the custom colors by completing the following steps:
   a. Select the current text in the *Name* text box.
   b. Type your first and last names.
   c. Click the Save button.
9. Close the document without saving it.

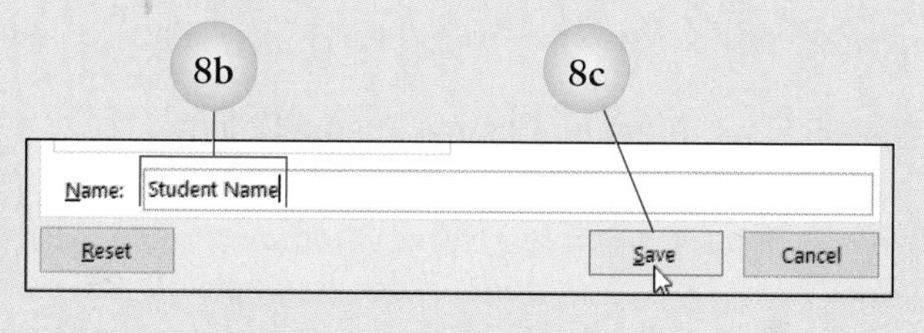

Tutorial

Creating and Applying Custom Theme Fonts

Creating Custom Fonts

To create a custom theme font, click the Design tab, click the Fonts button, and then click *Customize Fonts* at the drop-down gallery. This displays the Create New Theme Fonts dialog box. At this dialog box, choose a font for headings and a font for body text. Type a name for the custom fonts in the *Name* text box and then click the Save button.

Quick Steps

Create Custom Fonts

1. Click Design tab.
2. Click Fonts button.
3. Click *Customize Fonts.*
4. Choose fonts.
5. Type name for custom theme fonts.
6. Click Save button.

Project 1b Creating Custom Theme Fonts

Part 2 of 5

1. At a blank document, click the Design tab.
2. Click the Fonts button in the Document Formatting group and then click the *Customize Fonts* option at the drop-down gallery.
3. At the Create New Theme Fonts dialog box, click the *Heading font* option box arrow, scroll up the drop-down list, and then click *Arial*.
4. Click the *Body font* option box arrow, scroll down the drop-down list, and then click *Cambria*.
5. Save the custom fonts by completing the following steps:
   a. Select the current text in the *Name* text box.
   b. Type your first and last names.
   c. Click the Save button.
6. Close the document without saving it.

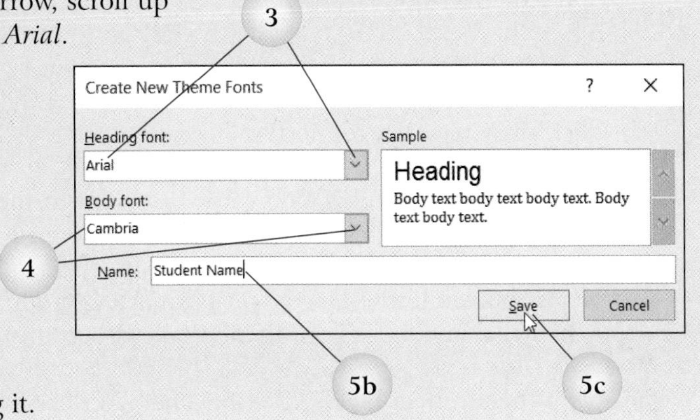

Applying Custom Theme Colors and Fonts

Apply custom theme colors to a document by clicking the Colors button in the Document Formatting group on the Design tab and then clicking the custom theme colors option at the top of the drop-down gallery in the *Custom* section. Complete similar steps to apply custom theme fonts.

Applying Theme Effects

The options in the Theme Effects button drop-down gallery apply sets of line and fill effects to the graphics in a document. Custom theme effects cannot be created but a theme effect can be applied to a document and the formatting can then be saved in a custom theme.

Tutorial

Saving a Custom Document Theme

Quick Steps

Save a Custom Document Theme

1. Click Design tab.
2. Click Themes button.
3. Click *Save Current Theme.*
4. Type name for theme.
5. Click Save button.

Saving a Custom Document Theme

A custom document theme containing custom theme colors and fonts and effects can be saved. To do this, create and apply custom theme colors and fonts and theme effects to a document, click the Themes button on the Design tab, and then click *Save Current Theme* at the drop-down gallery. This displays the Save Current Theme dialog box, which has many of the same options as the Save As dialog box. Type a name for the custom document theme in the *File name* text box and then click the Save button.

Project 1c Applying Theme Effects and Saving a Custom Document Theme

1. Open **NSSServices.docx** and then save it with the name **4-NSSServices**.
2. Make the following changes to the document:
   a. Apply the Title style to the company name *Northland Security Systems*.
   b. Apply the Heading 1 style to the heading *Northland Security Systems Mission*.
   c. Apply the Heading 2 style to the remaining headings, *Security Services* and *Security Software*.
   d. Apply the Word 2010 style set (the last option in the expanded style sets gallery).
3. Apply the custom theme colors you saved by completing the following steps:
   a. Click the Design tab.
   b. Click the Colors button in the Document Formatting group.
   c. Click the theme colors option with your name at the top of the drop-down gallery in the *Custom* group.
4. Apply the custom theme fonts you saved by clicking the Fonts button in the Document Formatting group and then clicking the custom theme font with your name.
5. Apply a theme effect by clicking the Theme Effects button in the Document Formatting group and then clicking *Glossy* at the drop-down gallery (last option).

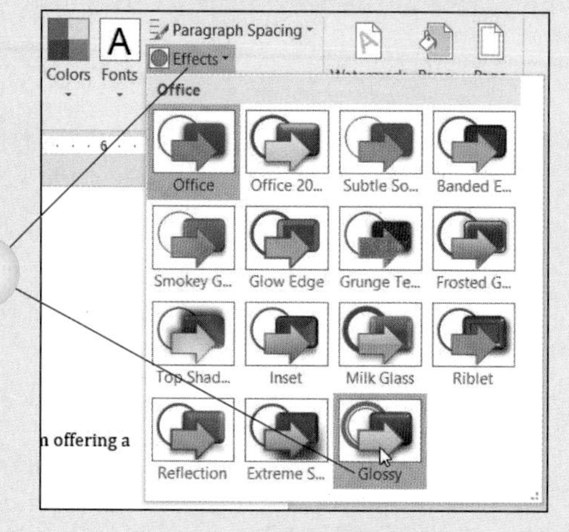

6. Make the following changes to the SmartArt graphic:
   a. Click near the graphic to select it. (When the graphic is selected, a gray border displays around it.)
   b. Click the SmartArt Tools Design tab.
   c. Click the Change Colors button and then click *Colorful Range - Accent Colors 5 to 6* (last option in the *Colorful* section).
   d. Click the More SmartArt Styles button in the SmartArt Styles group and then click *Cartoon* (third column, first row in the *3-D* section).
   e. Click outside the SmartArt graphic to deselect it.
7. Save the custom theme colors and fonts, as well as the Glossy theme effect, as a custom document theme by completing the following steps:
   a. Click the Design tab.
   b. Click the Themes button in the Document Formatting group.
   c. Click the *Save Current Theme* option at the bottom of the drop-down gallery.
   d. At the Save Current Theme dialog box, type your first and last names in the *File name* text box and then click the Save button.

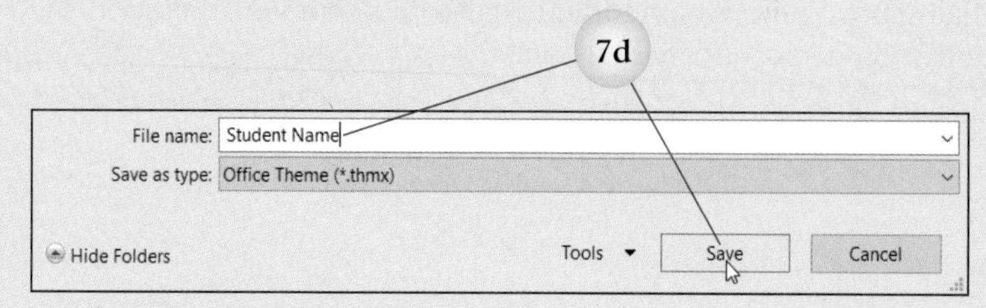

8. Save and then print **4-NSSServices.docx**.

Check Your Work

Tutorial

Editing a Custom Theme

Quick Steps

Edit Custom Theme Colors or Fonts

1. Click Design tab.
2. Click Colors button or Fonts button.
3. Right-click custom theme colors or fonts.
4. Click *Edit*.
5. Make changes.
6. Click Save button.

Editing Custom Themes

Custom theme colors and theme fonts can be edited. To edit custom theme colors, click the Design tab and then click the Colors button in the Document Formatting group. At the drop-down gallery of custom and built-in theme colors, right-click the custom theme colors and then click *Edit* at the shortcut menu. This displays the Edit Theme Colors dialog box, which contains the same options as the Create New Theme Colors dialog box. Make changes to the theme colors and then click the Save button.

To edit custom theme fonts, click the Fonts button in the Document Formatting group on the Design tab, right-click the custom theme fonts, and then click *Edit* at the shortcut menu. This displays the Edit Theme Fonts dialog box, which contains the same options as the Create New Theme Fonts dialog box. Make changes to the theme fonts and then click the Save button.

Project 1d Editing Custom Themes

Part 4 of 5

1. With **4-NSSServices.docx** open, edit the theme colors by completing the following steps:
   a. If necessary, click the Design tab.
   b. Click the Colors button.
   c. Right-click the custom theme colors named with your first and last names.
   d. Click *Edit* at the shortcut menu.
   e. At the Edit Theme Colors dialog box, click the color button to the right of the *Text/ Background - Dark 2* option.
   f. Click the *More Colors* option below the color palette.
   g. At the Colors dialog box, click the Standard tab.
   h. Click the dark green color. (This is the same color you chose for *Accent 1* in Project 1a.)
   i. Click OK to close the dialog box.
   j. Click the Save button.

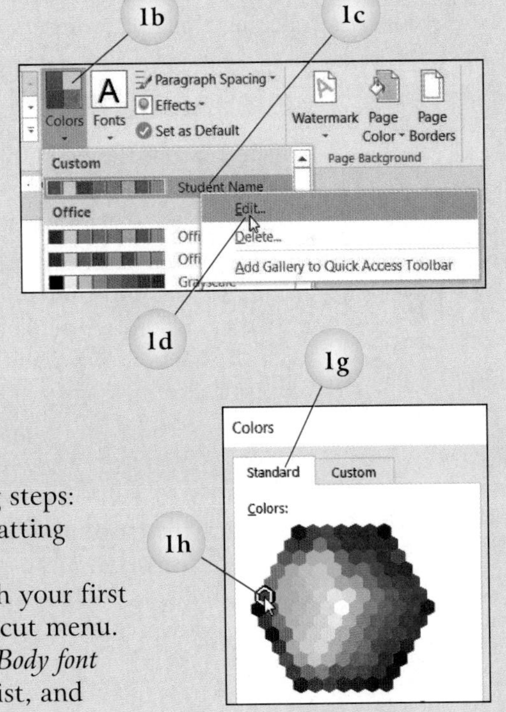

2. Edit the theme fonts by completing the following steps:
   a. Click the Fonts button in the Document Formatting group.
   b. Right-click the custom theme fonts named with your first and last names and then click *Edit* at the shortcut menu.
   c. At the Edit Theme Fonts dialog box, click the *Body font* option box arrow, scroll down the drop-down list, and then click *Constantia*.
   d. Click the Save button.

3. Apply a different theme effect by clicking the Theme Effects button in the Document Formatting group and then clicking *Extreme Shadow* at the drop-down gallery. (This applies a shadow behind each shape.)
4. Save the changes to the custom theme by completing the following steps:
   a. Click the Themes button and then click *Save Current Theme* at the drop-down gallery.
   b. At the Save Current Theme dialog box, click the theme named with your first and last names in the content pane.
   c. Click the Save button.
   d. At the message telling you that the theme already exists and asking if you want to replace it, click Yes.
5. Save, print, and then close **4-NSSServices.docx**.

Check Your Work

Resetting a Template Theme

Quick Steps

Reset a Template Theme

1. Click Design tab.
2. Click Themes button.
3. Click *Reset to Theme from Template*.

If a built-in theme other than the Office default theme or a custom theme is applied to a document, the theme can be reset to the default by clicking the Themes button and then clicking the *Reset to Theme from Template* at the drop-down gallery. If the document is based on the default template provided by Word, clicking this option resets the theme to the Office default theme.

Deleting Custom Themes

Tutorial

Deleting Custom Themes

Quick Steps

Delete Custom Theme Colors or Fonts

1. Click Design tab.
2. Click Colors or Fonts button.
3. Right-click custom theme.
4. Click *Delete*.
5. Click Yes.

Delete a Custom Theme

1. Click Design tab.
2. Click Themes button.
3. Right-click custom theme.
4. Click *Delete*.
5. Click Yes.

Delete custom theme colors from the Colors button drop-down gallery, delete custom theme fonts from the Fonts drop-down gallery, and delete custom themes from the Save Current Theme dialog box.

To delete custom theme colors, click the Colors button, right-click the theme to be deleted, and then click *Delete* at the shortcut menu. At the confirmation message, click Yes. To delete custom theme fonts, click the Fonts button, right-click the theme to be deleted, and then click *Delete* at the shortcut menu. At the confirmation message, click Yes.

Delete a custom theme (including custom colors, fonts, and effects) at the Themes button drop-down gallery or the Save Current Theme dialog box. To delete a custom theme from the drop-down gallery, click the Themes button, right-click the custom theme, click *Delete* at the shortcut menu, and then click Yes at the confirmation message. To delete a custom theme from the Save Current Theme dialog box, click the Themes button and then click *Save Current Theme* at the drop-down gallery. At the dialog box, click the custom theme document name, click the Organize button on the dialog box toolbar, and then click *Delete* at the drop-down list. If a confirmation message displays, click Yes.

Changing Default Settings

If formatting is applied to a document—such as a specific style set, theme, and paragraph spacing—it can be saved as the default formatting. To do this, click the Set as Default button in the Document Formatting group on the Design tab. At the message asking if the current style set and theme should be set as the default and indicating that the settings will be applied to new documents, click Yes.

Project 1e Applying and Deleting Custom Themes

Part 5 of 5

1. Open **NSSSecurity.docx** and then save it with the name **4-NSSSecurity**.
2. Apply the Title style to the company name, apply the Heading 1 style to the two headings in the document, and then apply the Word 2010 style set.
3. Apply your custom theme by completing the following steps:
   a. If necessary, click the Design tab.
   b. Click the Themes button.
   c. Click the custom theme named with your first and last names at the top of the drop-down gallery in the *Custom* section.
4. Save and then print **4-NSSSecurity.docx**.
5. Reset the theme to the Office default theme by clicking the Themes button and then clicking *Reset to Theme from Template* at the drop-down gallery.
6. Save and then close **4-NSSSecurity.docx**.
7. Press Ctrl + N to display a new blank document.
8. Delete the custom theme colors by completing the following steps:
   a. Click the Design tab.
   b. Click the Colors button in the Document Formatting group.
   c. Right-click the custom theme colors named with your first and last names.
   d. Click *Delete* at the shortcut menu.

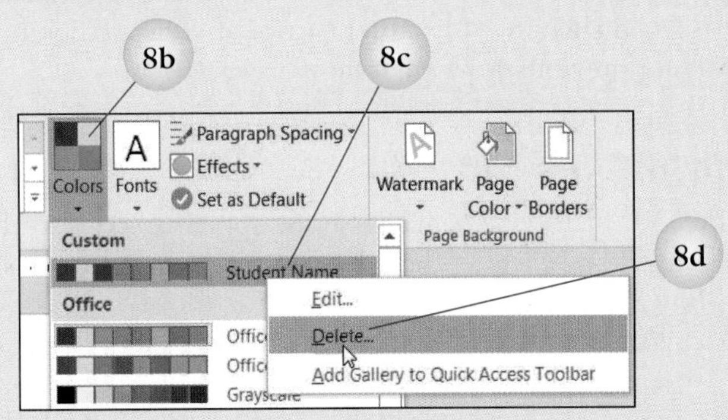

   e. At the message that displays asking if you want to delete the theme colors, click Yes.
9. Complete steps similar to those in Step 8 to delete the custom theme fonts named with your first and last names.
10. Delete the custom theme by completing the following steps:
    a. Click the Themes button.
    b. Right-click the custom theme named with your first and last names.
    c. Click *Delete* at the shortcut menu.
    d. At the message asking if you want to delete the theme, click Yes.
11. Close the document without saving it.

Check Your Work

Project 2 Format a Travel Document with Styles

1 Part

You will open a travel document, change the style set, and apply styles.

Preview Finished Project

Formatting with Styles

A style is a set of formatting instructions that can be applied to text. Word provides a number of predesigned styles and groups those that apply similar formatting into style sets. Whereas a theme changes the overall colors, fonts, and effects used in a document, a style set changes the font and paragraph formatting for the document. Using the styles within a style set, formatting can be applied to a document to give it a uniform and professional appearance.

Displaying Styles in a Style Set

The styles in a style set are available in the Styles group on the Home tab. Generally, the visible styles include Normal, No Spacing, Heading 1, Heading 2, Title, Subtitle, and Subtitle Emphasis. (Depending on the monitor and screen resolution, more or fewer styles may display in the Styles group.) The styles change to reflect the style set that has been applied to the active document. Click the More Styles button in the Styles group and a drop-down gallery displays containing all the styles available in the default style set. Hover the mouse pointer over a style in the drop-down gallery to see how the style will format the text in the document.

Another method for displaying additional styles is to click either the up arrow or the down arrow at the right of the styles. Clicking the down arrow scrolls down the styles, displaying subsequent rows of styles. Clicking the up arrow scrolls up, displaying previous rows of styles.

Tutorial

Applying and Modifying a Style

Quick Steps

Apply a Style

Click style in Styles group on Home tab.
OR
1. Click More Styles button in Styles group on Home tab.
2. Click style.
OR
1. Display Styles task pane.
2. Click style in task pane.

Hint You can also display the Styles task pane by pressing Alt + Ctrl + Shift + S.

Applying a Style

A variety of methods are available for applying styles to the text in a document. Apply a style by clicking the style in the Styles group on the Home tab or by clicking the More Styles button and then clicking the style at the drop-down gallery. The Styles task pane provides another method for applying a style. Display the Styles task pane, shown in Figure 4.2, by clicking the Styles group task pane launcher.

The styles in the currently selected style set display in the task pane followed by the paragraph symbol (¶), indicating that the style applies paragraph formatting, or the character symbol (**a**), indicating that the style applies character formatting. If both characters display to the right of a style, the style applies both paragraph and character formatting. In addition to displaying styles that apply formatting, the Styles task pane also displays a *Clear All* option that removes all formatting from the selected text.

Hover the mouse pointer over a style in the Styles task pane and a ScreenTip displays with information about the formatting applied by the style. Apply a style in the Styles task pane by clicking the style. Close the Styles task pane by clicking the Close button in the upper right corner of the task pane.

Modifying a Style

If a predesigned style contains most but not all the desired formatting, consider modifying the style. To modify a predesigned style, right-click the style in the Styles group or in the Styles task pane and then click *Modify* at the shortcut menu. This displays the Modify Style dialog box, shown in Figure 4.3. Use options at this dialog box to make changes such as renaming the style, applying or changing the formatting, and specifying whether the modified style should be available only in the current document or in all new documents.

The *Formatting* section of the Modify Style dialog box contains a number of buttons and options for applying formatting. Additional options are available by clicking the Format button in the lower left corner of the dialog box and then clicking an option at the drop-down list. For example, display the Font dialog box by clicking the Format button and then clicking *Font* at the drop-down list.

Hint You can also apply styles at the Apply Styles window. Display this window with the keyboard shortcut Ctrl + Shift + S or by clicking the More Styles button at the right side of the styles in the Styles group on the Home tab and then clicking *Apply Styles* at the drop-down gallery.

Figure 4.2 Styles Task Pane

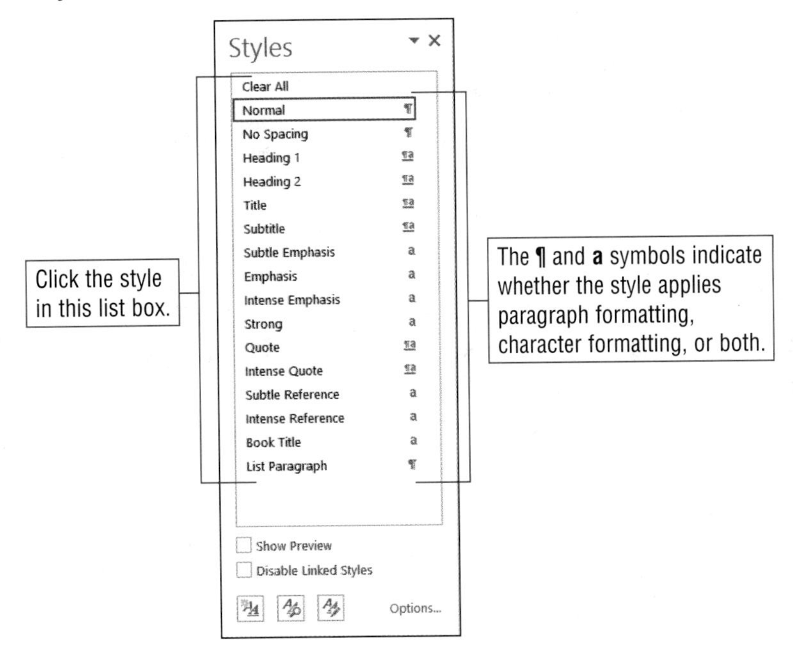

Figure 4.3 Modify Style Dialog Box

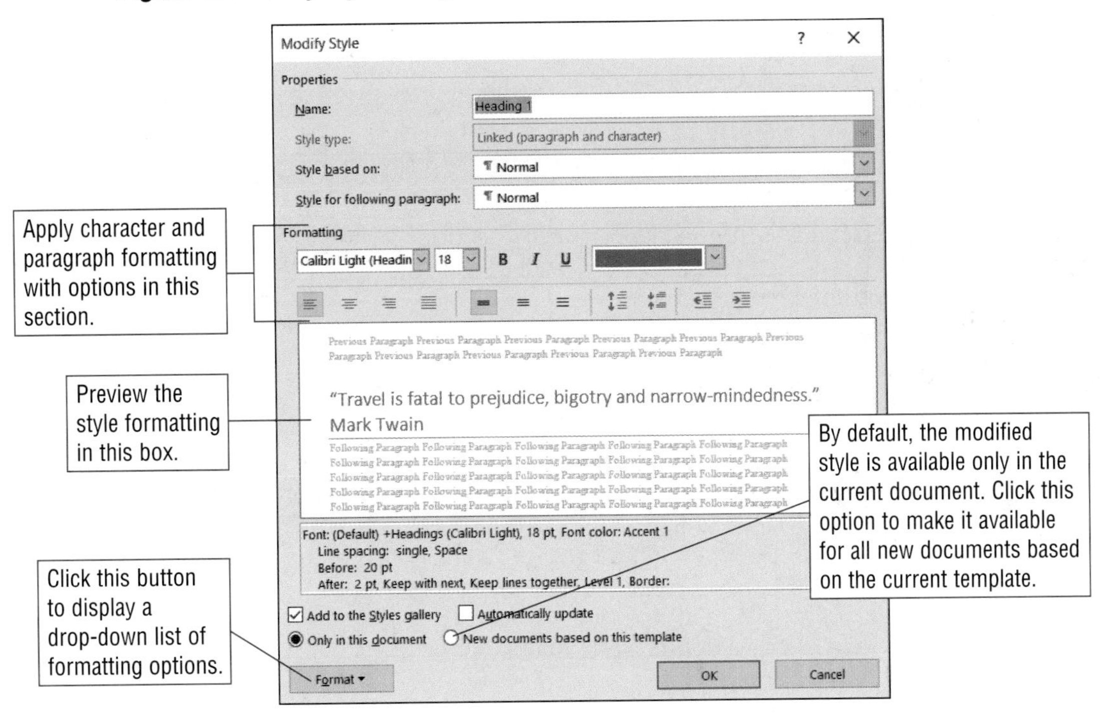

Project 2 Applying and Modifying Styles

Part 1 of 1

1. Open **BTAdventures.docx** and then save it with the name **4-BTAdventures**.
2. Apply styles using the Styles task pane by completing the following steps:
   a. Move the insertion point to the end of the document and then select the last paragraph.
   b. With the Home tab active, click the Styles group task pane launcher. (This displays the Styles task pane.)
   c. Click the *Subtle Reference* style in the Styles task pane. (Notice that the style is followed by the character symbol **a**, indicating that the style applies character formatting.)
   d. Select the bulleted text below the heading *Disneyland Adventure* and then click the *Subtle Emphasis* style in the Styles task pane.
   e. Apply the Subtle Emphasis style to the bulleted text below the heading *Florida Adventure* and the heading *Cancun Adventure*.
   f. Select the quote by Mark Twain and his name at the beginning of the document and then click *Quote* in the Styles task pane.
   g. After noticing the formatting of the quote, remove the formatting by making sure the text is selected and then clicking *Clear All* at the top of the Styles task pane.
   h. With the Mark Twain quote still selected, click the *Intense Quote* style in the Styles task pane.
   i. Click anywhere in the document to deselect the text.
3. Modify the Heading 1 style by completing the following steps:
   a. Right-click the *Heading 1* style in the Styles group.
   b. Click *Modify* at the shortcut menu.

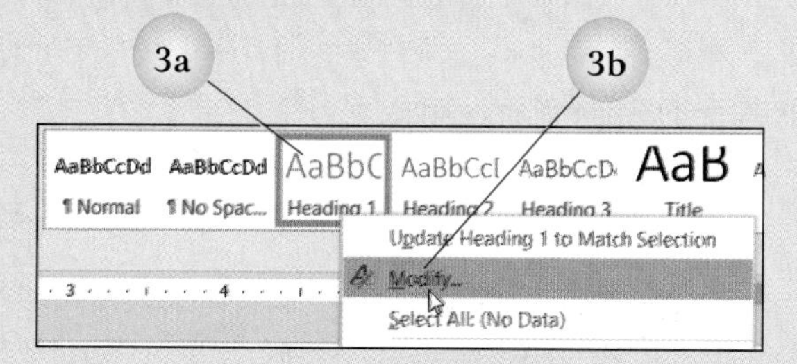

   c. At the Modify Style dialog box, click the Bold button in the *Formatting* section.
   d. Click the Center button in the *Formatting* section.

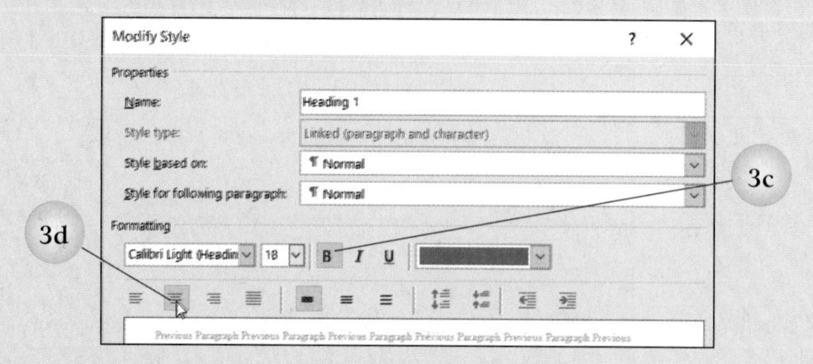

   e. Click OK to close the Modify Style dialog box.

4. Modify the Heading 2 style by completing the following steps:
   a. Right-click the *Heading 2* style in the Styles task pane and then click *Modify* at the shortcut menu.
   b. At the Modify Style dialog box, click the Format button in the lower left corner and then click *Font* at the drop-down list.
   c. At the Font dialog box, click the *Font color* option box arrow and then click *Dark Red* (first option in the *Standard Colors* section).
   d. Click the *Small caps* check box to insert a check mark.
   e. Click OK to close the Font dialog box.
   f. Click the Format button in the dialog box and then click *Paragraph* at the drop-down list.
   g. At the Paragraph dialog box, click the *After* measurement box up arrow. (This displays *6 pt* in the measurement box.)
   h. Click OK to close the Paragraph dialog box and then click OK to close the Modify Style dialog box.
5. Close the Styles task pane.
6. Save, print, and then close **4-BTAdventures.docx**.

Check Your Work

Project 3 Record and Run Macros in Documents **4 Parts**

You will record several macros, run the macros in a document on writing resumes, assign a macro to a keyboard command, run macros in a business letter, and delete a macro.

Preview Finished Project

Tutorial

Recording and Running a Macro

Creating a Macro

A macro is a time-saving tool that automates the formatting of Word documents. The word *macro* was coined by computer programmers for a collection of commands used to make a large programming job easier and thus save time. Two basic steps are involved in working with macros: recording a macro and running a macro. When recording a macro, all the keys pressed and dialog boxes displayed are recorded and become part of the macro. After a macro is recorded, running it carries out the recorded actions.

Recording a Macro

Recording a macro involves turning on the macro recorder, performing the steps to be recorded, and then turning off the recorder. Both the View tab and Developer tab contain buttons for recording a macro. If the Developer tab does not appear on the ribbon, turn on the display of this tab by opening the Word Options dialog box with *Customize Ribbon* selected in the left panel, inserting a check mark in the *Developer* check box in the list box at the right, and then clicking OK to close the dialog box.

Figure 4.4 Record Macro Dialog Box

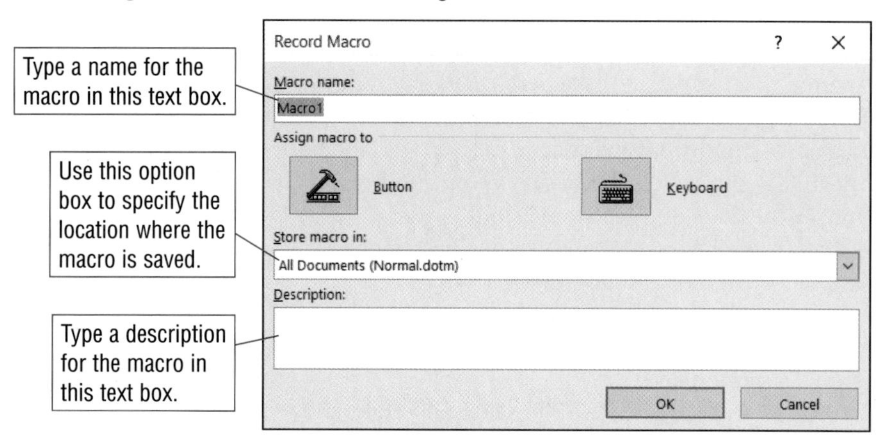
Type a name for the macro in this text box.
Use this option box to specify the location where the macro is saved.
Type a description for the macro in this text box.
Record Macro
?
Macro name:
Macro1
Assign macro to
Button
Keyboard
Store macro in:
All Documents (Normal.dotm)
Description:
OK
Cancel

Record Macro

Macros

Quick Steps

Record a Macro

1. Click Developer tab.
2. Click Record Macro button.

OR

1. Click View tab.
2. Click Macros button arrow.
3. Click *Record Macro.*
4. Make changes at Record Macro dialog box.
5. Click OK.
6. Complete macro steps.
7. Click Stop Recording button.

OR

7. Click macro icon on Status bar.

Stop Recording

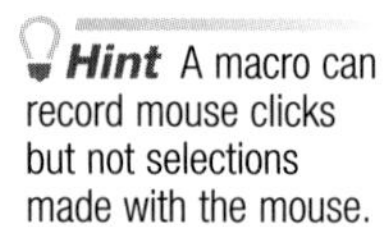
Hint A macro can record mouse clicks but not selections made with the mouse.

To record a macro, click the Record Macro button in the Code group on the Developer tab. Or click the View tab, click the Macros button arrow in the Macros group, and then click *Record Macro* at the drop-down list. This displays the Record Macro dialog box, shown in Figure 4.4. At the Record Macro dialog box, type a name for the macro in the *Macro name* text box. A macro name must begin with a letter and can contain only letters and numbers.

By default, Word stores macros in the Normal.dotm template. Macros stored here are available for any document based on this template. In a company or school setting, where computers may be networked, consider storing macros in personalized documents or templates. Specify the location for a macro with the *Store macro in* option box at the Record Macro dialog box (shown in Figure 4.4).

Type a description of the macro in the *Description* text box at the dialog box. A macro description can contain a maximum of 255 characters and may include spaces. After typing the macro name, specifying where the macro is to be stored, and typing a description of the macro, click OK to close the Record Macro dialog box. At the open document, a macro icon displays near the left side of the Status bar and the mouse displays with a cassette icon attached. In the document, perform the actions to be recorded. A macro can record mouse clicks and key presses. However, if part of the macro is selecting text, use the keyboard to select text because a macro cannot record selections made by the mouse. When all the steps have been completed, click the Stop Recording button (previously the Record Macro button) in the Code group on the Developer tab or click the macro icon near the left side of the Status bar.

When you record macros in Project 3a, you will be instructed to name the macros beginning with your initials. Recorded macros are stored in the Normal.dotm template by default and display in the Macros dialog box. If the computer you are using is networked, macros recorded by other students will also display at the Macros dialog box. Naming macros with your initials will enable you to distinguish your macros from those of other users.

Project 3a Recording Macros

Part 1 of 4

1. Turn on the display of the Developer tab by completing the following steps. (Skip to Step 2 if the Developer tab is already visible.)
   a. Click the File tab and then click *Options*.
   b. At the Word Options dialog box, click *Customize Ribbon* in the left panel.
   c. In the list box at the right, click the *Developer* check box to insert a check mark.
   d. Click OK to close the dialog box.
2. Record a macro that selects text, indents a paragraph of text, and then applies italic formatting by completing the following steps:
   a. Open **MacroText.docx** and then position the insertion point at the left margin of the paragraph that begins with *This is text to use for creating a macro.*
   b. Click the Developer tab.
   c. Click the Record Macro button in the Code group on the Developer tab.

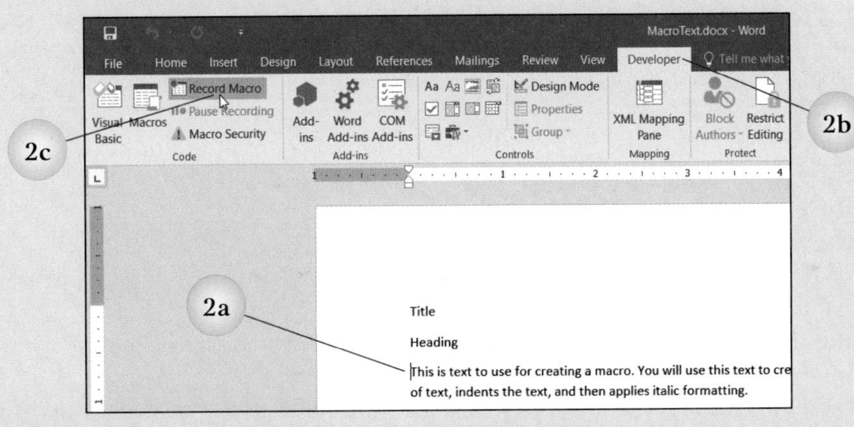

   d. At the Record Macro dialog box, type XXXIndentItalics in the *Macro name* text box. (Type your initials in place of *XXX*.)
   e. Click inside the *Description* text box and then type Select text, indent text, and apply italic formatting. (If text displays in the *Description* text box, select it and then type the description.)
   f. Click OK.
   g. At the document, press the F8 function key to turn on the Extend mode.
   h. Press and hold down the Shift key and the Ctrl key, press the Down Arrow key, and then release the Shift and Ctrl keys. (Shift + Ctrl + Down Arrow is the keyboard shortcut to select a paragraph.)

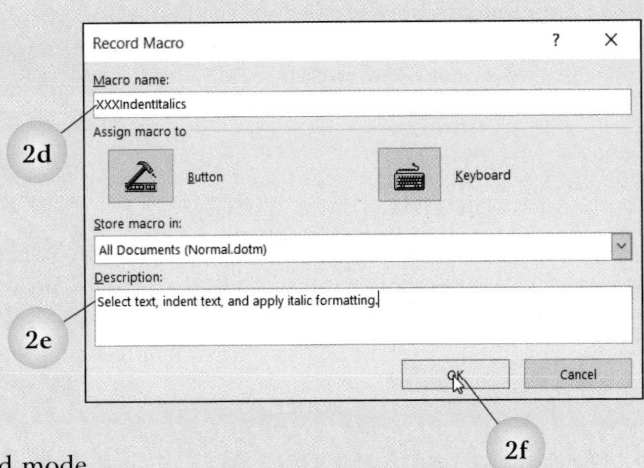

i. Click the Home tab.
j. Click the Paragraph group dialog box launcher.
k. At the Paragraph dialog box, click the *Left* measurement box up arrow until *0.5*" displays.
l. Click the *Right* measurement box up arrow until *0.5*" displays.
m. Click OK.
n. Press Ctrl + I to apply italic formatting.
o. Press the Esc key and then press the Left Arrow key. (This deselects the text.)
p. Click the macro icon on the Status bar to turn off the macro recording.

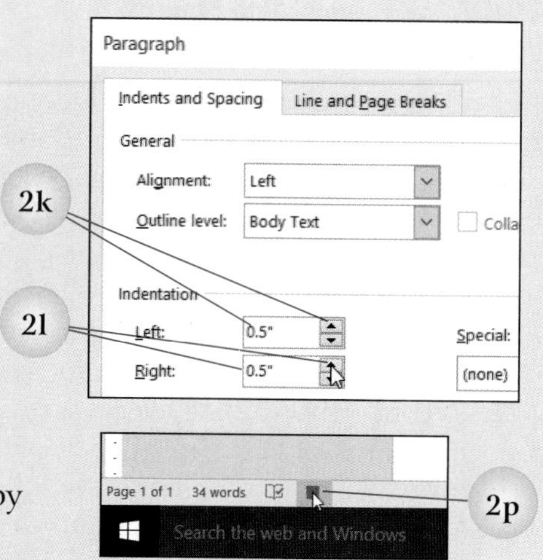

3. Record a macro that applies formatting to a heading by completing the following steps:
   a. Move the insertion point to the beginning of the text *Heading*.
   b. Click the Developer tab and then click the Record Macro button in the Code group.
   c. At the Record Macro dialog box, type XXXHeading in the *Macro name* text box. (Type your initials in place of *XXX*.)
   d. Click inside the *Description* text box and then type Select text, change font size, turn on bold and italic, and insert bottom border line. (If text displays in the *Description* text box, select it and then type the description.)
   e. Click OK.
   f. At the document, press the F8 function key and then press the End key.
   g. Click the Home tab.
   h. Click the Bold button in the Font group.
   i. Click the Italic button in the Font group.
   j. Click the *Font Size* option box arrow in the Font group and then click *12* at the drop-down gallery.
   k. Click the Borders button arrow in the Paragraph group and then click *Bottom Border* at the drop-down list.
   l. Press the Home key. (This moves the insertion point back to the beginning of the heading and deselects the text.)
   m. Click the macro icon on the Status bar to turn off the macro recording.
4. Close the document without saving it.

Running a Macro

Quick Steps

Run a Macro

1. Click Developer tab.
2. Click Macros button.
3. At Macros dialog box, double-click macro in list box.

OR

1. Click View tab.
2. Click Macros button.
3. At Macros dialog box, double-click macro in list box.

To run a recorded macro, click the Macros button in the Code group on the Developer tab or click the Macros button on the View tab. This displays the Macros dialog box, shown in Figure 4.5. At this dialog box, double-click a macro in the list box or click a macro and then click the Run button.

Figure 4.5 Macros Dialog Box

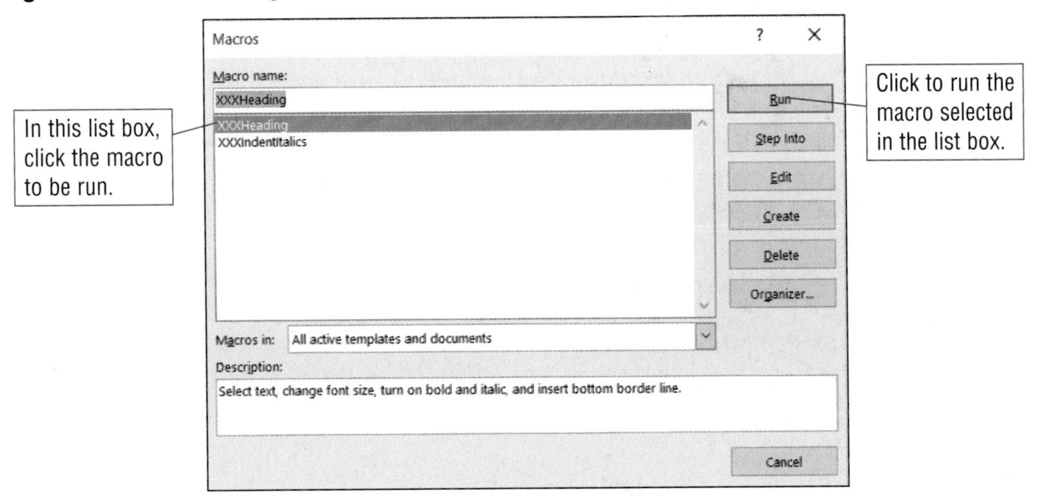

Project 3b Running Macros

Part 2 of 4

1. Open **WriteResumes.docx** and then save it with the name **4-WriteResumes**.
2. With the insertion point positioned at the beginning of the heading *Resume Strategies*, run the XXXHeading macro by completing the following steps:
   a. Click the View tab.
   b. Click the Macros button in the Macros group.
   c. At the Macros dialog box, click *XXXHeading* in the list box.
   d. Click the Run button.

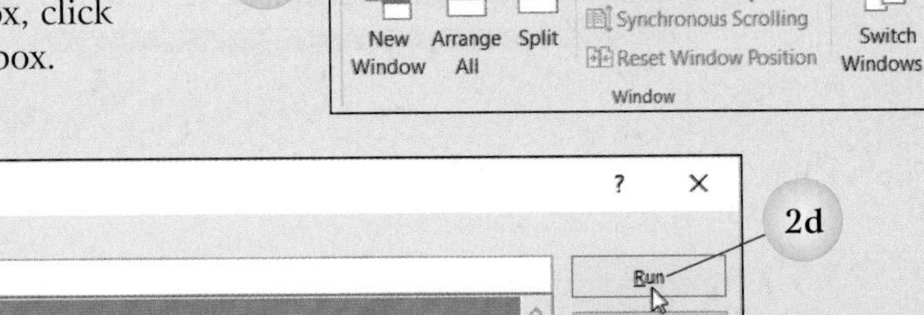

3. Complete steps similar to those in Steps 2a–2d to run the macro for the two other headings in the document: *Writing Style* and *Phrases to Avoid*.
4. Move the insertion point to the beginning of the paragraph below *First Person* and then complete the following steps to run the XXXIndentItalics macro:
   a. Click the Developer tab.
   b. Click the Macros button in the Code group.
   c. At the Macros dialog box, double-click *XXXIndentItalics* in the list box.
5. Complete steps similar to those in Step 4a–4c to run the XXXIndentItalics macro for the paragraph below *Third Person*, the paragraph that begins *Responsible for all marketing and special events*, and the paragraph that begins *Orchestrated a series of marketing and special-event programs*.
6. Save, print, and then close **4-WriteResumes.docx**.

Check Your Work

Pausing and Resuming a Macro

When recording a macro, the recording can be suspended temporarily to perform actions that should not be included in the recording. To pause the recording of a macro, click the Pause Recording button in the Code group on the Developer tab or click the Macros button on the View tab and then click *Pause Recording* at the drop-down list. To resume recording the macro, click the Resume Recorder button (previously the Pause Recording button).

Deleting a Macro

If a macro is no longer needed, delete it. To delete a macro, display the Macros dialog box, click the macro name in the list box, and then click the Delete button. At the confirmation message, click Yes. Click the Close button to close the Macros dialog box.

Project 3c Deleting a Macro

Part 3 of 4

1. At a blank document, delete the XXXIndentItalics macro by completing the following steps:
   a. Click the Developer tab and then click the Macros button in the Code group.
   b. At the Macros dialog box, click *XXXIndentItalics* in the list box.
   c. Click the Delete button.

   d. At the message asking if you want to delete the macro, click Yes.
   e. Click the Close button to close the Macros dialog box.
2. Close the document without saving it.

Tutorial

Assigning a Macro to a Keyboard Command

Assigning a Macro to a Keyboard Command

Consider assigning regularly used macros to keyboard commands. To run a macro that has been assigned to a keyboard command, simply press the assigned keys. A macro can be assigned to a keyboard command with the following combinations:

Alt + letter
Ctrl + letter
Alt + Ctrl + letter
Alt + Shift + letter
Ctrl + Shift + letter
Alt + Ctrl + Shift + letter

Word already uses many combinations for Word functions. For example, pressing Alt + Ctrl + C inserts the copyright symbol (©).

Assign a macro to a keyboard command at the Customize Keyboard dialog box, shown in Figure 4.6. Specify the keyboard command by pressing the keys, such as Alt + D. The keyboard command entered displays in the *Press new shortcut key* text box. Word inserts the message *Currently assigned to:* below the *Current keys* list box. If the keyboard command is already assigned to a command, the command is listed after the *Currently assigned to:* message. If Word has not used the keyboard command, *[unassigned]* displays after the *Currently assigned to:* message. When assigning a keyboard command to a macro, use an unassigned keyboard command.

In Project 3d, you will record a macro and then assign it to a keyboard command. When you delete a macro, the keyboard command is no longer assigned to that action. This allows using the key combination again.

Figure 4.6 Customize Keyboard Dialog Box

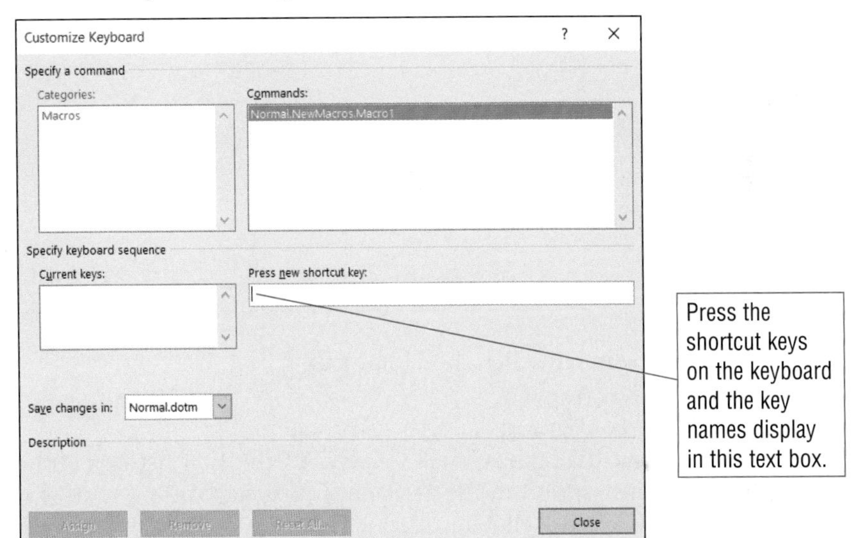

Project 3d Assigning a Macro to a Keyboard Command

Part 4 of 4

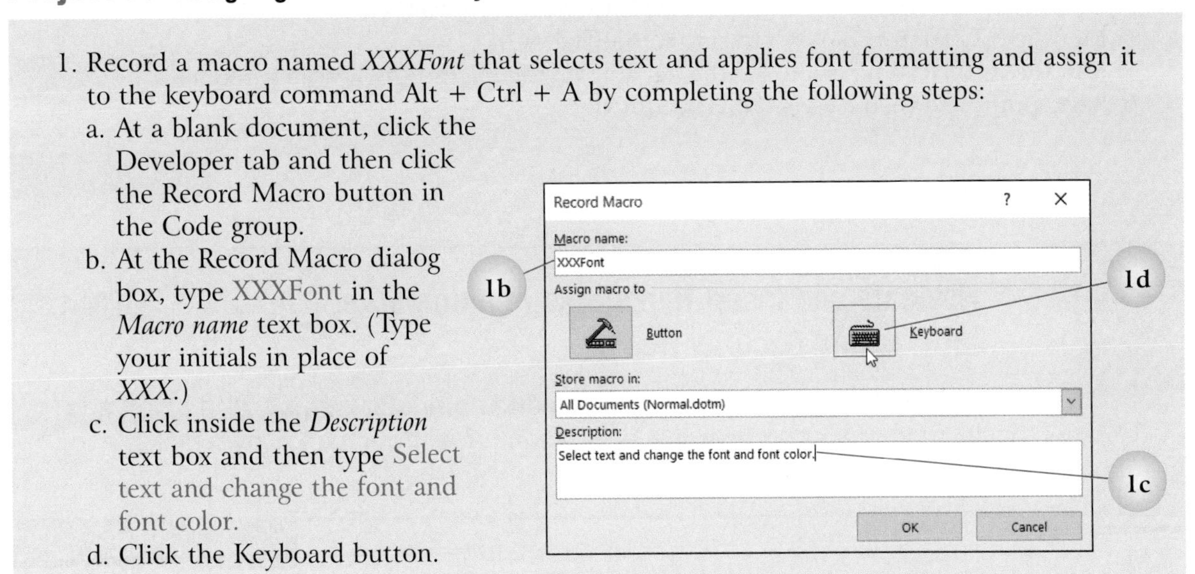

1. Record a macro named *XXXFont* that selects text and applies font formatting and assign it to the keyboard command Alt + Ctrl + A by completing the following steps:
   a. At a blank document, click the Developer tab and then click the Record Macro button in the Code group.
   b. At the Record Macro dialog box, type XXXFont in the *Macro name* text box. (Type your initials in place of *XXX*.)
   c. Click inside the *Description* text box and then type Select text and change the font and font color.
   d. Click the Keyboard button.

e. At the Customize Keyboard dialog box with the insertion point positioned in the *Press new shortcut key* text box, press Alt + Ctrl + A.
f. Check to make sure *[unassigned]* displays after *Currently assigned to:*.
g. Click the Assign button.
h. Click the Close button.

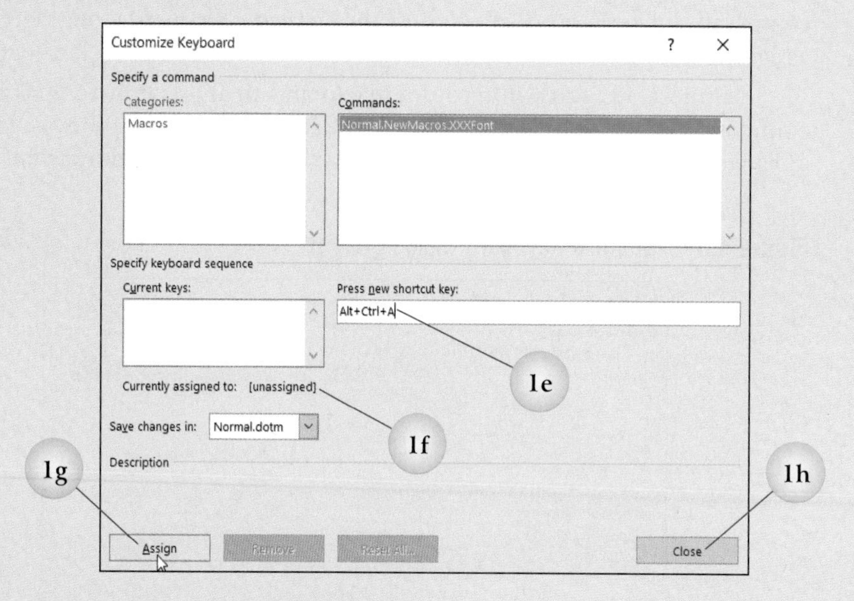

i. At the document, click the Home tab.
j. Press Ctrl + A.
k. Click the Font group dialog box launcher.
l. At the Font dialog box, click *Cambria* in the *Font* list box and click the *Dark Blue* font color (ninth option in the *Standard Colors* section).
m. Click OK to close the Font dialog box.
n. At the document, press the Down Arrow on the keyboard.
o. Click the macro icon on the Status bar to turn off the macro recording.

2. Close the document without saving it.
3. Open **GSHLtr.docx** and then save it with the name **4-GSHLtr**.
4. Run the XXXFont macro by pressing Alt + Ctrl + A.
5. Run the XXXHeading macro for the heading *Procedural* and the heading *Teaching*.
6. Save, print, and then close **4-GSHLtr.docx**.

Check Your Work

Project 4 Navigate and Insert Hyperlinks in a Computer Viruses and Security Report — 6 Parts

You will open a report on computer viruses and computer security and insert and then navigate in the report with the Navigation pane, bookmarks, hyperlinks, and cross-references.

Preview Finished Project

Navigating in a Document

Word provides a number of features for navigating in a document. Navigate in a document using the Navigation pane or using bookmarks, hyperlinks, or cross-references.

Tutorial

Review: Navigating Using the Navigation Pane

Quick Steps

Display the Navigation Pane

1. Click View tab.
2. Click *Navigation Pane* check box.

Navigating Using the Navigation Pane

As explained in Level 1, Chapter 4, the Navigation pane can be used to navigate in a document. To navigate with the Navigation pane, click the View tab and then click the *Navigation Pane* check box in the Show group to insert a check mark. The Navigation pane displays at the left side of the screen and includes a search text box and a pane with three tabs.

Click the first Navigation pane tab, Headings, and titles and headings with certain styles applied display in the Navigation pane. Click a title or heading and the insertion point moves to it. Click the Pages tab and a thumbnail of each page displays in the pane. Click a thumbnail to move the insertion point to that specific page. Click the Results tab to browse the current search results in the document.

Close the Navigation pane by clicking the *Navigation Pane* check box in the Show group on the View tab to remove the check mark. Another option is to click the Close button in the upper right corner of the pane.

Project 4a **Navigating Using the Navigation Pane** **Part 1 of 6**

1. Open **Security.docx** and then save it with the name **4-Security**.
2. Since this document has heading styles applied, you can easily navigate in the document with the Navigation pane by completing the following steps:
   a. Click the View tab.
   b. Click the *Navigation Pane* check box in the Show group to insert a check mark. (This displays the Navigation pane at the left side of the screen.)
   c. With the Headings tab active, click the heading *CHAPTER 2: INFORMATION THEFT* in the Navigation pane.

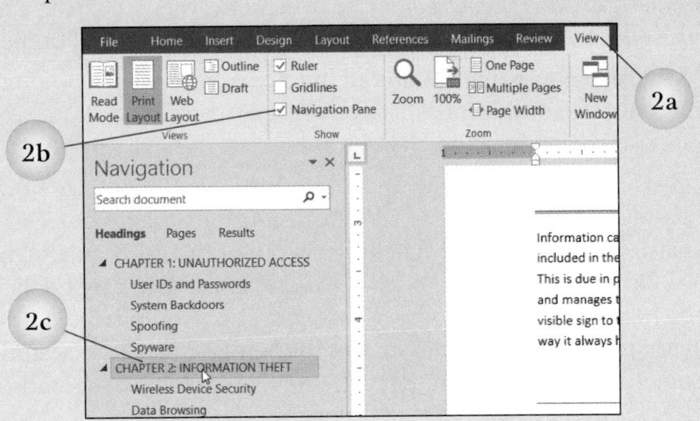

   d. Click *CHAPTER 3: COMPUTER VIRUSES* in the Navigation pane.
   e. Click *Systems Failure* in the Navigation pane.

3. Navigate in the document using thumbnails by completing the following steps:
   a. Click the Pages tab in the Navigation pane. (This displays thumbnails of the pages in the pane.)
   b. Click the page 1 thumbnail in the Navigation pane. (You may need to scroll up the Navigation pane to display this thumbnail.)

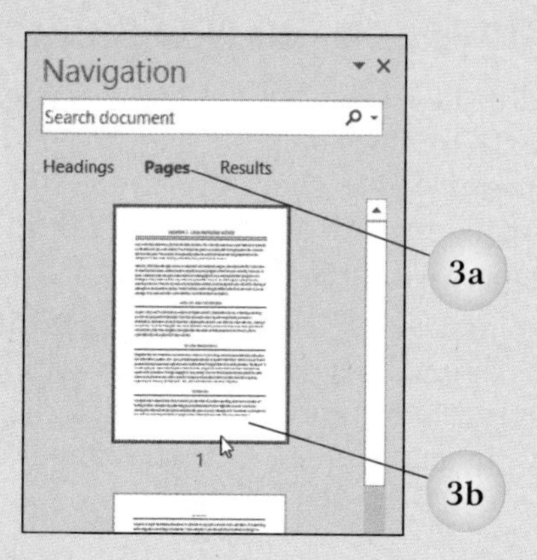

   c. Click the page 3 thumbnail in the Navigation pane.
4. Close the Navigation pane by clicking the Close button in the upper right corner of the Navigation pane.
5. Save **4-Security.docx**.

Tutorial

Inserting and Navigating with Bookmarks

Bookmark

Quick Steps

Insert a Bookmark

1. Position insertion point at specific location.
2. Click Insert tab.
3. Click Bookmark button.
4. Type name for bookmark.
5. Click Add button.

Inserting and Navigating with Bookmarks

When working in a long document, marking a place in it with a bookmark may be useful for moving the insertion point to that specific location. Create bookmarks for locations in a document at the Bookmark dialog box.

To create a bookmark, position the insertion point at the specific location, click the Insert tab, and then click the Bookmark button in the Links group. This displays the Bookmark dialog box, as shown in Figure 4.7. Type a name for the bookmark in the *Bookmark name* text box and then click the Add button. Repeat these steps as many times as needed to insert additional bookmarks.

Give each bookmark a unique name. A bookmark name must begin with a letter and can contain numbers but not spaces. To separate words in a bookmark name, use the underscore character.

By default, the bookmarks inserted in a document are not visible. Turn on the display of bookmarks at the Word Options dialog box with *Advanced* selected. Display this dialog box by clicking the File tab and then clicking *Options*. At the Word Options dialog box, click *Advanced* in the left panel. Click the *Show bookmarks* check box in the *Show document content* section to insert a check mark. Complete similar steps to turn off the display of bookmarks. A bookmark displays in the document as an I-beam marker.

Figure 4.7 Bookmark Dialog Box

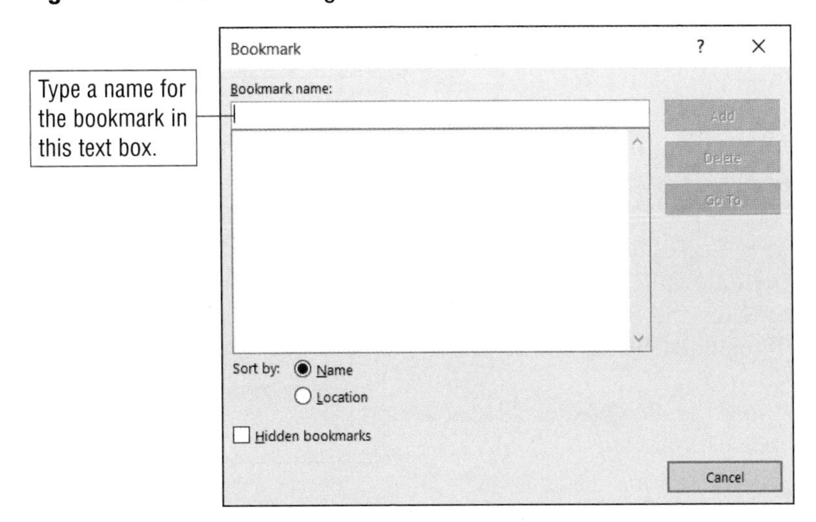

Hint Bookmark brackets do not print.

A bookmark can be created for selected text. To do this, first select the text and then complete the steps to create a bookmark. A bookmark created with selected text displays a left bracket ([) indicating the beginning of the selected text and a right bracket (]) indicating the end of the selected text.

Quick Steps

Navigate with Bookmarks

1. Click Insert tab.
2. Click Bookmark button.
3. Double-click bookmark name.

Navigate in a document by moving the insertion point to a specific bookmark. To do this, display the Bookmark dialog box and then double-click the bookmark name or click the bookmark name and then click the Go To button. When Word stops at the location of the bookmark, click the Close button to close the dialog box. When moving to a bookmark created with selected text, Word moves the insertion point to the bookmark and then selects the text. Delete a bookmark in the Bookmark dialog box by clicking the bookmark name in the list box and then clicking the Delete button.

Project 4b Inserting and Navigating with Bookmarks

Part 2 of 6

1. With **4-Security.docx** open, turn on the display of bookmarks by completing the following steps:
   a. Click the File tab and then click *Options*.
   b. At the Word Options dialog box, click *Advanced* in the left panel.
   c. Scroll down the dialog box and then click the *Show bookmarks* check box in the *Show document content* section to insert a check mark.
   d. Click OK to close the dialog box.
2. Insert a bookmark by completing the following steps:
   a. Move the insertion point to the beginning of the paragraph in the section *TYPES OF VIRUSES* (the paragraph that begins *Viruses can be categorized*).
   b. Click the Insert tab.
   c. Click the Bookmark button in the Links group.

d. At the Bookmark dialog box, type Viruses in the *Bookmark name* text box.
e. Click the Add button.

3. Using steps similar to those in Steps 2a–2e, insert a bookmark named *Electrical* at the beginning of the paragraph in the section *SYSTEMS FAILURE*.
4. Navigate to the Viruses bookmark by completing the following steps:
   a. If necessary, click the Insert tab.
   b. Click the Bookmark button in the Links group.
   c. At the Bookmark dialog box, click *Viruses* in the list box.
   d. Click the Go To button.
5. With the Bookmark dialog box open, delete the Electrical bookmark by clicking *Electrical* in the list box and then clicking the Delete button.
6. Click the Close button to close the Bookmark dialog box.
7. Save **4-Security.docx**.

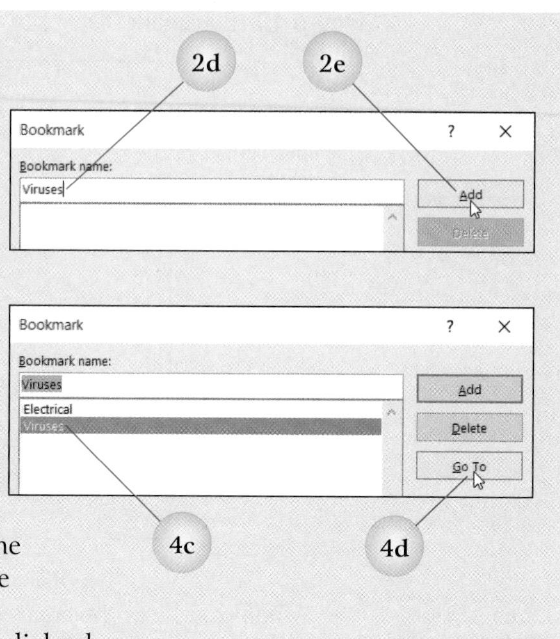

Tutorial

Inserting and Editing a Hyperlink

Hyperlink

Quick Steps

Insert a Hyperlink

1. Click Insert tab.
2. Click Hyperlink button.
3. Make changes at Insert Hyperlink dialog box.
4. Click OK.

Inserting Hyperlinks

Hyperlinks can serve a number of purposes in a document. They can be used to navigate to a specific location in the document, to display a different document, to open a file in a different program, to create a new document, and to link to an email address.

Insert a hyperlink by clicking the Hyperlink button in the Links group on the Insert tab. This displays the Insert Hyperlink dialog box, as shown in Figure 4.8. This dialog box can also be displayed by pressing Ctrl + K. At the Insert Hyperlink dialog box, identify what to link to and where to find the link. Click the ScreenTip button to customize the ScreenTip for the hyperlink.

Figure 4.8 Insert Hyperlink Dialog Box

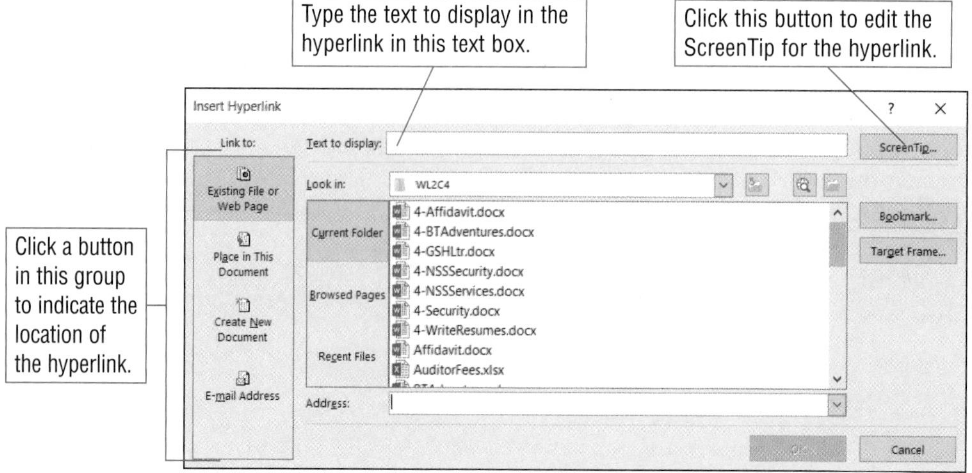

Linking to a Place in the Document To create a hyperlink to another location in the document, first mark the location by applying a heading style to the text or inserting a bookmark. To hyperlink to that heading or bookmark, display the Insert Hyperlink dialog box and then click the Place in This Document button in the *Link to* section. This displays text with heading styles applied and bookmarks in the *Select a place in this document* list box. Click the heading style or bookmark name and the heading or bookmark name displays in the *Text to display* text box. Leave the text as displayed or select the text and then type the text that will appear in the document.

Navigating Using Hyperlinks Navigate to a hyperlink by hovering the mouse pointer over the hyperlink text, pressing and holding down the Ctrl key, clicking the left mouse button, and then releasing the Ctrl key. When hovering the mouse pointer over the hyperlink text, a ScreenTip displays with the name of the heading or bookmark. To display specific information in the ScreenTip, click the ScreenTip button in the Insert Hyperlink dialog box, type the text in the Set Hyperlink ScreenTip dialog box, and then click OK.

Project 4c Inserting and Navigating with Hyperlinks

Part 3 of 6

1. With **4-Security.docx** open, insert a hyperlink to a bookmark in the document by completing the following steps:
   a. Position the insertion point at the immediate right of the period that ends the first paragraph of text in the section *CHAPTER 4: SECURITY RISKS* (located on page 4).
   b. Press the spacebar.
   c. If necessary, click the Insert tab.
   d. Click the Hyperlink button in the Links group.
   e. At the Insert Hyperlink dialog box, click the Place in This Document button in the *Link to* section.
   f. Scroll down the *Select a place in this document* list box and then click *Viruses,* which displays below *Bookmarks* in the list box.
   g. Select the text in the *Text to display* text box and then type Click to view types of viruses.
   h. Click the ScreenTip button in the upper right corner of the dialog box.
   i. At the Set Hyperlink ScreenTip dialog box, type View types of viruses and then click OK.
   j. Click OK to close the Insert Hyperlink dialog box.
2. Navigate to the hyperlinked location by hovering the mouse pointer over the Click to view types of viruses hyperlink, pressing and holding down the Ctrl key, clicking the left mouse button, and then releasing the Ctrl key.

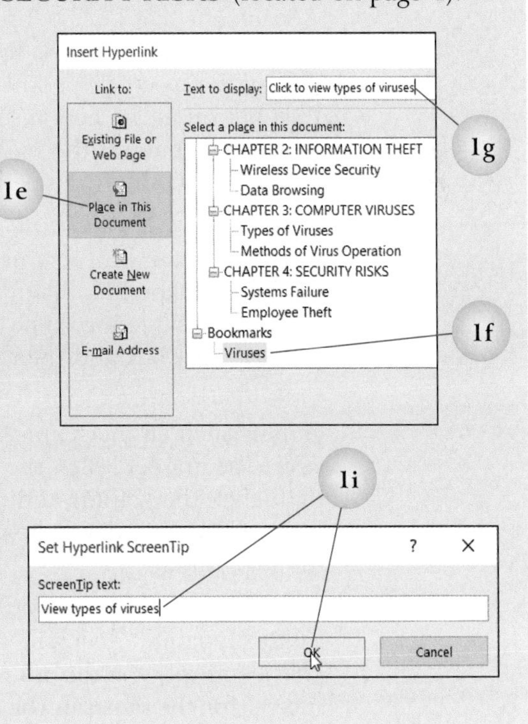

3. Insert a hyperlink to a heading in the document by completing the following steps:
   a. Press Ctrl + Home to move the insertion point to the beginning of the document.
   b. Move the insertion point to the immediate right of the period that ends the second paragraph in the document and then press the spacebar.
   c. Click the Hyperlink button on the Insert tab.
   d. At the Insert Hyperlink dialog box with Place in This Document button active in the *Link To* section, click the *Methods of Virus Operation* heading in the *Select a place in this document* list box.
   e. Click OK to close the Insert Hyperlink dialog box.

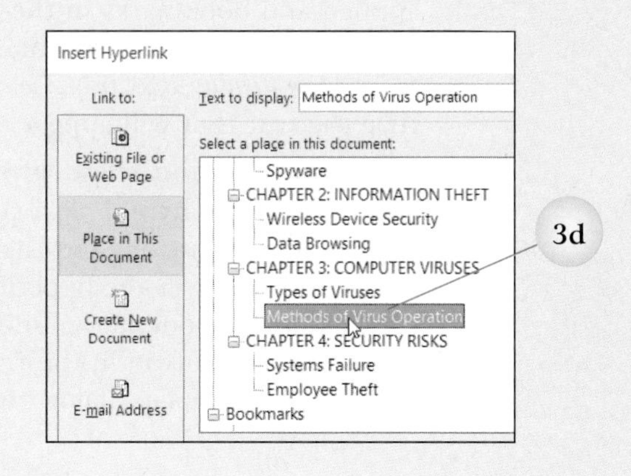

4. Navigate to the hyperlinked heading by hovering the mouse pointer over the Methods of Virus Operation hyperlink, pressing and holding down the Ctrl key, clicking the left mouse button, and then releasing the Ctrl key.
5. Save **4-Security.docx**.

Check Your Work

Linking to a File in Another Application A hyperlink can be inserted in a document that links to another Word document, an Excel worksheet, or a PowerPoint presentation. To link a Word document to a file in another application, display the Insert Hyperlink dialog box and then click the Existing File or Web Page button in the *Link to* section. Use the *Look in* option box to navigate to the folder that contains the specific file and then click the file name. Make other changes in the Insert Hyperlink dialog box as needed and then click OK.

Linking to a New Document In addition to linking to an existing document, a hyperlink can link to a new document. To insert this kind of hyperlink, display the Insert Hyperlink dialog box and then click the Create New Document button in the *Link to* section. Type a name for the new document in the *Name of new document* text box and then specify if the document is to be edited now or later.

Linking Using a Graphic A hyperlink to a file or website can be inserted in a graphic such an image, picture, or text box. To create a hyperlink with a graphic, select the graphic, click the Insert tab, and then click the Hyperlink button or right-click the graphic and then click *Hyperlink* at the shortcut menu. At the Insert Hyperlink dialog box, specify where to link to and what text to display in the hyperlink.

Linking to an Email Address Insert a hyperlink to an email address at the Insert Hyperlink dialog box. To do this, click the E-Mail Address button in the *Link to* group, type the address in the *E-mail address* text box, and then type a subject for the email in the *Subject* text box. Click in the *Text to display* text box and then type the text to display in the document. To use this feature, the email address must be set up in Outlook.

Project 4d Inserting a Hyperlink to Another Program, a New Document, and Using a Graphic

Part 4 of 6

1. The **4-Security.docx** document contains information used by Northland Security Systems. The company also has a PowerPoint presentation that contains similar information. Link the document with the presentation by completing the following steps:
   a. Move the insertion point to the immediate right of the period that ends the first paragraph in the section *CHAPTER 3: COMPUTER VIRUSES* and then press the spacebar.
   b. If necessary, click the Insert tab.
   c. Click the Hyperlink button in the Links group.
   d. At the Insert Hyperlink dialog box, click the Existing File or Web Page button in the *Link to* section.
   e. Click the *Look in* option box arrow, at the drop-down list that displays, navigate to the WL2C4 folder on your storage medium, and then click the folder.
   f. Click ***NSSPres.pptx*** in the list box.
   g. Select the text in the *Text to display* text box and then type Computer Virus Presentation.
   h. Click OK to close the Insert Hyperlink dialog box.

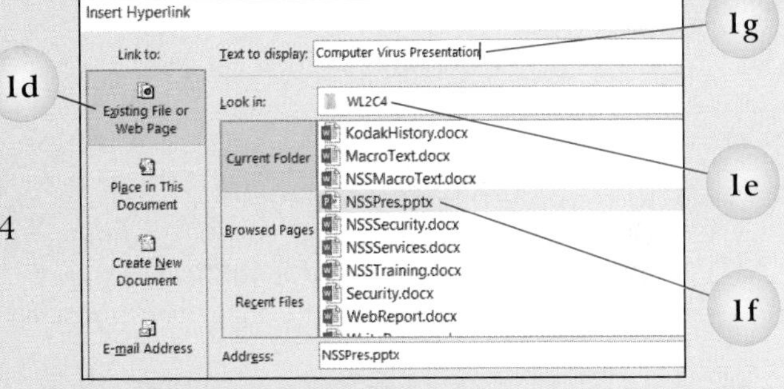

2. View the PowerPoint presentation by completing the following steps:
   a. Position the mouse pointer over the Computer Virus Presentation hyperlink, press and hold down the Ctrl key, click the left mouse button, and then release the Ctrl key.
   b. At the PowerPoint presentation, click the Slide Show button in the view area on the Status bar.
   c. Click the left mouse button to advance each slide.
   d. Click the left mouse button at the black screen that displays the message *End of slide show, click to exit.*
   e. Close the presentation and PowerPoint by clicking the Close button (which contains an X) in the upper right corner of the screen.

2b

65%

3. Insert a hyperlink with a graphic by completing the following steps:
   a. Press Ctrl + End to move the insertion point to the end of the document.
   b. Click the compass image to select it.
   c. Click the Hyperlink button on the Insert tab.
   d. At the Insert Hyperlink dialog box, make sure the Existing File or Web Page button is active in the *Link to* group.
   e. Navigate to the WL2C4 folder on your storage medium and then double-click ***NSSTraining.docx***. (This selects the document name and closes the dialog box.)
   f. Click outside the compass image to deselect it.
4. Navigate to **NSSTraining.docx** by hovering the mouse pointer over the compass image, pressing and holding down the Ctrl key, clicking the left mouse button, and then releasing the Ctrl key.
5. Close the document by clicking the File tab and then clicking the *Close* option.

6. Insert a hyperlink to a new document by completing the following steps:
   a. Move the insertion point to the immediate right of the period that ends the paragraph in the section *USER IDS AND PASSWORDS* and then press the spacebar.
   b. Click the Hyperlink button on the Insert tab.
   c. Click the Create New Document button in the *Link to* section.
   d. In the *Name of new document* text box, type 4-PasswordSuggestions.
   e. Edit the text in the *Text to display* text box so it displays as *Password Suggestions*.
   f. Make sure the *Edit the new document now* option is selected.
   g. Click OK.
   h. At the blank document, turn on bold formatting, type Please type any suggestions you have for creating secure passwords:, turn off bold formatting, and then press the Enter key.
   i. Save and then close the document. 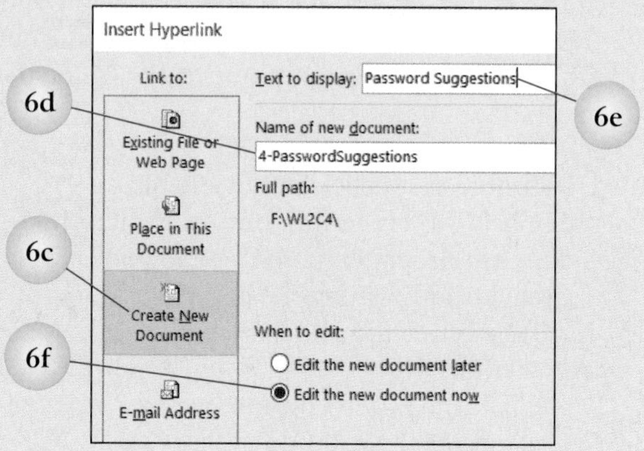
7. Press Ctrl + End to move the insertion point to the end of the document and then press the Enter key four times.
8. Insert a hyperlink to your email address or your instructor's email address by completing the following steps:
   a. Click the Hyperlink button.
   b. At the Insert Hyperlink dialog box, click the E-mail Address button in the *Link to* group.
   c. Type your email address or your instructor's email address in the *E-mail address* text box.
   d. Select the current text in the *Text to display* text box and then type Click to send an email.
   e. Click OK to close the dialog box.

Optional:* *If you have Outlook set up, press and hold down the Ctrl key, click the Click to send an email hyperlink, release the Ctrl key, and then send a message indicating that you have completed inserting hyperlinks in 4-Security.docx.

9. Save **4-Security.docx**.

Check Your Work

Editing a Hyperlink

The hyperlink or the hyperlink destination can be edited with options at the Edit Hyperlink dialog box. The Edit Hyperlink dialog box contains the same options as the Insert Hyperlink dialog box. Display the Edit Hyperlink dialog box by selecting the hyperlinked text and then clicking the Hyperlink button on the Insert tab or by right-clicking the hyperlinked text and then clicking *Edit Hyperlink* at the shortcut menu. In addition to editing the hyperlink, the hyperlinked text can be edited. For example, a different font, font size, text color, or text effect can be applied to the hyperlink text. Remove a hyperlink from a document by right-clicking the hyperlinked text and then clicking *Remove Hyperlink* at the shortcut menu.

Project 4e Editing and Removing a Hyperlink

1. With **4-Security.docx** open, edit a hyperlink by completing the following steps:
   a. Display the hyperlink that displays at the end of the paragraph below the title CHAPTER 3: COMPUTER VIRUSES.
   b. Right-click the Computer Virus Presentation hyperlink and then click *Edit Hyperlink* at the shortcut menu.

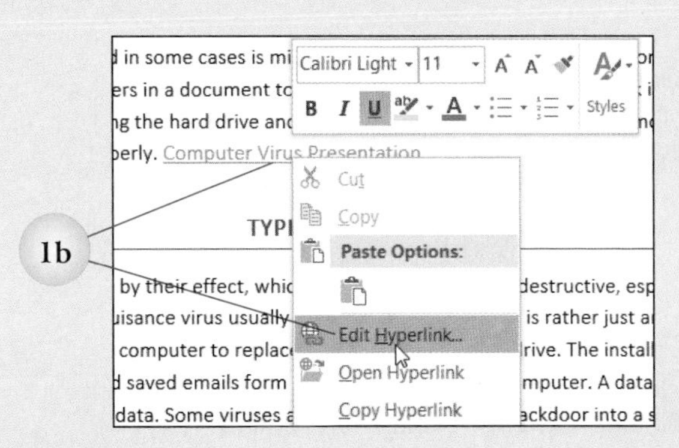

   c. At the Edit Hyperlink dialog box, select the text in the *Text to display* text box and then type Click to view a presentation on computer viruses.
   d. Click the ScreenTip button in the upper right corner of the dialog box.
   e. At the Set Hyperlink ScreenTip dialog box, type View the Computer Viruses PowerPoint presentation and then click OK.
   f. Click OK to close the Edit Hyperlink dialog box.
2. Remove a hyperlink by completing the following steps:
   a. Press Ctrl + Home to move the insertion point to the beginning of the document.
   b. Right-click the Methods of Virus Operation hyperlink that displays at the end of the second paragraph below the title *CHAPTER 1: UNAUTHORIZED ACCESS*.
   c. At the shortcut menu that displays, click the *Remove Hyperlink* option.
3. Save **4-Security.docx**.

Check Your Work

Tutorial

Creating a Cross-Reference

Quick Steps

Insert a Cross-Reference

1. Type text or position insertion point.
2. Click Insert tab.
3. Click Cross-reference button.
4. Identify reference type, location, and text.
5. Click Insert.
6. Click Close.

Cross-reference

Creating a Cross-Reference

A *cross-reference* in a Word document refers readers to another location within the document. Providing cross-references is useful in a long document or a document containing related information. References to items such as headings, figures, and tables are helpful to readers. For example, a cross-reference can be inserted that refers readers to a location with more information about the topic, to a specific table, or to a specific page. Cross-references are inserted in a document as hyperlinks.

To insert a cross-reference, type introductory text or position the insertion point at a specific location, click the Insert tab, and then click the Cross-reference button in the Links group. This displays the Cross-reference dialog box similar to the one shown in Figure 4.9. At the Cross-reference dialog box, identify the type of reference, the location to reference, and the specific text to reference.

The reference identified in the Cross-reference dialog box displays immediately after the introductory text. To move to the specified reference, press and hold down the Ctrl key, position the mouse pointer over the text (the pointer turns into a hand), click the left mouse button, and then release the Ctrl key.

Figure 4.9 Cross-reference Dialog Box

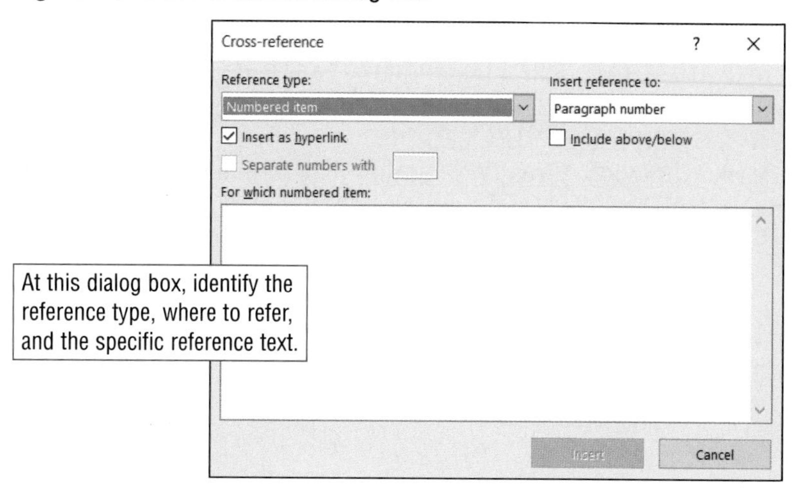

Project 4f Inserting and Navigating with Cross-References

Part 6 of 6

1. With **4-Security.docx** open, insert a cross-reference in the document by completing the following steps:
   a. Move the insertion point immediately right of the period that ends the paragraph in the section *TYPES OF VIRUSES*.
   b. Press the spacebar and then type (For more information, refer to.
   c. Press the spacebar.
   d. If necessary, click the Insert tab.
   e. Click the Cross-reference button in the Links group.
   f. At the Cross-reference dialog box, click the *Reference type* option box arrow and then click *Heading* at the drop-down list.
   g. Click *Spyware* in the *For which heading* list box.
   h. Click the Insert button.
   i. Click the Close button to close the dialog box.
   j. At the document, type a period followed by a right parenthesis.

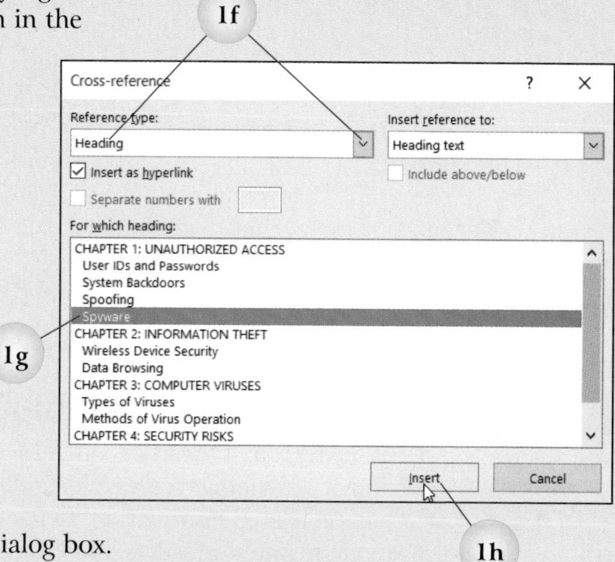

2. Move to the referenced text by pressing and holding down the Ctrl key, positioning the mouse pointer over *Spyware* until the pointer turns into a hand, clicking the left mouse button, and then releasing the Ctrl key.
3. Save and then print **4-Security.docx**.
4. Turn off the display of bookmarks by completing the following steps:
   a. Click the File tab and then click *Options*.
   b. At the Word Options dialog box, click *Advanced* in the left panel.
   c. Click the *Show bookmarks* check box in the *Show document content* section to remove the check mark.
   d. Click OK to close the dialog box.
5. Close **4-Security.docx**.

Check Your Work

Chapter Summary

- Create custom theme colors with options at the Create New Theme Colors dialog box and create custom theme fonts with options at the Create New Theme Fonts dialog box.
- Click the Reset button in the Create New Theme Colors dialog box to reset the colors back to the default Office theme colors.
- Create custom theme colors and custom theme fonts, apply a theme effect, and then save the changes in a custom theme. Save a custom theme at the Save Current Theme dialog box. Display this dialog box by clicking the Themes button in the Document Formatting group on the Design tab and then clicking *Save Current Theme* at the drop-down gallery.
- Apply custom theme colors by clicking the Colors button and then clicking the custom theme at the top of the drop-down gallery. Complete similar steps to apply custom theme fonts and a custom theme.
- Delete a custom theme at the Themes button drop-down gallery or at the Save Current Theme dialog box.
- Click the *Reset to Theme from Template* option at the Themes button drop-down gallery to reset the theme to the template default.
- A style is a set of formatting instructions that can be applied to text in a document. Word provides a number of predesigned styles grouped into style sets.
- Styles within a style set are available in the Styles group on the Home tab or the Styles task pane.
- Apply a style by clicking the style in the Styles group on the Home tab or clicking a style in the Styles task pane. Display the Styles task pane by clicking the Styles group task pane launcher.
- Modify a predesigned style with options at the Modify Style dialog box. Display this dialog box by right-clicking the style in the Styles group or in the Styles task pane and then clicking *Modify* at the shortcut menu.
- A macro automates the formatting of a document. Recording a macro involves turning on the macro recorder, performing the steps to be recorded, and then turning off the recorder.
- Both the View tab and the Developer tab contain buttons for recording a macro. Turn on the display of the Developer tab by inserting a check mark in the *Developer* check box at the Word Options dialog box with *Customize Ribbon* selected in the left panel.
- Name and describe a macro at the Record Macro dialog box. Display the dialog box by clicking the Record Macro button on the Developer tab or clicking the Macros button arrow on the View tab and then clicking *Record Macro* at the drop-down list.
- Run a macro by displaying the Macros dialog box and then double-clicking the macro name or clicking the macro name and then clicking the Run button.
- Temporarily suspend the recording of a macro by clicking the Pause Recording button in the Code group on the Developer tab.
- Delete a macro by displaying the Macros dialog box, clicking the macro name, and then clicking the Delete button.

- Assign a macro to a keyboard command at the Customize Keyboard dialog box. Display this dialog box by clicking the Keyboard button at the Record Macro dialog box. To run a macro that has been assigned a keyboard command, press the combination of keys assigned to the macro.
- Navigate in a document using the Navigation pane or by inserting bookmarks, hyperlinks, or cross-references.
- Insert bookmarks with options at the Bookmark dialog box.
- Insert hyperlinks in a document with options at the Insert Hyperlink dialog box. Insert a hyperlink to an existing file or web page, a location in the current document, a new document, or an email. A graphic can also be used to link to a file or website.
- Create a cross-reference with options at the Cross-reference dialog box.

Commands Review

FEATURE	RIBBON TAB, GROUP	BUTTON, OPTION	KEYBOARD SHORTCUT
Bookmark dialog box	Insert, Links		
Create New Theme Colors dialog box	Design, Document Formatting	, *Customize Colors*	
Create New Theme Fonts dialog box	Design, Document Formatting	, *Customize Fonts*	
Cross-reference dialog box	Insert, Links		
Insert Hyperlink dialog box	Insert, Links		Ctrl + K
Macros dialog box	Developer, Code OR View, Macros		Alt + F8
Record Macro dialog box	Developer, Code OR View, Macros		
Save Current Theme dialog box	Design, Document Formatting	, *Save Current Theme*	
Styles task pane	Home, Styles		Alt + Ctrl + Shift + S
theme effects	Design, Document Formatting		

Workbook

Chapter study tools and assessment activities are available in the *Workbook* ebook. These resources are designed to help you further develop and demonstrate mastery of the skills learned in this chapter.

Unit assessment activities are also available in the *Workbook*. These activities are designed to help you demonstrate mastery of the skills learned in this unit.

Microsoft®

Word Level 2

Unit 2

Editing and Formatting Documents

Chapter 5 Inserting Special Features and References

Chapter 6 Creating Specialized Tables and Indexes

Chapter 7 Working with Shared Documents

Chapter 8 Protecting and Preparing Documents

Microsoft®

Word

Inserting Special Features and References

CHAPTER 5

Performance Objectives

Upon successful completion of Chapter 5, you will be able to:

1 Sort text in paragraphs, columns, and tables
2 Sort records in a data source file
3 Select specific records in a data source file
4 Find specific records in a data source file
5 Create and use specialized templates
6 Insert footnotes and endnotes
7 Insert and edit sources and citations
8 Insert, modify, and format source lists

Precheck

Check your current skills to help focus your study.

In Word, you can sort text in paragraphs, columns, tables, and records in a data source file. You can also select specific records in a data source file and merge them with a main document. Use the default template provided by Word to create a document or create and use your own specialized template. When you prepare research papers and reports, citing sources of information properly is important. In this chapter, you will learn to reference documents and acknowledge sources using footnotes, endnotes, citations, and source lists.

Data Files

Before beginning chapter work, copy the WL2C5 folder to your storage medium and then make WL2C5 the active folder.

SNAP

If you are a SNAP user, launch the Precheck and Tutorials from your Assignments page.

Project 1 **Sort Company Information** **2 Parts**

You will open a document containing information on company employees and then sort data in paragraphs, columns, and tables.

Preview Finished Project

Tutorial

Sorting Text in Paragraphs

Sorting Text in Paragraphs

Paragraphs of text in a document can be sorted alphanumerically, numerically, or chronologically. For example, a list of company employees can be sorted to create an internal telephone directory or a list for a company-wide mailing. Sorting items in a Word document is also an effective way to organize a list of customers by zip code or by product purchased.

In an alphanumeric sort, punctuation marks and special symbols are sorted first, followed by numbers, and then text. If paragraphs are sorted alphanumerically or numerically, dates are treated as regular text. During a paragraph sort, blank lines in a document are moved to the beginning of the sorted text.

Sort

Quick Steps

Sort Text in Paragraphs

1. Click Sort button.
2. Make changes at Sort Text dialog box.
3. Click OK.

Display the Sort Options Dialog Box

1. Click Sort button.
2. Click Options button.

To sort text, select the text and then click the Sort button in the Paragraph group on the Home tab. This displays the Sort Text dialog box, which contains sorting options. The *Sort by* option box has a default setting of *Paragraphs*. This setting changes depending on the text in the document. For example, when items within a table are being sorted, the *Sort by* option box has a default setting of *Column 1*. The *Sort by* options also vary depending on selections at the Sort Options dialog box, shown in Figure 5.1. To display this dialog box, click the Options button in the Sort Text dialog box. At the Sort Options dialog box, specify how fields are separated.

Figure 5.1 Sort Options Dialog Box

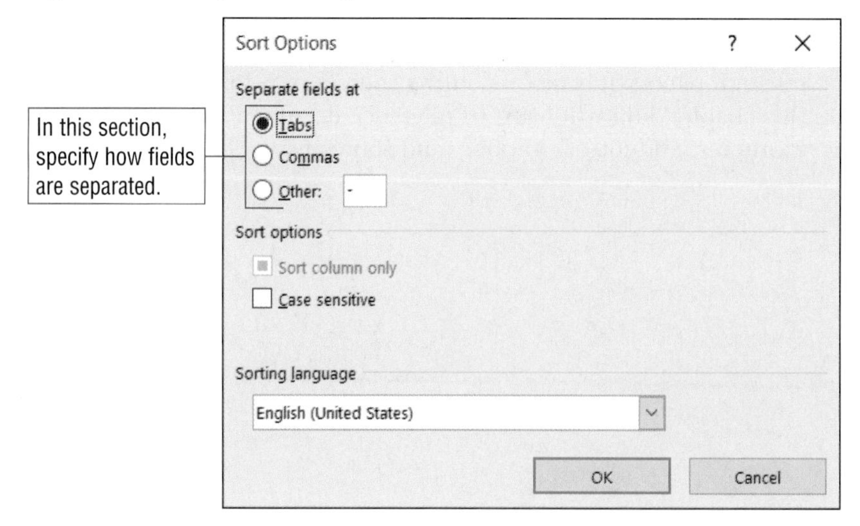

Tutorial

Sorting Text in Columns

Quick Steps

Sort Text in Columns

1. Select specific text.
2. Click Sort button.
3. Click Options button.
4. Specify *Tabs* as separator.
5. Click OK.
6. Make changes at Sort Text dialog box.
7. Click OK.

Sorting Text in Columns

To sort text set in columns, the text must be separated with tabs. When sorting text in columns, Word considers the left margin *Field 1*, text typed at the first tab *Field 2*, and so on. When sorting text in columns, make sure the columns are separated with only one tab because Word recognizes each tab as beginning a separate column. Thus, using more than one tab may result in field numbers that correspond to empty columns.

Sorting on More Than One Field

Text can be sorted on more than one field. For example, in Project 1a, Step 6, the department entries will be sorted alphabetically and then the employee names will be sorted alphabetically within the departments. To do this, specify the *Department* column in the *Sort by* option box and then specify the *Employee* column in the *Then by* option box. If a document contains columns with heading text, click the *Header row* option in the *My list has* section.

Project 1a Sorting Text

Part 1 of 2

1. Open **Sorting.docx** and then save it with the name **5-Sorting**.
2. Sort the text alphabetically by first name by completing the following steps:
   a. Select the seven lines of text at the beginning of the document.
   b. Click the Sort button in the Paragraph group on the Home tab.
   c. At the Sort Text dialog box, click OK.
3. Sort the text by last name by completing the following steps:
   a. With the seven lines of text still selected, click the Sort button.
   b. At the Sort Text dialog box, click the Options button.
   c. At the Sort Options dialog box, click *Other* and then press the spacebar. (This indicates that the first and last names are separated by a space.)
   d. Click OK.
   e. At the Sort Text dialog box, click the *Sort by* option box arrow and then click *Word 2* at the drop-down list.
   f. Click OK.

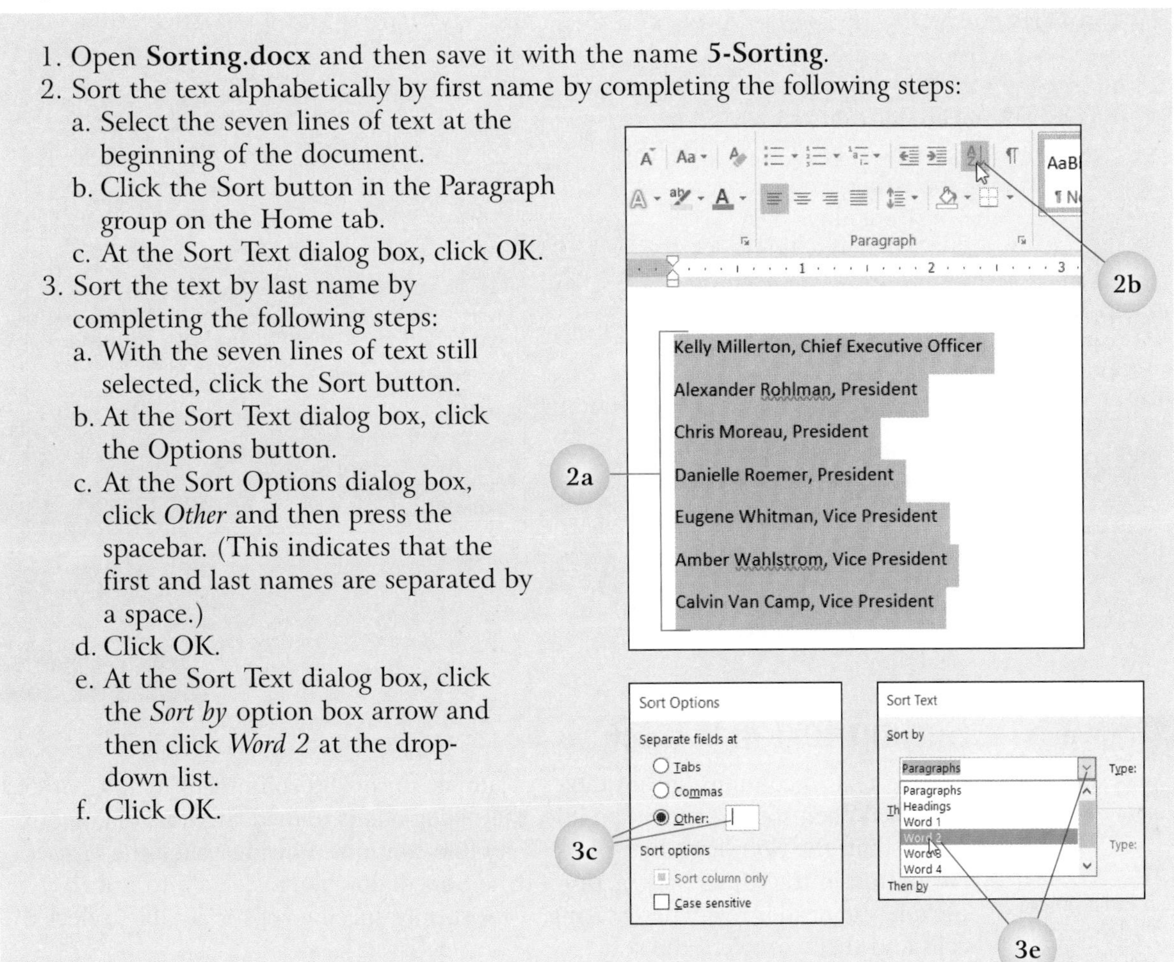

4. Sort text in columns by completing the following steps:
   a. Select the six lines of text below each of these column headings: *Employee*, *Department*, and *Ext*.
   b. Click the Sort button in the Paragraph group on the Home tab.
   c. At the Sort Text dialog box, click the Options button.
   d. At the Sort Options dialog box, make sure the *Tabs* option is selected in the *Separate fields at* section and then click OK to close the dialog box.
   e. At the Sort Text dialog box, click the *Sort by* option box arrow and then click *Field 2* at the drop-down list. (The left margin is *Field 1* and the first tab is *Field 2*.)
   f. Click OK.
5. With the six lines of text still selected, sort the third column of text numerically by completing the following steps:
   a. Click the Sort button.
   b. Click the *Sort by* option box arrow and then click *Field 4* at the drop-down list.
   c. Click OK.
6. Sort the text in the first two columns by completing the following steps:
   a. Select the seven lines of text set in the columns, including the headings.
   b. Click the Sort button.
   c. At the Sort Text dialog box, click the *Header row* option in the *My list has* section.
   d. If necessary, click the *Sort by* option box arrow and then click *Department*.
   e. Click the *Type* option box arrow in the *Sort by* section and then click *Text*.
   f. Click the *Then by* option box arrow and then click *Employee* at the drop-down list.
   g. Click OK.
7. Save **5-Sorting.docx**.

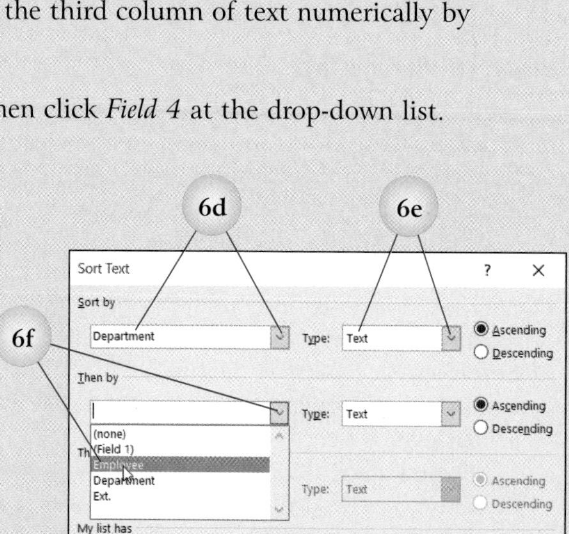

Check Your Work

Tutorial

Sorting Text in a Table

Quick Steps

Sort Text in a Table

1. Position insertion point in table.
2. Click Sort button.
3. Make changes at Sort dialog box.
4. Click OK.

Sorting Text in a Table

Sorting text in columns within tables is similar to sorting columns of text separated by tabs. When sorting text in a table, the dialog box is named the Sort dialog box rather than the Sort Text dialog box. If a table contains a header, click the *Header row* option in the *My list has* section of the Sort dialog box to tell Word not to include the header row when sorting. To sort only specific cells in a table, select the cells and then complete the sort.

Project 1b Sorting Text in a Table

Part 2 of 2

1. With **5-Sorting.docx** open, sort the text in the first column of the table by completing the following steps:
   a. Position the insertion point in any cell in the table.
   b. Click the Sort button.
   c. At the Sort dialog box, make sure the *Header row* option is selected in the *My list has* section.
   d. Click the *Sort by* option box arrow and then click *Sales, First Half* at the drop-down list.
   e. Click OK.
2. Sort the numbers in the third column in descending order by completing the following steps:
   a. Select all the cells in the table except the cells in the first row.
   b. Click the Sort button.
   c. Click the *Sort by* option box arrow and then click *Column 3* at the drop-down list.
   d. Click *Descending*.
   e. Click OK.
3. Save, print, and then close **5-Sorting.docx**.

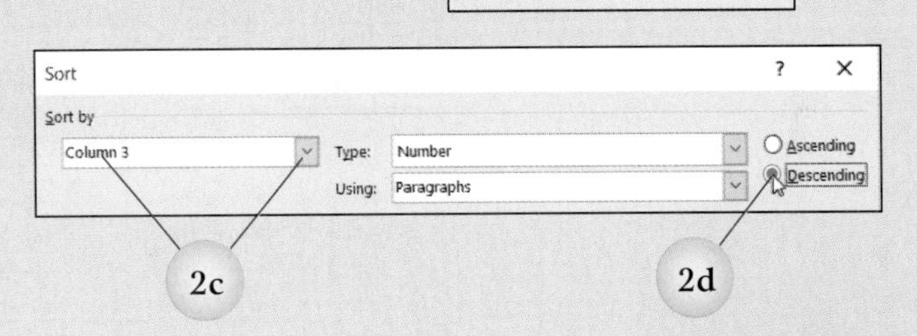

Check Your Work

Project 2 Sort, Select, and Find Records in a Data Source File

4 Parts

You will sort data in a data source file and create a labels main document. You will select and merge records and find specific records in a data source file.

Preview Finished Project

Sorting, Selecting, and Finding Records in a Data Source File

If a project requires sorting or selecting data and merging documents, consider the order in which the merged documents are to be printed or which records are to be merged and then sort and select the data before merging.

Tutorial

Sorting Records in a Data Source File

Sorting Records in a Data Source File

To sort records in a data source file, click the Mailings tab, click the Select Recipients button, and then click *Use an Existing List*. At the Select Data Source dialog box, navigate to the folder containing the data source file and then double-click the file. Click the Edit Recipient List button in the Start Mail Merge group on the Mailings tab and the Mail Merge Recipients dialog box displays, similar to the one shown in Figure 5.2.

Quick Steps

Sort Records in a Data Source File

1. Click Mailings tab.
2. Click Select Recipients button.
3. Click *Use an Existing List.*
4. Double-click file.
5. Click Edit Recipient List button.
6. At Mail Merge Recipients dialog box, sort by specific field by clicking field column heading.
7. Click OK.

Click the column heading to sort data in a specific column in ascending order. To perform an additional sort, click the down arrow at the right side of the column heading and then click the sort order. Another method for performing an additional sort is to click the Sort hyperlink in the *Refine recipient list* section of the Mail Merge Recipients dialog box. Clicking this hyperlink displays the Filter and Sort dialog box with the Sort Records tab selected, as shown in Figure 5.3. The options at the dialog box are similar to the options available at the Sort Text (and Sort) dialog box.

Figure 5.2 Mail Merge Recipients Dialog Box

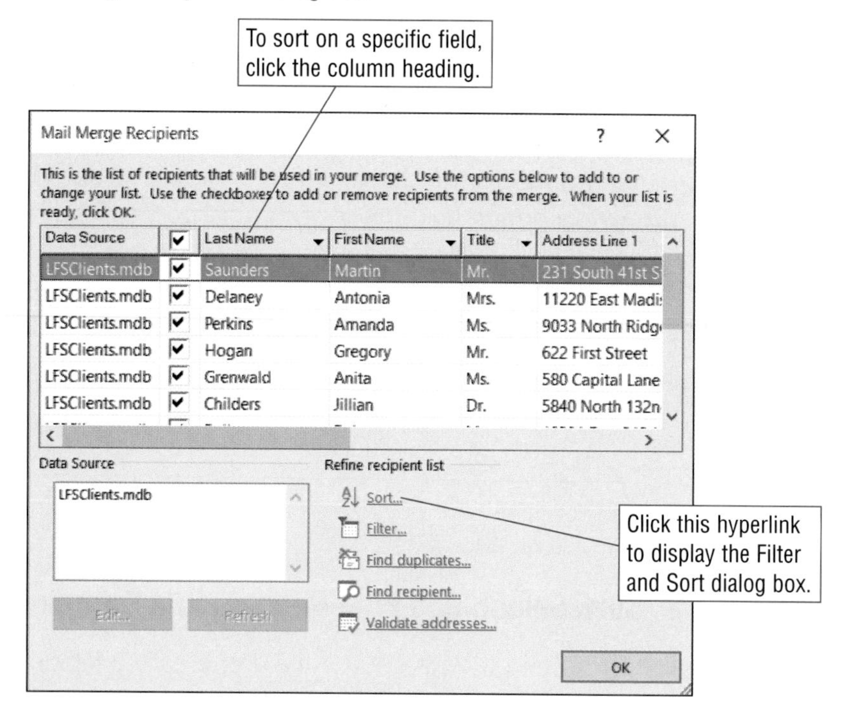

Figure 5.3 Filter and Sort Dialog Box with Sort Records Tab Selected

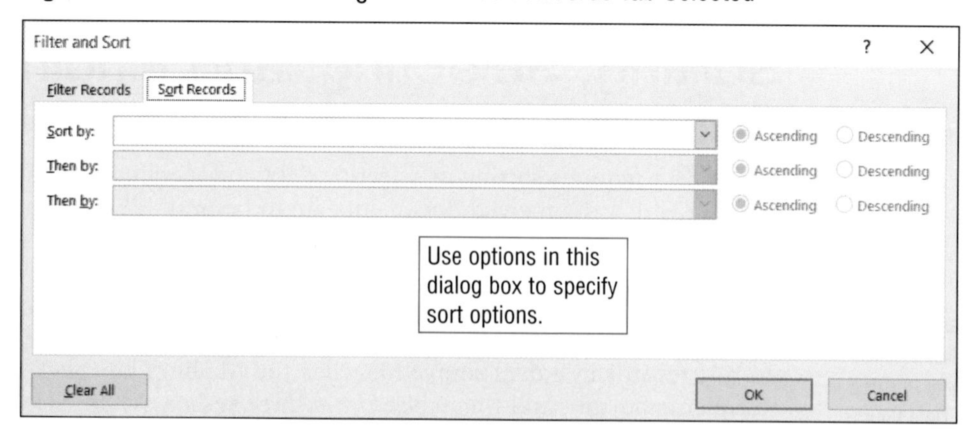

Project 2a Sorting Data in a Data Source File

Part 1 of 4

1. At a blank document, click the Mailings tab, click the Start Mail Merge button in the Start Mail Merge group, and then click *Labels* at the drop-down list.
2. At the Label Options dialog box, click the *Label vendors* option box arrow and then click *Avery US Letter* at the drop-down list.
3. Scroll down the *Product number* list box, click *5160 Easy Peel Address Labels*, and then click OK.

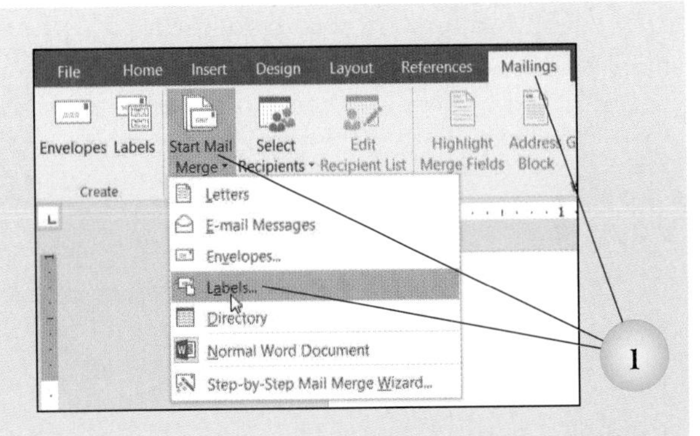

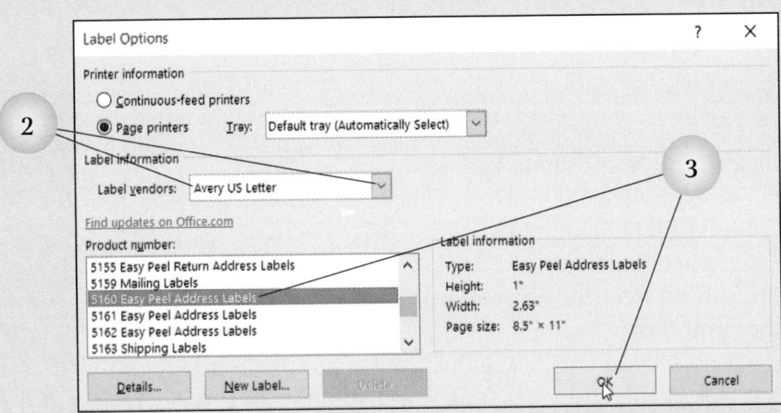

4. Click the Select Recipients button in the Start Mail Merge group and then click *Use an Existing List* at the drop-down list.
5. At the Select Data Source dialog box, navigate to the WL2C5 folder on your storage medium and then double-click the data source file named ***LFSClients.mdb***.
6. Click the Edit Recipient List button in the Start Mail Merge group on the Mailings tab.
7. At the Mail Merge Recipients dialog box, click the *Last Name* column heading. (This sorts the last names in ascending alphabetical order.)
8. Scroll right to display the *City* field and then click the *City* column heading.
9. Sort records by zip code and then by last name by completing the following steps:
   a. Click the Sort hyperlink in the *Refine recipient list* section of the Mail Merge Recipients dialog box.

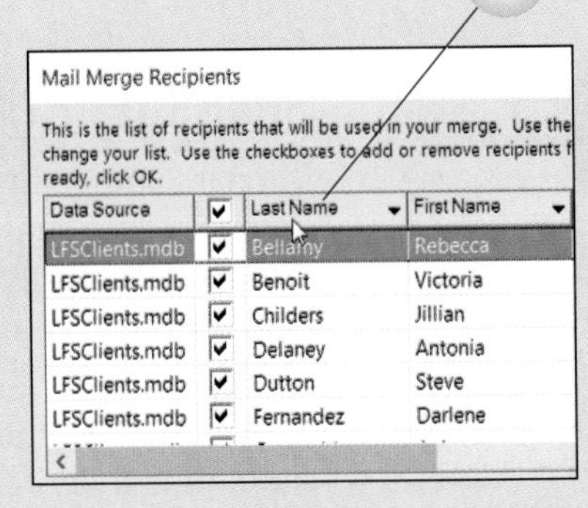

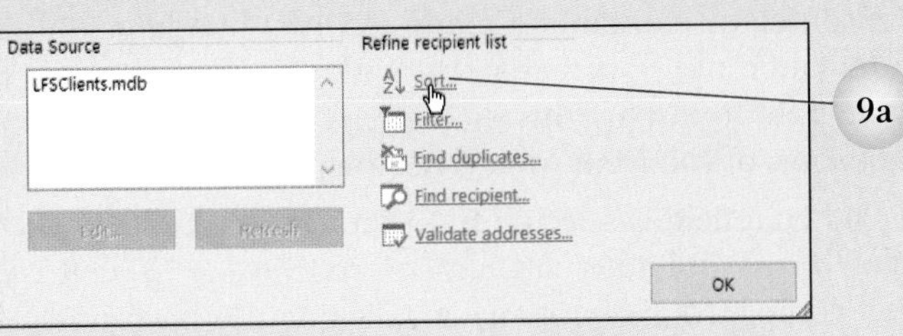

b. At the Filter and Sort dialog box with the Sort Records tab selected, click the *Sort by* option box arrow and then click *ZIP Code* at the drop-down list. (You will need to scroll down the list to display the *ZIP Code* field.)
c. Make sure *Last Name* displays in the *Then by* option box.
d. Click OK to close the Filter and Sort dialog box.

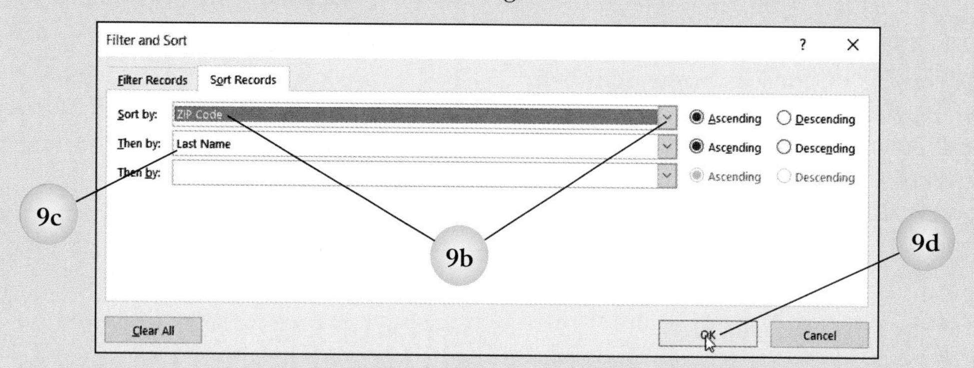

e. Click OK to close the Mail Merge Recipients dialog box.

10. At the labels document, click the Address Block button in the Write & Insert Fields group.
11. At the Insert Address Block dialog box, click OK.
12. Click the Update Labels button in the Write & Insert Fields group.
13. Click the Finish & Merge button in the Finish group and then click *Edit Individual Documents* at the drop-down list.
14. At the Merge to New Document dialog box, make sure *All* is selected and then click OK.
15. Press Ctrl + A to select the entire document and then click the *No Spacing* style in the Styles group on the Home tab.
16. Save the merged labels and name the document **5-Lbls01**.
17. Print and then close **5-Lbls01.docx**.
18. Close the labels main document without saving it.

Check Your Work

Tutorial

Selecting Specific Records for Merging

Hint Including or excluding certain records from a merge is referred to as *filtering*.

Selecting Records in a Data Source File

If a data source file contains numerous records, specific records can be selected from the data source file and then merged with a main document. For example, records with a specific zip code or city can be selected from a data source file. One method for selecting records is to display the Mail Merge Recipients dialog box and then insert or remove check marks from specific records.

Using check boxes to select specific records is useful in a data source file containing a limited number of records; however, it may not be practical in a data source file containing many records. In a large data source file, use options at the Filter and Sort dialog box with the Filter Records tab selected, as shown in Figure 5.4. To display this dialog box, click the Filter hyperlink in the *Refine recipient list* section of the Mail Merge Recipients dialog box.

When a field is selected from the *Field* drop-down list at the Filter and Sort dialog box, Word automatically inserts *Equal to* in the *Comparison* option box but other comparisons can be made. Clicking the *Comparison* option box arrow displays a drop-down list with these additional options: *Not equal to*, *Less than*, *Greater than*, *Less than or equal*, *Greater than or equal*, *Is blank*, and *Is not blank*. Use one of these options to create a select equation.

Figure 5.4 Filter and Sort Dialog Box with Filter Records Tab Selected

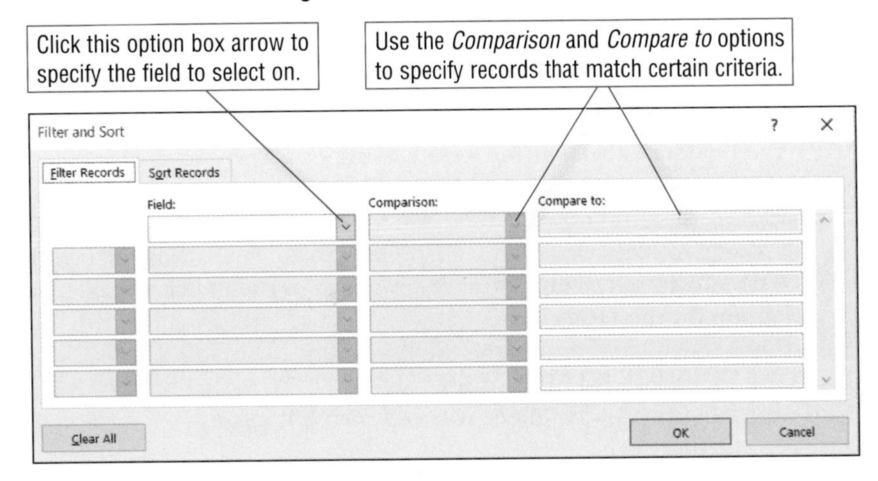

Project 2b Selecting Records in a Data Source File

Part 2 of 4

1. At a blank document, click the Mailings tab, click the Start Mail Merge button in the Start Mail Merge group, and then click *Labels* at the drop-down list.
2. At the Label Options dialog box, make sure *Avery US Letter* displays in the *Label vendors* option box and *5160 Easy Peel Address Labels* displays in the *Product number* list box and then click OK.
3. Click the Select Recipients button in the Start Mail Merge group and then click *Use an Existing List* at the drop-down list.
4. At the Select Data Source dialog box, navigate to the WL2C5 folder on your storage medium and then double-click the data source file named ***LFSClients.mdb***.
5. Click the Edit Recipient List button.
6. At the Mail Merge Recipients dialog box, click the Filter hyperlink in the *Refine recipient list* section.
7. At the Filter and Sort dialog box with the Filter Records tab selected, click the *Field* option box arrow and then click *ZIP Code* at the drop-down list. (You will need to scroll down the list to display *ZIP Code*. When *ZIP Code* is inserted in the *Field* option box, *Equal to* is inserted in the *Comparison* option box, and the insertion point is positioned in the *Compare to* text box.)
8. Type 21000 in the *Compare to* text box.
9. Click the *Comparison* option box arrow and then click *Greater than* at the drop-down list.

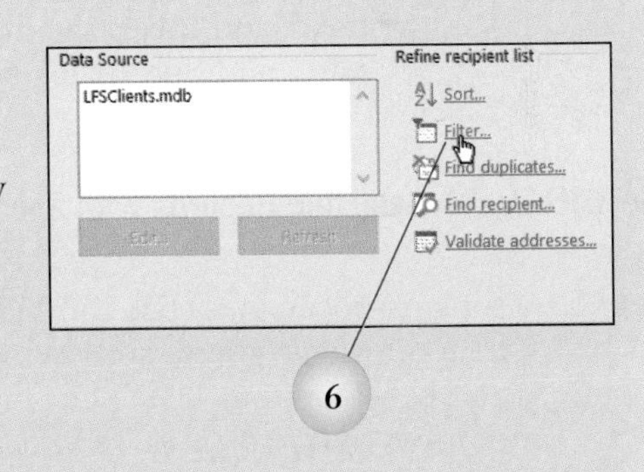

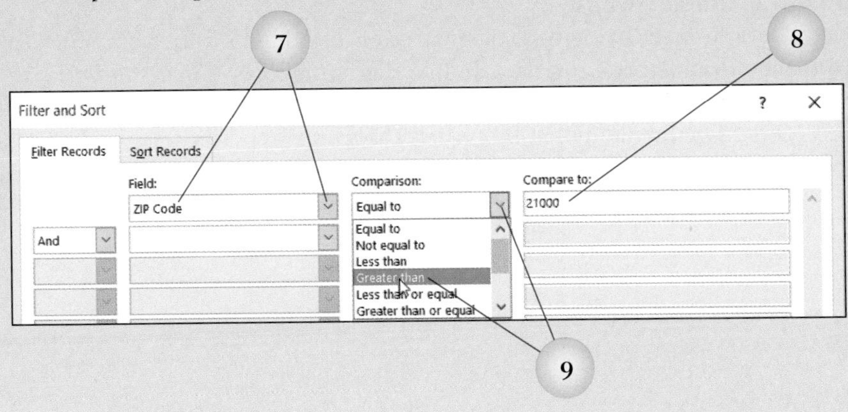

10. Click OK to close the Filter and Sort dialog box.
11. Click OK to close the Mail Merge Recipients dialog box.
12. At the labels document, click the Address Block button in the Write & Insert Fields group and then click OK at the Insert Address Block dialog box.
13. Click the Update Labels button in the Write & Insert Fields group.
14. Click the Finish & Merge button in the Finish group and then click *Edit Individual Documents* at the drop-down list.
15. At the Merge to New Document dialog box, make sure *All* is selected and then click OK.
16. Press Ctrl + A to select the entire document and then click the *No Spacing* style in the Styles group on the Home tab.
17. Save the merged labels and name the document **5-Lbls02**.
18. Print and then close **5-Lbls02.docx**.
19. Close the labels main document without saving it.

Check Your Work

When a field is selected from the *Field* option box, Word automatically inserts *And* in the first box at the left side of the dialog box but this can be changed to *Or* if necessary. With the *And* and *Or* options, more than one condition for selecting records can be specified. For example, in Project 2c, all the records of clients living in the cities Rosedale or Towson will be selected. If the data source file contained another field, such as a specific financial plan for each customer, all the customers living in these two cities that subscribe to a specific financial plan could be selected. In this situation, the *And* option would be used.

To clear the current options at the Filter and Sort dialog box with the Filter Records tab selected, click the Clear All button. This clears all the text from text boxes and leaves the dialog box on the screen. Click the Cancel button to close the Filter and Sort dialog box without specifying any records.

Project 2c Selecting Records with Specific Cities in a Data Source File — Part 3 of 4

1. At a blank document, click the Mailings tab, click the Start Mail Merge button in the Start Mail Merge group, and then click *Labels* at the drop-down list.
2. At the Label Options dialog box, make sure *Avery US Letter* displays in the *Label vendors* option box and *5160 Easy Peel Address Labels* displays in the *Product number* list box and then click OK.
3. Click the Select Recipients button in the Start Mail Merge group and then click *Use an Existing List* at the drop-down list.
4. At the Select Data Source dialog box, navigate to the WL2C5 folder on your storage medium and then double-click the data source file named ***LFSClients.mdb***.
5. Click the Edit Recipient List button.
6. At the Mail Merge Recipients dialog box, click the Filter hyperlink in the *Refine recipient list* section.

7. At the Filter and Sort dialog box with the Filter Records tab selected, click the *Field* option box arrow and then click *City* at the drop-down list. (You will need to scroll down the list to display this field.)
8. Type Rosedale in the *Compare to* text box.
9. Click the option box arrow for the option box containing the word *And* (at the left side of the dialog box) and then click *Or* at the drop-down list.
10. Click the second *Field* option box arrow and then click *City* at the drop-down list. (You will need to scroll down the list to display this field.)
11. With the insertion point positioned in the second *Compare to* text box (the one below the box containing *Rosedale*), type Towson.
12. Click OK to close the Filter and Sort dialog box.

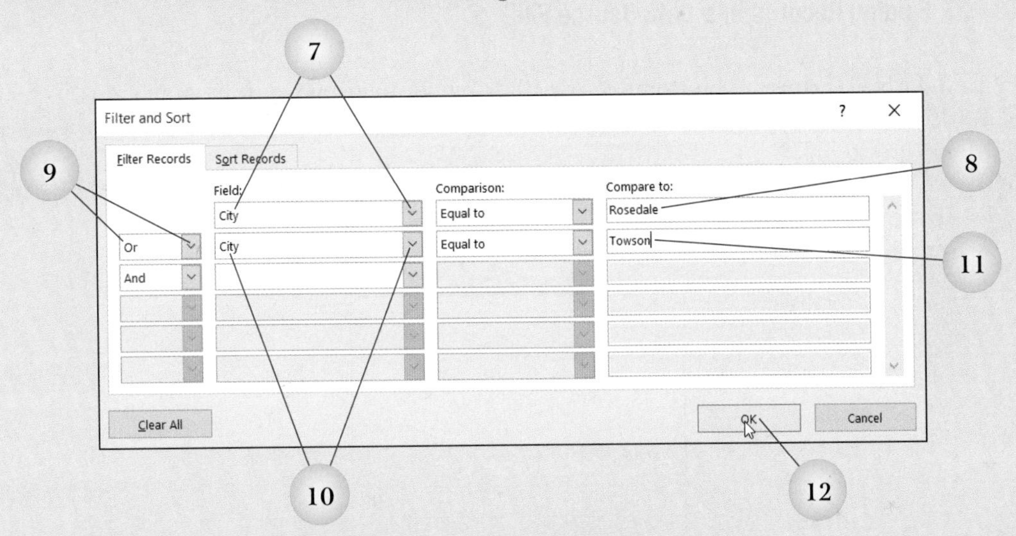

13. Click OK to close the Mail Merge Recipients dialog box.
14. At the labels document, click the Address Block button in the Write & Insert Fields group and then click OK at the Insert Address Block dialog box.
15. Click the Update Labels button in the Write & Insert Fields group.
16. Click the Finish & Merge button in the Finish group and then click *Edit Individual Documents* at the drop-down list.
17. At the Merge to New Document dialog box, make sure *All* is selected and then click OK.
18. Press Ctrl + A to select the entire document and then click the *No Spacing* style in the Styles group on the Home tab.
19. Save the merged labels and name the document **5-Lbls03**.
20. Print and then close **5-Lbls03.docx**.
21. Save the labels main document and name it **5-LblsMD**.

Check Your Work

Tutorial

Finding Records in a Data Source File

Hint Visit the Microsoft Office website to find more information about address validation software.

Finding Records in a Data Source File

The Find duplicates and Find recipient hyperlinks in the *Refine recipient list* section of the Mail Merge Recipients dialog box can be useful for finding records in an extensive data source file. Use the Find duplicates hyperlink to locate duplicate records that appear in the data source file. Use the Find recipient hyperlink to find a record or records that meet a specific criterion. The Validate addresses hyperlink in the *Refine recipient list* section is available only if address validation software has been installed.

Click the Find duplicates hyperlink and any duplicate records display in the Find Duplicates dialog box. At this dialog box, remove the check mark from the duplicate record check box that should not be included in the merge. To find a specific record in a data source file, click the Find recipient hyperlink. At the Find Entry dialog box, type the find text and then click the Find Next button. Continue clicking the Find Next button until a message displays indicating that there are no more entries that contain the text. By default, Word searches for the specified text in all of the fields of all of the records in the data source file. The search can be limited by clicking the *This field* option box arrow and then clicking the specific field. Type the text to find in the *Find* text box and then click OK.

Project 2d Finding Records in a Data Source File

Part 4 of 4

1. With **5-LblsMD.docx** open, remove the filter by completing the following steps:
   a. With the Mailings tab active, click the Edit Recipient List button in the Start Mail Merge group.
   b. At the Mail Merge Recipients dialog box, click the Filter hyperlink in the *Refine recipient list* section.
   c. At the Filter and Sort dialog box, click the Clear All button.

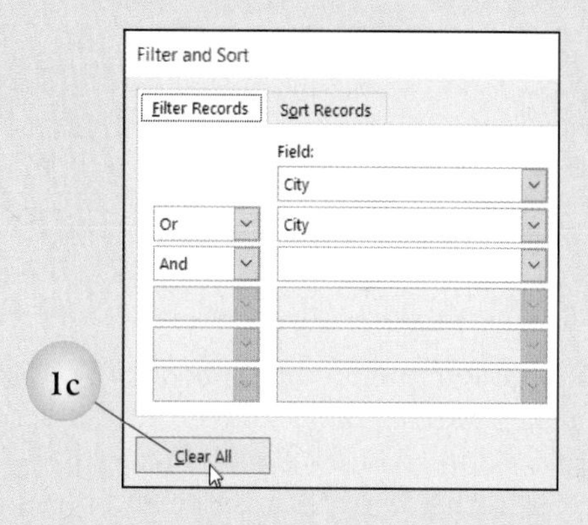

   d. Click OK to close the Filter and Sort dialog box.
   e. At the Mail Merge Recipients dialog box, click the Find duplicates hyperlink in the *Refine recipient list* section.
   f. At the Find Duplicates dialog box, which indicates that there are no duplicate items, click OK.
2. Find all records containing the zip code *20376* by completing the following steps:
   a. At the Mail Merge Recipients dialog box, click the Find recipient hyperlink in the *Refine recipient list* section.
   b. At the Find Entry dialog box, type 20376 in the *Find* text box.
   c. Click the *This field* option box arrow and then click *ZIP Code* at the drop-down list. (You will need to scroll down the list to display this option.)
   d. Click the Find Next button.
   e. When the first record is selected containing the zip code *20376*, click the Find Next button.
   f. When the second record is selected containing the zip code *20376*, click the Find Next button.

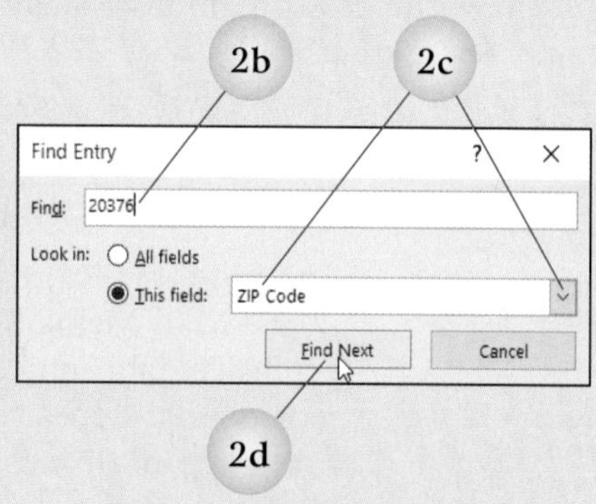

g. At the message indicating that there are no more entries that contain the text you typed, click OK.
h. Click the Cancel button to close the Find Entry dialog box.
3. Select and then merge records of those clients with a zip code of *20376* by completing the following steps:
a. At the Mail Merge Recipients dialog box, click the Filter hyperlink in the *Refine recipient list* section of the dialog box.
b. At the Filter and Sort dialog box, click the *Field* option box arrow and then click *ZIP Code* at the drop-down list. (You will need to scroll down the list to display this field.)
c. Type 20376 in the *Compare to* text box.
d. Click OK to close the Filter and Sort dialog box.
e. Click OK to close the Mail Merge Recipients dialog box.
4. At the label document, click the Finish & Merge button in the Finish group and then click *Edit Individual Documents* at the drop-down list.
5. At the Merge to New Document dialog box, make sure that *All* is selected and then click OK.
6. Save the merged labels and name the document **5-Lbls-04**.
7. Print and then close **5-Lbls-04.docx**.
8. Save and then close **5-LblsMD.docx**.

Check Your Work

Project 3 Save and Use a Summons Template

2 Parts

You will open a summons legal document, save it as a template, and then use it to create other summons documents.

Preview Finished Project

Tutorial

Saving and Using a Template

Quick Steps

Save a Template

1. Display Save As dialog box.
2. Change *Save as type* to *Word Template (*.dotx)*.
3. Type template name in *File name* text box.
4. Click Save.

Saving and Using a Template

If the content of a document is used to create other documents, consider saving the document as a template. Save a personal template in the Custom Office Templates folder in the Documents folder on the hard drive. A template saved in the Custom Office Templates folder will display in the New backstage area with the *PERSONAL* option selected.

To save a document as a template, display the Save As dialog box, change the *Save as type* option to *Word Template (*.dotx)*, type a name for the template, and then press the Enter key. When the *Save as type* option is changed to *Word Template (*.dotx)*, Word automatically makes Custom Office Templates the active folder. Word templates are saved with the .dotx file extension. A template also can be saved as a macro-enabled template with the .dotm file extension.

Another method for saving a template is to display the Export backstage area, click the *Change File Type* option, click the *Template (*.dotx)* option, and then click the Save As button. At the Save As dialog box, type a name for the template, and then click the Save button.

Project 3a Saving a Document as a Template

Part 1 of 2

Note: Before completing this project, check to make sure you can save a template in the Custom Office Templates folder in the Documents folder on the hard drive. If not, please check with your instructor.

1. Open **Summons.docx**.
2. Save the document as a template in the Custom Office Templates folder by completing the following steps:
   a. Press the F12 function key.
   b. At the Save As dialog box, click the *Save as type* option box and then click *Word Template (*.dotx)*. (When the *Save as type* option is changed to *Word Template (*.dotx)*, Word automatically makes Custom Office Templates the active folder.)
   c. Select the name in the *File name* text box and then type your last name followed by *Summons*.
   d. Press the Enter key or click the Save button.
3. Close the summons template.

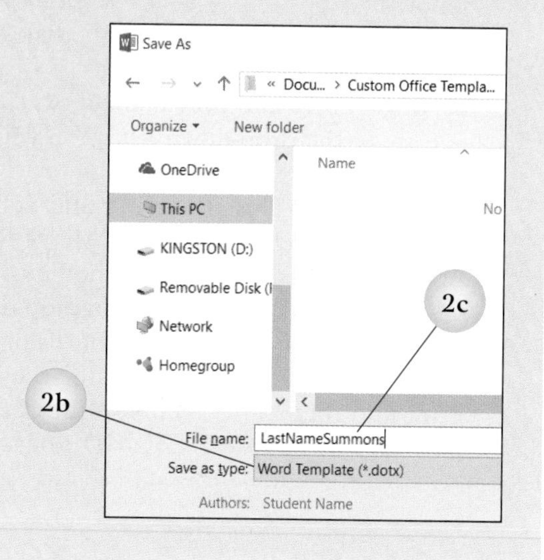

Quick Steps

Open a Document Based on a Template

1. Click File tab.
2. Click *New* option.
3. Click *PERSONAL*.
4. Click template.

To open a document based on a template saved in the Custom Office Templates folder, click the File tab and then click the *New* option. At the New backstage area, click the *PERSONAL* option. This displays the templates available in the Custom Office Templates folder. Click a template to open a document based on that template.

Project 3b Opening a Document Based on a Template

Part 2 of 2

1. Open a document based on the summons template by completing the following steps:
   a. Click the File tab.
   b. Click the *New* option.
   c. At the New backstage area, click the *PERSONAL* option.
   d. Click the summons template that is preceded by your last name.
2. With the summons document open, find and replace text as follows:
   a. Find *NAME1* and replace all occurrences with *AMY GARCIA*.
   b. Find *NAME2* and replace all occurrences with *NEIL CARLIN*.
   c. Find *NUMBER* and replace with *C-98002*.
3. Save the document in the WL2C5 folder on your storage medium and name it **5-Summons**.

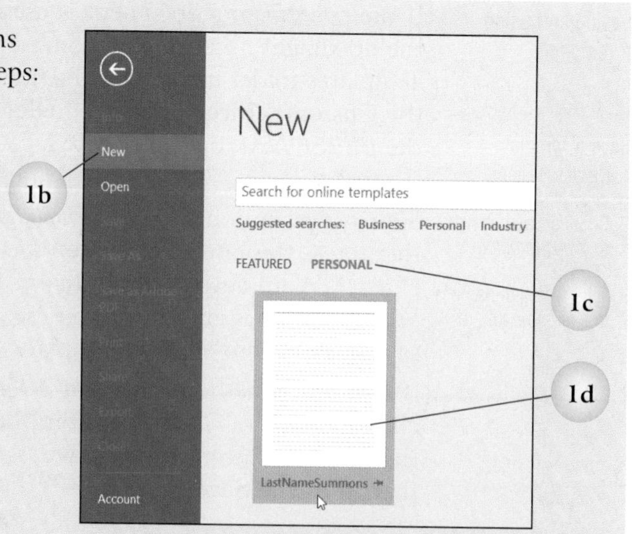

4. Print and then close **5-Summons.docx**.
5. Delete the summons template from the hard drive by completing the following steps:
   a. Press Ctrl + F12 to display the Open dialog box.
   b. At the Open dialog box, click *Documents* in the Navigation pane.
   c. Double-click the *Custom Office Templates* folder in the Content pane.
   d. Click the summons template that begins with your last name.
   e. Click the Organize button and then click *Delete* at the drop-down list.
   f. At the message asking if you want to move the file to the Recycle Bin, click the Yes button.
6. Close the Open dialog box.

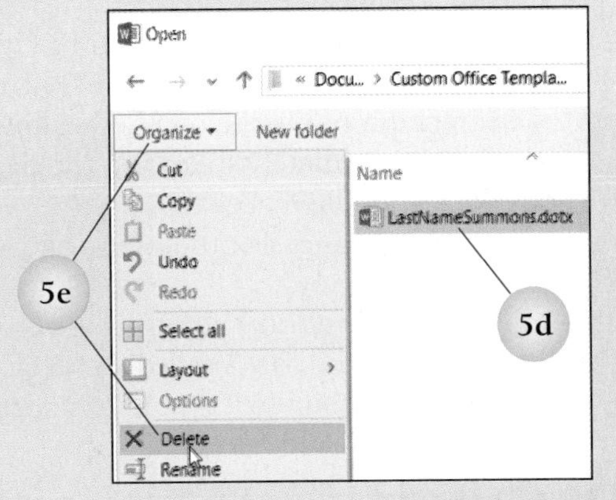

Check Your Work

Project 4 Insert Footnotes and Endnotes in Reports — 3 Parts

You will open a report on pioneers of computing intelligence and then insert, format, and modify footnotes. You will also open a report on technology visionaries and then insert endnotes.

Preview Finished Project

Tutorial

Inserting Footnotes and Endnotes

Hint Ctrl + Alt + F is the keyboard shortcut to insert a footnote and Ctrl + Alt + D is the keyboard shortcut to insert an endnote.

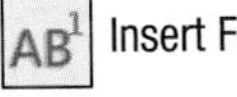

Insert Footnote

Insert Endnote

Quick Steps

Insert a Footnote
1. Click References tab.
2. Click Insert Footnote button.
3. Type footnote text.

Insert an Endnote
1. Click References tab.
2. Click Insert Endnote button.
3. Type endnote text.

Inserting Footnotes and Endnotes

A research paper or report contains information from a variety of sources. To give credit to those sources, footnotes or endnotes can be inserted in a document formatted in a specific reference style, such as that of the *Chicago Manual of Style*. (You will learn more about different reference styles in the next project.) A footnote is an explanatory note or source reference that is printed at the bottom of the page on which the corresponding information appears. An endnote is also an explanatory note or reference but it is printed at the end of the document.

Two steps are involved in creating a footnote or endnote. First, the note reference number is inserted in the document where the corresponding information appears. Second, the note entry text is typed. Footnotes and endnotes are created in a similar manner.

To create a footnote, position the insertion point where the reference number is to appear, click the References tab, and then click the Insert Footnote button in the Footnotes group. This inserts a number in the document along with a separator line at the bottom of the page and a superscript number below it. With the insertion point positioned immediately right of the superscript number, type the note entry text. By default, Word numbers footnotes with superscript arabic numbers and endnotes with superscript lowercase roman numerals.

Project 4a Creating Footnotes

Part 1 of 3

1. Open **CompPioneers.docx** and then save it with the name **5-CompPioneers.**
2. Create the first footnote shown in Figure 5.7 by completing the following steps:
   a. Position the insertion point at the end of the first paragraph of text below the heading *Konrad Zuse* (immediately following the period).
   b. Click the References tab.
   c. Click the Insert Footnote button in the Footnotes group.
   d. With the insertion point positioned at the bottom of the page immediately following the superscript number, type the first footnote shown in Figure 5.7.

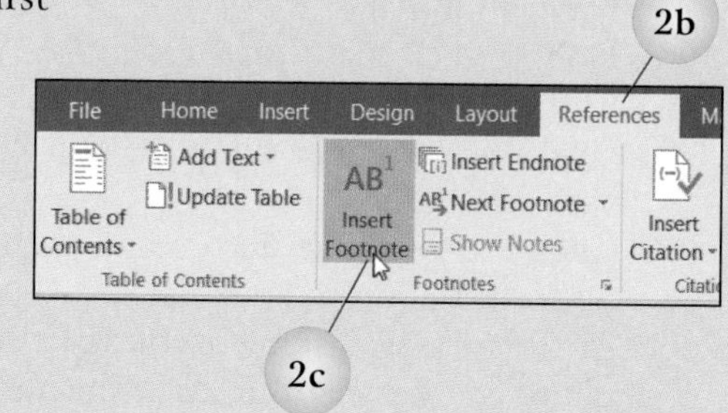

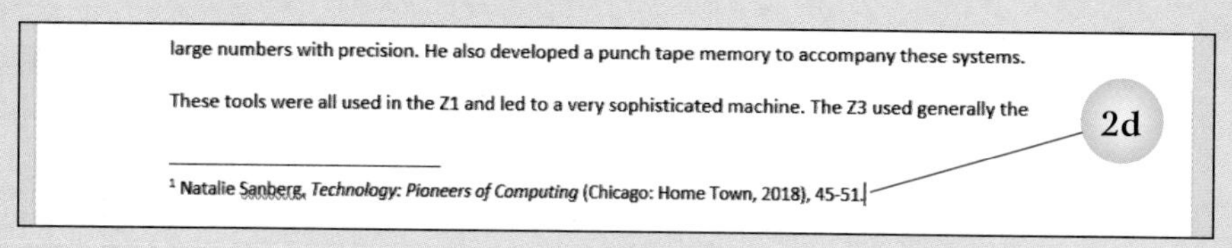

3. Move the insertion point to the end of the third paragraph below the heading *Konrad Zuse*. Using steps similar to those in Steps 2c and 2d, create the second footnote shown in Figure 5.7.
4. Move the insertion point to the end of the last paragraph below the heading *Konrad Zuse* and then create the third footnote shown in Figure 5.7.
5. Move the insertion point to the end of the third paragraph below the heading *William Hewlett and David Packard* and then create the fourth footnote shown in Figure 5.7.
6. Move the insertion point to the end of the last paragraph in the document and then create the fifth foonote shown in Figure 5.7.
7. Save, print, and then close **5-CompPioneers.docx**.

Check Your Work

Figure 5.7 Project 5a

Natalie Sanberg, *Technology: Pioneers of Computing* (Chicago: Home Town, 2018), 45-51.

Miguel Whitworth and Danielle Reyes, "Development of Computing," *Design Technologies* (2017): 24-26.

Sam Wells, *Biographies of Computing Pioneers* (San Francisco: Laurelhurst, 2018), 20-23.

Terrell Montgomery, *History of Computers* (Boston: Langley-Paulsen, 2018), 13-15.

Justin Evans, "Hewlett-Packard's Impact on Computing," *Computing Technologies* (2018): 7-12.

Printing Footnotes and Endnotes

When printing a document containing footnotes, Word automatically reduces the number of lines of text on each page to create the space needed for the footnotes and separator line. If a page does not have enough space, the footnote number and entry text are moved to the next page. Word separates the footnotes from the text with a 2-inch separator line that begins at the left margin. When endnotes are created in a document, Word prints all the endnote references at the end of the document, separated from the text by a 2-inch line.

Project 4b Creating Endnotes

Part 2 of 3

1. Open **TechVisionaries.docx** and then save it with the name **5-TechVisionaries**.
2. Create the first endnote shown in Figure 5.8 by completing the following steps:
   a. Position the insertion point at the end of the second paragraph below the heading *Gordon E. Moore*.
   b. Click the References tab.
   c. Click the Insert Endnote button in the Footnotes group.
   d. Type the first endnote shown in Figure 5.8.
3. Move the insertion point to the end of the fourth paragraph below the heading *Jack S. Kilby* and then complete steps similar to those in Steps 2c and 2d to create the second endnote shown in Figure 5.8.
4. Move the insertion point to the end of the first paragraph below the heading *Linus Torvalds* and then create the third endnote shown in Figure 5.8.
5. Move the insertion point to the end of the last paragraph in the document and then create the fourth endnote shown in Figure 5.8.
6. Save **5-TechVisionaries.docx**.

Check Your Work

Figure 5.8 Project 4b

Gina Shaw, *History of Computing Technologies* (Los Angeles: Gleason Rutherford, 2018), 11-14.

Ellen Littleton, "Jack Kilby: Nobel Prize Winner," *Horizon Computing* (Boston: Robison, 2018): 23-51.

Eric Ventrella, "Computer Nerd Hero," *Computing Today* (2018): 5-10.

Joseph Daniels, "Linus Torvalds: Technology Visionary," *Connections* (2018): 13-17.

Tutorial

Viewing and Editing Footnotes and Endnotes

Next Footnote

Show Notes

Hint To view the entry text for a footnote or endnote where the note occurs within the document, position the mouse pointer on the note reference number. The footnote or endnote text displays in a box above the number.

Viewing and Editing Footnotes and Endnotes

To view the footnotes in a document, click the Next Footnote button in the Footnotes group on the References tab. This moves the insertion point to the first footnote reference number following the insertion point. To view the endnotes in a document, click the Next Footnote button arrow and then click *Next Endnote* at the drop-down list. Use other options at the Next Footnote button drop-down list to view the previous footnote, next endnote, or previous endnote. Move the insertion point to specific footnote text with the Show Notes button.

If a footnote or endnote reference number is moved, copied, or deleted, all the remaining footnotes or endnotes automatically renumber. To move a footnote or endnote, select the reference number and then click the Cut button in the Clipboard group on the Home tab. Position the insertion point at the new location and then click the Paste button in the Clipboard group. To delete a footnote or endnote, select the reference number and then press the Delete key. This deletes the reference number as well as the footnote or endnote text.

Click the Footnotes group dialog box launcher and the Footnote and Endnote dialog box displays, as shown in Figure 5.9. Use options at this dialog box to convert footnotes to endnotes and endnotes to footnotes; change the locations of footnotes or endnotes; change the number formatting; start footnote or endnote numbering with a specific number, letter, and symbol; or change numbering within sections in a document.

Figure 5.9 Footnote and Endnote Dialog Box

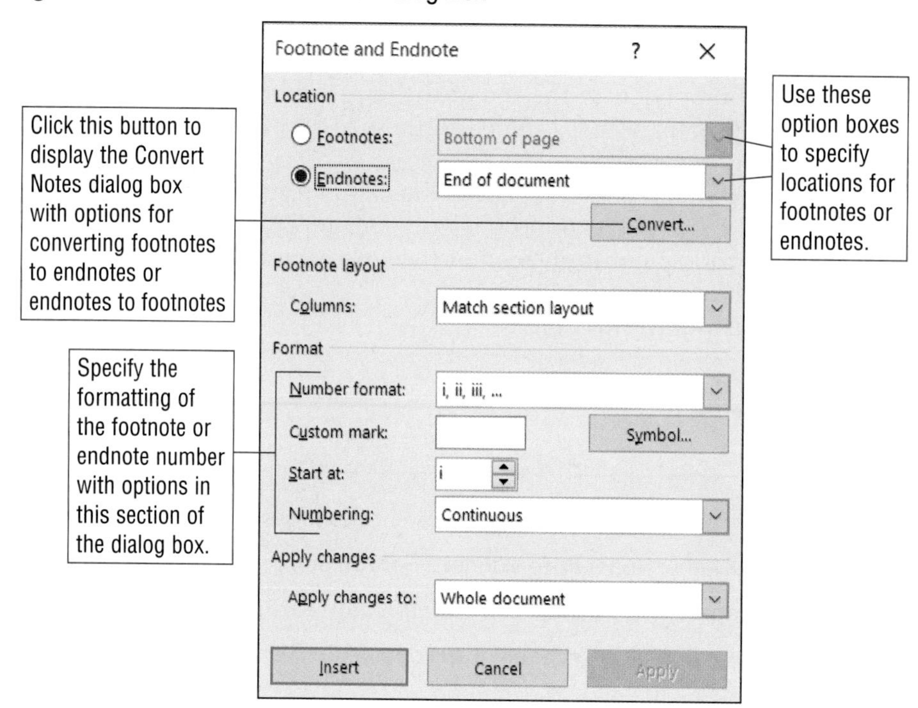

Project 4c Editing Endnotes, Converting Endnotes to Footnotes, and Editing Footnotes — Part 3 of 3

1. With **5-TechVisionaries.docx** open, press Ctrl + Home to move the insertion point to the beginning of the document and then edit the endnotes by completing the following steps:
   a. If necessary, click the References tab.
   b. Click the Next Footnote button arrow and then click *Next Endnote* at the drop-down list.
   c. Click the Show Notes button to display the endnote text.
   d. Change the page numbers for the Gina Shaw entry from *11-14* to *6-10*.
   e. Click the Show Notes button again to return to the reference number in the document.
2. Press Ctrl + A to select the document (but not the endnote entry text) and then change the font to Constantia.
3. Change the font for the endnotes by completing the following steps:
   a. Press Ctrl + End to move the insertion point to the end of the document.
   b. Click in any endnote entry and then press Ctrl + A to select all the endnote entries.
   c. Change the font to Constantia.
   d. Press Ctrl + Home.

4. Convert the endnotes to footnotes by completing the following steps:
   a. Click the References tab and then click the Footnotes group dialog box launcher.
   b. At the Footnote and Endnote dialog box, click the Convert button.
   c. At the Convert Notes dialog box with the *Convert all endnotes to footnotes* option selected, click OK.
   d. Click the Close button to close the Footnote and Endnote dialog box.
5. Change the footnote number format by completing the following steps:
   a. Click the Footnotes group dialog box launcher.
   b. Click the *Footnotes* option in the *Location* section of the dialog box.
   c. Click the *Footnotes* option box arrow and then click *Below text* at the drop-down list.
   d. Click the *Number format* option box arrow in the *Format* section and then click *a, b, c, …* at the drop-down list.
   e. Change the starting number by clicking the *Start at* measurement box up arrow until *d* displays in the measurement box.
   f. Click the Apply button and then scroll through the document and notice the renumbering of the footnotes.

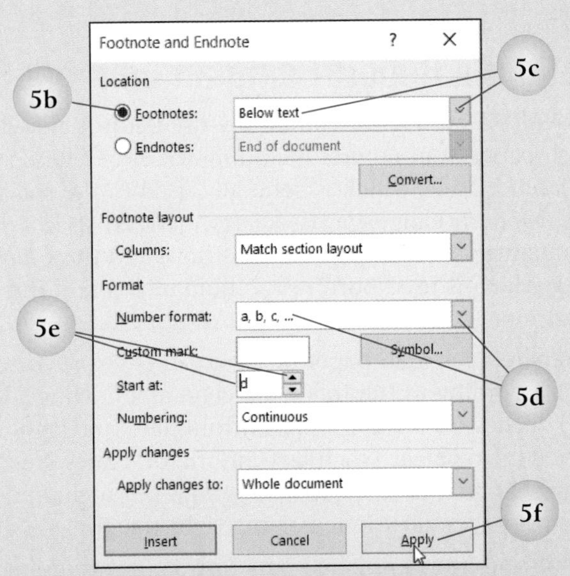

6. Change the footnote number format back to arabic numbers by completing the following steps:
   a. With the References tab active, click the Footnotes group dialog box launcher.
   b. At the Footnote and Endnote dialog box, click the *Footnotes* option in the *Location* section.
   c. Click the *Number format* option box arrow in the *Format* section and then click *1, 2, 3, …* at the drop-down list.
   d. Change the starting number back to 1 by clicking the *Start at* measurement box down arrow until *1* displays in the measurement box.
   e. Click the Apply button.
7. Delete the third footnote by completing the following steps:
   a. Press Ctrl + Home.
   b. Make sure the References tab is active and then click the Next Footnote button in the Footnotes group three times.
   c. Select the third footnote reference number (superscript number) and then press the Delete key.
8. Save, print, and then close **5-TechVisionaries.docx**.

Check Your Work

Project 5 Cite Sources in a Mobile Security Report **8 Parts**

You will open a report on securing mobile devices, add information and insert source citations and a bibliography, and then modify and customize citation styles.

Preview Finished Project

Citing and Editing Sources

In addition to using footnotes and endnotes to credit sources in a research paper or manuscript, consider inserting in-text citations and a works cited page to identify sources of quotations, facts, theories, and other borrowed or summarized material. An in-text citation acknowledges that information is being borrowed from a source. Not acknowledging someone else's words or ideas is called *plagiarizing*.

Tutorial

Formatting a Report in MLA Style

Formatting a Report Using an Editorial Style

Word provides a number of commonly used editorial styles for citing references in research papers and reports including the American Psychological Association (APA) reference style, which is generally used in the social sciences and research fields; the Modern Language Association (MLA) style, which is generally used in the humanities and English composition; and the *Chicago Manual of Style* (Chicago), which is used both in the humanities and the social sciences and is considered more complex than either APA or MLA style.

To prepare a research paper or report in APA or MLA style, format the document according to the following general guidelines: Use standard-sized paper (8.5 × 11 inches); set 1-inch top, bottom, left, and right margins; format text in a 12-point serif typeface (such as Cambria or Times New Roman); double-space text; indent the first line of each paragraph 0.5 inch; and insert page numbers in the header of pages, positioned at the right margin.

When formatting a research paper or report according to the MLA or APA style, follow certain guidelines for properly formatting the first page of the document. With MLA style, at the beginning of the first page, at the left margin, insert the author's name (person writing the report), the instructor's name, the course title, and the current date. Double space after each of the four lines. Type the title of the document a double-space below the current date and then center the title. Also double-space between the title and the first line of text. The text should be left aligned and double spaced. Finally, insert a header in the upper right corner of the document that includes the author's last name and page number.

When using APA style, create a title page that is separate from the body of the document. On this page, include the title of the paper, the author's name, and the school's name, all double-spaced, centered, and positioned on the upper half of the page. Also include a header with the text *Running Head:* followed by the title of the paper in uppercase letters at the left margin and the page number at the right margin.

Project 5a Formatting the First Page of a Research Paper in MLA Style

1. Open **MobileSecurity.docx** and then save it with the name **5-MobileSecurity**.
2. Format the document in MLA Style by completing the following steps:
   a. Press Ctrl + A to select the entire document.
   b. Change the font to Cambria and the font size to 12 points.
   c. Change the line spacing to double spacing (2.0).
   d. Remove extra spacing after paragraphs by clicking the Layout tab, clicking in the *After* measurement box in the *Spacing* section in the Paragraph group, typing 0, and then pressing the Enter key.
   e. Press Ctrl + Home to position the insertion point at the beginning of the document. Type your first and last names and then press the Enter key.
   f. Type your instructor's name and then press the Enter key.
   g. Type your course title and then press the Enter key.
   h. Type the current date and then press the Enter key.
   i. Type the document title Mobile Security and then center it.

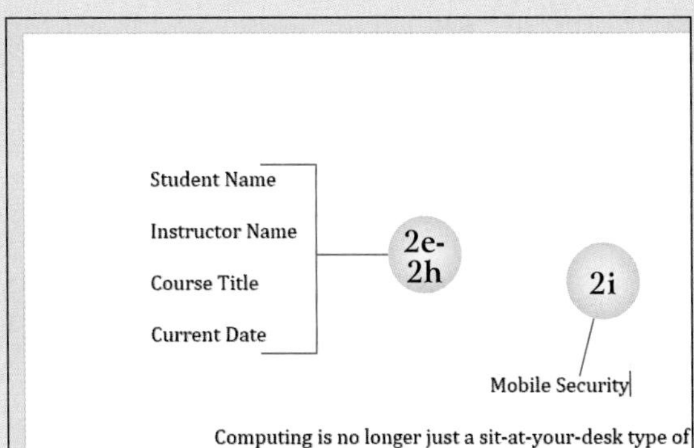

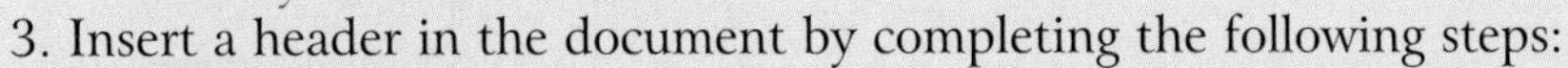

3. Insert a header in the document by completing the following steps:
   a. Click the Insert tab.
   b. Click the Header button in the Header & Footer group and then click *Edit Header* at the drop-down list.
   c. Press the Tab key two times to move the insertion point to the right margin in the Header pane.
   d. Type your last name and then press the spacebar.
   e. Click the Page Number button in the Header & Footer group on the Header & Footer Tools Design tab, point to *Current Position*, and then click the *Plain Number* option.

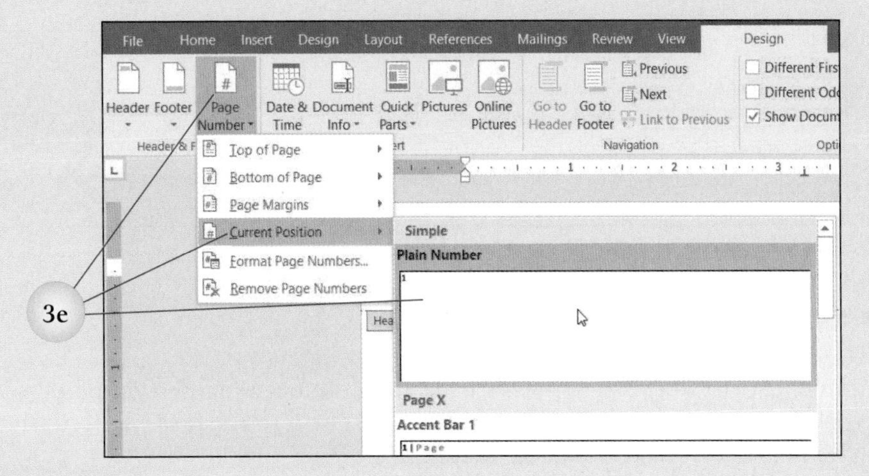

   f. Select the header text and change the font to 12-point Cambria.
   g. Double-click in the body of the document.
4. Save **5-MobileSecurity.docx**.

Check Your Work

Tutorial

Inserting Sources and Citations

Insert Citation

Inserting Source Citations

When creating an in-text source citation, enter the information about the source in fields at the Create Source dialog box. To insert a citation in a document, click the References tab, click the Insert Citation button in the Citations & Bibliography group, and then click *Add New Source* at the drop-down list. At the Create Source dialog box, shown in Figure 5.10, select the type of source to be cited (such as a book, journal article, or report) and then type the bibliographic information in the required fields. To include more information than required in the displayed fields, click the *Show All Bibliography Fields* check box to insert a check mark and then type the additional bibliographic details in the extra fields. After filling in the necessary source information, click OK. The citation is automatically inserted in the document at the location of the insertion point.

Quick Steps

Insert a New Citation
1. Click References tab.
2. Click Insert Citation button.
3. Click *Add New Source.*
4. Type source information.
5. Click OK.

Insert a Citation Placeholder
1. Click References tab.
2. Click Insert Citation button.
3. Click *Add New Placeholder.*
4. Type citation name.
5. Click OK.

Inserting Citation Placeholders

If information for an in-text source citation will be inserted later, insert a citation placeholder. To do this, click the Insert Citation button in the Citations & Bibliography group and then click *Add New Placeholder* at the drop-down list. At the Placeholder Name dialog box, type a name for the citation placeholder and then press the Enter key or click OK. Insert the citation text later at the Edit Source dialog box, which contains the same options as the Create Source dialog box.

Figure 5.10 Create Source Dialog Box

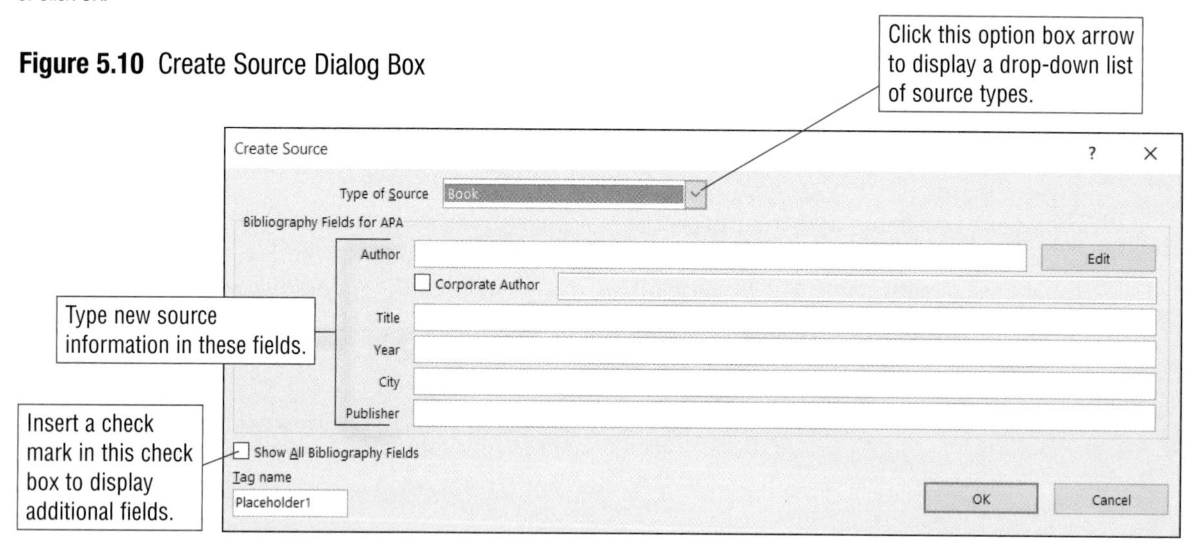

Project 5b Inserting Sources and a Citation Placeholder

Part 2 of 8

1. With **5-MobileSecurity.docx** open, press Ctrl + End to move the insertion point to the end of the document. Type the text shown in Figure 5.11 up to the first citation—the text *(Jefferson)*. To insert the citation, complete these steps:
   a. Press the spacebar once after typing the text *laptop*.

b. Click the References tab.
c. Make sure the *Style* option box in the Citations & Bibliography group is set to *MLA*. If not, click the *Style* option box arrow and then click *MLA* at the drop-down list.
d. Click the Insert Citation button in the Citations & Bibliography group and then click *Add New Source* at the drop-down list.

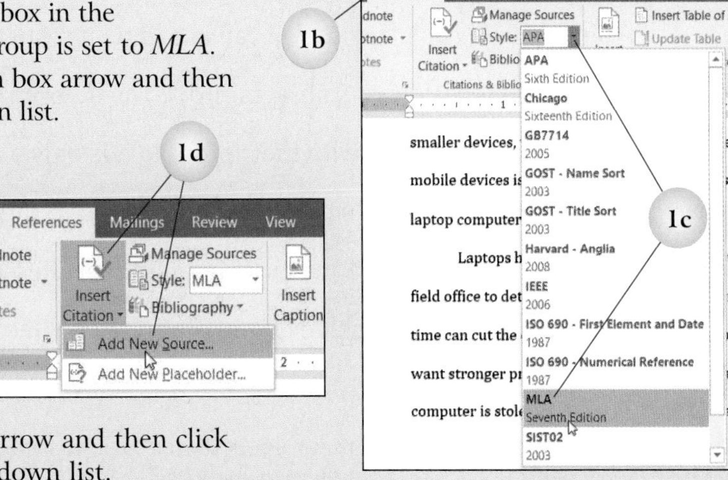

e. At the Create Source dialog box, click the *Type of Source* option box arrow and then click *Journal Article* at the drop-down list.
f. In the *Bibliography Fields for MLA* section, click in the *Author* text box, type Gabe Jefferson, and then press the Tab key three times.
g. In the *Title* text box, type Securing Laptops and Mobile Devices and then press the Tab key.
h. In the *Journal Name* text box, type Computing Technologies and then press the Tab key.
i. In the *Year* text box, type 2018 and then press the Tab key.
j. In the *Pages* text box, type 8-10.
k. Click OK.
l. Type a period to end the sentence in the document.

2. Continue typing the text up to the next citation—the text *(Lopez)*—and then insert the following source information for a book. (Click the *Type of Source* option box arrow and then click *Book* at the drop-down list.)

Author	Rafael Lopez
Title	Technology World
Year	2018
City	Chicago
Publisher	Great Lakes

3. Continue typing the text up to the next citation—the text *(Nakamura)*—and then insert a citation placeholder by completing the following steps. (You will create the citation and fill in the source information in the next project.)
   a. Click the Insert Citation button in the Citations & Bibliography group.
   b. Click *Add New Placeholder* at the drop-down list.
   c. At the Placeholder Name dialog box, type Nakamura and then press the Enter key.
4. Type the remaining text shown in Figure 5.11.
5. Save **5-MobileSecurity.docx**.

Check Your Work

Figure 5.11 Project 5b

A laptop has a cable device you can use to tie it to an airport chair or desk in a field office to deter potential thieves from stealing it. The determined thief with enough time can cut the cable and get away with the laptop, so it is only a slight deterrent. If you want stronger protection, consider a service that allows you to remotely delete data if your computer is stolen and uses GPS to track your laptop (Jefferson).

Many newer laptops include fingerprint readers. Because fingerprints are unique to each individual, being able to authenticate yourself with your own set of prints to gain access to your computer is a popular security feature. If somebody without a fingerprint match tries to get into the computer data, the system locks up. If you travel with a laptop, activating password protection and creating a secure password is a good idea. If somebody steals your laptop and cannot get past the password feature, he or she cannot immediately get at your valuable data (Lopez).

Stopping thieves is one concern when you are on the road, but stopping employees from making costly mistakes regarding company data is another area in which companies must take precautions. Making sure that employees who take company laptops outside the office are responsible for safe and secure storage offsite is vital to company security (Nakamura). Policies might require them to keep backups of data on physical storage media or to back up data to a company network.

Quick Steps

Insert a Citation with an Existing Source

1. Click References tab.
2. Click Insert Citation button.
3. Click source.

Inserting a Citation with an Existing Source

Once source information is inserted at the Create Source dialog box, Word automatically saves it. To insert a citation in a document for source information that has already been saved, click the Insert Citation button in the Citations & Bibliography group and then click the source at the drop-down list.

Tutorial

Editing a Citation and Source

Editing a Citation and Source

After source information is inserted in a document, it may need to be edited to correct errors or change data. Or perhaps the citation needs to be edited to add page numbers or suppress specific fields. Edit a citation at the Edit Citation dialog box. Display this dialog box by clicking the citation, clicking the Citations Options arrow, and then clicking the *Edit Citation* option.

In addition to the citation, the source information of a citation can be edited. Edit a source at the Edit Source dialog box. Display this dialog box by clicking the citation in the document, clicking the Citations Options arrow, and then clicking the *Edit Source* option.

Project 5c Editing an Existing Source and Inserting a Citation with an Existing Source — Part 3 of 8

1. With **5-MobileSecurity.docx** open, add the Nakamura source information by completing the following steps:
   a. Click the *Nakamura* citation in the document.
   b. Click the Citation Options arrow that displays at the right side of the selected citation.
   c. Click *Edit Source* at the drop-down list.
   d. At the Edit Source dialog box, click the *Type of Source* option box arrow and then click *Journal Article.*
   e. Type the following information in the specified text boxes:

      Author Janet Nakamura
      Title Computer Security
      Journal Name Current Technology Times
      Year 2018
      Pages 20-28
      Volume 6

      (Display the *Volume* field by clicking the *Show All Bibliography Fields* check box and then scrolling down the options list.)
   f. Click OK to close the Edit Source dialog box.
2. Press Ctrl + End to move the insertion point to the end of the document and then press the Enter key. Type the text shown in Figure 5.12 up to the citation text *(Jefferson)* and then insert a citation from an existing source by completing the following steps:
   a. If necessary, click the References tab.
   b. Click the Insert Citation button in the Citations & Bibliography group.
   c. Click the *Jefferson, Gabe* reference at the drop-down list.
   d. Type the remaining text in Figure 5.12.
3. Save **5-MobileSecurity.docx**.

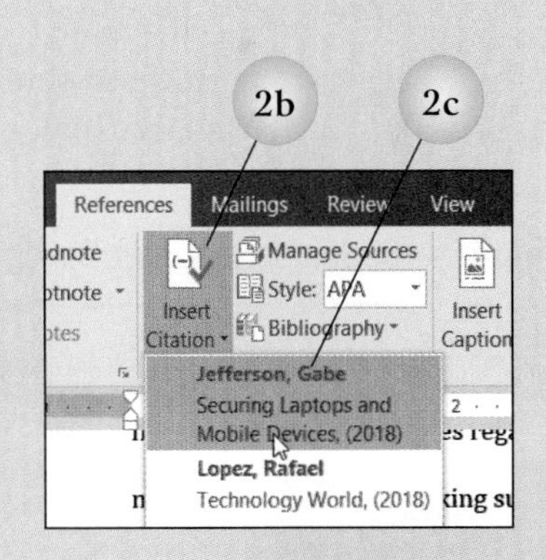

Check Your Work

Figure 5.12 Project 5c

> If you travel and access the Internet using a public location, you have to be very careful not to expose private information (Jefferson). Anything you send over a public network can be accessed by malicious hackers and cybercriminals. Limit your use of online accounts to times when it is essential.

Quick Steps

Insert a Page Number in a Citation

1. Click citation to display placeholder.
2. Click Citation Options arrow.
3. Click *Edit Citation*.
4. Type page number(s).
5. Click OK.

Inserting Page Numbers in a Citation

If a direct quote from a source is included in a report, insert quotation marks around the text used from that source and insert in the citation the page number or numbers of the quoted material. To insert specific page numbers in a citation, click the citation to select the citation placeholder. Click the Citation Options arrow and then click *Edit Citation* at the drop-down list. At the Edit Citation dialog box, type the page number or numbers of the source from which the quote was borrowed and then click OK.

Tutorial

Managing Sources

Quick Steps

Manage Sources

1. Click References tab.
2. Click Manage Sources button.
3. Edit, add, and/or delete sources.
4. Click Close.

Hint Click the Browse button in the Source Manager dialog box to select another master list.

Managing Sources

All the sources cited in the current document and in previous documents display in the Source Manager dialog box, as shown in Figure 5.13. Display this dialog box by clicking the References tab and then clicking the Manage Sources button in the Citations & Bibliography group. The *Master List* list box in the Source Manager dialog box displays all the sources that have been created in Word. The *Current List* list box displays all the sources used in the currently open document.

Use options at the Source Manager dialog box to copy a source from the master list to the current list, delete a source, edit a source, and create a new source. To copy a source from the master list to the current list, click the source in the *Master List* list box and then click the Copy button between the two list boxes. Click the Delete button to delete a source. Edit a source by clicking the source, clicking the Edit button, and then making changes at the Edit Source dialog box that displays. Click the New button to create a new source at the Create Source dialog box.

If the *Master List* list box contains a large number of sources, search for a specific source by typing keywords in the *Search* text box. As text is typed, the list narrows to sources that match the text. After making all the changes at the Source Manager dialog box, click the Close button.

Figure 5.13 Source Manager Dialog Box

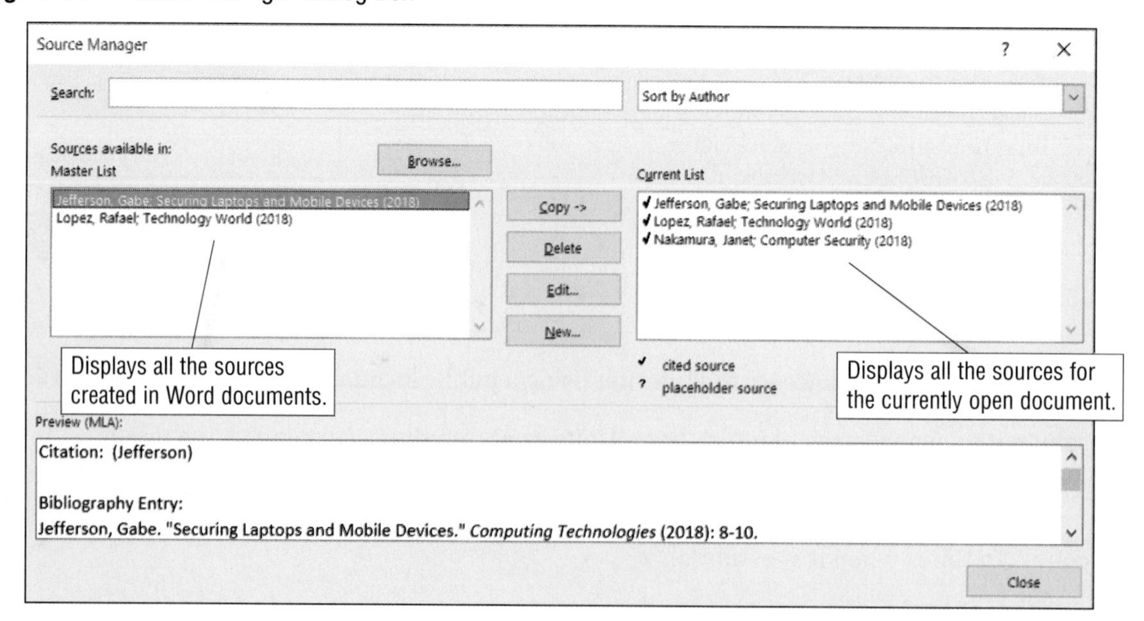

Project 5d Managing Sources

1. With **5-MobileSecurity.docx** open, edit a source by completing the following steps:
   a. If necessary, click the References tab.
   b. Click the Manage Sources button in the Citations & Bibliography group.
   c. At the Source Manager dialog box, click the *Jefferson, Gabe* source entry in the *Master List* list box.
   d. Click the Edit button.
   e. At the Edit Source dialog box, delete the text in the *Author* text box and then type Gabriel Jackson.
   f. Click OK to close the Edit Source dialog box.

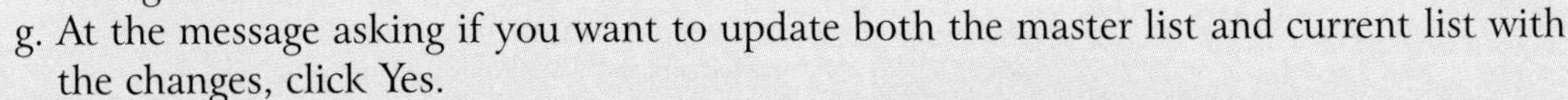

   g. At the message asking if you want to update both the master list and current list with the changes, click Yes.
   h. Click the Close button to close the Source Manager dialog box. (Notice that the last name changed in both of the Jefferson citations to reflect the edit.)
2. Delete a source by completing the following steps:
   a. Select and then delete the last sentence in the fourth paragraph in the document (the sentence beginning *If somebody steals your laptop*), including the citation.
   b. Click the Manage Sources button in the Citations & Bibliography group.
   c. At the Source Manager dialog box, click the *Lopez, Rafael* entry in the *Current List* list box. (This entry will not contain a check mark because you deleted the citation from the document.)
   d. Click the Delete button.

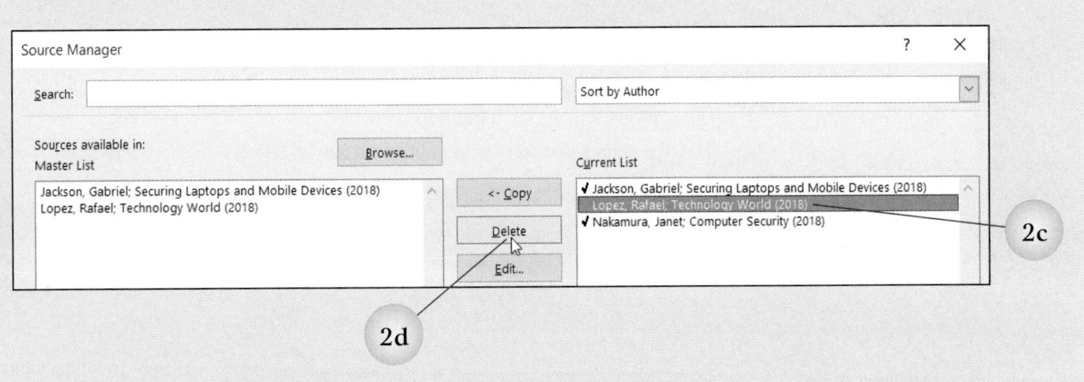

   e. Click the Close button to close the Source Manager dialog box.
3. Create and insert a new source in the document by completing the following steps:
   a. Click the Manage Sources button in the Citations & Bibliography group.
   b. Click the New button in the Source Manager dialog box.
   c. Type the following book information in the Create Source dialog box. (Change the *Type of Source* option to *Book*.)

Author	Georgia Miraldi
Title	Evolving Technology
Year	2018
City	Houston
Publisher	Rio Grande

d. Click OK to close the Create Source dialog box.
e. Click the Close button to close the Source Manager dialog box.
f. Position the insertion point one space after the period that ends the last sentence in the document and then type this sentence: "Be especially on guard when accessing your bank accounts, investment accounts, and retail accounts that store your credit card for purchases, and avoid entering your social security number" (Press the spacebar after typing the quotation mark that follows the word *number*.)
g. Insert a citation for Georgia Miraldi at the end of the sentence by clicking the Insert Citation button in the Citations & Bibliography group and then clicking *Miraldi, Georgia* at the drop-down list.

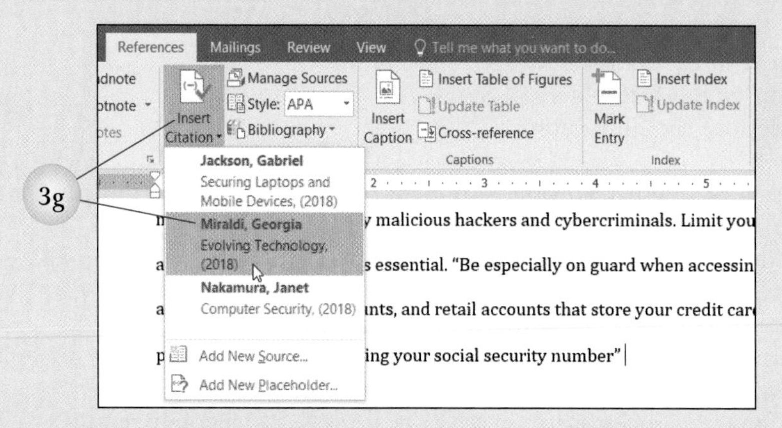

h. Type a period (.) to end the sentence.
4. To correctly acknowledge the direct quote from Georgia Miraldi, the page on which the quote appears in the book needs to be added. Insert the page number in the citation by completing the following steps:
a. Click the *Miraldi* citation in the document.
b. Click the Citation Options arrow that displays at the right of the citation placeholder and then click *Edit Citation* at the drop-down list.

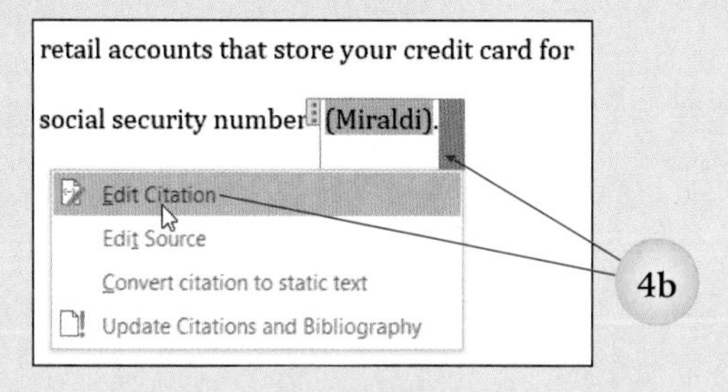

c. At the Edit Citation dialog box, type 19 in the *Pages* text box.
d. Click OK.

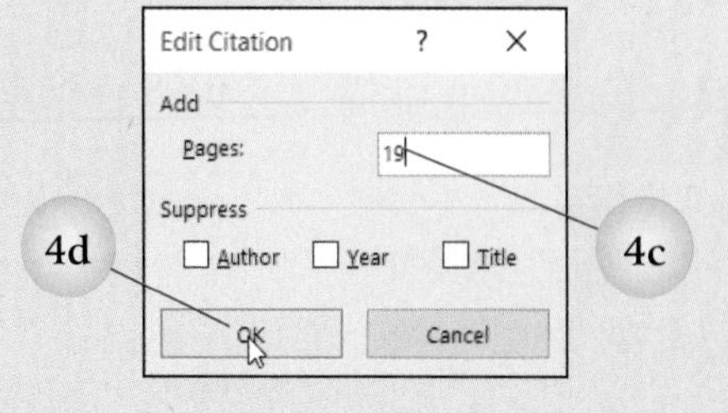

5. Save **5-MobileSecurity.docx**.

Check Your Work

Tutorial

Inserting a Works Cited Page

Quick Steps

Insert a Sources List

1. Insert new page at end of document.
2. Click References tab.
3. Click Bibliography button.
4. Click works cited, reference, or bibliography option.

Inserting a Sources List

If citations are included in a report or research paper, a sources list needs to be inserted as a separate page at the end of the document. A sources list is an alphabetical list of the books, journal articles, reports, and other sources referenced in the report or paper. Depending on the reference style applied to the document, the sources list may be a bibliography, a references page, or a works cited page.

When source information for citations is typed in the document, Word automatically saves the information from all the fields and compiles a sources list. The sources are alphabetized by the authors' last names and/or the titles of the works. To include the sources list in a report or research paper, insert a works cited page for a document formatted in MLA style, insert a references page for a document formatted in APA style, and insert a bibliography for a document formatted in Chicago style.

To insert a works cited page, move the insertion point to the end of the document and then insert a new page. Click the References tab and make sure the *Style* option box is set to *MLA*. Click the Bibliography button in the Citations & Bibliography group and then click the *Works Cited* option. Complete similar steps to insert a bibliography in an APA-style document, except click the *Bibliography* option.

Project 5e Inserting a Works Cited Page

Part 5 of 8

1. With **5-MobileSecurity.docx** open, insert a works cited page at the end of the document by completing these steps:
   a. Press Ctrl + End to move the insertion point to the end of the document.
   b. Press Ctrl + Enter to insert a page break.
   c. If necessary, click the References tab.
   d. Click the Bibliography button in the Citations & Bibliography group.
   e. Click the *Works Cited* option in the *Built-In* section of the drop-down list.
2. Save **5-MobileSecurity.docx**.

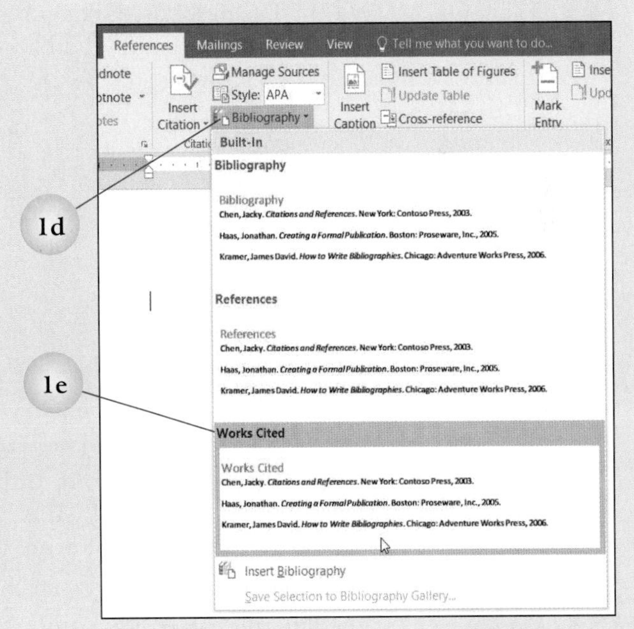

Check Your Work

Quick Steps

Update a Sources List

1. Click in sources list.
2. Click Update Citations and Bibliography tab.

Modifying and Updating a Sources List

If a new source is inserted at the Source Manager dialog box or an existing source is modified, Word automatically inserts the source information in the sources list. If a new citation requires a new source to be added, Word will not automatically update the sources list. To update the sources list, click in the list and then click the Update Citations and Bibliography tab. The updated sources list reflects any changes made to the citations and source information in the document.

Project 5f Modifying and Updating a Works Cited Page

Part 6 of 8

1. With **5-MobileSecurity.docx** open, create a new source and citation by completing the following steps:
   a. Position the insertion point immediately left of the period that ends the last sentence in the first paragraph of the document (after the word *safer*).
   b. Press the spacebar.
   c. If necessary, click the References tab.
   d. Click the Insert Citation button in the Citations & Bibliography group and then click *Add New Source* at the drop-down list.
   e. At the Create Source dialog box, insert the following source information for a website. (Change the *Type of Source* option to *Web site* and click the *Show All Bibliography Fields* check box to display all the fields.)

Author	Chay Suong
Name of Web Page	Securing and Managing Mobile Devices
Year	2018
Month	April
Day	20
Year Accessed	(type current year in numbers)
Month Accessed	(type current month in letters)
Day Accessed	(type current day in numbers)
URL	www.emcp.net/publishing

   f. Click OK to close the Create Source dialog box.
2. Update the works cited page to include the new source by completing the following steps:
   a. Press Ctrl + End to move the insertion point to the end of the document.
   b. Click in the works cited text.
   c. Click the Update Citations and Bibliography tab above the heading *Works Cited*. (Notice that the updated sources list includes the Suong reference.)
3. Save **5-MobileSecurity.docx**.

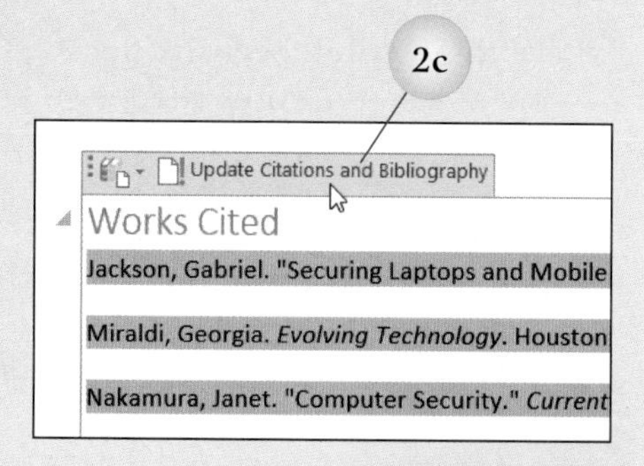

Check Your Work

Formatting a Sources List

The formatting applied by Word to the sources list may need to be changed to meet the specific guidelines of MLA, APA, or Chicago style. For example, MLA and APA styles require the following formats for a sources list:

- Begin the sources list on a separate page after the last page of text in the report.
- Include the title *Works Cited*, *References*, or *Bibliography* at the top of the page and center it on the width of the page.
- Use the same font for the sources list as for the main document.
- Double-space between and within entries.
- Begin each entry at the left margin and format subsequent lines in each entry with a hanging indent.
- Alphabetize the entries.

The general formatting requirements for Chicago style are similar except that single spacing is applied within entries and double spacing is applied between entries.

Project 5g Formatting a Works Cited Page

Part 7 of 8

1. With **5-MobileSecurity.docx** open, make the following formatting changes to the works cited page:
   a. Select the *Works Cited* title and the entries below the title.
   b. Click the Home tab and then click the *No Spacing* style in the Styles group.
   c. With the text still selected, change the font to Cambria, the font size to 12 points, and the line spacing to double spacing (2.0).
   d. Click in the title *Works Cited* and then click the Center button in the Paragraph group.
   e. Select only the works cited entries and then press Ctrl + T. (This formats the entries with a hanging indent.)
2. Press Ctrl + Home to move the insertion point to the beginning of the document.
3. Save and then print **5-MobileSecurity.docx**.

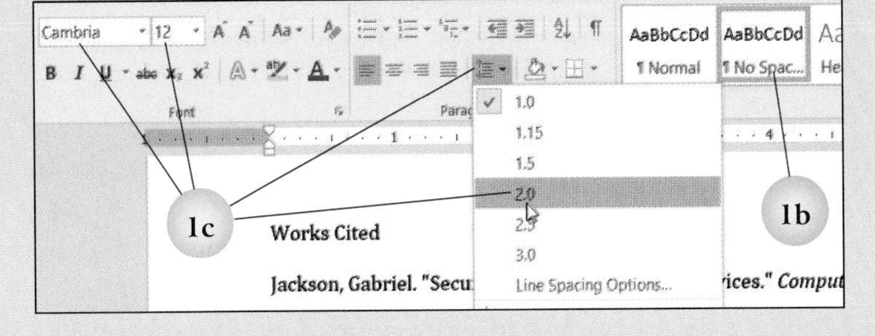

Check Your Work

Choosing a Citation Style

Quick Steps

Change the Citation Style

1. Click References tab.
2. Click *Style* option box arrow.
3. Click a style.

Different subjects and different instructors or professors may require different forms of citation or reference styles. The citation or reference style can be changed before beginning a new document or while working in an existing document. To change the reference style of an existing document, click the References tab, click the *Style* option box arrow, and then click the style at the drop-down list.

Project 5h Choosing a Citation Style

Part 8 of 8

1. With **5-MobileSecurity.docx** open, change the document and works cited page from MLA style to APA style by completing the following steps:
   a. With the insertion point positioned at the beginning of the document, click the References tab.
   b. Click the *Style* option box arrow in the Citations & Bibliography group and then click *APA* at the drop-down list.
   c. Scroll to the last page in the document (notice the changes to the citations), change the title *Works Cited* to *References*, select the four references, change the font to 12-point Cambria, remove the extra spacing after paragraphs, and then change the line spacing to double spacing (2.0).
2. Save the document and then print only the references page.
3. Close **5-MobileSecurity.docx**.
4. Display a blank document, click the References tab, change the style to *MLA*, and then close the document without saving it.

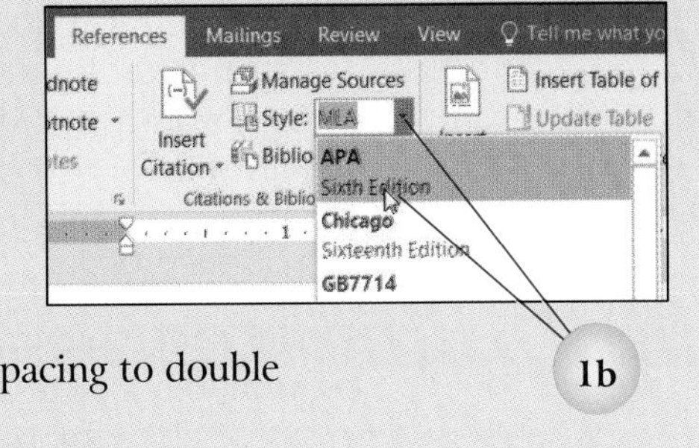

Check Your Work

Chapter Summary

- Text in paragraphs, columns, and tables can be sorted alphabetically, numerically, and chronologically. Use the Sort button in the Paragraph group on the Home tab to sort text in paragraphs, columns, and tables.
- When sorting text set in columns, Word considers text typed at the left margin *Field 1*, text typed at the first tab *Field 2*, and so on.
- Sort on more than one field with the *Sort by* and *Then by* options at the Sort dialog box.
- Use the *Header row* option in the *My list has* section in the Sort Text dialog box to sort all the text in columns except the first row.
- Sort records in a data source file at the Mail Merge Recipients dialog box. Sort by clicking the column heading or using options at the Filter and Sort dialog box with the Sort Records tab selected.
- Select specific records in a data source file with options at the Filter and Sort dialog box with the Filter Records tab selected.
- Use the *Comparison* option box at the Filter and Sort dialog box to refine a search to records that meet specific criteria.
- Use the Find duplicates hyperlink in the *Refine recipient list* section of the Mail Merge Recipients dialog box to find duplicate records in a data source file, and use the Find recipient hyperlink to search for records that match a specific criterion.
- Save a document as a template by changing the *Save as type* option at the Save As dialog box to *Word Template (*.dotx)*. Or display the Export backstage area, click the *Change File Type* option, click the *Template (*.dotx)* option, and then click the Save As button.
- Word adds the file extension *.dotx* to a template.
- Open a document based on a template from the Custom Office Templates folder by displaying the New backstage area, clicking the *PERSONAL* option, and then clicking the template.
- Footnotes and endnotes provide explanatory notes and source citations. Footnotes are inserted and printed at the bottoms of pages and endnotes are inserted and printed at the end of the document.
- By default, footnotes are numbered with arabic numbers and endnotes are numbered with lowercase roman numerals.
- When printing a document containing footnotes, Word automatically reduces the number of lines on each page to create space for the footnotes and the separator line. In a document containing endnotes, the notes are separated from the last line of text by a separator line.
- Move, copy, or delete a footnote/endnote reference number in a document and all the other footnotes/endnotes automatically renumber.
- Delete a footnote or endnote by selecting the reference number and then pressing the Delete key.
- Use options at the Footnote and Endnote dialog box to convert footnotes to endnotes and endnotes to footnotes and to change note numbering and number formatting.

- Consider using in-text citations to acknowledge sources in a report or research paper. Commonly used citation and reference styles include American Psychological Association (APA), Modern Language Association (MLA), and *Chicago Manual of Style* (Chicago).
- Insert a citation using the Insert Citation button in the Citations & Bibliography group on the References tab. Specify source information at the Create Source dialog box.
- Insert a source citation placeholder in a document if the source information will be added later.
- When source information is inserted at the Create Source dialog box, Word automatically saves it. New citations can be added using this saved source information.
- Edit a citation at the Edit Citation dialog box—for instance, to add the page numbers of quoted material. To display this dialog box, click the citation, click the Citation Options arrow, and then click the *Edit Citation* option.
- Edit a source at the Edit Source dialog box. Display this dialog box by clicking the source citation in the document, clicking the Citation Options arrow, and then clicking *Edit Source* at the drop-down list. Another option is to display the Source Manager dialog box, click the source to be edited, and then click the Edit button.
- Use options at the Source Manager dialog box to copy, delete, and edit existing sources and create new sources. Display this dialog box by clicking the Manage Sources button in the Citations & Bibliography group on the References tab.
- Insert a sources list—such as a works cited page, references page, or bibliography—at the end of the document on a separate page. To do so, use the Bibliography button in the Citations & Bibliography group on the References tab.
- To update a sources list, click in the list and then click the Update Citations and Bibliography tab.
- Apply APA, MLA, or Chicago style to the sources list in a new or existing document using the *Style* option box in the Citations & Bibliography group on the References tab.

Commands Review

FEATURE	RIBBON TAB, GROUP/OPTION	BUTTON, OPTION	KEYBOARD SHORTCUT
bibliography or works cited	References, Citations & Bibliography		
citation style	References, Citations & Bibliography		
Create Source dialog box	References, Citations & Bibliography	, *Add New Source*	
Filter and Sort dialog box with Select Records tab selected	Mailings, Start Mail Merge	, Filter	
Filter and Sort dialog box with Sort Records tab selected	Mailings, Start Mail Merge	, Sort	
endnote	References, Footnotes		Alt + Ctrl + D
footnote	References, Footnotes		Alt + Ctrl + F
Footnote and Endnote	References, Footnotes		dialog box
next footnote	References, Footnotes		
personal template	File, *New*, *PERSONAL*		
show footnotes and endnotes	References, Footnotes		
Sort Options dialog box	Home, Paragraph	, Options	
Sort Text dialog box	Home, Paragraph		
Source Manager dialog box	References, Citations & Bibliography		

Workbook

Chapter study tools and assessment activities are available in the *Workbook* ebook. These resources are designed to help you further develop and demonstrate mastery of the skills learned in this chapter.

Microsoft®

Word

Creating Specialized Tables and Indexes

CHAPTER 6

Performance Objectives

Upon successful completion of Chapter 6, you will be able to:

1 Create, insert, and update a table of contents
2 Create, insert, and update a table of figures
3 Create and customize captions
4 Create, insert, and update an index

Precheck

Check your current skills to help focus your study.

A book, textbook, report, or manuscript often includes sections such as a table of contents, table of figures, and index. Creating these sections manually can be tedious. However, using Word's automated features, these sections can be created quickly and easily. In this chapter, you will learn how to mark text for a table of contents, table of figures, and index and then insert the table or index in a document.

Data Files

Before beginning chapter work, copy the WL2C6 folder to your storage medium and then make WL2C6 the active folder.

SNAP

If you are a SNAP user, launch the Precheck and Tutorials from your Assignments page.

Project 1 Create a Table of Contents for a Computer Interface Report — 2 Parts

You will open a report on computer interfaces, mark text for a table of contents, and then insert the table of contents in the document. You will also customize and update the table of contents.

Preview Finished Project

Creating a Table of Contents

A table of contents appears at the beginning of a book, manuscript, or report and contains headings and subheadings with page numbers. In Chapter 3, a table of contents was created using the Quick Parts button in the Text group on the Insert tab. A table of contents can also be created using the Table of Contents button in the Table of Contents group on the References tab. Identify the text to be included in a table of contents by applying built-in heading styles or custom styles, assigning levels, or marking text.

Applying Styles

Hint If you apply heading styles to the text in a document, you can easily insert a table of contents later.

To create a table of contents with built-in styles, open the document and then apply the styles. All the text with the Heading 1 style applied is used for the first level of the table of contents, all the text with the Heading 2 style applied is used for the second level, and so on. Apply built-in styles with options in the Styles group on the Home tab.

Tutorial

Inserting a Table of Contents

Quick Steps

Insert a Table of Contents

1. Apply heading styles.
2. Click References tab.
3. Click Table of Contents button.
4. Click option at drop-down list.

Number the Table of Contents Page

1. Click Insert tab.
2. Click Page Number button.
3. Click *Format Page Numbers*.
4. Change number format to lowercase roman numerals at Page Number Format dialog box.
5. Click OK.

Page Number

Inserting a Table of Contents

After applying styles to the headings, insert the table of contents in the document. To do this, position the insertion point where the table of contents is to appear, click the References tab, click the Table of Contents button, and then click the specific option at the drop-down list.

Numbering the Table of Contents Page

Generally, the pages that contain the table of contents are numbered with lowercase roman numerals (*i*, *ii*, *iii*). Change the format of the page number to lowercase roman numerals at the Page Number Format dialog box, shown in Figure 6.1. Display this dialog box by clicking the Insert tab, clicking the Page Number button in the Header & Footer group, and then clicking *Format Page Numbers* at the drop-down list.

The first page of text in the main document, which usually comes immediately after the table of contents, should begin with arabic number 1. To change from roman to arabic page numbers within the same document, separate the table of contents from the first page of the document with a section break that begins a new page.

Figure 6.1 Page Number Format Dialog Box

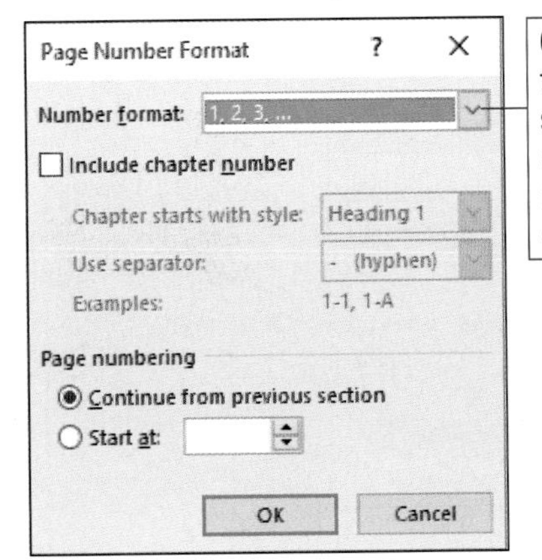

Change the number format from the default setting shown here to lowercase roman numerals when numbering the page or pages of the table of contents.

Navigating Using a Table of Contents

Hint You can use a table of contents to navigate quickly in a document and to get an overview of the topics it covers.

When a table of contents is inserted in a document, the headings contained in the table of contents can be used to navigate within the document. The headings in the table of contents are hyperlinks that connect to the headings where they appear within the document.

To navigate in a document using the table of contents headings, click in the table of contents to select it. Position the mouse pointer over a heading and a box displays with the path and file name as well as the text *Ctrl+Click to follow link*. Press and hold down the Ctrl key, click the left mouse button, and release the Ctrl key and the insertion point is positioned in the document at the location of the heading.

Project 1a Inserting a Table of Contents — Part 1 of 2

1. Open **AIReport.docx** and then save it with the name **6-AIReport**. (This document contains headings with heading styles applied.)
2. Position the insertion point immediately left of the first *N* in *NATURAL INTERFACE APPLICATIONS* and then insert a section break by completing the following steps:
   a. Click the Layout tab.
   b. Click the Breaks button in the Page Setup group.
   c. Click the *Next Page* option in the *Section Breaks* section.
3. With the insertion point positioned below the section break, insert page numbers and change the beginning number to 1 by completing the following steps:
   a. Click the Insert tab.
   b. Click the Page Number button in the Header & Footer group, point to *Bottom of Page*, and then click *Plain Number 2*.

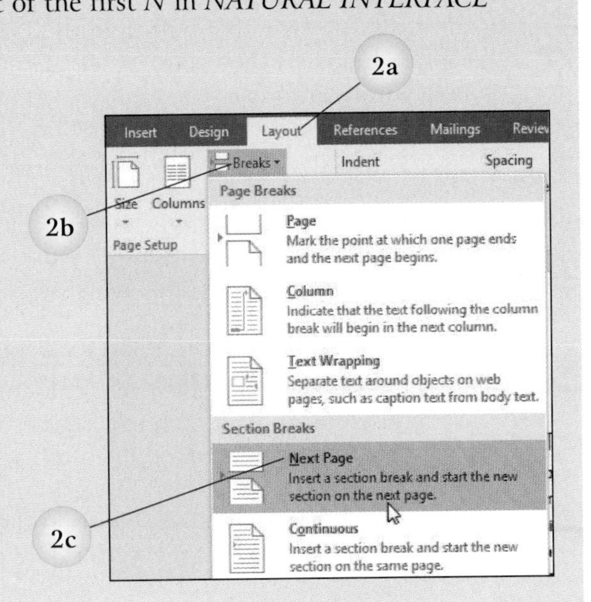

c. Click the Page Number button in the Header & Footer group on the Header & Footer Tools Design tab and then click *Format Page Numbers* at the drop-down list.

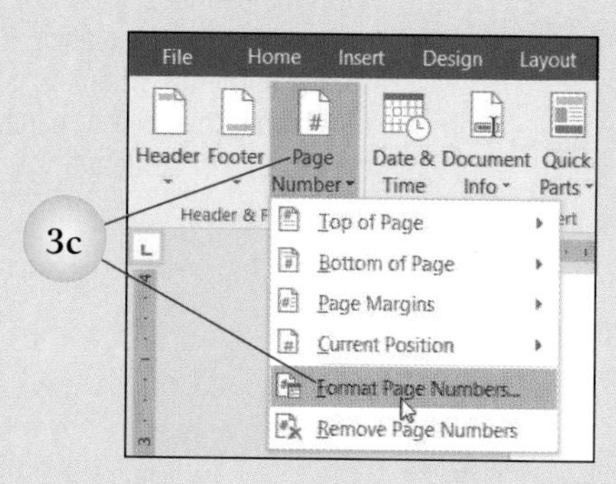

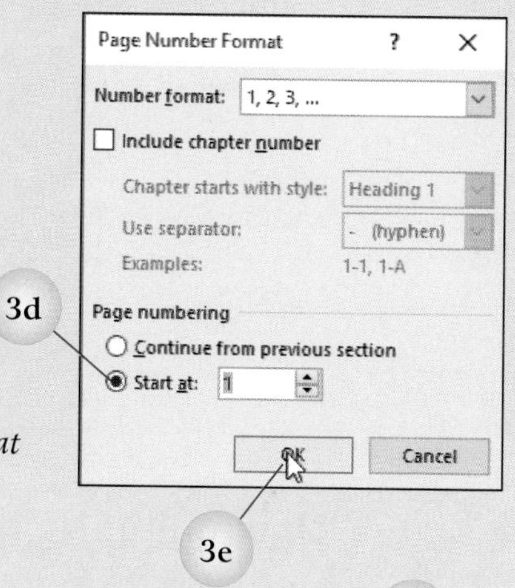

d. At the Page Number Format dialog box, click *Start at* in the *Page numbering* section. (This inserts *1* in the *Start at* measurement box.)
e. Click OK to close the Page Number Format dialog box.
f. Double-click in the document to make it active.

4. Insert a table of contents at the beginning of the document by completing the following steps:
   a. Press Ctrl + Home to move the insertion point to the beginning of the document.
   b. Click the References tab.
   c. Click the Table of Contents button in the Table of Contents group and then click the *Automatic Table 1* option in the *Built-In* section of the drop-down list.

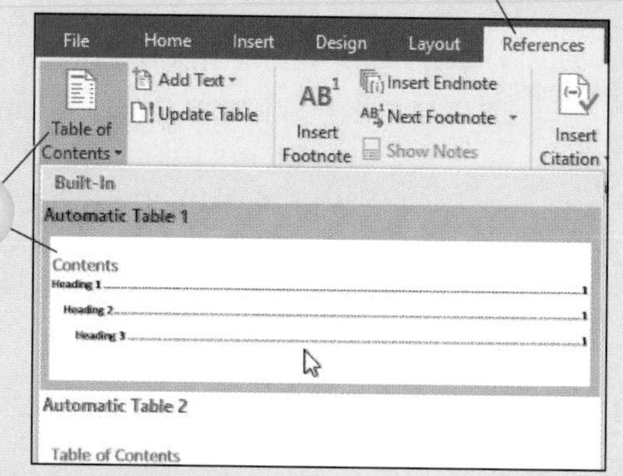

5. Insert a page number on the table of contents page by completing the following steps:
   a. Scroll up the document and then click in the heading *Contents*.
   b. Click the Insert tab.
   c. Click the Page Number button in the Header & Footer group and then click *Format Page Numbers* at the drop-down list.
   d. At the Page Number Format dialog box, click the *Number format* option box arrow and then click *i, ii, iii, …* at the drop-down list.
   e. Click OK to close the dialog box.

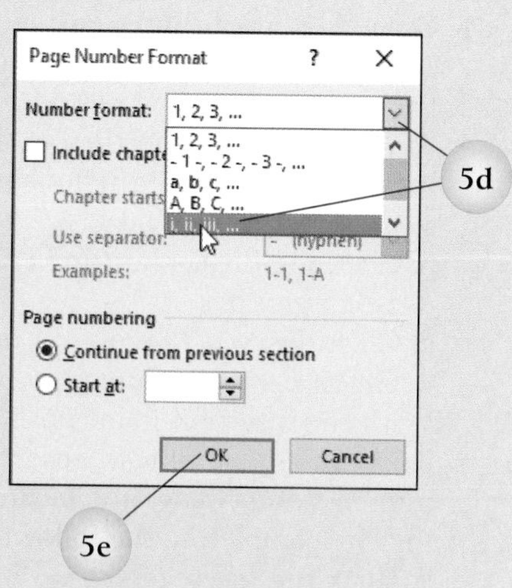

6. Navigate in the document using the table of contents by completing the following steps:
   a. Click in the table of contents.
   b. Position the mouse pointer on the heading *Virtual Reality*, press and hold down the Ctrl key, click the left mouse button, and then release the Ctrl key. (This moves the insertion point to the beginning of the heading *Virtual Reality* in the document.)
   c. Press Ctrl + Home to move the insertion point to the beginning of the document.
7. Save **6-AIReport.docx** and then print only page 1 (the table of contents page).

Check Your Work

Tutorial

Customizing and Updating a Table of Contents

Customizing a Table of Contents

Customize an existing table of contents in a document with options at the Table of Contents dialog box, shown in Figure 6.2. Display this dialog box by clicking the Table of Contents button on the References tab and then clicking *Custom Table of Contents* at the drop-down list.

At the Table of Contents dialog box, a sample table of contents displays in the *Print Preview* section. Change the table of contents format by clicking the *Formats* option box arrow in the *General* section. At the drop-down list that displays, click a format. When a different format is selected, that format displays in the *Print Preview* section.

Page numbers in a table of contents will display after the text or aligned at the right margin, depending on what option is selected. Page number alignment can also be specified with the *Right align page numbers* option. The possible number of levels in the contents list that display in a table of contents depends on the number of heading levels in the document. Control the number of levels that display with the *Show levels* measurement box in the *General* section. Tab leaders help guide readers' eyes from the table of contents heading to the page number. The default tab leader is a period. To choose a different leader, click the *Tab leader* option box arrow and then click a character at the drop-down list.

Figure 6.2 Table of Contents Dialog Box

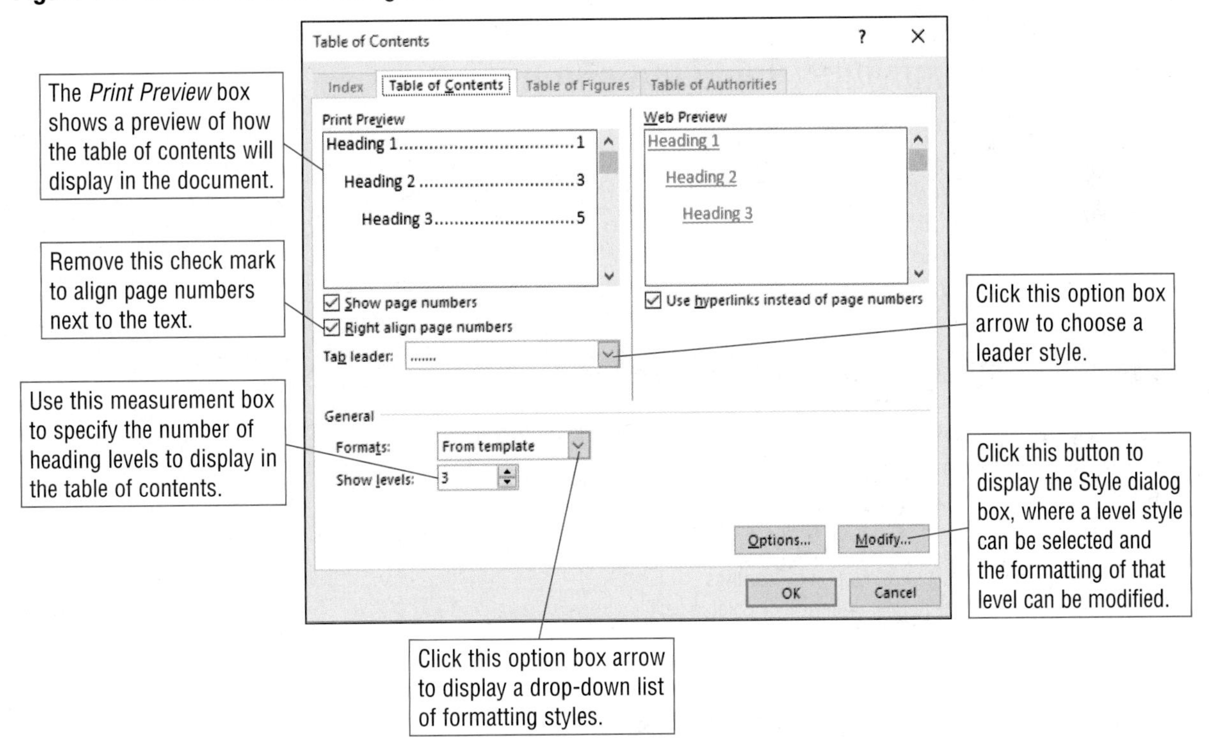
Table of Contents
Index
Table of Contents
Table of Figures
Table of Authorities
Print Preview
Heading 1....1
Heading 2....3
Heading 3....5
Web Preview
Heading 1
Heading 2
Heading 3
Show page numbers
Right align page numbers
Tab leader:
Use hyperlinks instead of page numbers
General
Formats:
From template
Show levels:
3
Options...
Modify...
OK
Cancel
The *Print Preview* box shows a preview of how the table of contents will display in the document.
Remove this check mark to align page numbers next to the text.
Use this measurement box to specify the number of heading levels to display in the table of contents.
Click this option box arrow to choose a leader style.
Click this button to display the Style dialog box, where a level style can be selected and the formatting of that level can be modified.
Click this option box arrow to display a drop-down list of formatting styles.

Word automatically formats the headings in a table of contents as hyperlinks and inserts page numbers. Each hyperlink can be used to move the insertion point to a specific location in the document. Word automatically inserts a check mark in the *Use hyperlinks instead of page numbers* check box so that if the document is posted to the web, readers will only need to click the hyperlink to view a specific page. Therefore readers of the document on the web do not need page numbers. Remove page numbering in the printed document by removing the check mark from the *Show page numbers* check box in the Table of Contents dialog box.

If changes are made to the options at the Table of Contents dialog box, clicking OK will cause a message to display asking if the selected table of contents should be replaced. At this message, click Yes.

Updating a Table of Contents

Update Table

Quick Steps

Update a Table of Contents

1. Click in table of contents.
2. Click References tab.
3. Click Update Table button, Update Table tab, or press F9.
4. Click *Update page numbers only* or *Update entire table.*
5. Click OK.

Remove a Table of Contents

1. Click References tab.
2. Click Table of Contents button.
3. Click *Remove Table of Contents.*

OR

1. Click in table of contents.
2. Click Table of Contents tab.
3. Click *Remove Table of Contents.*

If headings or other text in a document is deleted, moved, or edited after the table of contents is inserted, the table of contents will need to be updated. To do this, click in the current table of contents and then click the Update Table button in the Table of Contents group, the Update Table tab, or press the F9 function key (the Update Field key). At the Update Table of Contents dialog box, shown in Figure 6.3, click *Update page numbers only* if changes were made that only affected page numbers or click *Update entire table* if changes were made to the headings or subheadings in the document. Click OK or press the Enter key to close the dialog box.

Removing a Table of Contents

Remove a table of contents from a document by clicking the Table of Contents button on the References tab and then clicking *Remove Table of Contents* at the drop-down list. Another way to remove a table of contents is to click in the table of contents, click the Table of Contents tab in the upper left corner of the table of contents (immediately left of the Update Table tab), and then click *Remove Table of Contents* at the drop-down list.

Figure 6.3 Update Table of Contents Dialog Box

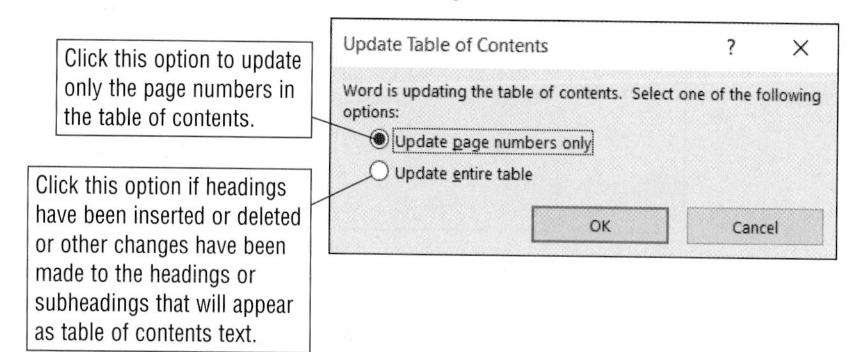
Click this option to update only the page numbers in the table of contents.
Click this option if headings have been inserted or deleted or other changes have been made to the headings or subheadings that will appear as table of contents text.
Update Table of Contents
?
Word is updating the table of contents. Select one of the following options:
Update page numbers only
Update entire table
OK
Cancel

1. With **6-AIReport.docx** open and the insertion point positioned at the beginning of the document, apply a different formatting style to the table of contents by completing the following steps:
   a. Click the References tab, click the Table of Contents button, and then click *Custom Table of Contents* at the drop-down list.
   b. At the Table of Contents dialog box with the Table of Contents tab selected, click the *Formats* option box arrow in the *General* section and then click *Formal* at the drop-down list.
   c. Click the *Tab leader* option box arrow and then click the solid line option (bottom option) at the drop-down list.
   d. Click the *Show levels* measurement box down arrow to change the number to *2*.
   e. Click OK to close the dialog box.
   f. At the message asking if you want to replace the selected table of contents, click the Yes button.

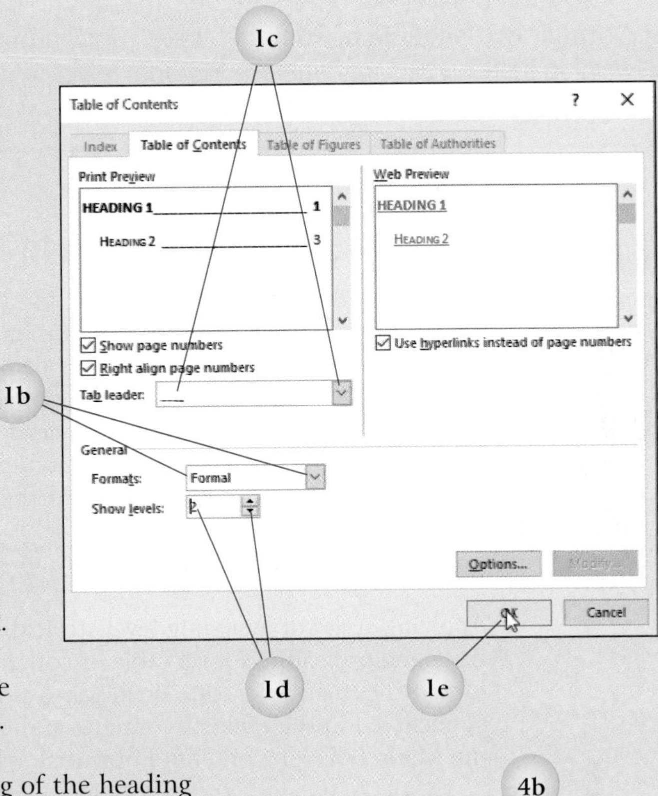

2. Use the table of contents to move the insertion point to the beginning of the heading *Navigation* at the bottom of page 3.
3. Press Ctrl + Enter to insert a page break.
4. Update the table of contents by completing the following steps:
   a. Press Ctrl + Home and then click in the table of contents.
   b. Click the Update Table tab.
   c. At the Update Table of Contents dialog box, make sure *Update page numbers only* is selected and then click OK.
5. Save the document, print only the table of contents page, and then close **6-AIReport.docx**.

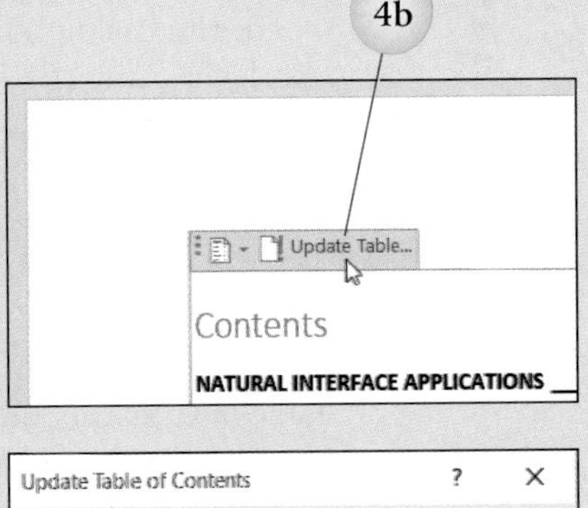

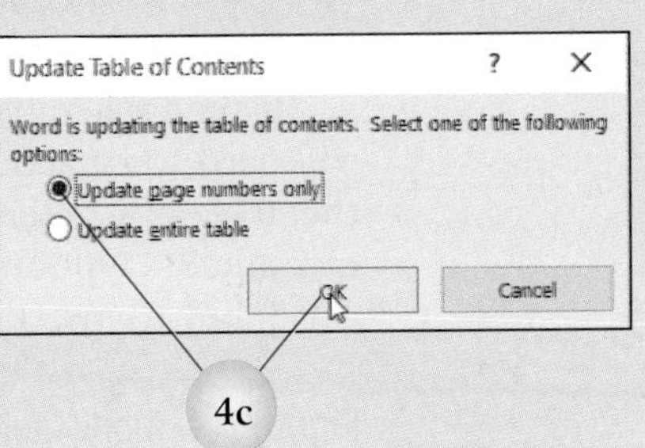

Check Your Work

Project 2 Mark Text for and Insert a Table of Contents in a Company Handbook

2 Parts

You will open a document that contains employee pay and evaluation information, mark text as table of contents fields, and then insert a table of contents. You will also insert a file containing additional information on employee classifications and then update the table of contents.

Preview Finished Project

Tutorial

Assigning Levels to Table of Contents Entries

Assigning Levels to Table of Contents Entries

Another method for identifying text for a table of contents is to use the Add Text button in the Table of Contents group on the References tab. Click this button and a drop-down list of level options displays. Click a level for the currently selected text and a heading style is applied to the text. For example, click the *Level 2* option and the Heading 2 style is applied to the selected text. After specifying levels, insert the table of contents by clicking the Table of Contents button and then clicking an option at the drop-down list.

Marking Table of Contents Entries as Fields

Applying styles or assigning levels to text applies specific formatting. To identify titles and/or headings for a table of contents without applying heading style formatting, mark each title or heading as a field entry. To do this, select the text to be included in the table of contents and then press Alt + Shift + O. This displays the Mark Table of Contents Entry dialog box, shown in Figure 6.4.

In the dialog box, the selected text displays in the *Entry* text box. Specify the text level using the *Level* measurement box and then click the Mark button. This turns on the display of nonprinting characters in the document and also inserts a field code immediately after the selected text.

For example, when the title is selected in Project 2a, the following code is inserted immediately after the title *COMPENSATION*: { TC "COMPENSATION" \f C \l "1" }. The Mark Table of Contents Entry dialog box also remains open. To mark the next entry for the table of contents, select the text and then click the Title bar of the Mark Table of Contents Entry dialog box. Specify the level and then click the Mark button. Continue in this manner until all the table of contents entries have been marked.

If the table of contents entries are marked as fields, the *Table entry fields* option will need to be activated when inserting the table of contents. To do this, display the Table of Contents dialog box and then click the Options button. At the Table of Contents Options dialog box, shown in Figure 6.5, click the *Table entry fields* check box to insert a check mark and then click OK.

Figure 6.4 Mark Table of Contents Entry Dialog Box

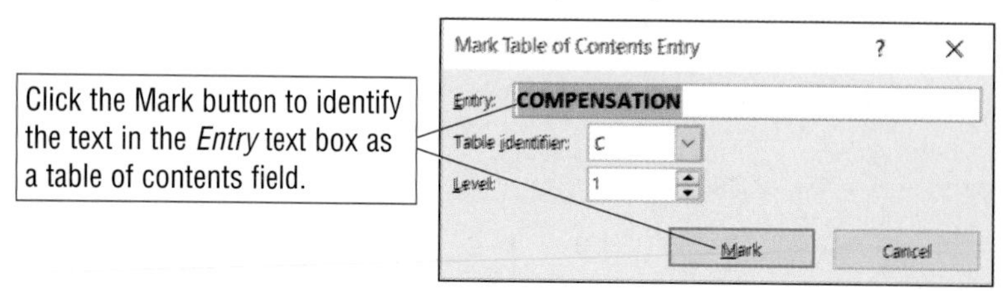

Figure 6.5 Table of Contents Options Dialog Box

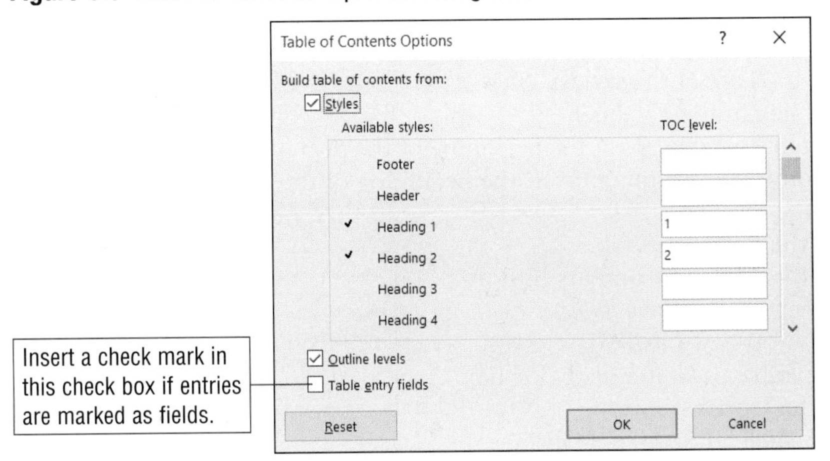

Project 2a Marking Headings as Fields

Part 1 of 2

1. Open **CompEval.docx** and then save it with the name **6-CompEval**.
2. Position the insertion point immediately left of the *C* in *COMPENSATION* and then insert a section break that begins a new page by clicking the Layout tab, clicking the Breaks button in the Page Setup group, and then clicking the *Next Page* option.
3. Mark the titles and headings as fields for insertion in a table of contents by completing the following steps:
   a. Select the title *COMPENSATION*.
   b. Press Alt + Shift + O.
   c. At the Mark Table of Contents Entry dialog box, make sure the *Level* measurement box is set at *1* and then click the Mark button. (This turns on the display of nonprinting characters.)
   d. Click in the document, scroll down, and then select the title *EVALUATION*.
   e. Click the dialog box Title bar and then click the Mark button.
   f. Click in the document, scroll up, and then select the heading *Rate of Pay*.
   g. Click the dialog box Title bar and then click the *Level* measurement box up arrow in the Mark Table of Contents Entry dialog box until *2* displays.
   h. Click the Mark button.
   i. Mark the following headings as level 2:
      Direct Deposit Option
      Pay Progression
      Overtime
      Work Performance Standards
      Performance Evaluation
      Employment Records
   j. Click the Close button to close the Mark Table of Contents Entry dialog box.

4. Position the insertion point at the beginning of the title *COMPENSATION*. Insert a page number at the bottom center of each page of the section and change the starting number to 1. ***Hint: Refer to Project 1a, Step 3.***
5. Double-click in the document.
6. Insert a table of contents at the beginning of the document by completing the following steps:
   a. Position the insertion point at the beginning of the document (on the new page).
   b. Type the title TABLE OF CONTENTS and then press the Enter key.
   c. Click the References tab.
   d. Click the Table of Contents button and then click *Custom Table of Contents* at the drop-down list.
   e. At the Table of Contents dialog box, click the Options button.
   f. At the Table of Contents Options dialog box, click the *Table entry fields* check box to insert a check mark.
   g. Click OK to close the Table of Contents Options dialog box.
   h. Click OK to close the Table of Contents dialog box.
   i. Apply bold formatting to and center the heading *TABLE OF CONTENTS*.

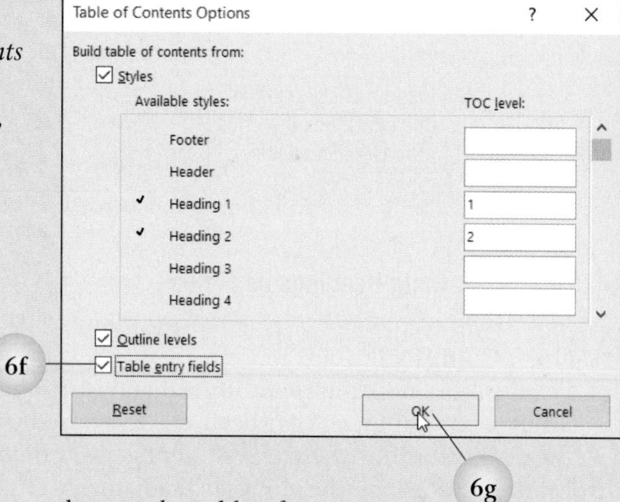

7. Insert a lowercase roman numeral page number on the table of contents page. ***Hint: Refer to Project 1a, Step 5.***
8. Click the Show/Hide ¶ button to turn off the display of nonprinting characters.
9. Save **6-CompEval.docx** and then print only page 1 (the table of contents page).

Check Your Work

If additional information is inserted in a document with headings marked as fields, the table of contents can be easily updated. To do this, insert the text and then mark the text with options at the Mark Table of Contents Entry dialog box. Click in the table of contents and then click the Update Table tab. At the Update Table of Contents dialog box, click the *Update entire table* option and then click OK.

Project 2b Updating an Entire Table of Contents

Part 2 of 2

1. With **6-CompEval.docx** open, insert a file into the document by completing the following steps:
   a. Press Ctrl + End to move the insertion point to the end of the document.
   b. Press Ctrl + Enter to insert a page break.
   c. Click the Insert tab.
   d. Click the Object button arrow in the Text group and then click *Text from File* at the drop-down list.
   e. At the Insert File dialog box, navigate to the WL2C6 folder on your storage medium and then double-click ***PosClass.docx***.

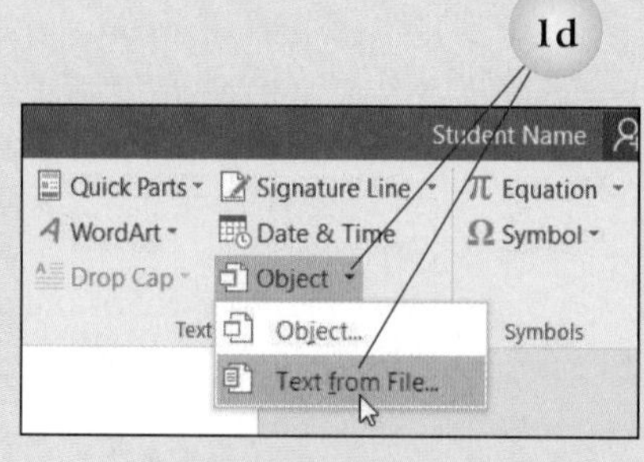

2. Select and then mark text for inclusion in the table of contents by completing the following steps:
   a. Select the title *POSITION CLASSIFICATION*.
   b. Press Alt + Shift + O.
   c. At the Mark Table of Contents Entry dialog box, make sure that *1* displays in the *Level* measurement box and then click the Mark button.
   d. Click the Close button to close the Mark Table of Contents Entry dialog box.
3. Update the table of contents by completing the following steps:
   a. Select the entire table of contents (excluding the title).
   b. Click the References tab.
   c. Click the Update Table button in the Table of Contents group.
   d. At the Update Table of Contents dialog box, click the *Update entire table* option.
   e. Click OK.
4. Turn off the display of nonprinting characters.
5. Save the document, print only the table of contents page, and then close **6-CompEval.docx**.

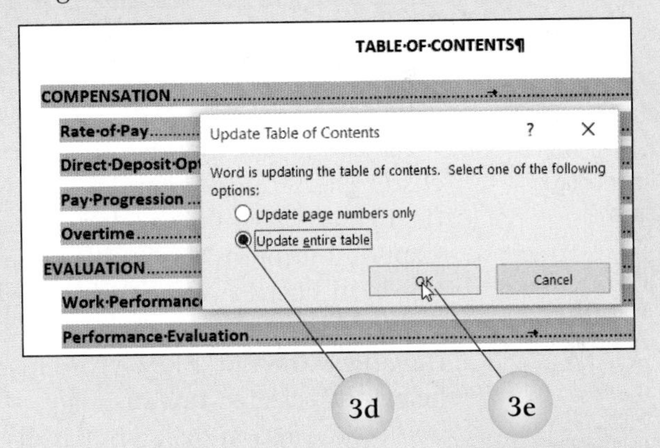

Check Your Work

Project 3 **Create a Table of Figures for a Technology Report and a Travel Document** **3 Parts**

You will open a report containing information on software, output devices, and the software development cycle, as well as images and a SmartArt diagram; insert captions; and then create a table of figures. You will also create and customize captions and insert a table of figures for an adventure document.

Preview Finished Project

Creating a Table of Figures

Insert Caption

Insert Table of Figures

A document that contains figures should include a table of figures so readers can quickly locate specific figures, images, tables, equations, and charts. Figure 6.6 shows an example of a table of figures. Create a table of figures by marking text or images with captions and then using the caption names to create the table. The Captions group on the References tab includes the Insert Caption button for creating captions and the Insert Table of Figures button for inserting a table of figures in a document.

Figure 6.6 Sample Table of Figures

TABLE OF FIGURES

Tutorial

Creating and Customizing Captions

Quick Steps

Create a Caption

1. Select text or image.
2. Click References tab.
3. Click Insert Caption button.
4. Type caption name.
5. Click OK.

Creating a Caption

A caption is text that describes an item such as a figure, image, table, equation, or chart. The caption generally displays below the item. Create a caption by selecting the figure text or image, clicking the References tab, and then clicking the Insert Caption button in the Captions group. This displays the Caption dialog box, shown in Figure 6.7. At the dialog box, *Figure 1* displays in the *Caption* text box and the insertion point is positioned after *Figure 1*. Type a name for the figure and then press the Enter key. Word inserts *Figure 1* followed by the typed caption below the selected text or image. If the insertion point is positioned in a table when the Caption dialog box is displayed, *Table 1* displays in the *Caption* text box instead of *Figure 1*.

Tutorial

Inserting a Table of Figures

Quick Steps

Insert a Table of Figures

1. Click References tab.
2. Click Insert Table of Figures button.
3. Select format.
4. Click OK.

Inserting a Table of Figures

After marking figures, images, tables, equations, or charts with captions in a document, insert the table of figures. A table of figures generally displays at the beginning of the document after the table of contents and on a separate page. To insert the table of figures, click the Insert Table of Figures button in the Captions group on the References tab. At the Table of Figures dialog box, shown in Figure 6.8, make any necessary changes and then click OK.

The options at the Table of Figures dialog box are similar to the options at the Table of Contents dialog box. They include choosing a format for the table of figures from the *Formats* option box, changing the alignment of the page numbers, and adding leaders before page numbers.

Figure 6.7 Caption Dialog Box

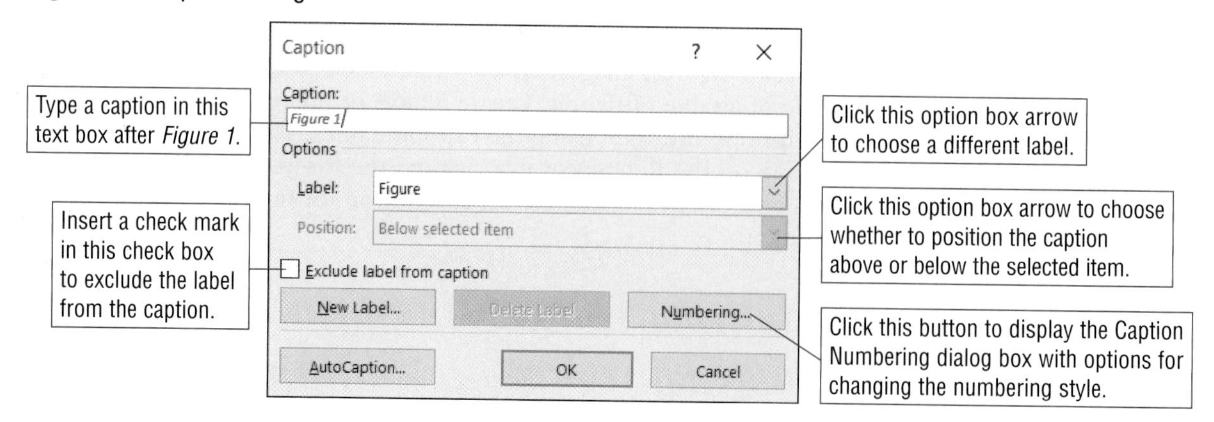

Caption
Caption:
Figure 1
Options
Label:
Figure
Position:
Below selected item
Exclude label from caption
New Label...
Delete Label
Numbering...
AutoCaption...
OK
Cancel
Type a caption in this text box after Figure 1.
Insert a check mark in this check box to exclude the label from the caption.
Click this option box arrow to choose a different label.
Click this option box arrow to choose whether to position the caption above or below the selected item.
Click this button to display the Caption Numbering dialog box with options for changing the numbering style.

Figure 6.8 Table of Figures Dialog Box

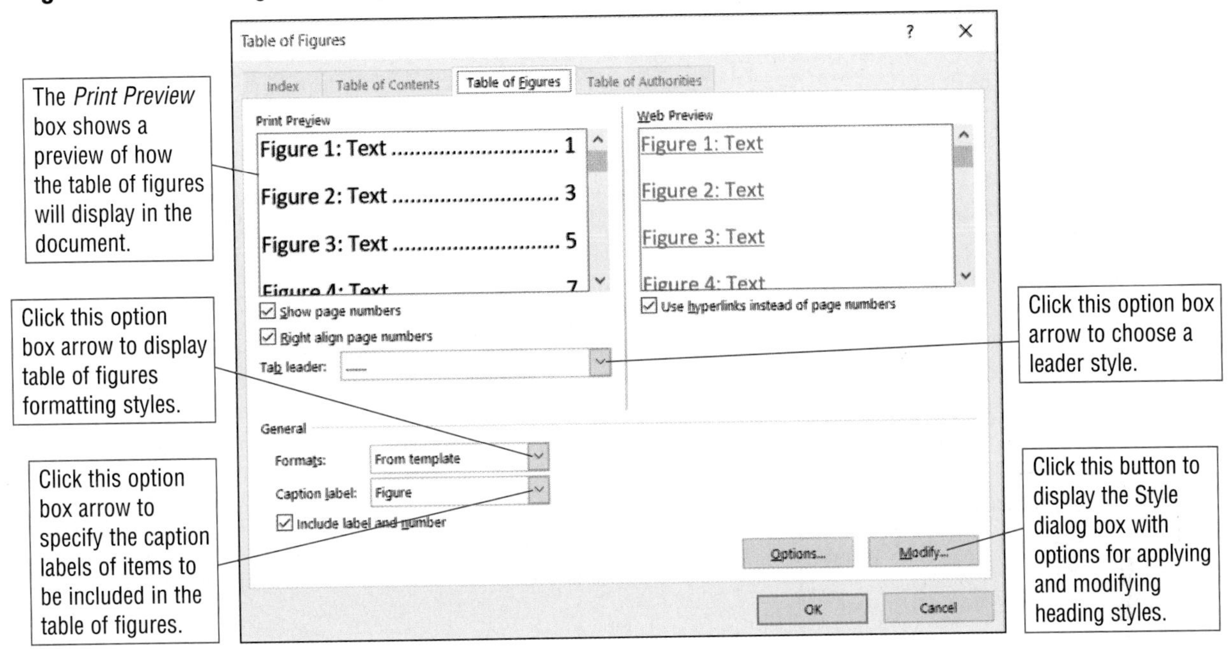

Project 3a Creating a Table of Figures

Part 1 of 3

1. Open **TechRpt.docx** and then save it with the name **6-TechRpt**.
2. Add the caption *Figure 1 Word Document* to an image by completing the following steps:
   a. Click the screen image in the *Word Processing Software* section.
   b. Click the References tab.
   c. Click the Insert Caption button in the Captions group.
   d. At the Caption dialog box with the insertion point positioned after *Figure 1* in the *Caption* text box, press the spacebar and then type Word Document.
   e. Click OK or press the Enter key.

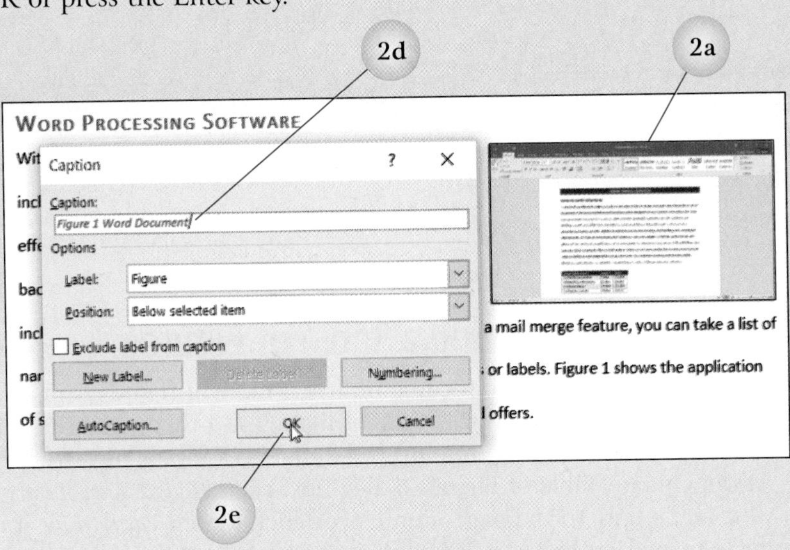

   f. Press Ctrl + E to center the caption in the text box.

3. Complete steps similar to those in Step 2 to create and center the caption *Figure 2 Excel Worksheet* for the image in the *SPREADSHEET SOFTWARE* section.
4. Complete steps similar to those in Step 2 to create and center the caption *Figure 3 Monitor* for the image in the *MONITOR* section.
5. Complete steps similar to those in Step 2 to create and center the caption *Figure 4 Software Life Cycle* for the SmartArt graphic in the *Developing Software* section.
6. Insert a table of figures at the beginning of the document by completing the following steps:
   a. Press Ctrl + Home to move the insertion point to the beginning of the document.
   b. Press Ctrl + Enter to insert a page break.
   c. Press Ctrl + Home to move the insertion point back to the beginning of the document, turn on bold formatting, change the paragraph alignment to center, and then type the title TABLE OF FIGURES.
   d. Press the Enter key, turn off bold formatting, and then change the paragraph alignment back to left alignment.
   e. If necessary, click the References tab.
   f. Click the Insert Table of Figures button in the Captions group.
   g. At the Table of Figures dialog box, click the *Formats* option box arrow and then click *Formal* at the drop-down list.

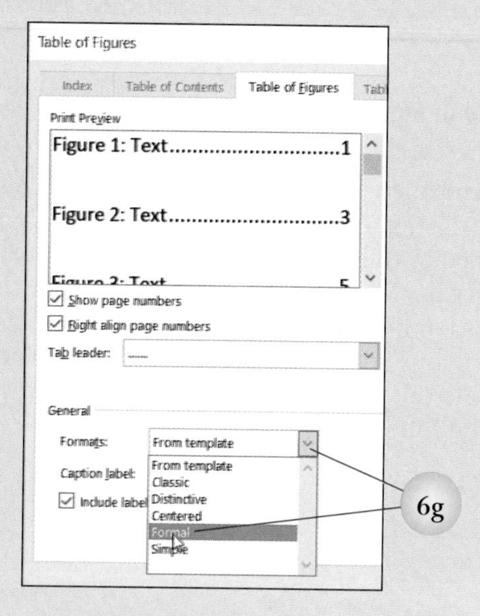

   h. Click OK.
7. Save **6-TechRpt.docx**.

Check Your Work

Quick Steps

Update a Table of Figures
1. Click in table of figures.
2. Click References tab.
3. Click Update Table button or press F9.
4. Click OK.

Delete a Table of Figures
1. Select entire table of figures.
2. Press Delete key.

Updating or Deleting a Table of Figures

If changes are made to a document after a table of figures is inserted, update the table. To do this, click in the table of figures and then click the Update Table button in the Captions group on the References tab or press the F9 function key. At the Update Table of Figures dialog box, click *Update page numbers only* if changes were made only to the page numbers or click *Update entire table* if changes were made to caption text. Click OK or press the Enter key to close the dialog box. To delete a table of figures, select the entire table using the mouse or keyboard and then press the Delete key.

Project 3b Updating a Table of Figures

Part 2 of 3

1. With **6-TechRpt.docx** open, insert an image of a laser printer by completing the following steps:
   a. Move the insertion point to the beginning of the second paragraph of text in the *PRINTERS* section.
   b. Click the Insert tab and then click the Pictures button in the Illustrations group.
   c. At the Insert Picture dialog box, navigate to the WL2C6 folder on your storage medium and then double-click the file named ***LaserPrinter.png***.
   d. Change the height of the image to 1.5 inches.
   e. Change to square text wrapping.
2. Add the caption *Figure 4 Laser Printer* to the printer image and then center the caption.
3. Click in the table of figures.
4. Press the F9 function key.
5. At the Update Table of Figures dialog box, click the *Update entire table* option and then click OK.
6. Save, print, and then close **6-TechRpt.docx**.

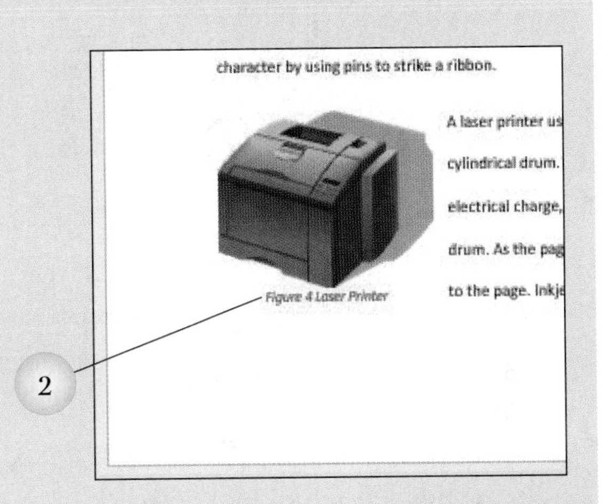

Check Your Work

Customizing a Caption

The Caption dialog box contains a number of options for customizing captions. Click the *Label* option box arrow to specify the caption label. The default is *Figure*, which can be changed to *Equation* or *Table*. The caption is positioned below the selected item. Use the *Position* option to change the position of the caption so it is above the selected item by default. A caption contains a label, such as *Figure*, *Table*, or *Equation*. To insert only a caption number and not a caption label, insert a check mark in the *Exclude label from caption* check box.

Click the New Label button and the Label dialog box displays. At this dialog box, type a custom label for the caption. Word automatically inserts an arabic number (*1, 2, 3,* and so on) after each caption label. To change the caption numbering style, click the Numbering button. At the Caption Numbering dialog box that displays, click the *Format* option box arrow and then click a numbering style at the drop-down list. For example, caption numbering can be changed to uppercase or lowercase letters or to roman numerals.

If items such as tables are inserted in a document on a regular basis, a caption can be inserted automatically with each item. To do this, click the AutoCaption button. At the AutoCaption dialog box, insert a check mark before the item (such as *Microsoft Word Table*) in the *Add caption when inserting* list box and then click OK. Each time a table is inserted in a document, Word inserts a caption above it.

Project 3c Creating and Customizing Captions and Inserting a Table of Figures Part 3 of 3

1. Open **TTSAdventures.docx** and then save it with the name **6-TTSAdventures**.
2. Insert a custom caption for the first table by completing the following steps:
   a. Click in any cell in the table.
   b. Click the References tab.
   c. Click the Insert Caption button.
   d. At the Caption dialog box, press the spacebar and then type Antarctic Zenith Adventures in the *Caption* text box.
   e. Remove the label (*Figure*) from the caption by clicking the *Exclude label from caption* check box to insert a check mark.
   f. Click the Numbering button.
   g. At the Caption Numbering dialog box, click the *Format* option box arrow and then click the *A, B, C, …* option at the drop-down list.
   h. Click OK to close the Caption Numbering dialog box.
   i. At the Caption dialog box, click the *Position* option box arrow and then click *Below selected item* at the drop-down list. (Skip this step if *Below selected item* is already selected.)
   j. Click OK to close the Caption dialog box.

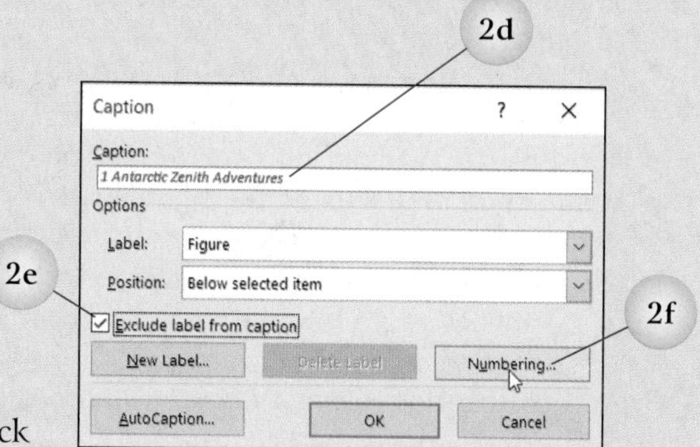

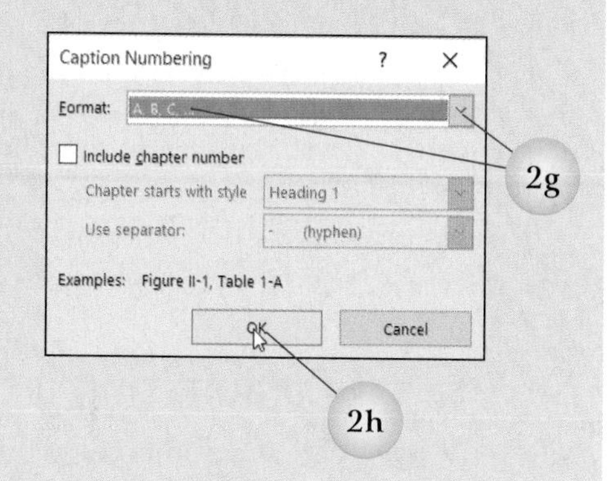

3. After looking at the caption, you decide to add a custom label and change the numbering. Do this by completing the following steps:
   a. Select the caption *A Antarctic Zenith Adventures*.
   b. Click the Insert Caption button in the Captions group on the References tab.
   c. At the Caption dialog box, click the *Exclude label from caption* check box to remove the check mark.
   d. Click the New Label button.
   e. At the New Label dialog box, type Adventure and then click OK.
   f. Click OK to close the Caption dialog box.

3e

New Label ? ×
Label:
Adventure
OK Cancel

4. Format the caption by completing the following steps:
   a. Select the caption *Adventure 1 Antarctic Zenith Adventures*.
   b. Click the Home tab.
   c. Click the Font Color button arrow.
   d. Click the *Dark Blue* color (ninth color in the *Standard Colors* section).
   e. Click the Bold button.
5. Insert a custom caption for the second table by completing the following steps:
   a. Click in any cell in the table.
   b. Click the References tab and then click the Insert Caption button.
   c. At the Caption dialog box, press the spacebar and then type Tall-Ship Adventures.
   d. Make sure *Below selected item* displays in the *Position* option box and then click OK to close the Caption dialog box.
6. Select the caption *Adventure 2 Tall-Ship Adventures*, apply the standard dark blue font color, and apply bold formatting.

7. Insert a table of figures by completing the following steps:
   a. Press Ctrl + Home and then press Ctrl + Enter to insert a page break.
   b. Press Ctrl + Home to move the insertion point above the page break.
   c. Turn on bold formatting, type TABLES, turn off bold formatting, and then press the Enter key.
   d. Click the References tab and then click the Insert Table of Figures button in the Captions group.
   e. At the Table of Figures dialog box, click OK.
8. Save, print, and then close **6-TTSAdventures.docx**.

Check Your Work

Project 4 Create an Index for a Desktop Publishing Report — 2 Parts

You will open a report containing information on desktop publishing, mark specific text for an index, and then insert the index in the document. You will also make changes to the document and then update the index.

Preview Finished Project

Creating an Index

An index is a list of the topics in a publication that includes the numbers of the pages those topics are discussed on. In Word, the process of creating an index is automated similarly to the process of creating a table of contents. When creating an index, single words and groups of words are marked to be included.

Creating an index takes careful thought and consideration. The author of the book, manuscript, or report must determine the main entries to be included, as well as the subentries to be added under the main entries. An index may include entries such as the main subject of a document, the main subjects of chapters and sections, variations of headings and subheadings, and abbreviations. Figure 6.9 shows an example of a portion of an index.

Figure 6.9 Sample Index

INDEX

A
Alignment, 12, 16
ASCII, 22, 24, 35
    data processing, 41
    word processing, 39

B
Backmatter, 120
    page numbering, 123
Balance, 67-69
Banners, 145

C
Callouts, 78
Captions, 156
Color, 192-195
    ink for offset printing, 193
    process color, 195

D
Databases, 124-129
    fields, 124
    records, 124
Directional flow, 70-71

Marking Text for an Index

Marking Text for an Index

Mark Entry

Quick Steps

Mark Text for an Index

1. Select text.
2. Click References tab.
3. Click Mark Entry button.
4. Click Mark button.

Hint You can also mark text for an index using the keyboard shortcut Alt + Shift + X.

A selected word or group of words can be marked for inclusion in an index. Before marking the text for an index, determine what main entries and subentries are to be included. Selected text is marked as an index entry at the Mark Index Entry dialog box.

To mark text for an index, select the word or group of words, click the References tab, and then click the Mark Entry button in the Index group. Another option is to use the keyboard shortcut Alt + Shift + X. At the Mark Index Entry dialog box, shown in Figure 6.10, the selected word or group of words appears in the *Main entry* text box. Click the Mark button to mark the word or groups of words and then click the Close button. Word automatically turns on the display of nonprinting characters and displays the index field code.

At the Mark Index Entry dialog box, if the selected word or group of words displayed in the *Main entry* text box is to be a main entry, leave it as displayed. However, if the selected text is to be a subentry, type the main entry in the *Main entry* text box, click in the *Subentry* text box, and then type the selected text. For example, suppose a publication includes the terms *Page layout* and *Portrait.* The group of words *Page layout* is to be marked as a main entry for the index and the word *Portrait* is to be marked as a subentry below *Page layout*. Marking these terms for use in an index would involve completing these steps:

1. Select *Page layout*.
2. Click the References tab and then click the Mark Entry button or press Alt + Shift + X.
3. At the Mark Index Entry dialog box, click the Mark button. (This turns on the display of nonprinting characters.)
4. With the Mark Index Entry dialog box still displayed, click in the document to make it active and then select the word *Portrait*.
5. Click the Mark Index Entry dialog box Title bar to make it active.
6. Select *Portrait* in the *Main entry* text box and then type Page layout.
7. Click in the *Subentry* text box and then type Portrait.
8. Click the Mark button.
9. Click the Close button.

Figure 6.10 Mark Index Entry Dialog Box

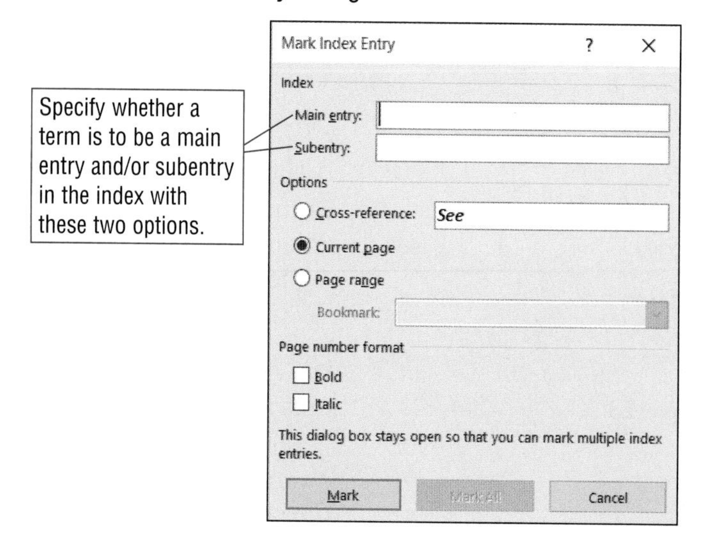

Hint To include a third-level index entry, type the subentry text, type a colon, and then type the third-level entry text.

Hint To delete an index entry, select the entire entry field, including the braces ({}), and then press the Delete key.

The main entry and subentry do not have to be the same as the selected text. Select text for an index, type specific text to be displayed in the document in the *Main entry* or *Subentry* text box, and then click the Mark button. At the Mark Index Entry dialog box, bold and/or italic formatting can be applied to the page numbers that will appear in the index. In the *Page number format* section, click *Bold* and/or *Italic* to insert a check mark in the check box.

In the *Options* section of the Mark Index Entry dialog box, *Current page* is the default. At this setting, the current page number will be provided in the index for the main entry and/or subentry. Click the *Cross-reference* option to cross reference specific text. To do this, type the text to be used as a cross-reference for the index entry in the *Cross-reference* text box. For example, the word *Serif* can be marked and cross referenced to *Typefaces*.

Click the Mark All button at the Mark Index Entry dialog box to mark all occurrences of the term in the document as index entries. Word marks only those entries whose uppercase and lowercase letters match the index entries.

Project 4a Marking Text for an Index

Part 1 of 2

1. Open **DTP.docx** and then save it with the name **6-DTP**.
2. Insert a page number at the bottom center of each page.
3. In the first paragraph, mark *software* for the index as a main entry and mark *word processing* as a subentry below *software* by completing the following steps:
   a. Select *software* (located in the second sentence of the first paragraph).
   b. Click the References tab and then click the Mark Entry button in the Index group.
   c. At the Mark Index Entry dialog box, click the Mark All button. (This turns on the display of nonprinting characters.)

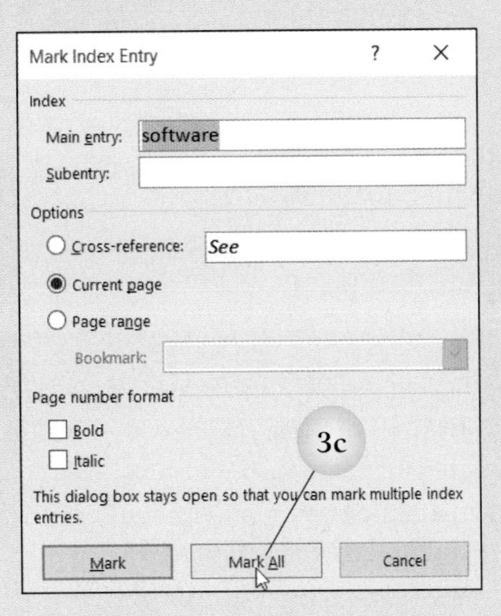

   d. With the Mark Index Entry dialog box still displayed, click in the document to make it active and then select *word processing* (located in the last sentence of the first paragraph). (You may want to drag the dialog box down the screen so more of the document text is visible.)
   e. Click the Title bar of the Mark Index Entry dialog box to make the dialog box active.

f. Select *word processing* in the *Main entry* text box and then type software.
g. Click in the *Subentry* text box and then type word processing.
h. Click the Mark All button.

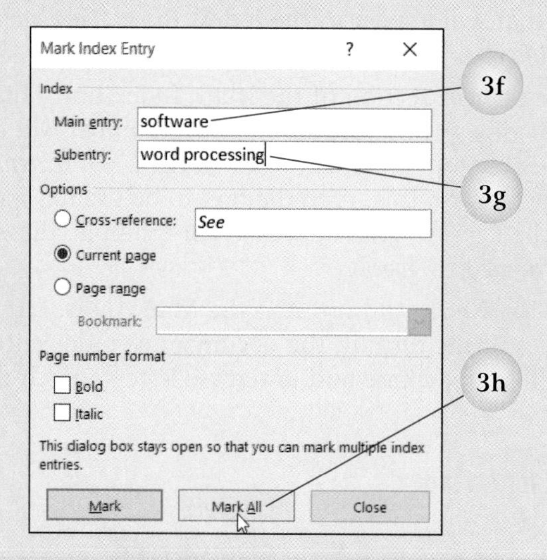

i. With the Mark Index Entry dialog box still displayed, complete steps similar to those in Steps 3d through 3h to select the first occurrence of each of the following words and then mark the word as a main entry or subentry for the index (click the Mark All button at the Mark Index Entry dialog box):
   1) In the first paragraph in the *Defining Desktop Publishing* section:
      spreadsheets = subentry (main entry = *software*)
      database = subentry (main entry = *software*)
   2) In the second paragraph in the *Defining Desktop Publishing* section:
      publishing = main entry
      desktop = subentry (main entry = *publishing*)
      printer = main entry
      laser = subentry (main entry = *printer*)
   3) In the third paragraph in the *Defining Desktop Publishing* section:
      design = main entry
   4) In the fourth paragraph in the *Defining Desktop Publishing* section:
      traditional = subentry (main entry = *publishing*)
   5) In the only paragraph in the *Initiating the Process* section:
      publication = main entry
      planning = subentry (main entry = *publication*)
      creating = subentry (main entry = *publication*)
      intended audience = subentry (main entry = *publication*)
      content = subentry (main entry = *publication*)
   6) In the third paragraph in the *Planning the Publication* section:
      message = main entry

j. Click Close to close the Mark Index Entry dialog box.

4. Turn off the display of nonprinting characters.
5. Save **6-DTP.docx**.

Figure 6.11 Index Dialog Box

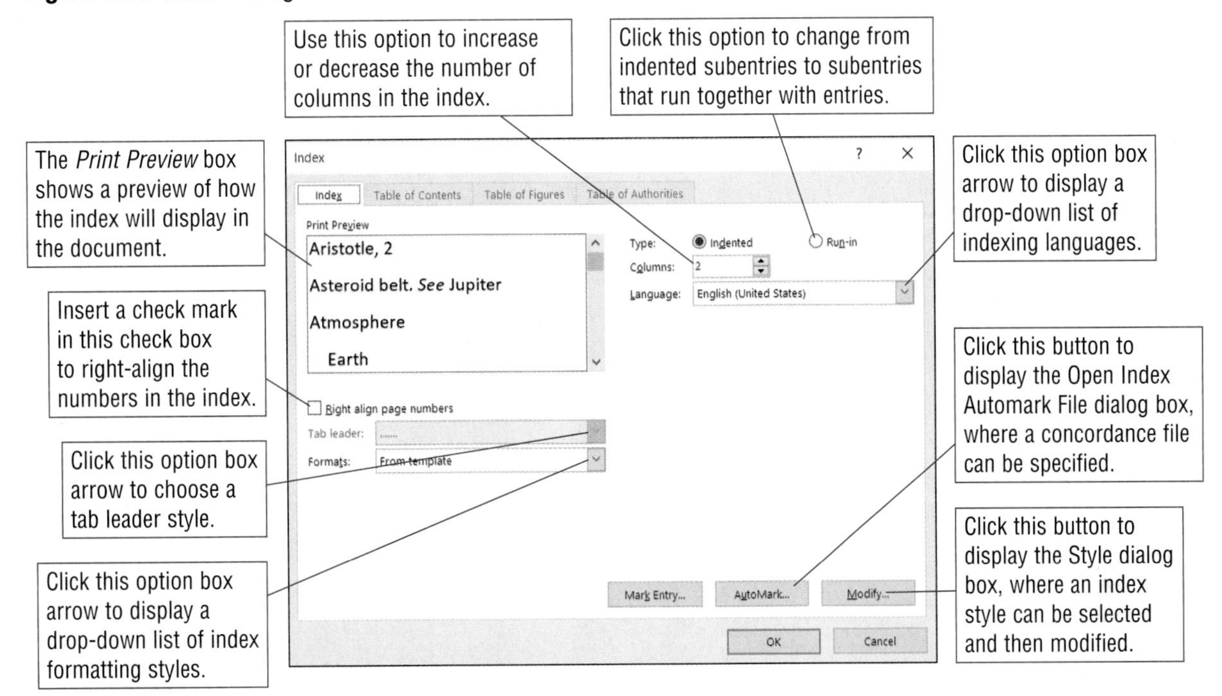
Use this option to increase or decrease the number of columns in the index.
Click this option to change from indented subentries to subentries that run together with entries.
The *Print Preview* box shows a preview of how the index will display in the document.
Click this option box arrow to display a drop-down list of indexing languages.
Insert a check mark in this check box to right-align the numbers in the index.
Click this button to display the Open Index Automark File dialog box, where a concordance file can be specified.
Click this option box arrow to choose a tab leader style.
Click this button to display the Style dialog box, where an index style can be selected and then modified.
Click this option box arrow to display a drop-down list of index formatting styles.
Index
Index
Table of Contents
Table of Figures
Table of Authorities
Print Preview
Aristotle, 2
Asteroid belt. See Jupiter
Atmosphere
Earth
Type:
Indented
Run-in
Columns:
2
Language:
English (United States)
Right align page numbers
Tab leader:
Formats:
From template
Mark Entry...
AutoMark...
Modify...
OK
Cancel

Tutorial

Inserting and Updating an Index

Inserting an Index

After marking all the terms to be included in an index as main entries or subentries, the next step is to insert the index. The index should appear at the end of the document and generally begins on a separate page.

Insert Index

To insert the index, position the insertion point at the end of the document and then insert a page break. With the insertion point positioned below the page break, type *INDEX*, center it, apply bold formatting, and then press the Enter key. With the insertion point positioned at the left margin, click the References tab and then click the Insert Index button in the Index group. At the Index dialog box, shown in Figure 6.11, select formatting options and then click OK. Word inserts the index at the location of the insertion point with the formatting selected at the Index dialog box. Word also inserts section breaks above and below the index text.

Insert an Index

1. Click References tab.
2. Click Insert Index button.
3. Select format.
4. Click OK.

At the Index dialog box, specify how the index entries are to appear. The *Print Preview* section shows how the index will display in the document. The *Columns* measurement box has a default setting of *2*. With this setting applied, the index will display in two columns; this number can be increased or decreased.

Insert a check mark in the *Right align page numbers* check box and the *Tab leader* options become active. Use these options to apply leaders before page numbers. The default tab leader is a period. To choose a different leader, click the *Tab leader* option box arrow and then click a character at the drop-down list.

In the *Type* section, the *Indented* option is selected by default. With this setting applied, subentries will appear indented below main entries. Click *Run-in* and subentries will display on the same lines as main entries.

Click the *Formats* option box arrow and a list of formatting choices displays. At this list, click a formatting choice and the *Print Preview* box displays how the index will appear in the document.

Project 4b Inserting an Index

Part 2 of 2

1. With **6-DTP.docx** open, insert the index in the document by completing the following steps:
   a. Press Ctrl + End to position the insertion point at the end of the document.
   b. Insert a page break.
   c. With the insertion point positioned below the page break, type INDEX and then press the Enter key.
   d. Click the References tab.
   e. Click the Insert Index button in the Index group.
   f. At the Index dialog box, click the *Formats* option box arrow and then click *Modern* at the drop-down list.
   g. Click OK to close the dialog box.
   h. Click in the title *INDEX*, apply the Heading 1 style (located in the Styles group on the Home tab), and then press Ctrl + E to center the title.
2. Save **6-DTP.docx** and then print the index page (the last page) of the document.
3. Close **6-DTP.docx**.

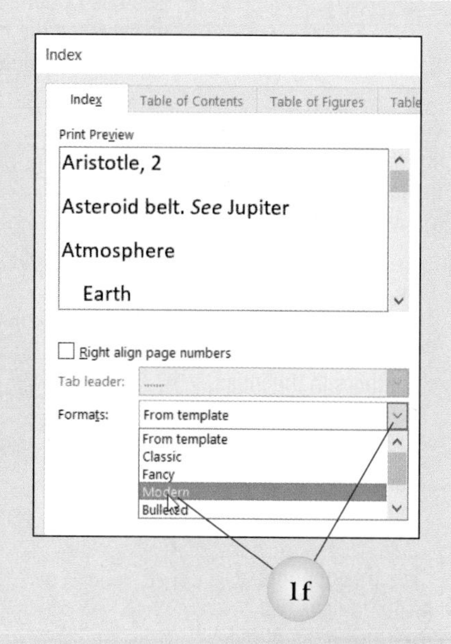

Check Your Work

Project 5 Mark Index Entries and Insert an Index

1 Part

You will create bookmarks in a document on computers, mark entries for an index, and then insert an index in the document.

Preview Finished Project

Marking Index Entry Options

The *Options* section of the Mark Index Entry dialog box provides additional options for marking text for an index. A bookmark can be marked as an index entry or text can be marked that refers readers to another index entry.

Marking Text That Spans a Range of Pages To use more than a few words as a single index entry, consider identifying the text as a bookmark and then marking the bookmark as an index entry. This option is especially useful when the text for an entry spans a range of pages. To mark text identified as a bookmark, position the insertion point at the end of the text, click the References tab, and then click the Mark Entry button in the Index group.

At the Mark Index Entry dialog box, type the index entry for the text and then click the *Page range* option in the *Options* section. Click the *Bookmark* option box arrow and then click the bookmark name at the drop-down list. Click the Mark button to mark the bookmark text and then close the dialog box.

Marking an Entry as a Cross-Reference Text that refers readers to another entry can be marked for inclusion in an index. For example, if the acronym *MIS* is used in a document to refer to *Management Information Systems*, *MIS* can be marked as an index entry that refers readers to the entry for *Management Information Systems*. To do this, select *MIS*, click the References tab, and then click the Mark Entry button in the Index group. At the Mark Index Entry dialog box, click *Cross-reference* in the *Options* section of the dialog box (to move the insertion point inside the text box), type *Management Information Systems*, and then click the Mark button.

Project 5 Marking Entries and Inserting an Index

Part 1 of 1

1. Open **Computers.docx** and then save it with the name **6-Computers**.
2. Make the following changes to the document:
   a. Apply the Heading 1 style to the title *COMPUTERS*.
   b. Apply the Heading 2 style to the five headings in the document (*Speed*, *Accuracy*, *Versatility*, *Storage*, and *Communications*).
   c. Apply the Lines (Stylish) style set.
   d. Apply the Blue theme colors.
   e. Change the theme fonts to Candara.
3. Create a bookmark for the *Speed* section of the document by completing the following steps:
   a. Select text from the beginning of the heading *Speed* through the paragraph of text that follows the heading.
   b. Click the Insert tab.
   c. Click the Bookmark button in the Links group.
   d. At the Bookmark dialog box, type Speed in the *Bookmark name* text box.
   e. Click the Add button.

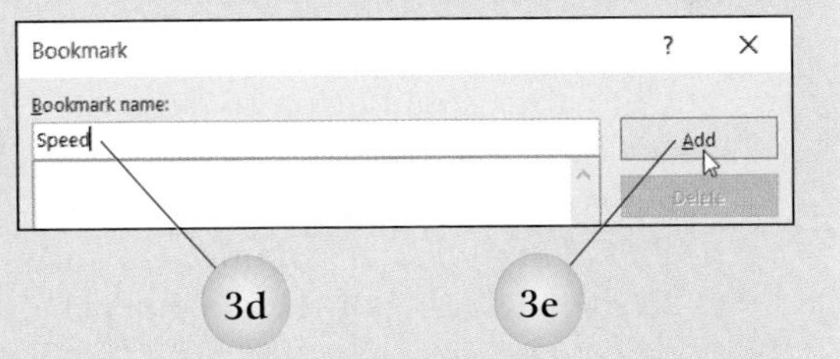

4. Complete steps similar to those in Step 3 to create the following bookmarks:
   a. Select text from the beginning of the *Accuracy* heading through the paragraph of text that follows the heading and then create a bookmark named *Accuracy*.
   b. Select text from the beginning of the *Versatility* heading through the paragraph of text that follows the heading and then create a bookmark named *Versatility*.
   c. Select text from the beginning of the *Storage* heading through the paragraph of text that follows the heading and then create a bookmark named *Storage*.
   d. Select text from the beginning of the *Communications* heading through the two paragraphs of text that follow the heading and then create a bookmark named *Communications*.
5. Mark the *Speed* bookmark as an index entry that spans multiple pages by completing the following steps:
   a. Move the insertion point so it is positioned immediately following the only paragraph of text in the *Speed* section.
   b. Click the References tab.
   c. Click the Mark Entry button in the Index group.
   d. At the Mark Index Entry dialog box, type Speed in the *Main entry* text box.
   e. Click the *Page range* option.
   f. Click the *Bookmark* option box arrow and then click *Speed* at the drop-down list.
   g. Click the Mark button.

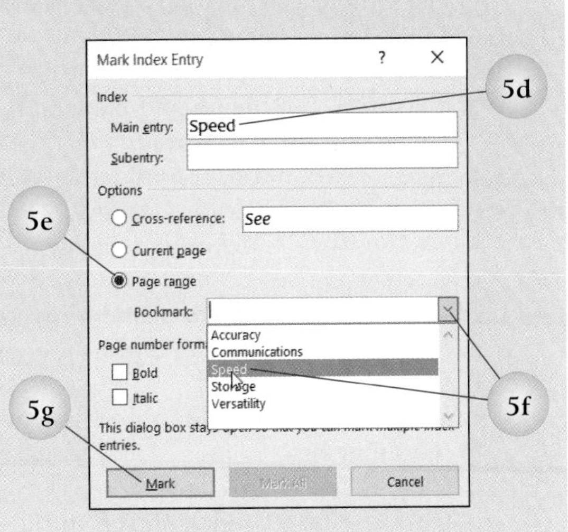

6. Complete steps similar to those in Step 5 to mark the following bookmarks as index entries: *Accuracy, Versatility, Storage,* and *Communications.*
7. With the Mark Index Entry dialog box open, mark the *first* occurrences of the following words (click the Mark All button) as main entries or subentries for the index:
   a. Mark *computers,* located in the first sentence of the first paragraph of text in the document as a main entry.
   b. Mark *personal computers,* located in the second paragraph of text in the document, as a main entry.
   c. Mark *supercomputers,* located in the *Speed* section of the document, as a main entry.
   d. Mark *GIGO,* located in the *Accuracy* section of the document, as a main entry.
   e. Mark the following text located in the *Versatility* section:

      Human Genome Project: main entry
      DNA: main entry

   f. Mark the following text located in the *Communications* section:

      wireless devices: main entry
      notebook computers: subentry (main entry: *wireless devices*)
      cell phones: subentry (main entry: *wireless devices*)
      local area network: main entry
      wide area network: main entry

   g. Click the Close button to close the Mark Index Entry dialog box.
8. Mark *microcomputers* as a cross-reference by completing the following steps:
   a. Press Ctrl + Home to move the insertion point to the beginning of the document.
   b. Select the word *microcomputers* that is located in the first sentence of the second paragraph of text.
   c. If necessary, click the References tab.
   d. Click the Mark Entry button in the Index group.
   e. At the Mark Index Entry dialog box, click the *Cross-reference* option in the *Options* section (after the word *See*) and then type personal computers.
   f. Click the Mark button.
   g. Click the Close button to close the Mark Index Entry dialog box.

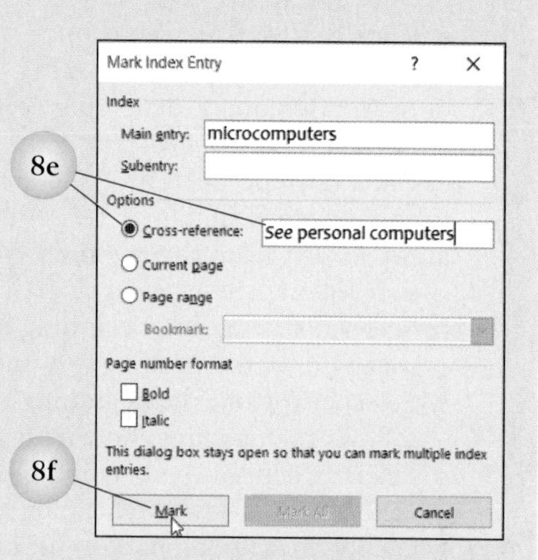

9. Complete steps similar to those in Step 8 to mark the following text as cross-references:
   a. Select *LAN* in the second paragraph of text in the *Communications* section and cross-reference it to *local area network.*
   b. Select *WAN* in the second paragraph of text in the *Communications* section and cross-reference it to *wide area network.*
10. Close the Mark Index Entry dialog box and then turn off the display of nonprinting characters.
11. Insert the index in the document by completing the following steps:
    a. Position the insertion point at the end of the document.
    b. Insert a page break.
    c. With the insertion point positioned below the page break, type INDEX, and then press the Enter key.
    d. Click the References tab.
    e. Click the Insert Index button in the Index group.

f. At the Index dialog box, click the *Formats* option box arrow, scroll down the drop-down list, and then click *Formal*.
g. Make sure *3* displays in the *Columns* measurement box.
h. Click OK to close the dialog box.
i. Apply the Heading 1 style to the title *INDEX*.
12. Save and then print the last page (the index page) of the document.
13. Close **6-Computers.docx**.

Check Your Work

Project 6 **Create an Index with a Concordance File for a Newsletter** **3 Parts**

You will create and then save a concordance file. You will then open a report containing information on designing newsletters and use the concordance file to create an index.

Preview Finished Project

Tutorial

Creating and Using a Concordance File

Quick Steps

Create a Concordance File

1. Click Insert tab.
2. Click Table button and drag to create table.
3. In first column, type word or words for index.
4. In second column, type corresponding main entry and subentry.
5. Save document.

Creating and Using a Concordance File

Another method for creating an index is to create a concordance file and use the information in it to create the index. Creating a concordance file avoids the need to mark each word or group of words in a document.

A concordance file is a Word document that contains a two-column table with no text outside the table. In the first column of the table, enter the word or group of words to be included in the index. In the second column, enter the corresponding main entry and subentry, if applicable, that should appear in the index. To create a subentry, type the main entry followed by a colon, a space, and then the subentry. Figure 6.12 shows an example of a completed concordance file.

In the concordance file shown in Figure 6.12, the word or group of words as it appears in the document text is inserted in the first column (such as *World War I*, *Technology*, and *technology*). The second column contains what is to appear in the index, identifying each item as a main entry or subentry. For example, the words *motion pictures* in the concordance file will appear in the index as a subentry under the main entry *Technology*.

Use a concordance file to quickly mark text for an index in a document. To do this, open the document containing the text to be marked for the index, display the Index dialog box with the Index tab selected, and then click the AutoMark button. At the Open Index AutoMark File dialog box, double-click the concordance file name in the list box. Word turns on the display of nonprinting characters, searches the document for text that matches the text in the concordance file, and then marks it accordingly. After marking text for the index, insert the index at the end of the document, as described earlier.

When creating the concordance file in Project 5a, Word's AutoCorrect feature will automatically capitalize the first letter of the first word entered in each cell. In Figure 6.12, several of the first words in the first column do not begin with capital letters. Before beginning the project, consider turning off this AutoCorrect capitalization feature. To do this, click the File tab and then click *Options*. At the Word Options dialog box, click *Proofing* in the left panel and then click the AutoCorrect Options button. At the AutoCorrect dialog box with the AutoCorrect tab selected, click the *Capitalize first letter of table cells* check box to remove the check mark. Click OK to close the dialog box and then click OK to close the Word Options dialog box.

Figure 6.12 Sample Concordance File

World War I	World War I
Technology	Technology
technology	Technology
Teletypewriters	Technology: teletypewriters
motion pictures	Technology: motion pictures
Television	Technology: television
Radio Corporation of America	Radio Corporation of America
coaxial cable	Coaxial cable
Telephone	Technology: telephone
Communications Act of 1934	Communications Act of 1934
World War II	World War II
radar system	Technology: radar system
Computer	Computer
Atanasoff Berry Computer	Computer: Atanasoff Berry Computer
Korean War	Korean War
Columbia Broadcasting System	Columbia Broadcasting System
Cold War	Cold War
Vietnam	Vietnam
artificial satellite	Technology: artificial satellite
Communications Satellite Act of 1962	Communications Satellite Act of 1962

Project 6a Creating a Concordance File

Part 1 of 3

1. At a blank document, create the text shown in Figure 6.13 as a concordance file by completing the following steps:
   a. Click the Insert tab.
   b. Click the Table button in the Tables group.
   c. Drag down and to the right until *2×1 Table* displays at the top of the grid and then click the left mouse button.

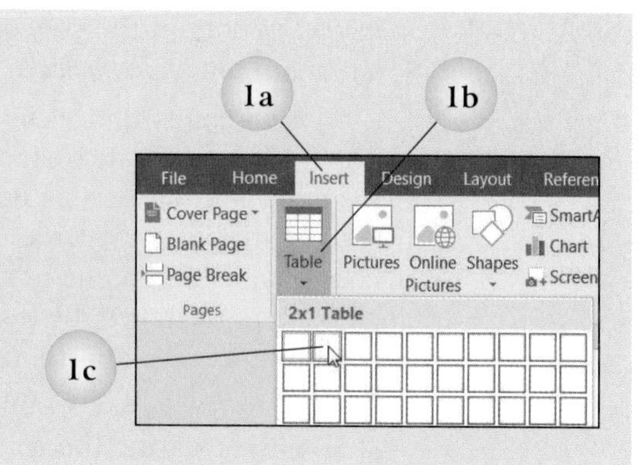

d. Type the text in the cells as shown in Figure 6.13. As you type the text shown in the figure, press the Tab key to move to the next cell. (If you did not remove the check mark before the *Capitalize first letter of table cells* option at the AutoCorrect dialog box, the *n* in the first word in the first cell, *newsletters*, is automatically capitalized. Hover the mouse pointer over the *N*, click the blue rectangle that displays below the *N*, and then click *Stop Auto-capitalizing First Letter of Table Cells*.)

2. Save the document and name it **6-CFile**.
3. Print and then close **6-CFile.docx**.

Check Your Work

Figure 6.13 Project 6a

newsletters	Newsletters
Newsletters	Newsletters
software	Software
desktop publishing	Software: desktop publishing
word processing	Software: word processing
printers	Printers
laser	Printers: laser
Design	Design
communication	Communication
consistency	Design: consistency
ELEMENTS	Elements
Elements	Elements
elements	Elements
Nameplate	Elements: nameplate
nameplate	Elements: nameplate
Logo	Elements: logo
logo	Elements: logo
Subtitle	Elements: subtitle
subtitle	Elements: subtitle
Folio	Elements: folio
folio	Elements: folio
Headlines	Elements: headlines
headlines	Elements: headlines
Subheads	Elements: subheads
subheads	Elements: subheads
Byline	Elements: byline
byline	Elements: byline
Body Copy	Elements: body copy
body copy	Elements: body copy

continues

Figure 6.13 Project 6a—*Continued*

Graphics Images	Elements: graphics images
Graphics images	Elements: graphics images
audience	Newsletters: audience
Purpose	Newsletters: purpose
purpose	Newsletters: purpose
focal point	Newsletters: focal point

If the check mark was removed from the *Capitalize first letter of table cells* option at the AutoCorrect dialog box, this feature may need to be turned back on. To do this, click the File tab and then click *Options*. At the Word Options dialog box, click *Proofing* in the left panel and then click the AutoCorrect Options button. At the AutoCorrect dialog box with the AutoCorrect tab selected, click the *Capitalize first letter of table cells* check box to insert a check mark. Click OK to close the dialog box and then click OK to close the Word Options dialog box.

Project 6b Inserting an Index Using a Concordance File

Part 2 of 3

1. Open **PlanNwsltr.docx** and then save it with the name **6-PlanNwsltr**.
2. Mark text for the index using the concordance file you created in Project 6a by completing the following steps:
   a. Click the References tab.
   b. Click the Insert Index button in the Index group.
   c. At the Index dialog box, click the AutoMark button.

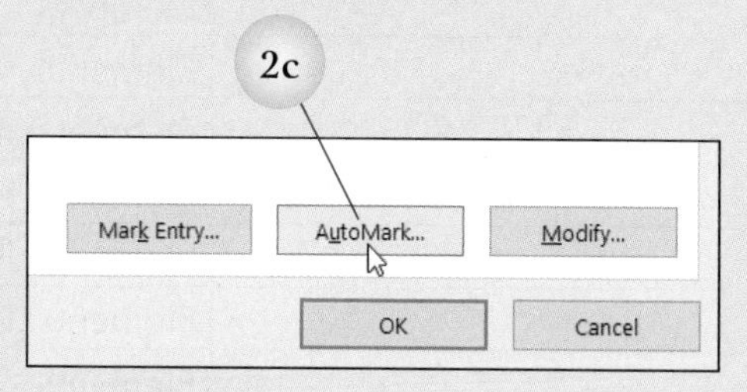

   d. At the Open Index AutoMark File dialog box, double-click ***6-CFile.docx*** in the Content pane. (This turns on the display of nonprinting characters.)
3. Insert the index in the document by completing the following steps:
   a. Position the insertion point at the end of the document.
   b. Insert a page break.
   c. Type INDEX and then press the Enter key.
   d. Click the Insert Index button in the Index group.
   e. At the Index dialog box, click the *Formats* option box arrow and then click *Formal* at the drop-down list.
   f. Click OK to close the dialog box.
4. Apply the Heading 1 style to the title *INDEX* and then center the title.
5. Turn off the display of nonprinting characters.
6. Save **6-PlanNwsltr.docx** and then print only the Index page.

Check Your Work

Updating and Deleting an Index

Update Index

Quick Steps

Update an Index
1. Click in index.
2. Click Update Index button or press F9.

Delete an Index
1. Select entire index.
2. Press Delete key.

If changes are made to a document after the index is inserted, update the index. To do this, click in the index and then click the Update Index button in the Index group or press the F9 function key. To delete an index, select the entire index using the mouse or keyboard and then press the Delete key.

Project 6c Updating an Index

Part 3 of 3

1. With **6-PlanNwsltr.docx** open, insert a page break at the beginning of the title *PLANNING A NEWSLETTER*.
2. Update the index by clicking in the index, clicking the References tab, and then clicking the Update Index button in the Index group.
3. Save **6-PlanNwsltr.docx** and then print only the index page.
4. Close **6-PlanNwsltr.docx**.

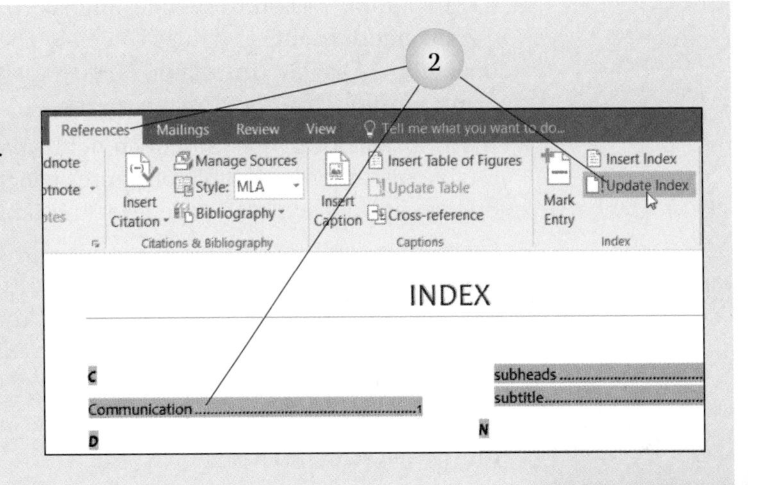

Check Your Work

Chapter Summary

- Word provides options for automating the creation of a table of contents, table of figures, and index.
- Identify the text to be included in a table of contents by applying heading styles, assigning levels, or marking text as field entries.
- Mark text as a field entry at the Mark Table of Contents dialog box. Display this dialog box by pressing Alt + Shift + O.
- Creating a table of contents using heading styles involves two steps: applying the appropriate styles to mark the text to be included and inserting the table of contents in the document.
- To insert a table of contents, position the insertion point where the table is to appear, click the References tab, click the Table of Contents button, and then click a specific option at the drop-down list.
- Generally, the pages containing the table of contents are numbered with lowercase roman numerals.
- The headings in a table of contents in a document are hyperlinks and these hyperlinks can be used to navigate within the document.

- If changes are made to a document after the table of contents is inserted, update the table of contents. To do this, click in the current table of contents and then click the Update Table button on the References tab click the Update Table tab, or press the F9 function key. Update a table of figures or index in a similar manner.
- Remove a table of contents by clicking the Table of Contents button on the References tab and then clicking *Remove Table of Contents* at the drop-down list.
- Another method for identifying text for a table of contents is to select the text, click the Add Text button on the References tab, and then click a specific level for the selected text.
- To identify text for a table of contents without applying styles, mark the text at the Mark Table of Contents Entry dialog box. Display this dialog box by pressing Alt + Shift + O.
- Create a table of figures by marking specific text or images with captions and then using the caption names to create the table. Mark captions at the Caption dialog box. Display this dialog box by clicking the Insert Caption button in the Captions group on the References tab.
- Insert a table of figures in a document in a manner similar to that for inserting a table of contents. A table of figures generally displays at the beginning of the document on a separate page after the table of contents.
- Customize captions at the Caption dialog box. Customizations include specifying a caption label, the position of the caption, and whether or not the label should be included in the caption. Click the Numbering button at the Caption dialog box and the Caption Numbering dialog box displays with options for specifying a numbering format and style.
- An index is a list of the topics in a publication and the numbers of the pages those topics are discussed on.
- Mark the words and groups of words to be included in an index at the Mark Index Entry dialog box. Display this dialog box by clicking the Mark Entry button in the Index group on the References tab or using the keyboard shortcut Alt + Shift + X.
- After all the words and groups of words have been marked as main entries and subentries, insert the index. Place it on a separate page at the end of the document.
- Insert an index in a document by clicking the Insert Index button on the References tab, selecting formatting at the Index dialog box, and then clicking OK.
- Text can be identified as a bookmark and then the bookmark can be marked as an index entry. This is especially useful when the text for an entry spans a range of pages.
- Mark text as a cross-reference to refer readers to another index entry.
- Words that appear frequently in a document can be saved in a concordance file and used in creating an index. A concordance file is a Word document that contains a two-column table. Using this table to create the index eliminates the need to mark all the words and groups of words in a document.

Commands Review

FEATURE	RIBBON TAB, GROUP	BUTTON, OPTION	KEYBOARD SHORTCUT
Caption dialog box	References, Captions		
Index dialog box	References, Index		
Mark Index Entry dialog box	References, Index		Alt + Shift + X
Mark Table of Contents Entry dialog box			Alt + Shift + O
Open Index AutoMark File dialog box	References, Index	, AutoMark button	
Page Number Format dialog box	Insert, Header & Footer	, *Format Page Numbers*	
Table of Contents dialog box	References, Table of Contents	, *Custom Table of Contents*	
Table of Contents Options dialog box	References, Table of Contents	, *Custom Table of Contents*, Options button	
Table of Figures dialog box	References, Captions		
update index	References, Index		F9
update table of contents	References, Table of Contents		F9

Workbook

Chapter study tools and assessment activities are available in the *Workbook* ebook. These resources are designed to help you further develop and demonstrate mastery of the skills learned in this chapter.

Microsoft®

Word

CHAPTER 7

Working with Shared Documents

Performance Objectives

Upon successful completion of Chapter 7, you will be able to:

1 Insert, edit, show, reply to, print, and delete comments
2 Navigate between comments
3 Distinguish comments from different users
4 Edit a document using the Track Changes feature
5 Customize the display of changes, markups, and review information
6 Navigate to and accept/reject revisions
7 Compare documents
8 Combine documents and show source documents
9 Embed and link data between Excel and Word

Precheck

Check your current skills to help focus your study.

In a workplace environment, you may need to share documents with and distribute them to coworkers and associates. You may be part of a workgroup, which is a networked collection of computers that share files, printers, and other resources. As a member of a workgroup, you can collaborate with other members and distribute documents for their review and/or revision. In this chapter, you will perform workgroup activities such as inserting comments, tracking changes, comparing documents, and combining documents from multiple users.

If a Word 2016 document (.docx format) is located on a server running Microsoft SharePoint Server, multiple users can edit it concurrently. Concurrent editing allows a group of users to work on a document at the same time or a single user to work on the same document from different computers. If a document is not located on a server running SharePoint Server, Word 2016 supports only single-user editing. Projects and assessments in this chapter assume that the files you are editing are not located on a server running SharePoint Server.

SNAP

If you are a SNAP user, launch the Precheck and Tutorials from your Assignments page.

Data Files

Before beginning chapter work, copy the WL2C7 folder to your storage medium and then make WL2C7 the active folder.

Project 1 Insert Comments in a New Employees Document 4 Parts

You will open a report containing company information for new employees and then insert and edit comments from multiple users.

Preview Finished Project

Tutorial

Inserting Comments

Quick Steps

Insert a Comment

1. Select text.
2. Click Review tab.
3. Click New Comment button.
4. Type comment.

New Comment

Hint Use comments to add notes, suggestions, and explanations and to communicate with members of your workgroup.

Inserting and Managing Comments

Use Word's comment feature to provide feedback on and suggest changes to a document that someone else has written. Similarly, get feedback on a document by distributing it electronically to others and having them insert comments in it.

To insert a comment in a document, select the text or item the comment pertains to or position the insertion point at the end of the text, click the Review tab, and then click the New Comment button in the Comments group. This displays a comment balloon at the right margin, as shown in Figure 7.1.

Depending on what settings have been applied, clicking the New Comment button may cause the Reviewing pane to display at the left side of the document, rather than the comment balloon. If this happens, click the Show Markup button in the Tracking group on the Review tab, point to *Balloons*, and then click *Show Only Comments and Formatting in Balloons* at the side menu. Also check to make sure the *Display for Review* option box in the Tracking group is set to *Simple Markup*. If it is not, click the *Display for Review* option box arrow and then click *Simple Markup* at the drop-down list.

Figure 7.1 Sample Comment Balloon

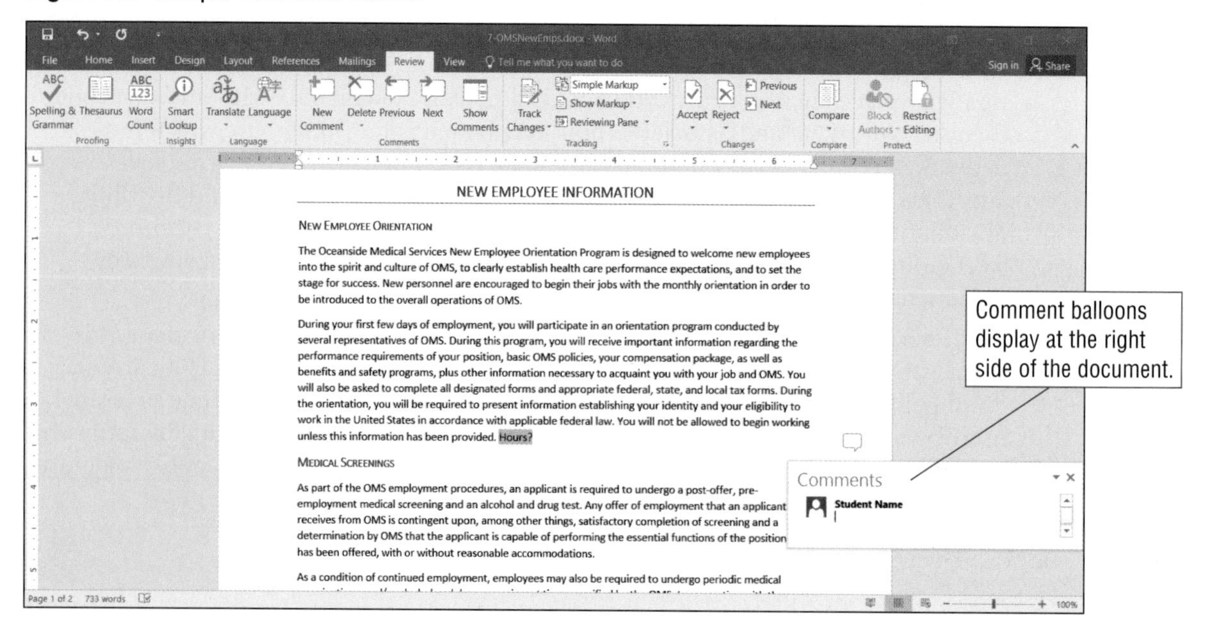

Project 1a Inserting Comments

1. Open **OMSNewEmps.docx** and then save it with the name **7-OMSNewEmps**.
2. Insert a comment by completing the following steps:
   a. Position the insertion point at the end of the second paragraph in the *New Employee Orientation* section.
   b. Press the spacebar and then type Hours?.
   c. Select *Hours?*.
   d. Click the Review tab.
   e. Make sure *Simple Markup* displays in the *Display for Review* option box. If it does not, click the *Display for Review* option box arrow and then click *Simple Markup* at the drop-down list.
   f. If the Show Comments button in the Comments group is active (displays with a gray background), click the button to deactivate it.
   g. Click the New Comment button in the Comments group.
   h. Type Please include the total number of orientation hours. in the comment balloon.

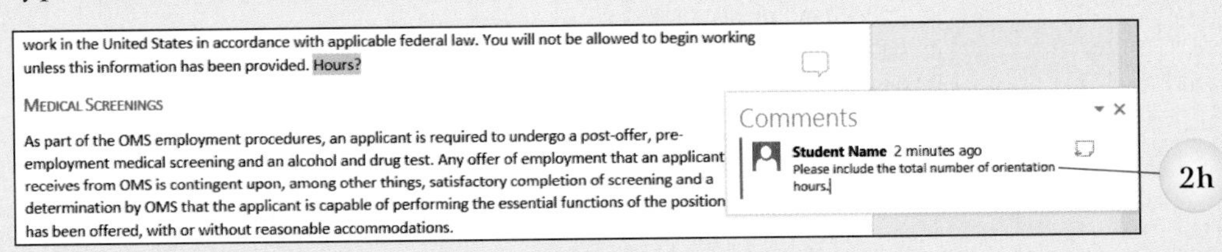

3. Insert another comment by completing the following steps:
   a. Move the insertion point to the end of the third (last) paragraph in the *Medical Screenings* section.
   b. Click the New Comment button in the Comments group.
   c. Type Specify the locations where drug tests are administered. in the comment balloon. (Since you did not select any text before clicking the New Comment button, Word selects the word immediately left of the insertion point.)
   d. Click in the document to close the comment balloons.
4. Save **7-OMSNewEmps.docx**.

Check Your Work

Inserting Comments in the Reviewing Pane

Reviewing Pane

Quick Steps

Insert a Comment in the Reviewing Pane
1. Click Review tab.
2. Click Reviewing Pane button.
3. Click New Comment button.
4. Type comment.

Comments can also be inserted with the Reviewing pane displayed on the screen. The Reviewing pane displays both inserted comments and changes recorded with the Track Changes feature. (Track Changes is covered later in this chapter.)

To display the Reviewing pane, click the Reviewing Pane button in the Tracking group on the Review tab. The Reviewing pane usually displays at the left side of the screen, as shown in Figure 7.2. Click the New Comment button in the Comments group and a comment icon and balloon displays in the right margin; the reviewer's name followed by "Commented" displays in the Reviewing pane. Type the comment and the text displays in the comment balloon and in the Reviewing pane. (The Reviewing pane might display along the bottom of the screen, rather than at the left side. To specify where the pane is to display, click the Reviewing Pane button arrow in the Tracking group on the Review tab and then click *Reviewing Pane Vertical* or *Reviewing Pane Horizontal*.)

Hint If your computer has a sound card and microphone, you can record voice comments.

A summary displays toward the top of the Reviewing pane and provides counts of the number of comments inserted and the types of changes that have been made to the document. After typing a comment in the Reviewing pane, close the pane by clicking the Reviewing Pane button in the Tracking group or by clicking the Close button in the upper right corner of the pane.

Figure 7.2 Vertical Reviewing Pane

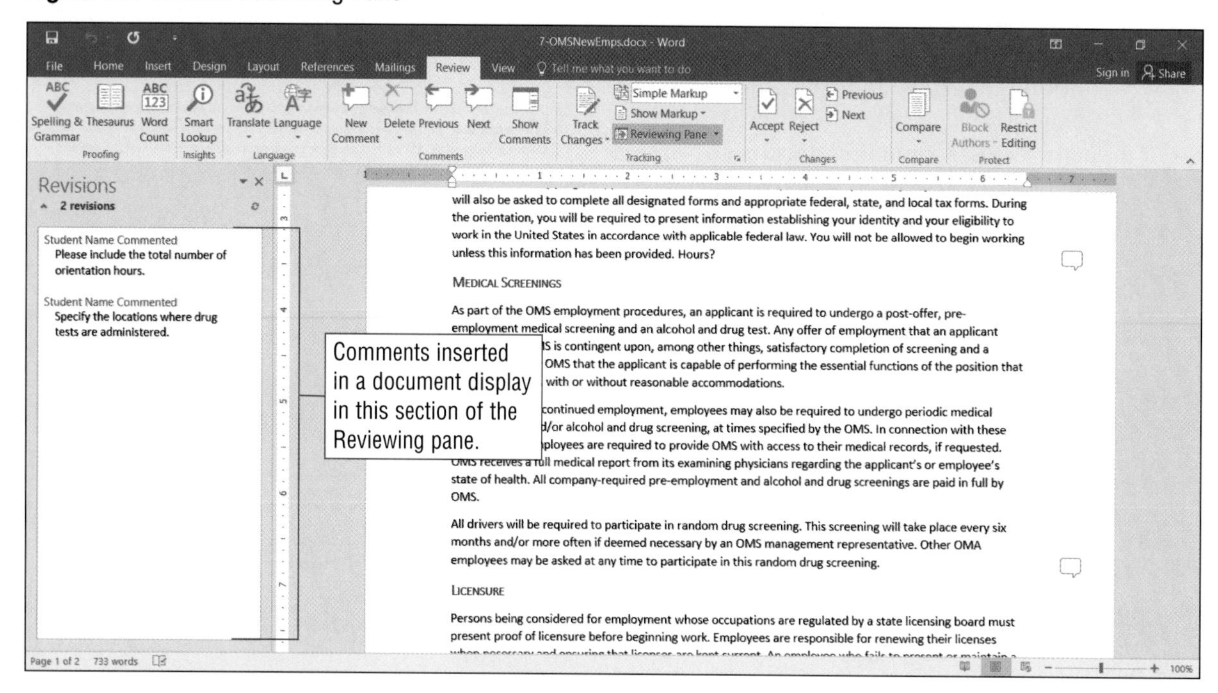

Project 1b Inserting a Comment in the Reviewing Pane

Part 2 of 4

1. With **7-OMSNewEmps.docx** open, show the comments in the Reviewing pane by completing the following steps:
   a. If necessary, click the Review tab.
   b. Click the Reviewing Pane button in the Tracking group.
   c. Click the Show Markup button in the Tracking group, point to *Balloons* at the drop-down list, and then click *Show All Revisions Inline* at the side menu.

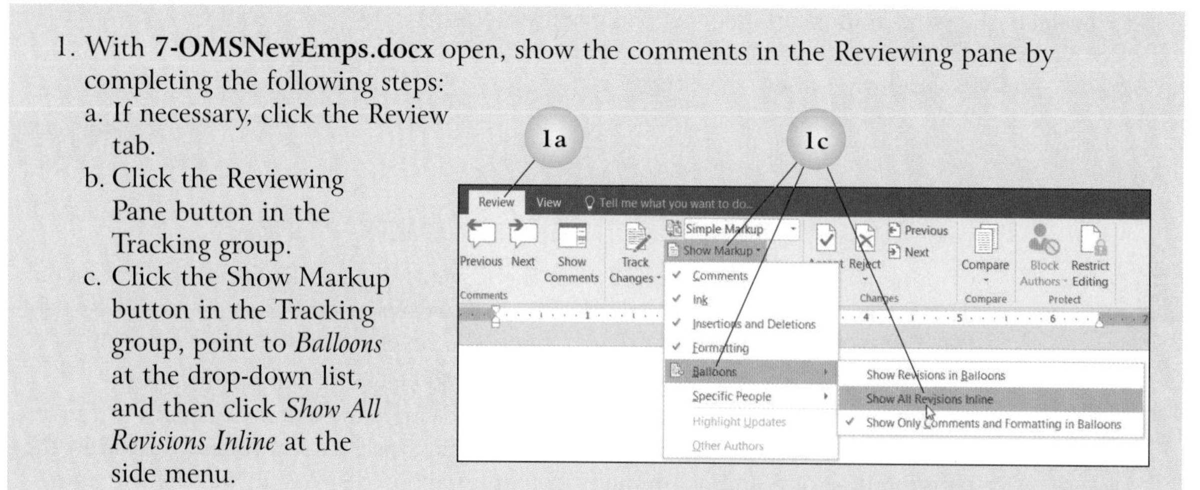

2. Insert a comment by completing the following steps:
   a. Move the insertion point to the end of the paragraph of text in the *Introductory Period* section.
   b. Press the spacebar once, type Maximum?, and then select *Maximum?*.
   c. Click the New Comment button in the Comments group on the Review tab.
   d. With the insertion point positioned in the Reviewing pane, type Please include in this section the maximum length of the probationary period.
3. Click the Reviewing Pane button in the Tracking group to turn off the display of the Reviewing pane.
4. Save **7-OMSNewEmps.docx**.

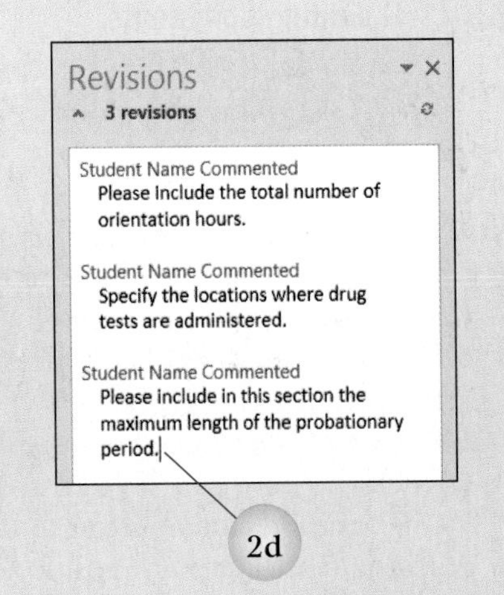

Check Your Work

Navigating between Comments

Previous

Next

When working in a long document with many comments, use the Previous and Next buttons in the Comments group on the Review tab to move easily from comment to comment. Click the Next button to move the insertion point to the next comment or click the Previous button to move the insertion point to the previous comment.

Tutorial

Managing Comments

Quick Steps

Edit a Comment

1. Click Review tab.
2. Click Reviewing Pane button.
3. Click in comment in pane.
4. Make changes.

OR

1. Click Review tab.
2. Turn on display of comment balloons.
3. Click in comment balloon.
4. Make changes.

Editing Comments

Edit a comment in the Reviewing pane or in a comment balloon. To edit a comment in the Reviewing pane, click the Reviewing Pane button to turn on the pane and then click in the comment to be edited. Make changes to the comment and then close the Reviewing pane. To edit a comment in a comment balloon, turn on the display of comment balloons, click in the comment balloon, and then make changes.

Showing Comments

The Comments group on the Review tab contains a Show Comments button. Click this button and comments display at the right side of the document. The Show Comments button is available only when the *Display for Review* option in the Tracking group is set to *Simple Markup*.

Project 1c Editing Comments

Part 3 of 4

1. With **7-OMSNewEmps.docx** open, navigate from one comment to another by completing the following steps:
   a. Press Ctrl + Home to move the insertion point to the beginning of the document.
   b. If necessary, click the Review tab.
   c. Click the Next button in the Comments group. (This moves the insertion point to the first comment, opens the Reviewing pane, and inserts the insertion point in the pane.)
   d. Click the Next button to display the second comment.
   e. Click the Next button to display the third comment.
   f. Click the Previous button to display the second comment.
2. With the insertion point positioned in the Reviewing pane, edit the second comment to read as follows: *Specify the locations within OMS where drug tests are administered as well as any off-site locations.*
3. Click the Reviewing Pane button to close the pane.
4. Edit a comment in a comment balloon by completing the following steps:
   a. Click the Show Markup button in the Tracking group, point to *Balloons*, and then click *Show Only Comments and Formatting in Balloons* at the side menu.
   b. Click the Show Comments button in the Comments group to display the balloons at the right side of the document.
   c. Display the paragraph of text in the *Introductory Period* section and then click in the comment balloon that displays at the right.
   d. Edit the comment to read as follows: *Please include in this section the maximum probationary period, if any.*

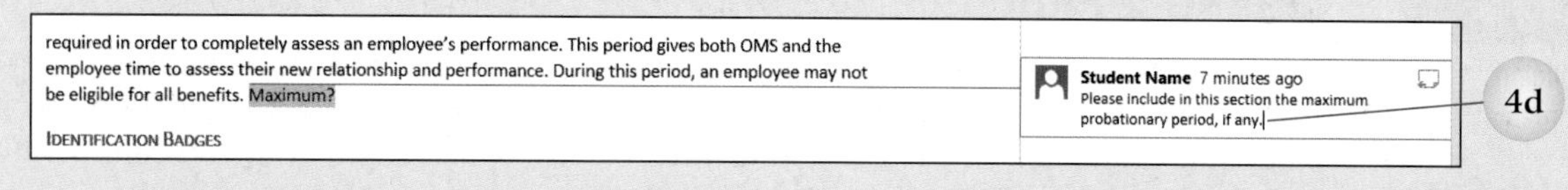

   e. Click in the document and then click the Show Comments button to turn off the display of comment balloons.
   f. Click the Show Markup button, point to *Balloons*, and then click *Show All Revisions Inline*.
5. Save **7-OMSNewEmps.docx**.

Check Your Work

Replying to Comments

Quick Steps

Reply to a Comment
1. Open comment balloon.
2. Hover mouse over comment text.
3. Click Reply button.
4. Type reply in reply window.

During the review of a document, a reply can be made to a comment. To reply to a comment, open the comment balloon, hover the mouse pointer over the comment text, and then click the Reply button to the right of the reviewer's name. Type the reply in the window that opens below the comment. Other methods of replying to a comment are to click in a comment and then click the New Comment button in the Comments group and to right-click in a comment and then click *Reply to Comment* at the shortcut menu.

Printing Comments

Quick Steps

Print a Document with the Comments

1. Click File tab.
2. Click *Print* option.
3. Click first gallery in *Settings* category.
4. If necessary, click *Print Markup* to insert check mark.
5. Click Print button.

Print Only the Comments

1. Click File tab.
2. Click *Print* option.
3. Click first gallery in *Settings* category.
4. Click *List of Markup*.
5. Click Print button.

 Delete

To print a document with the comments, display the Print backstage area and then click the first gallery in the *Settings* category (the gallery that contains the text *Print All Pages*). At the drop-down list, insert a check mark before the *Print Markup* option to print the document with the comments. To print the document without the comments, click *Print Markup* to remove the check mark.

To print only the comments and not the document, click *List of Markup* at the drop-down list. This prints the contents of the Reviewing pane, which may include comments, tracked changes, and changes to headers, footers, text boxes, footnotes, and endnotes.

Deleting Comments

Quick Steps

Delete a Comment

1. Click Review tab.
2. Click Next button until comment is selected.
3. Click Delete button.

Change the User Name and Initials

1. Click File tab.
2. Click *Options*.
3. Type name in *User name* text box.
4. Type initials in *Initials* text box.
5. Click OK.

Delete a comment by clicking the Next button in the Comments group on the Review tab until the specific comment is selected and then clicking the Delete button in the Comments group. To delete all the comments in a document, click the Delete button arrow and then click *Delete All Comments in Document* at the drop-down list. A comment can also be dimmed in a document without being deleted. To do this, right-click the comment and then click *Mark Comment Done* at the shortcut menu.

Distinguishing Comments from Different Users

More than one user can insert comments in the same document. Word uses different colors to distinguish comments inserted by different users, generally displaying the first user's comments in red and the second user's comments in blue. (These colors may vary.)

The user name and initials can be changed at the Word Options dialog box with *General* selected, as shown in Figure 7.3. To change the user name, select the name that displays in the *User name* text box and then type the new name. Complete similar steps to change the user initials in the *Initials* text box. A check mark may need to be inserted in the *Always use these values regardless of sign in to Office* check box.

Figure 7.3 Word Options Dialog Box with *General* Selected

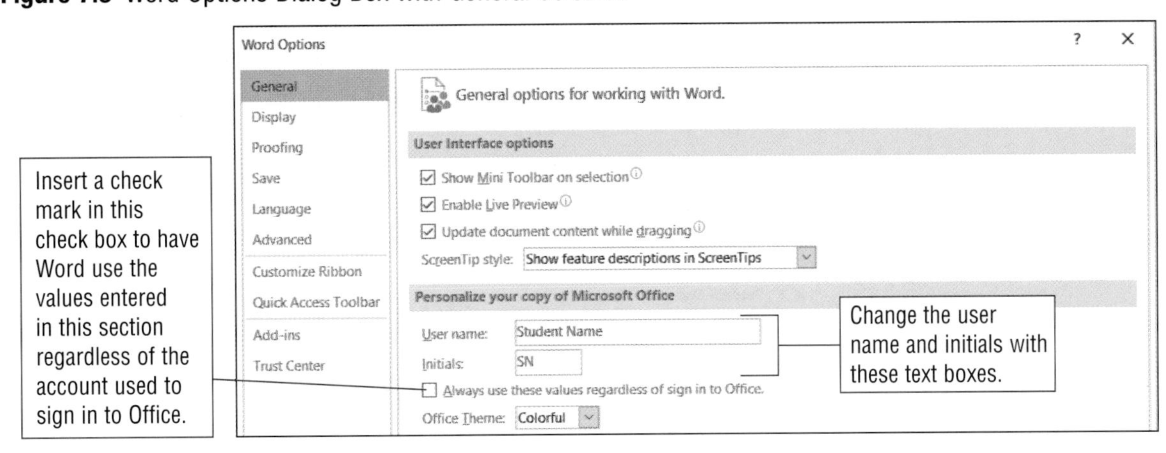

Project 1d Changing User Information and Inserting and Deleting Comments Part 4 of 4

1. With **7-OMSNewEmps.docx** open, change the user information by completing the following steps:
   a. Click the File tab.
   b. Click *Options*.
   c. At the Word Options dialog box, make sure *General* is selected in the left panel.
   d. Make a note of the current name and initials in the *Personalize your copy of Microsoft Office* section.
   e. Select the name displayed in the *User name* text box and then type Taylor Stanton.
   f. Select the initials displayed in the *Initials* text box and then type TS.
   g. Click the *Always use these values regardless of sign in to Office* check box to insert a check mark.
   h. Click OK to close the Word Options dialog box.

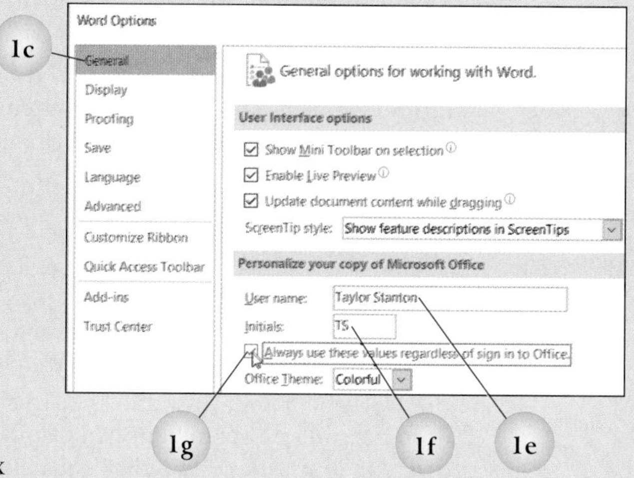

2. Insert a comment by completing the following steps:
   a. Move the insertion point to the end of the first paragraph of text in the section *Performance Review*.
   b. Click the New Comment button in the Comments group on the Review tab.
   c. Type Provide additional information on performance evaluation documentation. in the Reviewing pane.
   d. Click the Reviewing Pane button to close the pane.

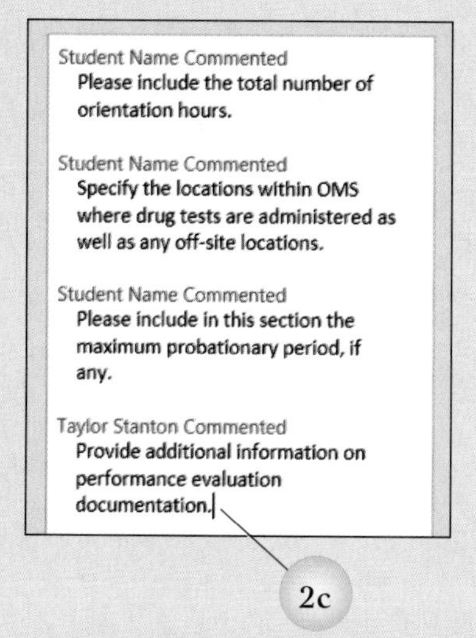

Student Name Commented
Please include the total number of orientation hours.
Student Name Commented
Specify the locations within OMS where drug tests are administered as well as any off-site locations.
Student Name Commented
Please include in this section the maximum probationary period, if any.
Taylor Stanton Commented
Provide additional information on performance evaluation documentation.
2c

3. Respond to a comment by completing the following steps:
   a. Press Ctrl + Home to move the insertion point to the beginning of the document.
   b. Click the Show Markup button, point to *Balloons*, and then click *Show Only Comments and Formatting in Balloons* at the drop-down list.
   c. Click the Next button in the Comments group. (This opens the comment balloon for the first comment.)
   d. Click the Reply button right of the reviewer's name in the comment balloon.

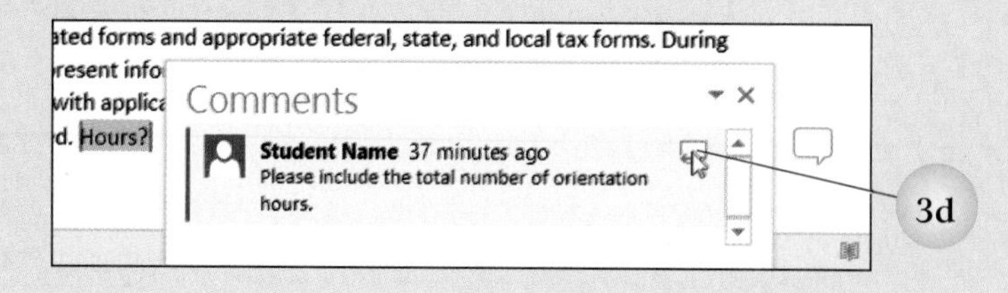

e. Type Check with Barb on the total number of orientation hours.

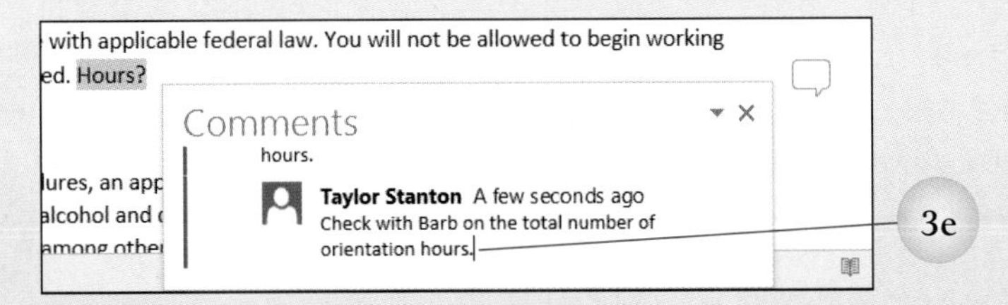

f. Click in the document to close the comment balloon.

4. Print only the information in the Reviewing pane by completing the following steps:
   a. Click the File tab and then click the *Print* option.
   b. At the Print backstage area, click the first gallery in the *Settings* category and then click *List of Markup* in the *Document Info* section of the drop-down list.

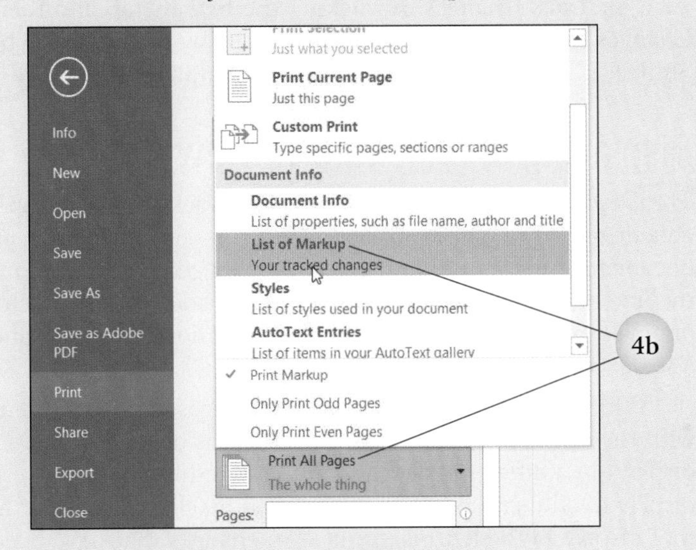

   c. Click the Print button.
5. Delete a comment by completing the following steps:
   a. Press Ctrl + Home.
   b. If necessary, click the Review tab.
   c. Click the Next button in the Comments group.
   d. Click the Next button again.
   e. Click the Next button again.
   f. Click the Delete button in the Comments group.
6. Print only the information in the Reviewing pane by completing Step 4.
7. Change the user information back to the default settings by completing the following steps:
   a. Click the File tab and then click *Options*.
   b. At the Word Options dialog box with *General* selected, select *Taylor Stanton* in the *User name* text box and then type the original name.
   c. Select the initials *TS* in the *Initials* text box and then type the original initials.
   d. Click the *Always use these values regardless of sign in to Office* check box to remove the check mark.
   e. Click OK to close the dialog box.
8. Save and then close **7-OMSNewEmps.docx**.

Check Your Work

Project 2 Track Changes in a Building Construction Agreement 4 Parts

You will open a building construction agreement, turn on Track Changes, and then make changes to the document. You will also customize Track Changes and accept and reject changes.

Preview Finished Project

Tutorial

Tracking Changes in a Document

Track Changes

Tracking Changes in a Document

If more than one person in a workgroup needs to review and edit a document, consider using Word's Track Changes feature. When Track Changes is turned on, Word tracks each deletion, insertion, and formatting change made in a document. Turn on Track Changes by clicking the Review tab and then clicking the Track Changes button in the Tracking group or by using the keyboard shortcut Ctrl + Shift + E. Turn off Track Changes by completing the same steps.

Tutorial

Displaying Changes for Review and Showing Markup

Quick Steps

Turn on Track Changes

1. Click Review tab.
2. Click Track Changes button.

OR

Press Ctrl + Shift + E.

Hint Each of the four options at the *Display for Review* option drop-down list displays a document at various stages in the editing process.

Displaying Changes for Review

The *Display for Review* option box in the Tracking group on the Review tab has a default setting of *Simple Markup*. With this setting applied, each change made to the document displays in it and a vertical change line displays in the left margin next to the line of text in which the change was made. To see the changes along with the original text, click the *Display for Review* option box arrow and then click the *All Markup* option.

With *All Markup* selected, all the changes display in the document along with the original text. For example, if text is deleted, it stays in the document but displays in a different color and with strikethrough characters through it. The display of all markups can be turned on by clicking one of the vertical change lines that display in the left margin next to changes that have been made or by clicking a comment balloon.

If changes have been made to a document with Track Changes turned on, the appearance of the final document with the changes applied can be previewed by clicking the *Display for Review* option box arrow and then clicking *No Markup* at the drop-down list. This displays the document with the changes made but does not actually make the changes to the document. To view the original document without any changes marked, click the *Display for Review* option box arrow and then click *Original* at the drop-down list.

Showing Markups

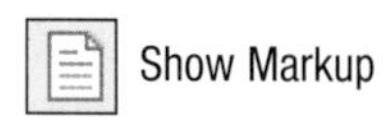

With the display of all markups turned on, specify what tracking information displays in the body of the document with options at the Balloons side menu. To show all the changes in balloons in the right margin, click the Show Markup button, point to *Balloons*, and then click *Show Revisions in Balloons* at the side menu. Click *Show All Revisions Inline* to display all the changes in the document with vertical change lines in the left margin next to the affected lines of text. Click the *Show Only Comments and Formatting in Balloons* option at the side menu and insertions and deletions display in the text while comments and formatting changes display in balloons in the right margin.

Project 2a Tracking Changes in a Document

1. Open **Agreement.docx** and then save it with the name **7-Agreement**.
2. Turn on Track Changes by clicking the Review tab and then clicking the Track Changes button in the Tracking group.

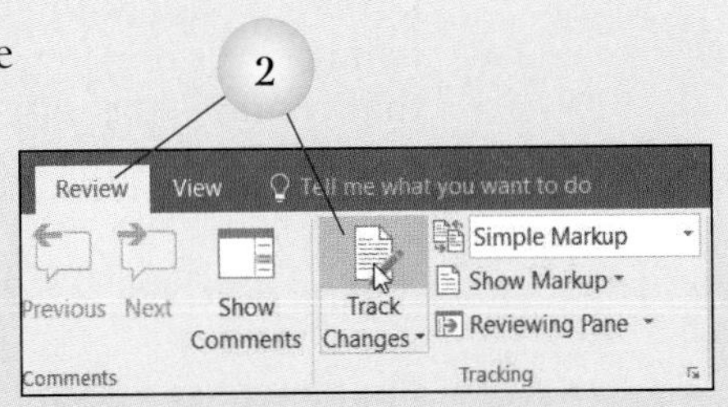

3. Type the word BUILDING between the words *THIS* and *AGREEMENT* in the first paragraph of the document.

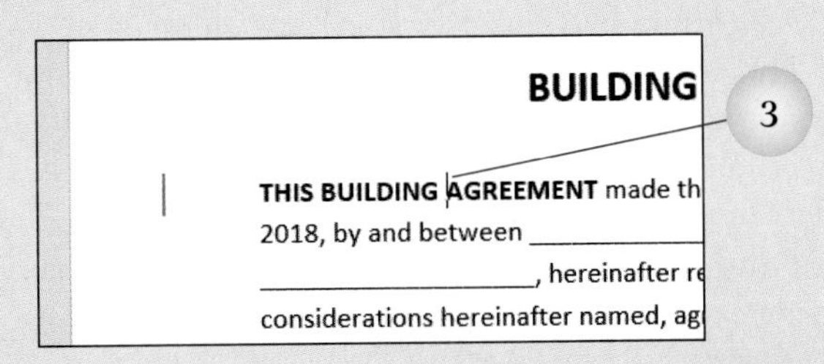

4. Show all markups by clicking the *Display for Review* option box arrow in the Tracking group and then clicking *All Markup* at the drop-down list. (Notice that the text *BUILDING* is underlined and displays in red in the document [the color may vary].)
5. Select and then delete *thirty (30)* in the second paragraph. (The deleted text displays in the document with strikethrough characters through it.)
6. Type sixty (60).

7. Move a paragraph of text by completing the following steps:
   a. Select the paragraph that begins *Supervision of Work* (including the paragraph mark that ends the paragraph).
   b. Press Ctrl + X to cut the text. (The text stays in the document and displays in red with strikethrough characters through it.)
   c. Position the insertion point immediately before the word *Start* (in the paragraph that begins *Start of Construction and Completion:*).
   d. Press Ctrl + V to paste the cut text in the new location. The inserted text displays in green and has a double underline below it. Notice that the text in the original location changes to green and has double-strikethrough characters through it.)
8. Turn off Track Changes by clicking the Track Changes button in the Tracking group.
9. Display revisions in balloons by clicking the Show Markup button, pointing to *Balloons*, and then clicking *Show Revisions in Balloons* at the side menu.
10. After looking at the revisions in balloons, click the Show Markup button, point to *Balloons,* and then click *Show All Revisions Inline* at the side menu.
11. Save **7-Agreement.docx**.

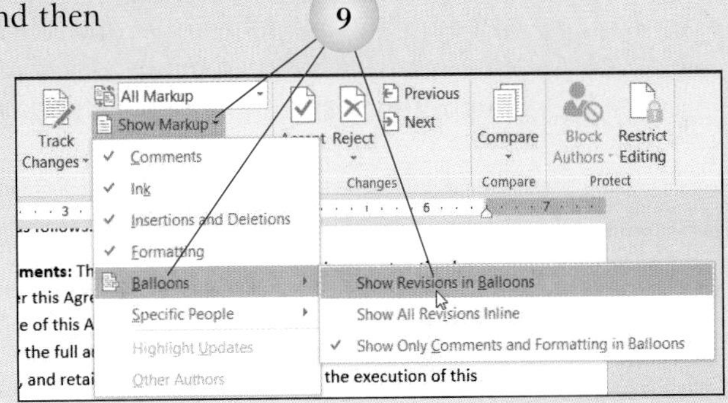

Check Your Work

Displaying Information about Tracked Changes

Display information about a specific tracked change by hovering the mouse pointer over it. After approximately one second, a box displays above the change that contains the author's name, the date and time the change was made, and the type of change (for example, whether it was a deletion or insertion). Information on tracked changes can also be displayed in the Reviewing pane, where each change is listed separately.

Changing User Information

Word uses different colors to record the changes made by different people (up to eight). This color coding allows anyone looking at the document to identify which users made which changes. How to change the user name and initials at the Word Options dialog box was covered earlier in the chapter (see the section *Distinguishing Comments from Different Users*). In Project 2b, the user name and initials will be changed and then additional tracked changes will be made.

Locking Track Changes

Quick Steps

Lock Track Changes

1. Click Review tab.
2. Click Track Changes button arrow.
3. Click *Lock Tracking*.
4. Type password.
5. Press Tab.
6. Type password.
7. Click OK.

To ensure that all the changes made to a document will be tracked, lock the Track Changes feature so it cannot be turned off. To do this, click the Track Changes button arrow and then click *Lock Tracking* at the drop-down list. At the Lock Tracking dialog box, type a password, press the Tab key, type the password again, and then click OK. Unlock Track Changes by clicking the Track Changes button arrow and then clicking *Lock Tracking*. At the Unlock Tracking dialog box, type the password and then click OK.

Tutorial

Customizing Track Changes Options

Customizing Track Changes Options

Customize how tracked changes display in a document with options at the Show Markup button drop-down list. To show only one particular type of tracked change, remove the check marks before all the options except the specific one. For example, to view only formatting changes and not other types of changes, such as insertions and deletions, remove the check mark before each option except *Formatting*. Another method of customizing which tracked changes display is to use options at the Track Changes Options dialog box, shown in Figure 7.4. Display this dialog box by clicking the Tracking group dialog box launcher.

If the changes made by multiple reviewers have been tracked in a document, the changes made by a particular reviewer can be displayed. To do this, click the Show Markup button, point to *Specific People* at the drop-down list, and then click the *All Reviewers* check box to remove the check mark. Click the Show Markup button, point to *Reviewers*, and then click the check box of the specific reviewer.

Figure 7.4 Track Changes Options Dialog Box

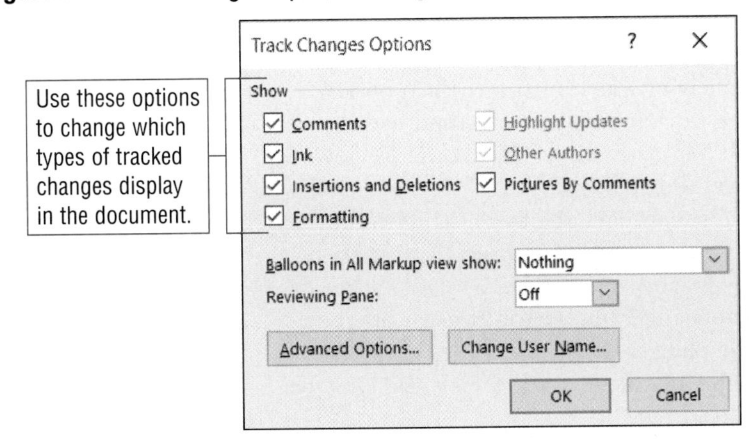

Project 2b Changing User Information and Tracking Changes

Part 2 of 4

1. With **7-Agreement.docx** open, change the user information by completing the following steps:
   a. Click the File tab and then click *Options*.
   b. At the Word Options dialog box with *General* selected, select the current name in the *User name* text box and then type Julia Moore.
   c. Select the initials in the *Initials* text box and then type JM.
   d. Click the *Always use these values regardless of sign in to Office* check box to insert a check mark.
   e. Click OK to close the dialog box.
2. Make additional changes to the contract and track the changes by completing the following steps:
   a. Click the Track Changes button on the Review tab to turn on tracking.
   b. Select the title *BUILDING CONSTRUCTION AGREEMENT* and then change the font size to 14 points.
   c. Delete the text *at his option* (located in the second sentence in the second paragraph).
   d. Delete the text *and Completion* (located near the beginning of the fourth paragraph).

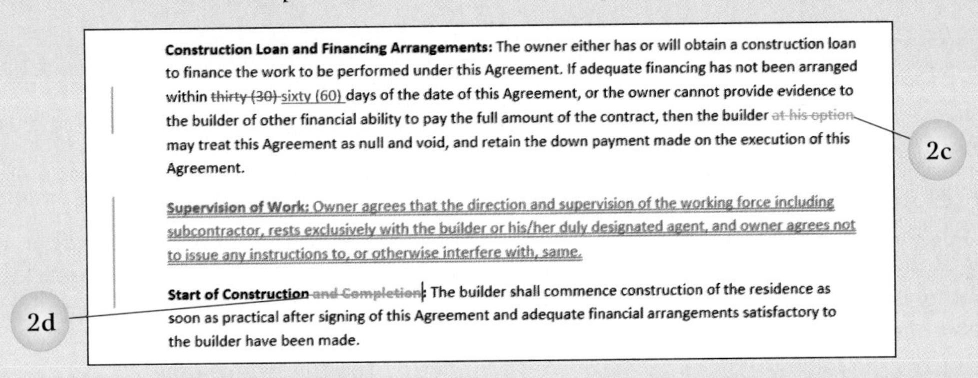

   e. Delete *thirty (30)* in the paragraph that begins *Builder's Right to Terminate the Contract:* (located on the second page).
   f. Type sixty (60).
   g. Select the text *IN WITNESS WHEREOF* (located near the bottom of the document) and then apply bold formatting.

3. Click the Review tab and then click the Track Changes button to turn off Track Changes.
4. Click the Reviewing Pane button to turn on the display of the Reviewing pane and then use the vertical scroll bar at the right side of the Reviewing pane to review the changes.
5. View the changes in balloons by clicking the Show Markup button, pointing to *Balloons*, and then clicking *Show Revisions in Balloons*.
6. Click the Reviewing Pane button to turn off the display of the pane.
7. Scroll through the document and view the changes in the balloons.
8. Click the Show Markup button, point to *Balloons*, and then click *Show All Revisions Inline* at the side menu.

Revisions
11 revisions
Julia Moore Formatted
Font: 14 pt
Student Name Inserted
BUILDING
Student Name Deleted
thirty (30)
Student Name Inserted
sixty (60)
Julia Moore Deleted
at his option
Student Name Moved (insertion) [1]
Supervision of Work: Owner
4

9. Change the user information back to the original information by completing the following steps:
   a. Click the File tab and then click *Options*.
   b. At the Word Options dialog box, select *Julia Moore* in the *User name* text box and then type the original name.
   c. Select the initials *JM* in the *Initials* text box and then type the original initials.
   d. Click the *Always use these values regardless of sign in to Office* check box to remove the check mark.
   e. Click OK to close the dialog box.
10. Display only those changes made by Julia Moore by completing the following steps:
   a. Click the Show Markup button in the Tracking group and then point to *Specific People* at the drop-down list.
   b. Click *All Reviewers* at the side menu.

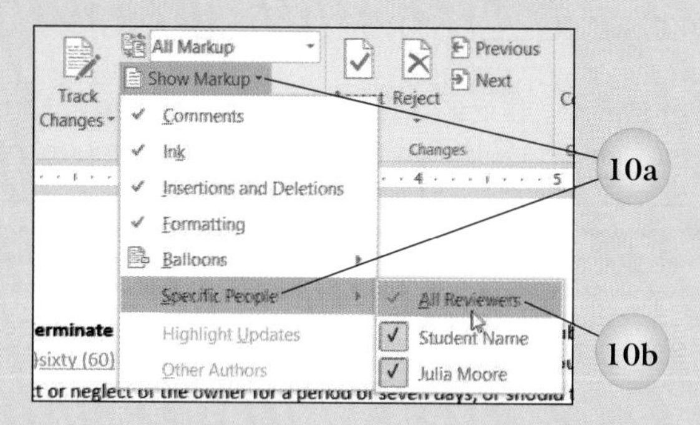

   c. Click the Show Markup button, point to *Specific People*, and then click *Julia Moore*.
   d. Scroll through the document and notice that only changes made by Julia Moore display.
   e. Return the display to all the reviewers by clicking the Show Markup button, pointing to *Specific People*, and then clicking *All Reviewers*.
11. Print the document with the markups by completing the following steps:
   a. Click the File tab and then click the *Print* option.
   b. At the Print backstage area, click the first gallery in the *Settings* category and then make sure a check mark displays before the *Print Markup* option. (If the *Print Markup* option is not preceded by a check mark, click the option.)
   c. Click the Print button.
12. Save **7-Agreement.docx**.

Check Your Work

Customizing Advanced Track Changes Options

How tracked changes display in a document is determined by default settings. For example, with all the markups showing, inserted text displays in red with an underline below it and deleted text displays in red with strikethrough characters through it. Moved text displays in the original location in green with double-strikethrough characters through it and in the new location in green with double-underlining below it.

Customize these options, along with others, at the Advanced Track Changes Options dialog box, shown in Figure 7.5. Use options at this dialog box to customize the display of markup text, moved text, table cell highlighting, formatting, and balloons. Display the dialog box by clicking the Tracking group dialog box launcher. At the Track Changes Options dialog box, click the Advanced Options button.

Figure 7.5 Advanced Track Changes Options Dialog Box

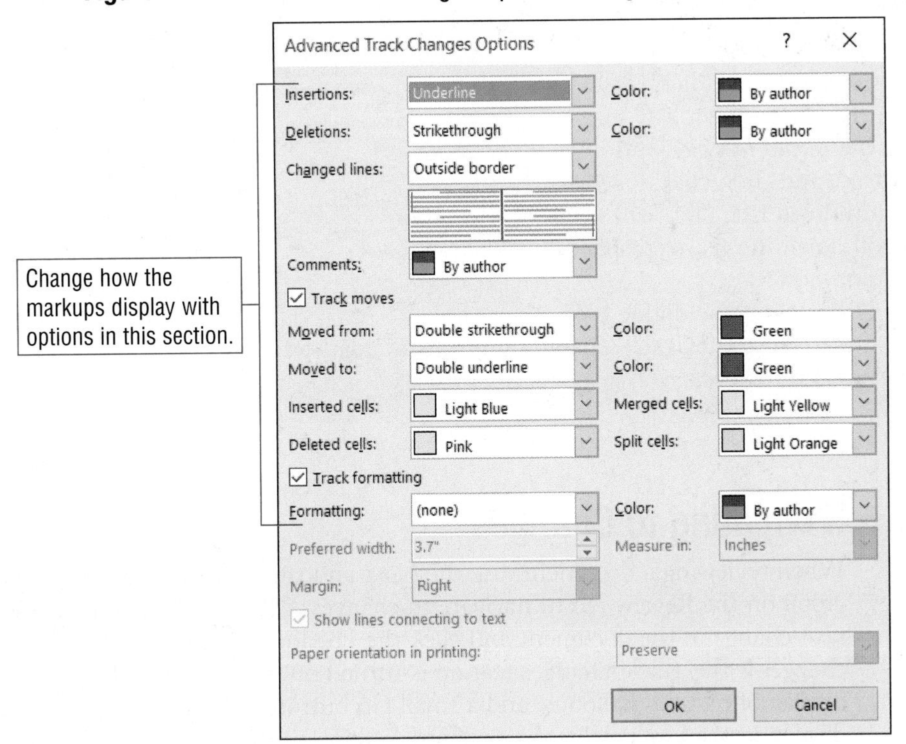

Project 2c Customizing Track Changes Options

Part 3 of 4

1. With **7-Agreement.docx** open, customize the Track Changes options by completing the following steps:
   a. If necessary, click the Review tab.
   b. Click the Tracking group dialog box launcher.
   c. Click the Advanced Options button at the Track Changes Options dialog box.
   d. At the Advanced Track Changes Options dialog box, click the *Insertions* option box arrow and then click *Double underline* at the drop-down list.
   e. Click the *Insertions Color* option box arrow and then click *Green* at the drop-down list. (You will need to scroll down the list to display this color.)
   f. Click the *Moved from Color* option box arrow and then click *Dark Blue* at the drop-down list.
   g. Click the *Moved to Color* option box arrow and then click *Violet* at the drop-down list. (You will need to scroll down the list to display this color.)
   h. Click OK to close the dialog box.
   i. Click OK to close the Track Changes Options dialog box.
2. Save **7-Agreement.docx**.

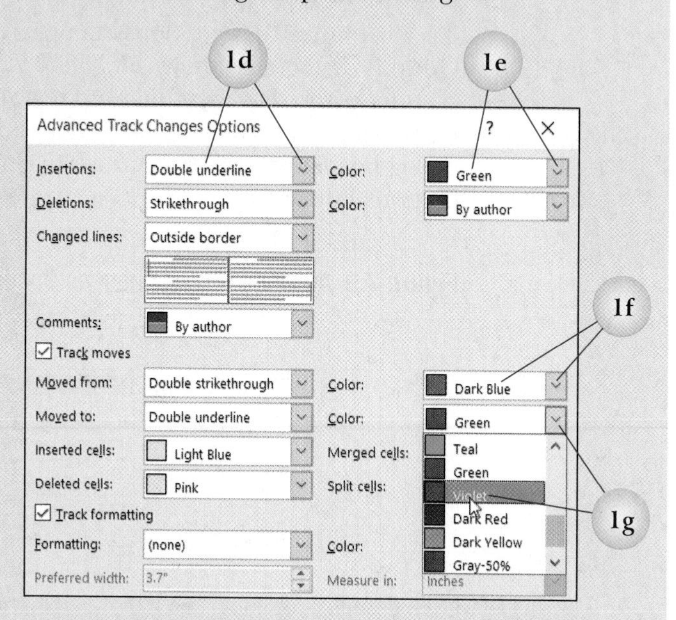

Check Your Work

Tutorial

Navigating, Accepting, and Rejecting Tracked Changes

Next

Previous

Navigating to Changes

When reviewing a document, use the Next and the Previous buttons in the Changes group on the Review tab to navigate to changes. Click the Next button to review the next change in the document and click the Previous button to review the previous change. If the Track Changes feature is turned on, move text and then turn on the display of revision balloons, and a small Go button (a blue right-pointing arrow) will display in the lower right corner of any balloon that identifies moved text. Click the Go button in the balloon identifying the original text to move the insertion point to the balloon identifying the moved text.

Accepting or Rejecting Changes

Accept

Reject

Tracked changes can be removed from a document only by accepting or rejecting them. Click the Accept button in the Changes group on the Review tab to accept a change and move to the next change or click the Reject button to reject a change and move to the next change. Click the Accept button arrow and a drop-down list displays with options to accept the change and move to the next change, accept the change, accept all the changes showing, and accept all the changes and stop tracking. Similar options are available at the Reject button drop-down list.

Project 2d Accepting or Rejecting Changes

Part 4 of 4

1. With **7-Agreement.docx** open, display all the tracked changes *except* formatting changes by completing the following steps:
   a. Click the Show Markup button in the Tracking group and then click *Formatting* at the drop-down list. (This removes the check mark before the option.)
   b. Scroll through the document and notice that the vertical change lines in the left margin next to the two formatting changes have been removed.
   c. Click the Show Markup button and then click *Formatting* at the drop-down list. (This inserts a check mark before the option.)
2. Navigate to review tracked changes by completing the following steps:
   a. Press Ctrl + Home to move the insertion point to the beginning of the document.
   b. Click the Next button in the Changes group to select the first change.
   c. Click the Next button again to select the second change.
   d. Click the Previous button to select the first change.
3. Navigate between the original and new locations of the moved text by completing the following steps:
   a. Press Ctrl + Home to move the insertion point to the beginning of the document.
   b. Click the Show Markup button, point to *Balloons*, and then click *Show Revisions in Balloons*.
   c. Click the Go button (a blue right-pointing arrow) in the lower right corner of the Moved balloon. (This selects the text in the Moved up balloon.)
   d. Click the Go button in the lower right corner of the Moved up balloon. (This selects the text in the Moved balloon.)
   e. Click the Show Markup button, point to *Balloons*, and then click *Show All Revisions Inline*.

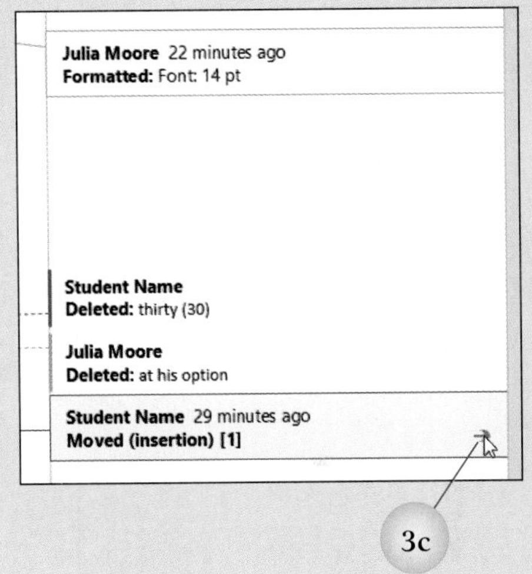

4. Press Ctrl + Home to move the insertion point to the beginning of the document.
5. Display and then accept only formatting changes by completing the following steps:
   a. Click the Tracking group dialog box launcher.
   b. At the Track Changes Options dialog box, click the *Comments* check box to remove the check mark.
   c. Click the *Ink* check box to remove the check mark.
   d. Click the *Insertions and Deletions* check box to remove the check mark.
   e. Click OK to close the Track Changes Options dialog box.

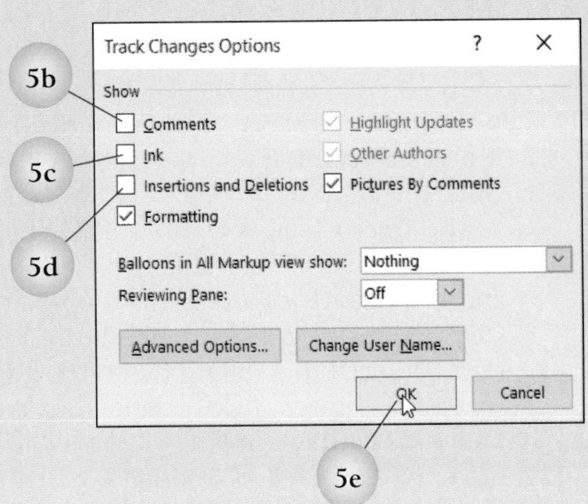

f. Click the Accept button arrow and then click *Accept All Changes Shown* at the drop-down list. (This accepts only the formatting changes in the document because those are the only changes showing.)

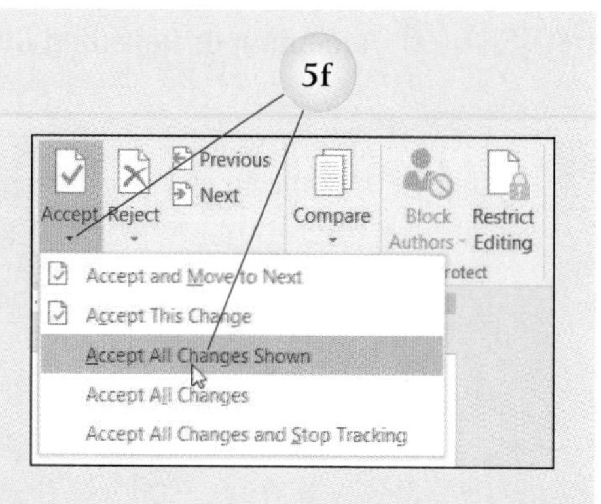

6. Redisplay all the changes by completing the following steps:
   a. Click the Tracking group dialog box launcher.
   b. Click the *Comments* check box to insert a check mark.
   c. Click the *Ink* check box to insert a check mark.
   d. Click the *Insertions and Deletions* check box to insert a check mark.
   e. Click OK to close the Track Changes Options dialog box.
7. Press Ctrl + Home to move the insertion point to the beginning of the document.
8. Reject the change that inserts the word *BUILDING* by clicking the Next button in the Changes group and then clicking the Reject button. (This rejects the change and moves to the next revision in the document.)
9. Click the Accept button to accept the change that deletes *thirty (30)*.
10. Click the Accept button to accept the change that inserts *sixty (60)*.
11. Click the Reject button to reject the change that deletes the words *at his option*.
12. Accept all the remaining changes by clicking the Accept button arrow and then clicking *Accept All Changes* at the drop-down list.

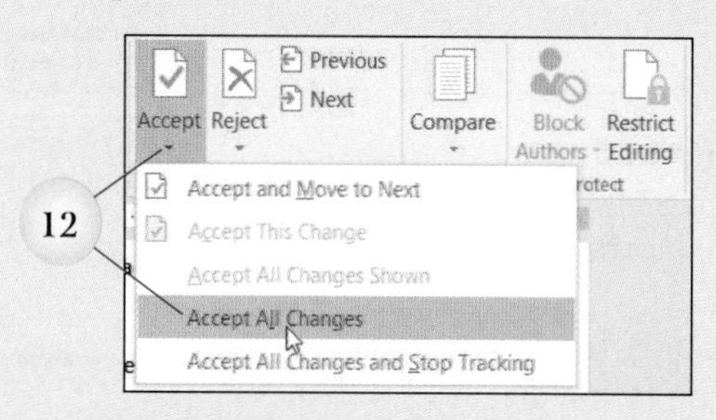

13. Return the track changes options to the default settings by completing the following steps:
    a. If necessary, click the Review tab.
    b. Click the Tracking group dialog box launcher.
    c. At the Track Changes Options dialog box, click the Advanced Options button.
    d. At the Advanced Track Changes Options dialog box, click the *Insertions* option box arrow and then click *Underline* at the drop-down list.
    e. Click the *Insertions Color* option box arrow and then click *By author* at the drop-down list. (You will need to scroll up the list to display this option.)
    f. Click the *Moved from Color* option box and then click *Green* at the drop-down list. (You may need to scroll down the list to display this color.)
    g. Click the *Moved to Color* option box arrow and then click *Green* at the drop-down list.
    h. Click OK to close the dialog box.
    i. Click OK to close the Track Changes Options dialog box.

14. Check to make sure all the tracked changes are accepted or rejected by completing the following steps:
    a. Click the Reviewing Pane button in the Tracking group.
    b. Check the summary information at the top of the Reviewing pane and make sure that each option is followed by a 0. (You may need to click the up arrow right of *0 revisions* to display all the options.)
    c. Close the Reviewing pane.
15. Save, print, and then close **7-Agreement.docx**.

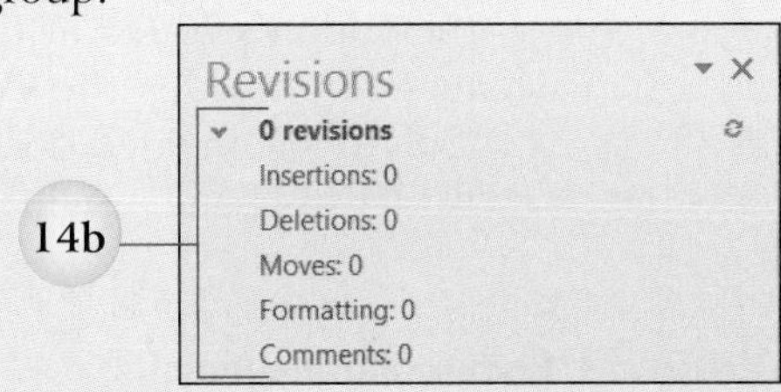

Check Your Work

Project 3 Compare Lease Agreement Documents — 2 Parts

You will compare the contents of a lease agreement and an edited version of the lease agreement. You will then customize compare options and then compare the documents again.

Preview Finished Project

Tutorial

Comparing Documents

Quick Steps

Compare Documents
1. Click Review tab.
2. Click Compare button.
3. Click *Compare*.
4. Click Browse for Original button.
5. Double-click document.
6. Click Browse for Revised button.
7. Double-click document.
8. Click OK.

Hint Word does not change the documents being compared.

Comparing Documents

Word contains a Compare feature that will compare two documents and display the differences between them as tracked changes in a third document. To use this feature, click the Review tab, click the Compare button in the Compare group, and then click *Compare* at the drop-down list. This displays the Compare Documents dialog box, shown in Figure 7.6. At this dialog box, click the Browse for Original button. At the Open dialog box, navigate to the folder that contains the original document, and then double-click the document. Click the Browse for Revised button in the Compare Documents dialog box, navigate to the folder containing the revised document, and then double-click the document.

Figure 7.6 Compare Documents Dialog Box

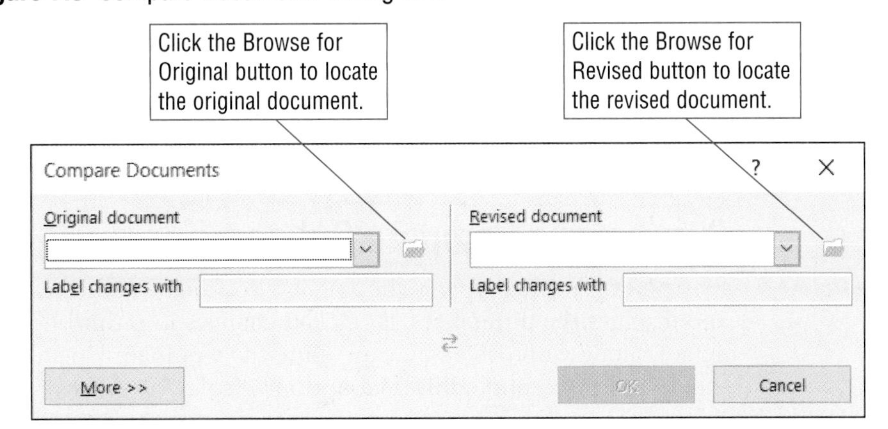

Viewing Compared Documents

Click OK at the Compare Documents dialog box and the compared document displays with the changes tracked. Other windows may also display, depending on the option selected at the Show Source Documents side menu. Display this side menu by clicking the Compare button and then pointing to *Show Source Documents*. Only the compared document may display or the compared document plus the Reviewing pane, original document, and/or revised document may display.

Project 3a Comparing Documents — Part 1 of 2

1. Close any open documents.
2. Click the Review tab.
3. Click the Compare button and then click *Compare* at the drop-down list.
4. At the Compare Documents dialog box, click the Browse for Original button.

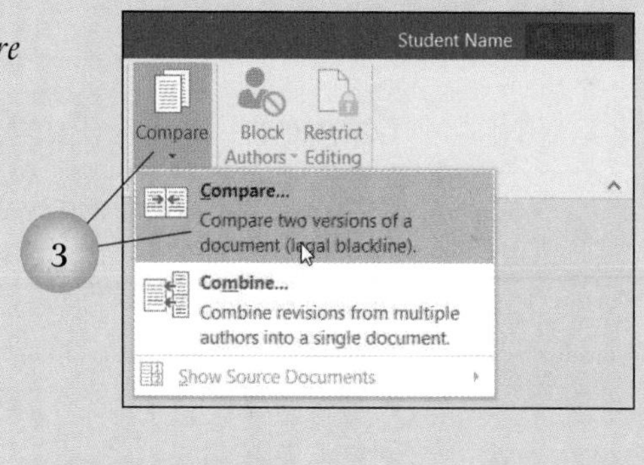

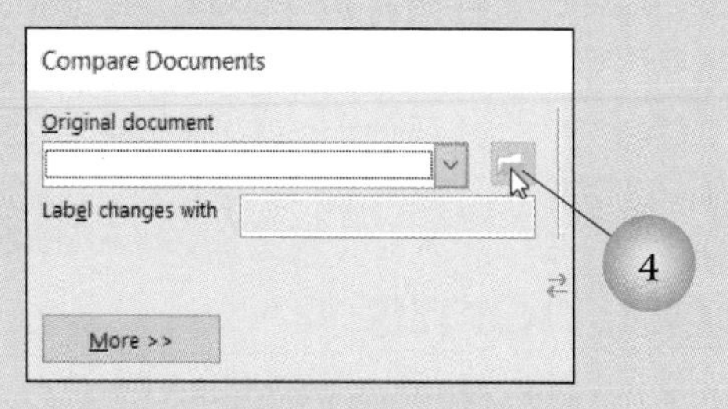

5. At the Open dialog box, navigate to the WL2C7 folder on your storage medium and then double-click ***ComAgrmnt.docx***.
6. At the Compare Documents dialog box, click the Browse for Revised button.
7. At the Open dialog box, double-click ***EditedComAgrmnt.docx***.
8. Click OK.
9. If the original and revised documents display along with the compared document, click the Compare button, point to *Show Source Documents* at the drop-down list, and then click *Hide Source Documents* at the side menu.
10. With the compared document active, print the document with markups.
11. Click the File tab and then click the *Close* option. At the message asking if you want to save changes, click the Don't Save button.

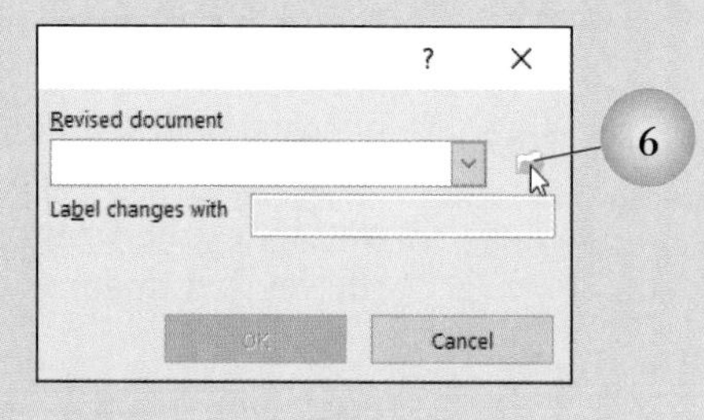

Check Your Work

Customizing Compare Options

By default, Word compares the original document with the revised document and displays the differences as tracked changes in a third document. Change this default along with others by expanding the Compare Documents dialog box. Click the More button and additional options display, as shown in Figure 7.7.

Figure 7.7 Expanded Compare Documents Dialog Box

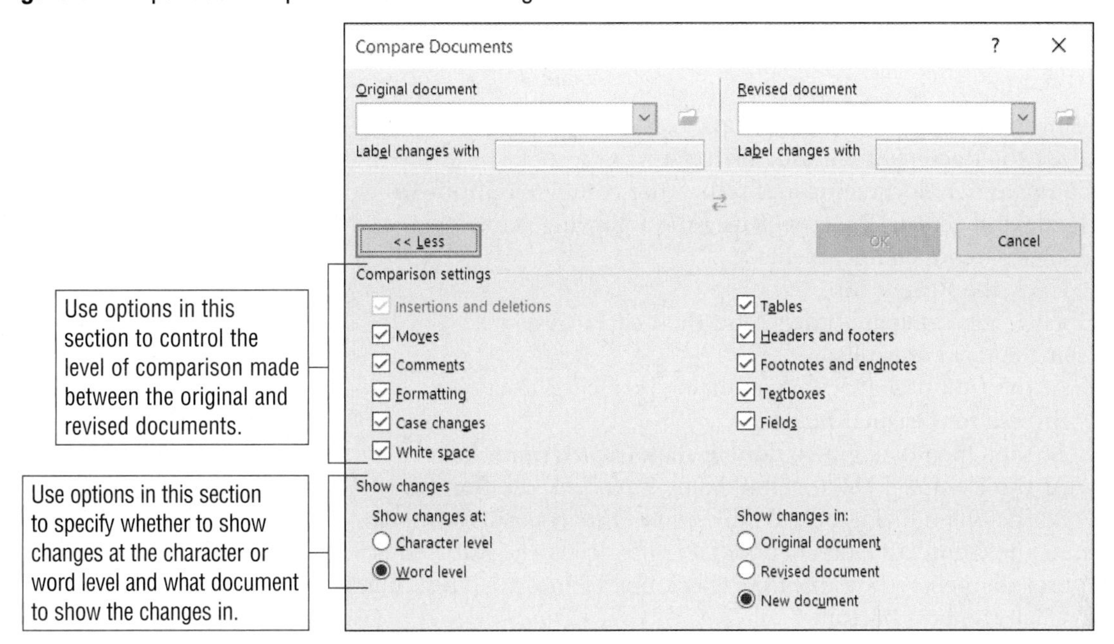

Control the level of comparison that Word makes between the original and revised documents with options in the *Comparison settings* section of the dialog box. The *Show changes at* option in the *Show changes* section of the dialog box has a default setting of *Word level*. With this setting applied, Word shows changes to whole words rather than individual characters within the word. For example, if the letters *ed* are deleted from the end of a word, Word will display the entire word as a change rather than just the *ed*. To show changes by character, click the *Character level* option.

By default, Word displays differences between compared documents in a new document. With options in the *Show changes in* section, this default can be changed to *Original document* or *Revised document*. If changes are made to options in the expanded Compare Documents dialog box, the selected options will be the defaults the next time the dialog box is opened.

Project 3b Customizing Compare Options and Comparing Documents — Part 2 of 2

1. Close any open documents.
2. Click the Review tab.
3. Click the Compare button and then click *Compare* at the drop-down list.
4. At the Compare Documents dialog box, click the Browse for Original button.
5. At the Open dialog box, navigate to the WL2C7 folder on your storage medium and then double-click ***ComAgrmnt.docx***.
6. At the Compare Documents dialog box, click the Browse for Revised button.
7. At the Open dialog box, double-click ***EditedComAgrmnt.docx***.
8. At the Compare Documents dialog box, click the More button. (Skip this step if the dialog box displays expanded and a Less button displays above the *Comparison settings* section.)

9. Click the *Moves* check box and then click the *Formatting* check box to remove the check marks.
10. Click OK.
11. Print the document with markups.
12. Close the document without saving it.
13. Compare two documents and return the compare options to the default settings by completing the following steps:
    a. Close any open documents.
    b. Click the Review tab.
    c. Click the Compare button and then click *Compare* at the drop-down list.
    d. At the Compare Documents dialog box, click the Browse for Original button.
    e. At the Open dialog box, double-click ***ComAgrmnt.docx***.
    f. At the Compare Documents dialog box, click the Browse for Revised button.
    g. At the Open dialog box, double-click ***EditedComAgrmnt.docx***.
    h. At the Compare Documents dialog box, click the *Moves* check box to insert a check mark and then click the *Formatting* check box to insert a check mark.
    i. Click the Less button.
    j. Click OK.
14. At the new document, accept all the changes.
15. Save the document and name it **7-ComAgrmnt**.
16. Print and then close the document.

Compare Documents
Original document
ComAgrmnt.docx
Label changes with
<< Less
Comparison settings
Insertions and deletions
Moves
Comments
Formatting
Case changes
White space
9

Check Your Work

Project 4 Combine Lease Agreement Documents — 2 Parts

You will open a lease agreement document and then combine edited versions of the agreement with the original document.

Preview Finished Project

Tutorial

Combining Documents

Combining Documents

If several people have made changes to a document, their changed versions can be combined with the original document. Each person's changed document can be combined with the original until all the changes have been incorporated into the original document. To do this, open the Combine Documents dialog box, shown in Figure 7.8, by clicking the Compare button on the Review tab and then clicking *Combine* at the drop-down list. The Combine Documents dialog box contains many of the same options as the Compare Documents dialog box.

To combine documents at the Combine Documents dialog box, click the Browse for Original button, navigate to the specific folder, and then double-click the original document. Click the Browse for Revised button, navigate to the specific folder, and then double-click one of the documents containing revisions. Click the *Original document* option box arrow or the *Revised document* option box arrow and a drop-down list displays with the most recently selected documents.

Quick Steps
Combine Documents
1. Click Review tab.
2. Click Compare button.
3. Click *Combine.*
4. Click Browse for Original button.
5. Double-click document.
6. Click Browse for Revised button.
7. Double-click document.
8. Click OK.

Figure 7.8 Combine Documents Dialog Box

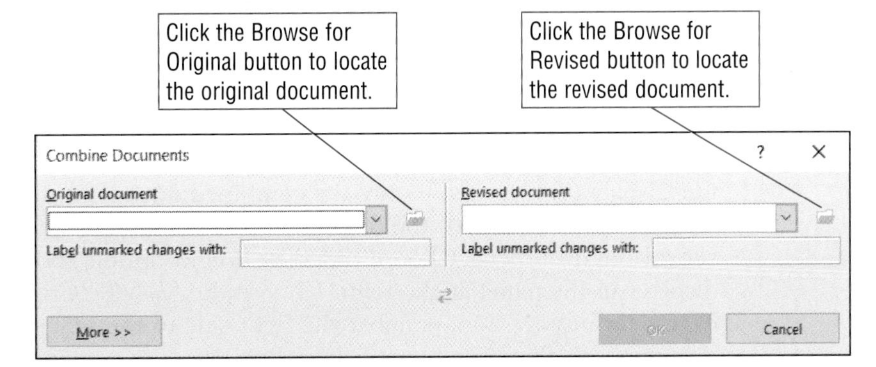

Combining and Merging Documents

Control how changes are combined with options at the expanded Combine Documents dialog box. This dialog box contains many of the same options as the expanded Compare Documents dialog box. By default, Word merges the changes in the revised document into the original document. Change this default setting with options in the *Show changes in* section. Use options in this section to show changes in the original document, the revised document, or a new document.

Project 4a Combining Documents

Part 1 of 2

1. Close all the open documents.
2. Click the Review tab.
3. Click the Compare button in the Compare group and then click *Combine* at the drop-down list.
4. At the Combine Documents dialog box, click the More button to expand the dialog box.
5. Click the *Original document* option in the *Show changes in* section.

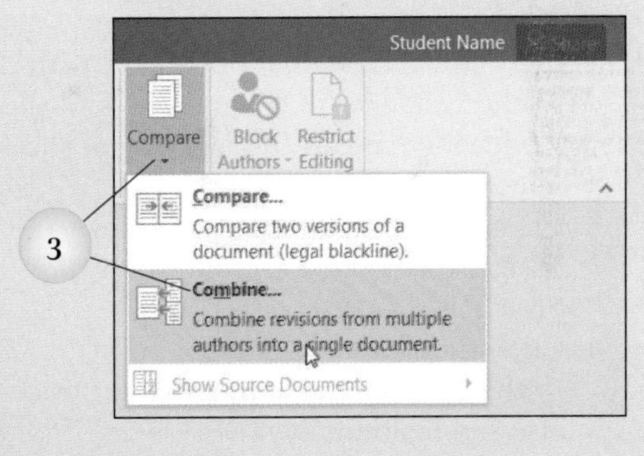

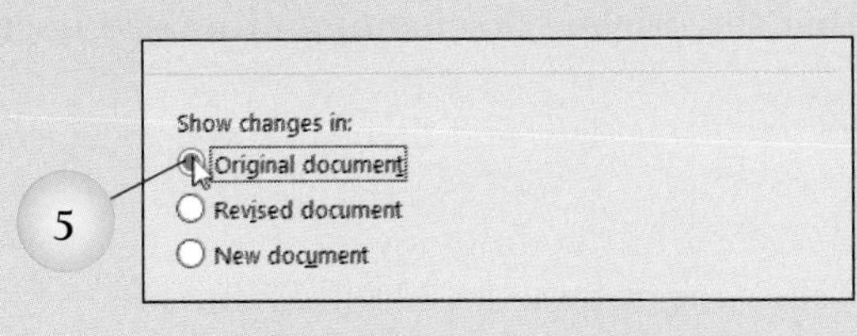

6. Click the Browse for Original button.
7. At the Open dialog box, navigate to the WL2C7 folder on your storage medium and then double-click ***OriginalLease.docx***.
8. At the Combine Documents dialog box, click the Browse for Revised button.
9. At the Open dialog box, double-click ***LeaseReviewer1.docx***.
10. Click OK.
11. Save the document and name it **7-CombinedLease**.

Check Your Work

Showing Source Documents

Use options in the Show Source Documents side menu to specify which source documents to display. Display this side menu by clicking the Compare button and then pointing to *Show Source Documents*. Four options display at the side menu: *Hide Source Documents*, *Show Original*, *Show Revised*, and *Show Both*. With the *Hide Source Documents* option selected, the original and revised documents do not display on the screen; only the combined document displays. With the *Show Original* option selected, the original document displays in a side panel at the right side of the document. Choose the *Show Revised* option and the revised document displays in the panel at the right. Choose the *Show Both* option and the original document displays in a panel at the right side of the screen and the revised document displays in a panel below the original document panel. Synchronous scrolling is selected by default, so scrolling in the combined document causes simultaneous scrolling in the other document.

Project 4b Combining and Showing Documents

Part 2 of 2

1. With **7-CombinedLease.docx** open, click the Compare button, point to *Show Source Documents*, and then click *Hide Source Documents* at the side menu if necessary. (This displays the original document with the combined document changes shown as tracked changes.)
2. Click the Compare button, point to *Show Source Documents*, and then click *Show Original* at the side menu. (This displays the original document at the right, the original document with tracked changes in the middle, and the Reviewing pane at the left side of the screen.)
3. Click the Compare button, point to *Show Source Documents*, and then click *Show Revised*.
4. Click the Compare button, point to *Show Source Documents*, and then click *Show Both*. Scroll in the combined document and notice that the original document and revised document also scroll simultaneously.
5. Click the Compare button, point to *Show Source Documents*, and then click *Hide Source Documents*.
6. Close the Reviewing pane.
7. Click the Compare button and then click *Combine* at the drop-down list.
8. At the Combine Documents dialog box, click the Browse for Original button.
9. At the Open dialog box, double-click ***7-CombinedLease.docx***.
10. At the Combine Documents dialog box, click the Browse for Revised button.
11. At the Open dialog box, double-click ***LeaseReviewer2.docx***.
12. At the Combine Documents dialog box, click OK.
13. Save **7-CombinedLease.docx**.
14. Print the document with markups.
15. Accept all the changes to the document.
16. Keep the heading *Damage to Premises* together with the next paragraph.
17. Save, print, and then close **7-CombinedLease.docx**.

Check Your Work

Project 5 Embed Data in and Link Data between Excel and Word — 3 Parts

You will copy and embed Excel data into a Word document and then update the embedded data. You will also copy and link an Excel chart into a Word document and then update the data in the chart.

Preview Finished Project

Embedding and Linking Objects

One of the reasons the Microsoft Office suite is used extensively in business is that it allows data from one program to be seamlessly integrated into another program. For example, a chart depicting sales projections created in Excel can easily be added to a corporate report prepared in Word.

Integration is the process of adding content from other sources to a file. Integrating content is different from simply copying and pasting it. While it makes sense to copy and paste objects from one application to another when the content is not likely to change, if the content is dynamic, the copy and paste method becomes problematic and inefficient.

To illustrate this point, assume that one of the outcomes of presenting sales projections to the company's board of directors is revision of the projections; this means that the chart originally created in Excel has to be updated to reflect the new projections. If the first version of the chart was copied and pasted into Word, it would need to be deleted and then the revised Excel chart would need to be copied and pasted into the Word document again. Both Excel and Word would need to be opened and edited to reflect the changes in sales projections. In this case, copying and pasting the chart would not be efficient.

To eliminate the inefficiency of the copy and paste method, objects can be integrated between programs. An object can be text in a document, data in a table, a chart, a picture, or any combination of data to be shared between programs. The program that was used to create the object is called the *source* and the program the object is linked or embedded to is called the *destination*.

Embedding and linking are two methods for integrating data. Embedding an object means that the object is stored independently in both the source and the destination programs. When an embedded object is edited in the destination program, the source program opens to provide buttons and options for editing the object; however, the changes will not be reflected in the version of the object stored in the source program. If the object is changed in the source program, the changes will not be reflected in the version of the object stored in the destination program.

Linking inserts a code in the destination file that connects the destination to the name and location of the source object. The object is not stored within the destination file. When an object is linked, changes made to the content in the source program are automatically reflected in the destination program.

The decision to integrate data by embedding or linking will depend on whether the data is dynamic or static. If the data is dynamic, then linking the object is the most efficient method of integration.

Tutorial

Embedding an Object

Embedding an Object

An object that is embedded is stored in both the source and the destination programs. The content of the object can be edited in *either* the source or the destination; however, a change made in one will not be reflected in the other. The difference between copying and pasting and copying and embedding is that an embedded object can be edited with the buttons and options of the source program.

Since an embedded object is edited within the source program, that program must reside on the computer when the file is opened for editing. When preparing a Word document that will be edited on another computer, determine whether the other computer has both Word and the source program before embedding any objects.

To embed an object, open both programs and both files. In the source program, click the object and then click the Copy button in the Clipboard group on the Home tab. Click the button on the taskbar that represents the destination program file and then position the insertion point at the location the object is to be embedded. Click the Paste button arrow in the Clipboard group and then click *Paste Special* at the drop-down list. At the Paste Special dialog box, click the source of the object in the *As* list box and then click OK.

Edit an embedded object by double-clicking it. This displays the object with the source program buttons and options. Make any changes and then click outside the object to close the source program buttons and options.

Quick Steps

Embed an Object

1. Open source and destination programs and files.
2. Click object in source program.
3. Click Copy button.
4. Click taskbar button for destination program file.
5. Position insertion point in specific location.
6. Click Paste button arrow.
7. Click *Paste Special*.
8. Click source file format in *As* list box.
9. Click OK.

Project 5a Embedding Excel Data in a Document — Part 1 of 3

1. Open **DIRevs.docx** and then save it with the name **7-DIRevs**.
2. Open Excel and then open **DISales.xlsx** in the WL2C7 folder on your storage medium.
3. Select the range A2:F9.
4. Click the Copy button in the Clipboard group on the Home tab.
5. Click the Word button on the taskbar.
6. Press Ctrl + End to move the insertion point to the end of the document.
7. Click the Paste button arrow and then click *Paste Special* at the drop-down list.
8. At the Paste Special dialog box, click *Microsoft Excel Worksheet Object* in the *As* list box and then click OK.
9. Save **7-DIRevs.docx**.
10. Click the Excel button on the taskbar, close the workbook, and then close Excel.
11. With **7-DIRevs.docx** open, double-click in any cell in the Excel data. (This displays the Excel buttons and options for editing the data.)
12. Click in cell E3 (contains the amount *$89,231*), type 95000, and then press the Enter key.
13. Click in cell F9 and then double-click the AutoSum button in the Editing group on the Home tab. (This inserts the total *$1,258,643* in the cell.)
14. Click outside the Excel data to remove the Excel buttons and options.
15. Save, print, and then close **7-DIRevs.docx**.

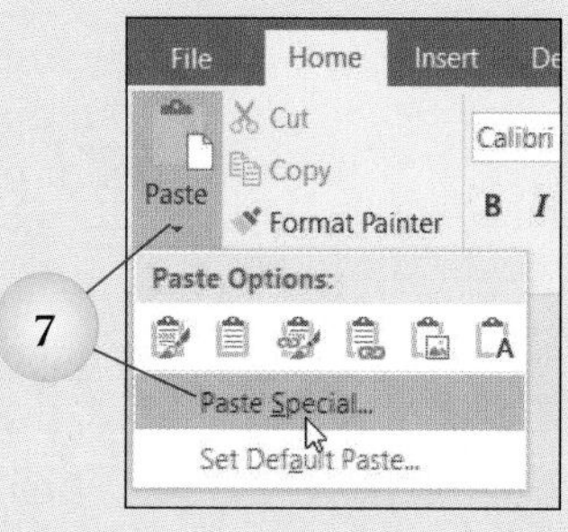

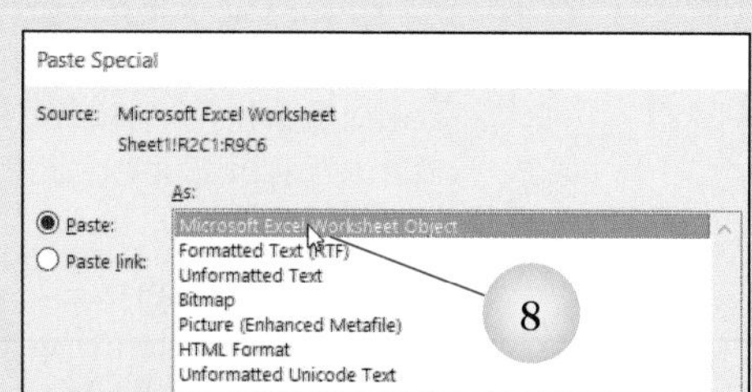

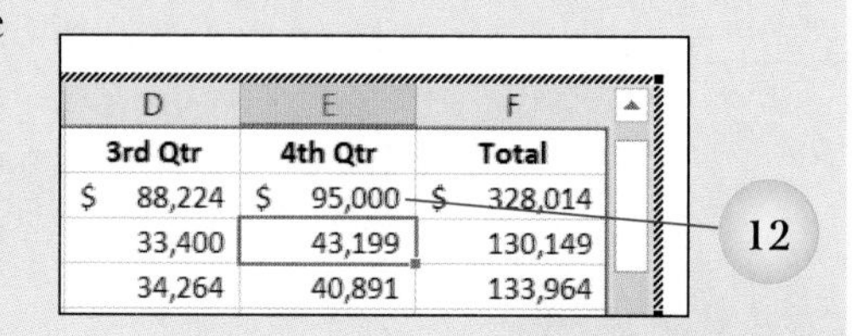

Check Your Work

Tutorial

Linking an Object

Linking an Object

If the content of the object to be integrated between programs is likely to change, link the object from the source program to the destination program. Linking the object establishes a direct connection between the source and destination programs. The object is stored only in the source program and the destination program contains a code that indicates the name and location of the source of the object. Whenever the document containing the link is opened, a message displays indicating that the document contains links and asking if the link should be updated.

To link an object, open both programs and program files. In the source program file, click the object and then click the Copy button in the Clipboard group on the Home tab. Click the button on the taskbar that represents the destination program file and then position the insertion point where the object is to be inserted. Click the Paste button arrow in the Clipboard group on the Home tab and then click *Paste Special* at the drop-down list. At the Paste Special dialog box, click the source program for the object in the *As* list box, click the *Paste link* option at the left side of the *As* list box, and then click OK.

Quick Steps

Link an Object

1. Open source and destination programs and files.
2. Click object in source program.
3. Click Copy button.
4. Click taskbar button for destination program file.
5. Position insertion point.
6. Click Paste button arrow.
7. Click *Paste Special*.
8. Click source program for object in *As* list box.
9. Click *Paste link* option.
10. Click OK.

Project 5b Linking an Excel Chart to a Document

Part 2 of 3

1. Open **NSSCosts.docx** and then save it with the name **7-NSSCosts**.
2. Open Excel and then open **NSSDept%.xlsx** located in the WL2C7 folder on your storage medium.
3. Save the workbook and name it **7-NSSDept%**.
4. Copy and link the chart to the Word document by completing the following steps:
   a. Click the chart to select it.
   b. Click the Copy button in the Clipboard group on the Home tab.
   c. Click the Word button on the taskbar.
   d. Press Ctrl + End to move the insertion point to the end of the document.
   e. Click the Paste button arrow and then click *Paste Special* at the drop-down list.
   f. At the Paste Special dialog box, click the *Paste link* option.
   g. Click *Microsoft Excel Chart Object* in the *As* list box.

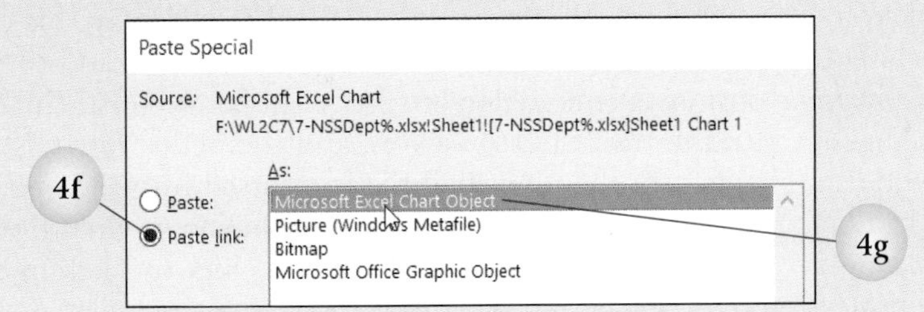

   h. Click OK.
5. Click the Excel button on the taskbar, close **7-NSSDept%.xlsx**, and then close Excel.
6. With **7-NSSCosts.docx** open on the screen, save, print, and then close the document.

Check Your Work

Editing a Linked Object

Edit a linked object in the source program in which it was created. Open the file containing the object, make the changes as required, and then save and close the file. If the source and destination programs are open at the same time, the changed content is reflected immediately in both.

Project 5c **Editing a Linked Excel Chart** **Part 3 of 3**

1. Open Excel and then open **7-NSSDept%.xlsx**.
2. Make the following changes to the data:
   a. In cell B4, change *18%* to *12%*.
   b. In cell B6, change *10%* to *13%*.
   c. In cell B8, change *5%* to *8%*.
3. Click the Save button on the Quick Access Toolbar to save the edited workbook.
4. Close **7-NSSDept%.xlsx** and then close Excel.
5. In Word, open **7-NSSCosts.docx**.
6. At the message stating that the document contains links, click the Yes button. (Notice the changes made to the chart data.)
7. Save, print, and then close **7-NSSCosts.docx**.

Check Your Work

Project 6 **Linking and Pasting Data into a Company Document** **2 Parts**

You will open a company document and then use the Insert File dialog box to paste a file into the company document as a linked object. You will also use the Paste Special dialog box to copy and paste the company name with formatting and copy and paste the company name and image as an object in a header.

Linking Data at the Insert File Dialog Box

In addition to linking an object using the Paste Special dialog box, data can be linked to a document at the Insert File dialog box. Display this dialog box by clicking the Insert tab, clicking the Object button arrow, and then clicking the *Text from File* option. At the dialog box, specify the file to be linked to the open document, click the Insert button arrow, and then click *Insert as Link* at the drop-down list. The data in the identified file is inserted into the open document as a linked object. If changes are made to the data in the original file, the data in the linked object will need to be updated. Update a link by clicking the object and then pressing the F9 function key or right-clicking the object and then clicking *Update Field* at the shortcut menu.

Project 6a Linking Data at the Insert File Dialog Box

Part 1 of 2

1. Open **ATSManagement.docx**, save it with the name **7-ATSManagement**, and then close the document.
2. Open **ATSDocument.docx** and then save it with the name **7-ATSDocument**.
3. Position the insertion point at the beginning of the heading *EMPLOYER COMMUNICATION*.
4. Link the table in *7-ATSManagement.docx* as an object to the open document by completing the following steps:
   a. Click the Insert tab.
   b. Click the Object button arrow and then click *Text from File* at the drop-down list.
   c. At the Insert File dialog box, click *7-ATSManagement.docx* in the Content pane.
   d. Click the Insert button arrow and then click *Insert as Link* at the drop-down list.

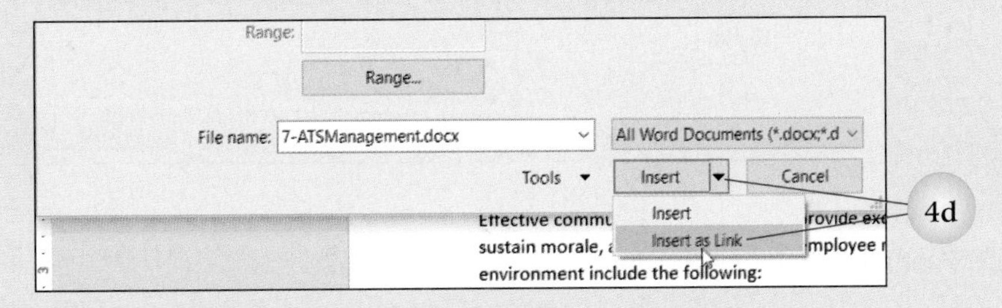

5. Save and then close **7-ATSDocument.docx**.
6. Open **7-ATSManagement.docx** and then make the following edits:
   a. Change the name *Genevieve Parkhurst* to *Noah Stein*.
   b. Change the extension *123* to *102*.

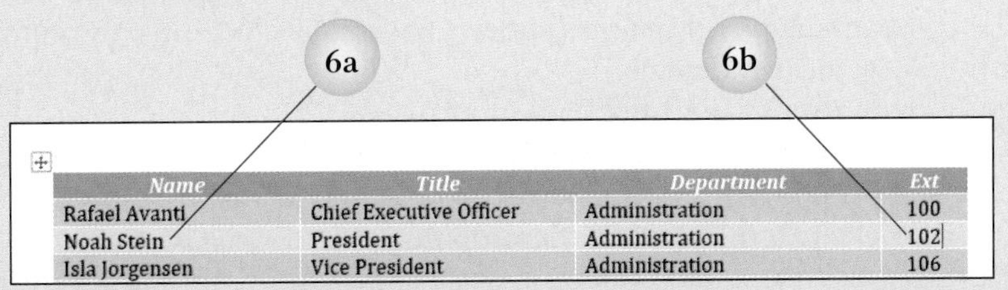

Name	Title	Department	Ext
Rafael Avanti	Chief Executive Officer	Administration	100
Noah Stein	President	Administration	102
Isla Jorgensen	Vice President	Administration	106

7. Save and then close **7-ATSManagement.docx**.
8. Open **7-ATSDocument.docx**.
9. Update the data in the table object by completing the following steps:
   a. Click in the table to select the table object.
   b. Press the F9 function key.
10. Save **7-ATSDocument.docx**.

Check Your Work

Using Paste Special

Use options at the Paste Special dialog box shown in Figure 7.9 to specify the formatting for pasted text and objects. Display the dialog box by clicking the Paste button arrow in the Clipboard group on the Home tab and then clicking *Paste Special* at the drop-down list. The options in the *As* list box vary depending on the cut or copied text or object and the source application. Text can be pasted with or without formatting and selected text can be pasted as an object. For example, in Project 6b, text will be copied in one document and then pasted into another document without the formatting. Also in the project, text and an image will be selected in one document and then pasted into another document as a Word object.

Figure 7.9 Paste Special Dialog Box

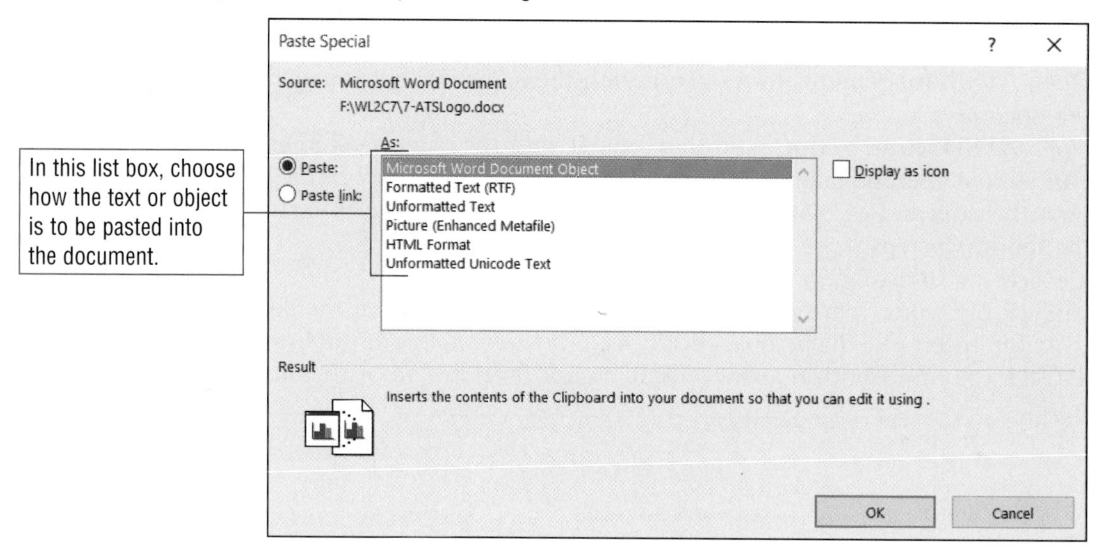

Project 6b Pasting Data Using the Paste Special Dialog Box

Part 2 of 2

1. With **7-ATSDocument.docx** open, press Ctrl + End to move the insertion point to the end of the document.
2. Open **ATSLogo.docx** and then save it with the name **7-ATSLogo.docx**.
3. Copy and paste the company name by completing the following steps:
   a. Select the company name *Advantage Transport Services*. (Select only the company name and not the image near the name.)
   b. Click the Copy button in the Clipboard group.
   c. Click the Word button on the taskbar and then click the *7-ATSDocument.docx* thumbnail.
   d. With the insertion point positioned at the end of the document, click the Paste button arrow and then click *Paste Special* at the drop-down list.
   e. At the Paste Special dialog box, click the *Unformatted Text* option in the *As* list box.
   f. Click OK.

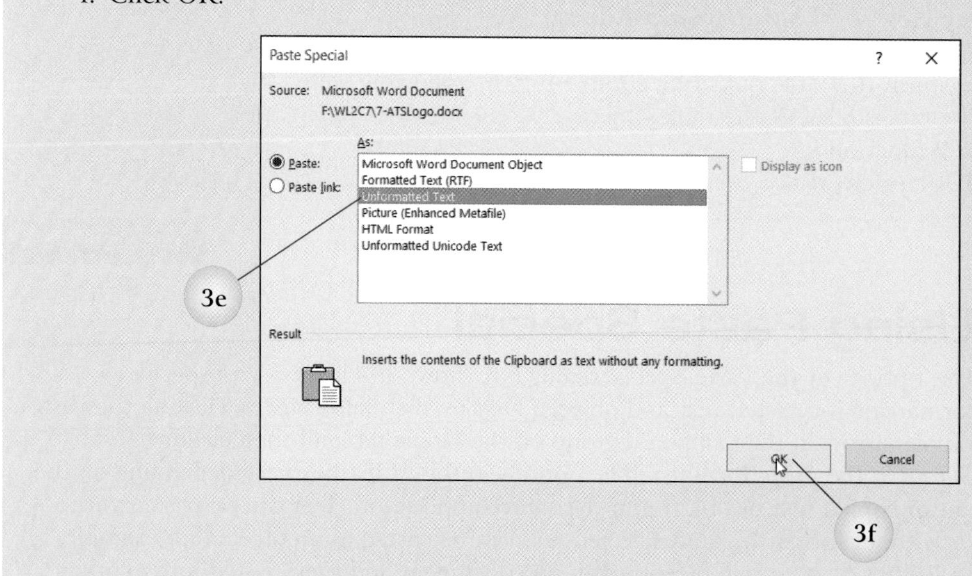

4. Copy the company name and image and then paste it as an object in the Header pane by completing the following steps:
   a. Click the Word button on the taskbar and then click the *7-ATSLogo.docx* thumbnail.
   b. Press Ctrl + A to select the entire document (the company name plus the road image).
   c. Click the Copy button.
   d. Click the Word button on the taskbar and then click the *7-ATSDocument.docx* thumbnail.
   e. Click the Insert tab.
   f. Click the Header button and then click *Edit Header* at the drop-down list.
   g. With the insertion point positioned in the Header pane, click the Home tab, click the Paste button arrow and then click *Paste Special* at the drop-down list.
   h. At the Paste Special dialog box, click the *Microsoft Word Document Object* option in the *As* list box.
   i. Click OK.

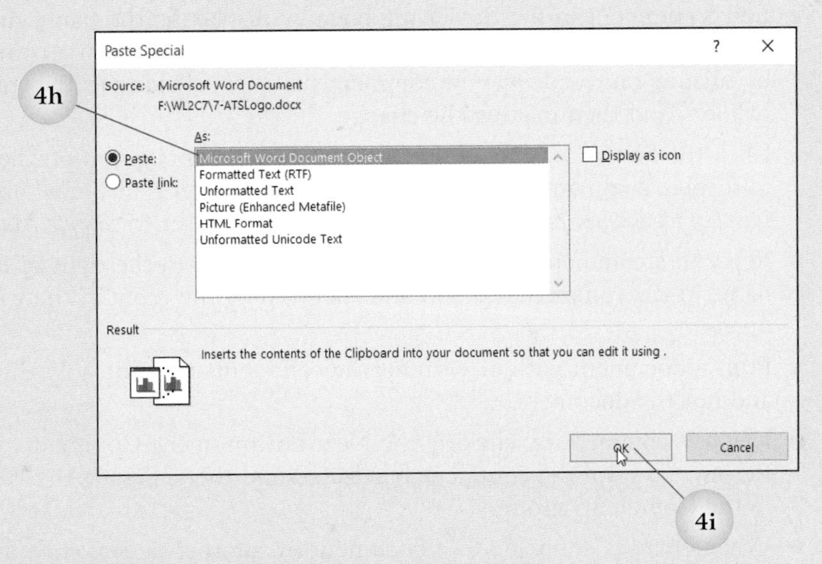

5. Increase the height of the pasted object by completing the following steps:
   a. Click the object to select it.
   b. Position the mouse pointer on the bottom middle sizing handle, click and hold down the mouse button, drag down approximately one-quarter inch, and then release the mouse button.
6. Close the Header pane by double-clicking in the document.
7. Save, print, and then close **7-ATSDocument.docx**.
8. Close **7-ATSLogo.docx**.

Check Your Work

Chapter Summary

- Insert a comment in a document by clicking the New Comment button in the Comments group on the Review tab; a comment balloon displays at the right margin. Depending on what previous settings have been applied, the Reviewing pane may display at the left side, rather than a comment balloon.
- Turn the display of the Reviewing pane on and off with the Reviewing Pane button in the Tracking group on the Review tab.
- Comments can be inserted in a document in the Reviewing pane. The summary that displays toward the top of the Reviewing pane provides counts of the numbers of comments inserted and changes made to the document.
- Navigate to review comments using the Previous and Next buttons in the Comments group on the Review tab.
- Edit a comment in the Reviewing pane by displaying the pane, clicking in the comment, and then making the change. Edit a comment in a comment balloon by turning on the display of comment balloons, clicking in the comment balloon, and then making the change.
- Click the Show Comments button in the Comments group on the Review tab to display comments. The Show Comments button is available only when the *Display for Review* option in the Tracking group is set to *Simple Markup*.
- Reply to a comment by clicking the Reply button to the right of the reviewer's name in the comment balloon and then typing the reply in the window that opens.
- Print a document with or without the comments or print only the comments and not the document.
- Delete a comment by clicking the Next button in the Comments group on the Review tab until the comment is selected and then clicking the Delete button in the Comments group.
- When changes are made to a document by another person with different user information, the changes display in a different color. Change the user name and initials at the Word Options dialog box with *General* selected.
- Use the Track Changes feature when more than one person is reviewing a document and making changes to it. Turn on Track Changes by clicking the Track Changes button in the Tracking group on the Review tab.
- Control how changes display in a document with the *Display for Review* option in the Tracking group on the Review tab. Control how markups display in a document with options at the Show Markup button drop-down list.
- Lock Track Changes so that all changes made to a document will be tracked. Lock Track Changes by clicking the Track Changes button arrow and then clicking *Lock Tracking*. Specify a password at the Lock Tracking dialog box that displays.
- Use options at the Show Markup button drop-down list or the Track Changes Options dialog box to customize the markup display. Click the Show Markup button in the Tracking group on the Review tab to display the drop-down list and click the Tracking group dialog box launcher to display the Track Changes Options dialog box.

- Display information about tracked changes—such as the author's name, date and time the change was made, and type of change—by hovering the mouse pointer over a change. After approximately one second, a box displays with the information. Information about tracked changes can also be displayed in the Reviewing pane.
- Change the Track Changes default settings with options at the Advanced Track Changes Options dialog box. Display this dialog box by clicking the Tracking group dialog box launcher. At the Track Changes Options dialog box, click the Advanced Options button.
- When reviewing a document, move to the next change by clicking the Next button in the Changes group on the Review tab and move to the previous change by clicking the Previous button.
- Use the Accept and Reject buttons in the Changes group on the Review tab to accept and reject changes made in a document.
- Use the Compare button in the Compare group on the Review tab to compare two documents and display the differences between them as tracked changes in a third document.
- Control how changes are combined with options at the expanded Compare Documents dialog box. Click the More button to display additional options.
- If several people have made changes to a document, their changed versions can be combined with the original document. Combine documents with options at the Combine Documents dialog box.
- Customize options for combining documents at the expanded Combine Documents dialog box. Click the More button to display additional options.
- Specify which source documents to display by clicking the Compare button in the Compare group on the Review tab, pointing to *Show Source Documents*, and then clicking an option at the side menu.
- An object created in one program in the Microsoft Office suite can be copied, linked, or embedded into another program in the suite. The program containing the original object is called the *source program* and the program in which it is inserted is called the *destination program*.
- An embedded object is stored in both the source and the destination programs. A linked object is stored only in the source program. Link an object if the content in the destination program should reflect changes made to the object stored in the source program.
- Data in one document can be linked to the open document at the Insert File dialog box by clicking the Insert button arrow in the dialog box and then clicking the *Insert as Link* option. Display the Insert File dialog box by clicking the Insert tab, clicking the Object button arrow, and then clicking the *Text from File* option.
- Use options at the Paste Special dialog box to specify the formatting for pasted text and objects. Display the Paste Special dialog box by clicking the Paste button arrow on the Home tab and then clicking *Paste Special* at the drop-down list.

Commands Review

FEATURE	RIBBON TAB, GROUP	BUTTON, OPTION	KEYBOARD SHORTCUT
accept change	Review, Changes		
Advanced Track Changes Options dialog box	Review, Tracking	, *Advanced Options*	
balloons	Review, Tracking	, *Balloons*	
Combine Documents dialog box	Review, Compare	, *Combine*	
Compare Documents dialog box	Review, Compare	, *Compare*	
delete comment	Review, Comments		
display for review	Review, Tracking		
Insert File dialog box	Insert, Text	, *Text from File*	
new comment	Review, Comments		
next comment	Review, Comments		
next revision	Review, Changes		
Paste Special dialog box	Home, Clipboard	, *Paste Special*	
previous comment	Review, Comments		
previous revision	Review, Changes		
reject change	Review, Changes		
Reviewing pane	Review, Tracking		
show markups	Review, Tracking		
show source documents	Review, Compare	, *Show Source Documents*	
Track Changes	Review, Tracking		Ctrl + Shift + E
Track Changes Options dialog box	Review, Tracking		

Workbook

Chapter study tools and assessment activities are available in the *Workbook* ebook. These resources are designed to help you further develop and demonstrate mastery of the skills learned in this chapter.

Microsoft®

Word

CHAPTER 8

Protecting and Preparing Documents

Performance Objectives

Upon successful completion of Chapter 8, you will be able to:

1. Restrict formatting and editing in a document and allow exceptions to restrictions
2. Protect a document with a password
3. Open a document in different views
4. Modify document properties
5. Mark a document as final
6. Encrypt a document with a password
7. Inspect a document for confidentiality, accessibility, and compatibility issues
8. Manage versions of a document

Precheck

Check your current skills to help focus your study.

In Chapter 7, you learned to perform workgroup activities such as inserting comments into a document, tracking changes made by other users, comparing documents, and combining documents from multiple users. In this chapter, you will learn how to protect the integrity of shared documents, limit the formatting and editing changes that users can make, and prepare documents for distribution.

Data Files

Before beginning chapter work, copy the WL2C8 folder to your storage medium and then make WL2C8 the active folder.

SNAP

If you are a SNAP user, launch the Precheck and Tutorials from your Assignments page.

Project 1 Restrict Formatting and Editing in a Company Report

3 Parts

You will open a company report document, restrict formatting and editing in the document, and insert a password.

Preview Finished Project

Tutorial

Restricting Formatting and Editing

Protecting Documents

Within an organization, copies of a document may be distributed among members of a group. In some situations, the document may need to be protected and the changes that can be made to it need to be limited. If a document contains sensitive, restricted, or private information, consider protecting it by saving it as a read-only document or securing it with a password.

Use options in the Restrict Editing task pane to limit what formatting and editing users can perform on a document. Limiting formatting and editing is especially useful in a workgroup environment, in which a number of people review and edit the same document.

For example, suppose a company's annual report is being prepared and it contains information from a variety of departments, such as Finance, Human Resources, and Sales and Marketing. Access to the report can be restricted so only certain employees are allowed to edit specific parts of the document. For instance, the part of the report pertaining to finance can be restricted to allow only someone in the Finance Department to make edits. Similarly, the part of the report on employees can be restricted so only someone in Human Resources can make edits. By limiting others' options for editing, the integrity of the document can be protected.

Restrict Editing

To protect a document, display the Restrict Editing task pane, shown in Figure 8.1, by clicking the Review tab and then clicking the Restrict Editing button in the Protect group. Use options in the *Formatting restrictions* section to

Figure 8.1 Restrict Editing Task Pane

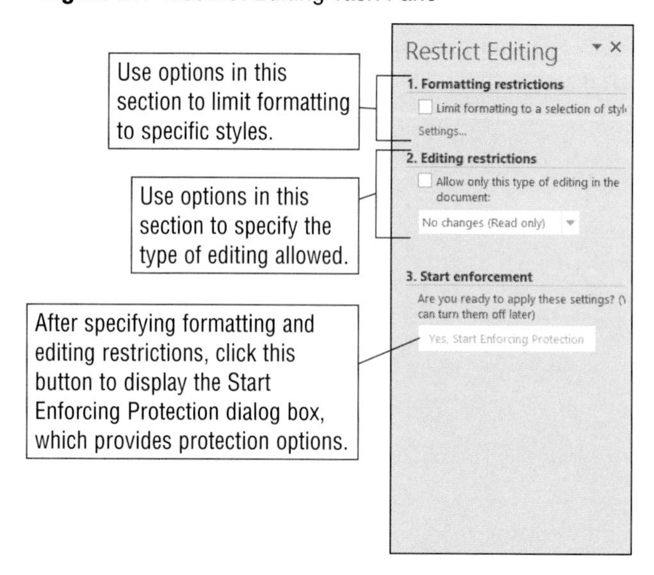
Use options in this section to limit formatting to specific styles.
Use options in this section to specify the type of editing allowed.
After specifying formatting and editing restrictions, click this button to display the Start Enforcing Protection dialog box, which provides protection options.
Restrict Editing
1. Formatting restrictions
Settings...
2. Editing restrictions
Allow only this type of editing in the document:
No changes (Read only)
3. Start enforcement
Yes, Start Enforcing Protection

limit formatting to specific styles and use options in the *Editing restrictions* section to specify the type of editing allowed in the document.

The Protect group on the Review tab contains a Block Authors button when a document is saved to a Microsoft SharePoint site that supports workspaces. If the button is active, select the portion of the document to block from editing and then click the Block Authors button. To unblock authors, click in the locked section of the document and then click the Block Authors button.

Restricting Formatting

Quick Steps

Display the Formatting Restrictions Dialog Box

1. Click Review tab.
2. Click Restrict Editing button.
3. Click Settings hyperlink.

Use options in the *Formatting restrictions* section of the Restrict Editing task pane to lock specific styles used in a document, thus allowing the use of only those styles and prohibiting users from making other formatting changes. Click the Settings hyperlink in the *Formatting restrictions* section and the Formatting Restrictions dialog box displays, as shown in Figure 8.2.

Insert a check mark in the *Limit formatting to a selection of styles* check box and the styles become available in the *Checked styles are currently allowed* list box. In this list box, insert check marks in the check boxes preceding the styles that are allowed and remove check marks from the check boxes preceding the styles that are not allowed. Limit formatting to a minimum number of styles by clicking the Recommended Minimum button. This allows formatting with styles that Word uses for certain features, such as bulleted and numbered lists. Click the None button to remove all the check marks and prevent all the styles from being used in the document. Click the All button to insert check marks in all the check boxes and allow all the styles to be used in the document.

Use options in the *Formatting* section of the dialog box to allow or not allow AutoFormat to make changes in a document. Also use options in this section of the dialog box to allow or not allow users to switch themes or style sets.

Figure 8.2 Formatting Restrictions Dialog Box

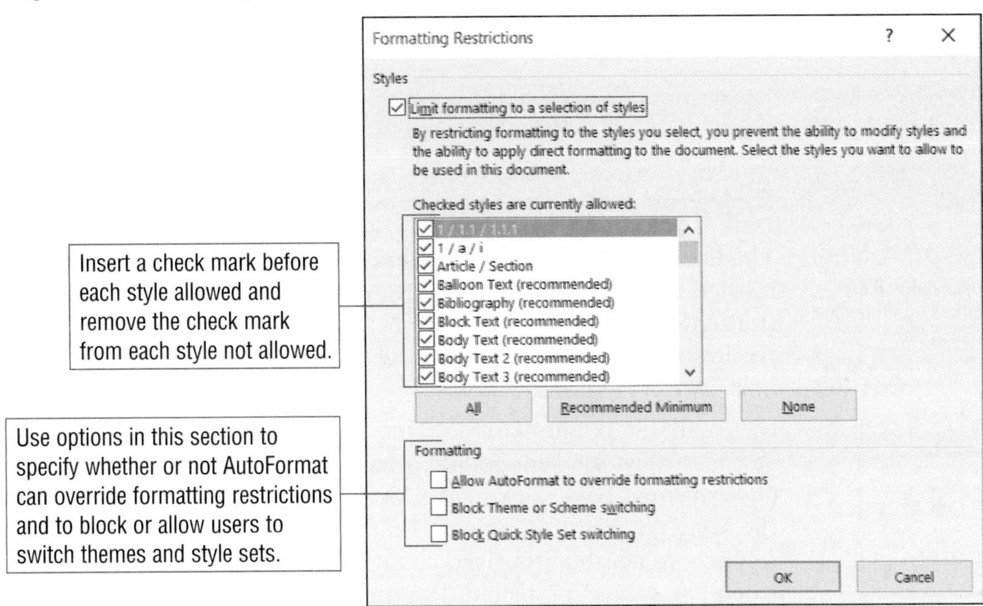

Project 1a Restricting Formatting of a Document

Part 1 of 3

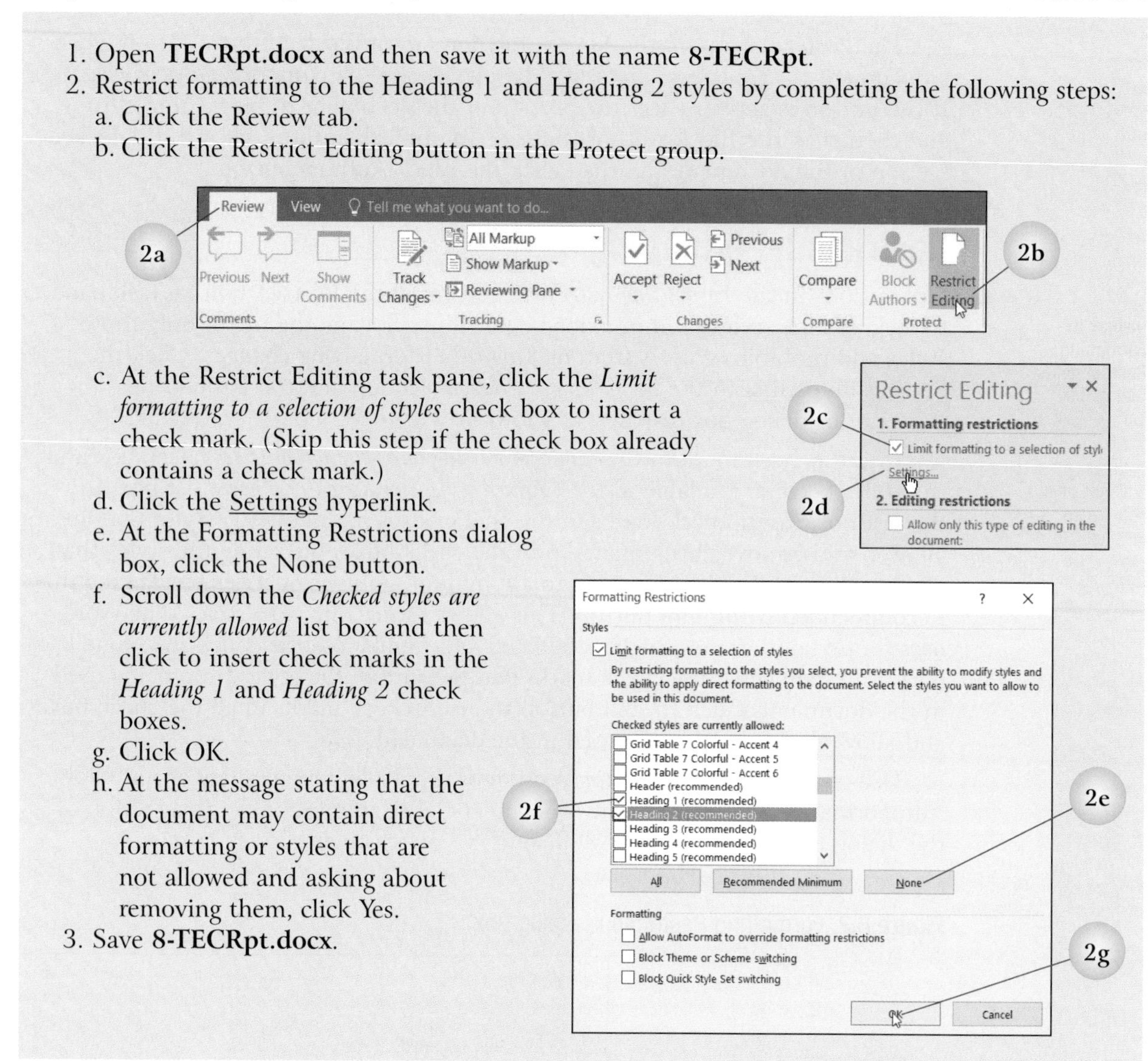

1. Open **TECRpt.docx** and then save it with the name **8-TECRpt**.
2. Restrict formatting to the Heading 1 and Heading 2 styles by completing the following steps:
   a. Click the Review tab.
   b. Click the Restrict Editing button in the Protect group.
   c. At the Restrict Editing task pane, click the *Limit formatting to a selection of styles* check box to insert a check mark. (Skip this step if the check box already contains a check mark.)
   d. Click the Settings hyperlink.
   e. At the Formatting Restrictions dialog box, click the None button.
   f. Scroll down the *Checked styles are currently allowed* list box and then click to insert check marks in the *Heading 1* and *Heading 2* check boxes.
   g. Click OK.
   h. At the message stating that the document may contain direct formatting or styles that are not allowed and asking about removing them, click Yes.
3. Save **8-TECRpt.docx**.

Enforcing Restrictions

Quick Steps

Display the Start Enforcing Protection Dialog Box

1. Click Review tab.
2. Click Restrict Editing button.
3. Specify formatting and/or editing options.
4. Click Yes, Start Enforcing Protection button.

The first step in protecting a document is to specify formatting and editing restrictions along with any exceptions to those restrictions. The second step is to start enforcing the restrictions. Click the Yes, Start Enforcing Protection button at the Restrict Editing task pane to display the Start Enforcing Protection dialog box, as shown in Figure 8.3.

At the Start Enforcing Protection dialog box, the *Password* option is automatically selected. To add a password, type it in the *Enter new password (optional)* text box. Click in the *Reenter password to confirm* text box and then type the same password again. Choose the *User authentication* option to use encryption to prevent any unauthorized changes. If Word does not recognize the password when a password-protected document is being opened, check to make sure Caps Lock is turned off and then try typing the password again.

Figure 8.3 Start Enforcing Protection Dialog Box

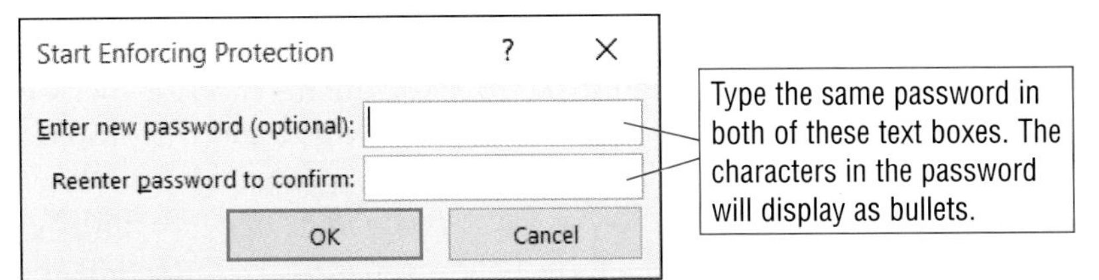

Project 1b Protecting a Document

Part 2 of 3

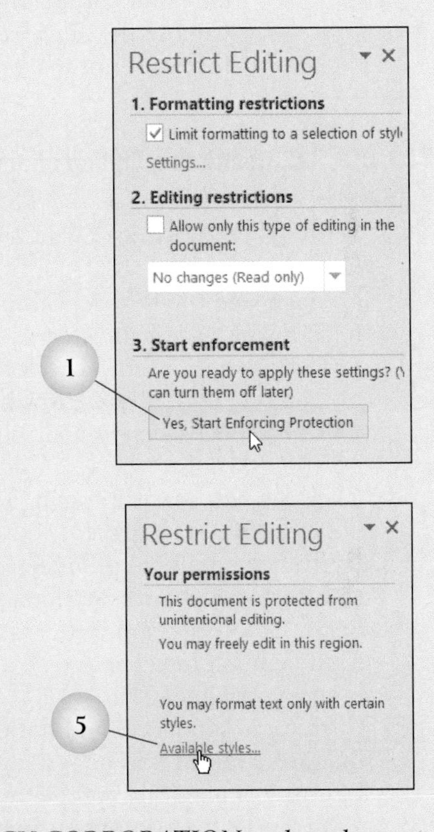

1. With **8-TECRpt.docx** open, click the Yes, Start Enforcing Protection button (at the bottom of the task pane).
2. At the Start Enforcing Protection dialog box, type formatting in the *Enter new password (optional)* text box. (Bullets will display in the text box, rather than the letters you type.)
3. Press the Tab key (which moves the insertion point to the *Reenter password to confirm* text box) and then type formatting. (Again, bullets will display in the text box, rather than the letters you type.)
4. Click OK to close the dialog box.

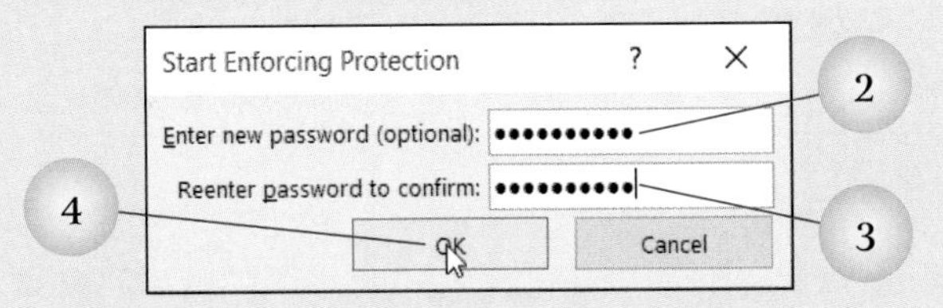

5. Read the information in the task pane stating that the document is protected and that text may be formatted only with certain styles. Click the Available styles hyperlink. (This displays the Styles task pane with four styles in the list box: *Clear All*, *Normal*, *Heading 1*, and *Heading 2*.)
6. Apply the Heading 1 style to the title *TANDEM ENERGY CORPORATION* and apply the Heading 2 style to the following headings: *Overview*, *Research and Development*, *Manufacturing*, and *Sales and Marketing*.
7. Close the Styles task pane.
8. Apply the Lines (Simple) style set.
9. At the message stating that some of the styles could not be updated, click OK.
10. Save the document.
11. Remove the password protection from the document by completing the following steps:
    a. Click the Stop Protection button at the bottom of the Restrict Editing task pane.
    b. At the Unprotect Document dialog box, type formatting in the *Password* text box.
    c. Click OK.
12. Save **8-TECRpt.docx**.

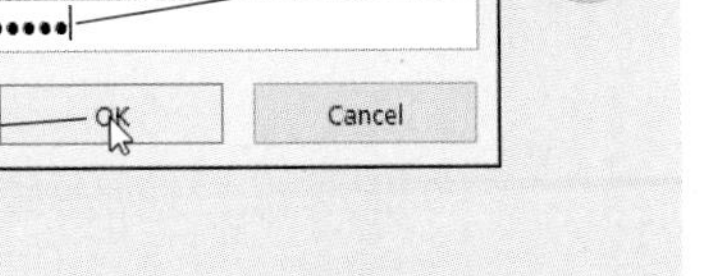

Check Your Work

Restricting Editing

Use the *Editing restrictions* option in the Restrict Editing task pane to limit the types of changes users can make to a document. Insert a check mark in the *Allow only this type of editing in the document* check box and the drop-down list below the option becomes active. Click the option box arrow and the following options become available: *Tracked changes*, *Comments*, *Filling in forms*, and *No changes (Read only)*.

To restrict users from making changes to a document, choose the *No changes (Read only)* option. Choose the *Tracked changes* option to allow users to make tracked changes in a document and choose the *Comments* option to allow users to insert comments in a document. These two options are useful in a workgroup environment, in which a document is routed to various individuals for review. Choose the *Filling in forms* option and users will be able to fill in the fields in a form but not make any other changes.

Project 1c Restricting Editing of and Protecting a Document — Part 3 of 3

1. With **8-TECRpt.docx** open, restrict editing to inserting comments by completing the following steps:
   a. Make sure the Restrict Editing task pane displays.
   b. Click the *Allow only this type of editing in the document* check box to insert a check mark.
   c. Click the option box arrow below *Allow only this type of editing in the document* and then click *Comments* at the drop-down list.

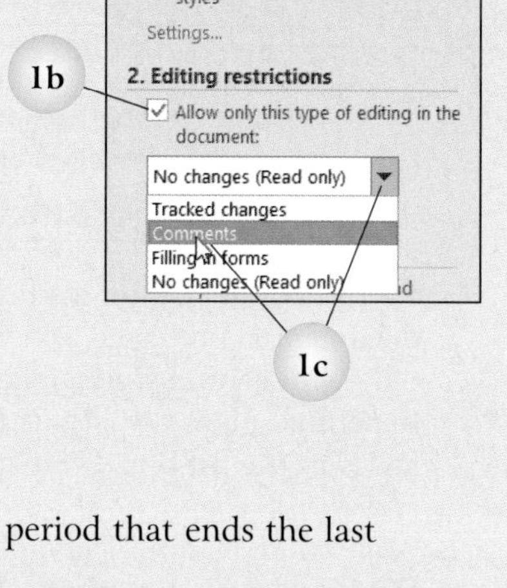

2. Click the Yes, Start Enforcing Protection button at the bottom of the task pane.
3. At the Start Enforcing Protection dialog box, click OK. (Adding a password is optional.)
4. Read the information in the task pane stating that the document is protected and that editing is restricted to inserting comments.
5. Click each ribbon tab and notice the buttons and options that are dimmed and unavailable.
6. Insert a comment by completing the following steps:
   a. Move the insertion point immediately to the right of the period that ends the last sentence in the second paragraph of the *Overview* section.
   b. Click the Review tab (if necessary), click the Show Markup button in the Tracking group, point to *Balloons*, and then click the *Show All Revisions Inline* option.
   c. Click the Reviewing Pane button to turn on the display of the Reviewing pane.
   d. Click the New Comment button in the Comments group on the Review tab.
   e. Type the following text in the Reviewing pane: Include additional information on the impact of this purchase.

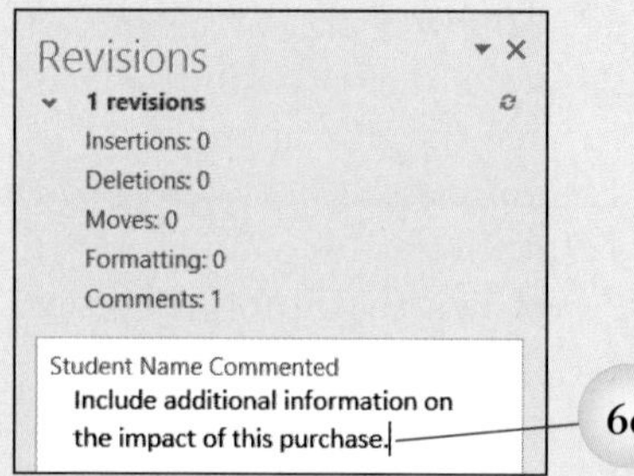

f. Close the Reviewing pane.
g. Click the Stop Protection button at the bottom of the Restrict Editing task pane.
h. Close the Restrict Editing task pane.
7. Save the document and then print only page 1.
8. Print only the comment. (To do this, display the Print backstage area, click the first gallery in the *Settings* category, click the *List of Markup* option, and then click the Print button.)
9. Close **8-TECRpt.docx**.

Check Your Work

Project 2 Protect a Contract Document and Identify a Training Document as Read-Only

2 Parts

You will open a contract document and then protect it with a password. You will also open documents in different views.

Preview Finished Project

Tutorial

Protecting a Document with a Password

Quick Steps

Protect a Document with a Password
1. Press F12.
2. Click Tools button.
3. Click *General Options.*
4. Type password in *Password to modify* text box.
5. Press Enter.
6. Type same password again.
7. Press Enter.

Hint A strong password contains a mix of uppercase and lowercase letters as well as numbers and symbols.

Protecting a Document with a Password

In addition to protecting a document with a password using options at the Start Enforcing Protection dialog box, a document can be protected with a password using options at the General Options dialog box, shown in Figure 8.4. Display this dialog box by pressing the F12 function key to display the Save As dialog box, clicking the Tools button at the bottom of the dialog box next to the Save button, and then clicking *General Options* at the drop-down list.

Use options at the General Options dialog box to assign a password to open the document, modify the document, or both. To insert a password to open the document, click in the *Password to open* text box and then type the password. A password can contain up to 15 characters, should be at least 8 characters, and is case sensitive. Consider combining uppercase letters, lowercase letters, numbers, and/or symbols to make a password secure. Use the *Password to modify* option to create a password that someone must enter before being allowed to make edits to the document.

At the General Options dialog box, insert a check mark in the *Read-only recommended* check box to save a document as read-only. If a read-only document is opened and then changes are made to it, it must be saved with a new name. Use this option if the contents of the original document should not be changed.

Figure 8.4 General Options Dialog Box

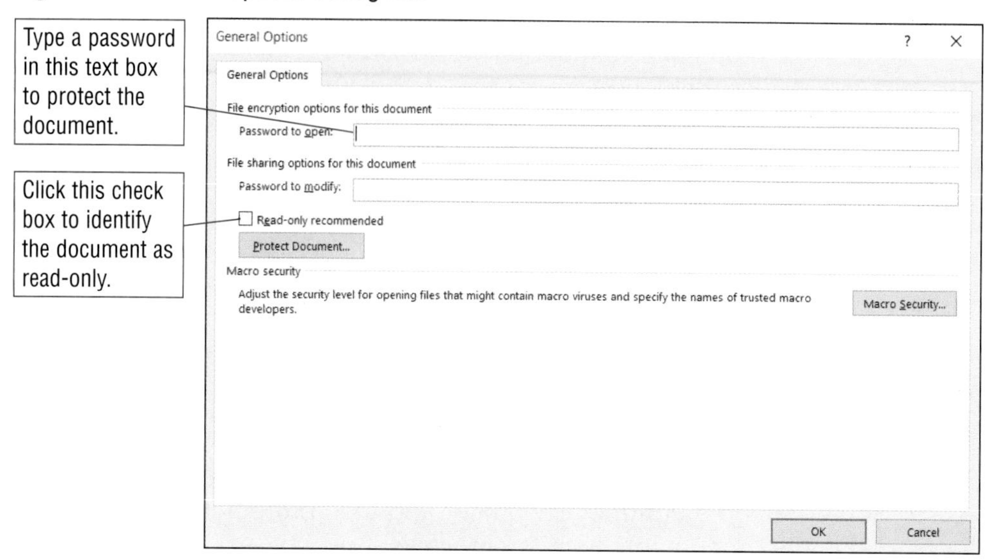

Project 2a Protecting a Document with a Password

Part 1 of 2

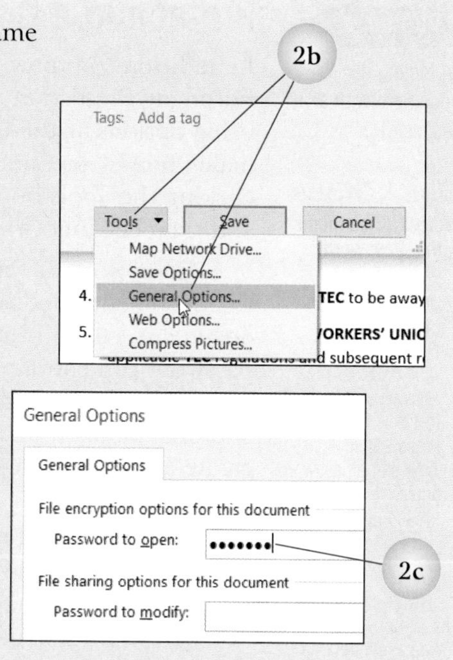

1. Open **TECContract.docx** and then save it with the name **8-TECContract**.
2. Save the document and protect it with a password by completing the following steps:
   a. Press the F12 function key to display the Save As dialog box.
   b. Click the Tools button at the bottom of the dialog box (next to the Save button) and then click *General Options* at the drop-down list.
   c. At the General Options dialog box, type your first name in the *Password to open* text box. (If your name is longer than 15 characters, abbreviate it. You will not see your name; Word inserts bullets in place of the letters.)
   d. After typing your name, press the Enter key.
   e. At the Confirm Password dialog box, type your name again in the *Reenter password to open* text box. (Be sure to type it exactly as you did in the *Password to open* text box, including the same uppercase and lowercase letters.) Press the Enter key.
   f. Click the Save button at the Save As dialog box.
3. Close **8-TECContract.docx**.
4. Open **8-TECContract.docx** and type your password when prompted in the *Enter password to open file* text box.
5. Close the document.

Opening a Document in Different Views

Quick Steps

Open a Document in Different Views

1. Display Open dialog box.
2. Click document name.
3. Click Open button arrow.
4. Click option at drop-down list.

Use the Open button at the Open dialog box to open a document in different views. At the Open dialog box, click the Open button arrow and a drop-down list of options displays. Click the *Open Read-Only* option and the document opens in Read Mode view and Read-Only mode. In Read-Only mode, changes can be made to the document but the document cannot be saved with the same name. Exit Read Mode view and display the document in Print Layout view by pressing the Esc key.

Click the *Open as Copy* option and a copy of the document opens with the text *Copy (1)* before the document name in the Title bar. Click the *Open in Protected View* option and the document opens with the text *(Protected View)* after the document name in the Title bar. A message bar displays above the document indicating that the file was opened in Protected view. To edit the document, click the Enable Editing button in the message bar. Open a document with the *Open and Repair* option and Word will open a new version of the document and attempt to resolve any issues.

Project 2b Opening a Document in Different Views

Part 2 of 2

1. Open **TECTraining.docx** and then save it with the name **8-TECTraining**.
2. Close **8-TECTraining.docx**.
3. Open a document as a read-only document by completing the following steps:
   a. Press Ctrl + F12 to display the Open dialog box and then navigate to the WL2C8 folder on your storage medium.
   b. Click the document name ***8-TECTraining.docx***. (Click only one time.)
   c. Click the Open button arrow (in the bottom right corner of the dialog box) and then click *Open Read-Only* at the drop-down list.

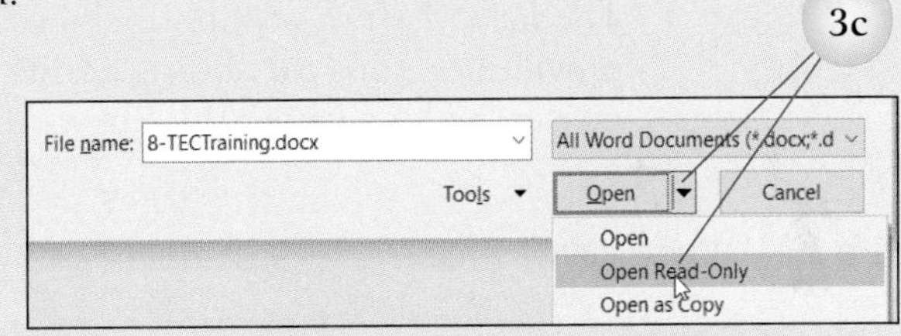

   d. The document opens in Read Mode view. Press the Esc key to exit Read Mode and display the document in Print Layout view. Notice that *[Read-Only]* displays after the name of the document in the Title bar.
   e. Close the document.
4. Open a document in Protected view by completing the following steps:
   a. Press Ctrl + F12 to display the Open dialog box.
   b. Click the document name ***PremPro.docx***.
   c. Click the Open button arrow and then click *Open in Protected View* at the drop-down list.
   d. Press the Esc key to exit Read Mode view and display the document in Print Layout view. Notice the message bar that displays stating that the file was opened in Protected view.
   e. Click each tab and notice that most of the formatting options are dimmed.
   f. Click in the document and then click the Enable Editing button in the message bar. This removes *(Protected View)* after the document name in the Title bar and makes available the options on the tabs.

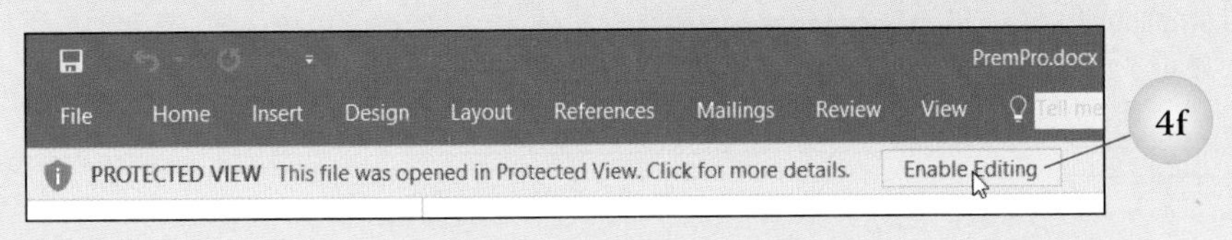

   g. Close the document.

Project 3 Prepare a Real Estate Agreement for Distribution — 3 Parts

You will open a real estate agreement and then prepare it for distribution by inserting document properties, marking it as final, and encrypting it with a password.

Preview Finished Project

Tutorial

Managing Document Properties

Managing Document Properties

Every document that is created has properties associated with it, such as the type of document, the location in which it has been saved, and when it was created, modified, and accessed. Document properties can be viewed and modified at the Info backstage area. To display information about the open document, click the File tab. Document property information displays at the right side of the Info backstage area, as shown in Figure 8.5.

The document property information that displays at the Info backstage area includes the file size, number of pages and words, total editing time, and any tags or comments that have been added. Add or update a document property by hovering the mouse pointer over the information that displays right of the property (a rectangular text box with a light-blue border displays), clicking in the text box, and then typing information. In the *Related Dates* section, dates display for when the document was created and when it was last modified and printed. The *Related People* section includes the name of the author of the document and provides options for adding additional author names. Display additional document properties by clicking the Show All Properties hyperlink.

Figure 8.5 Info Backstage Area

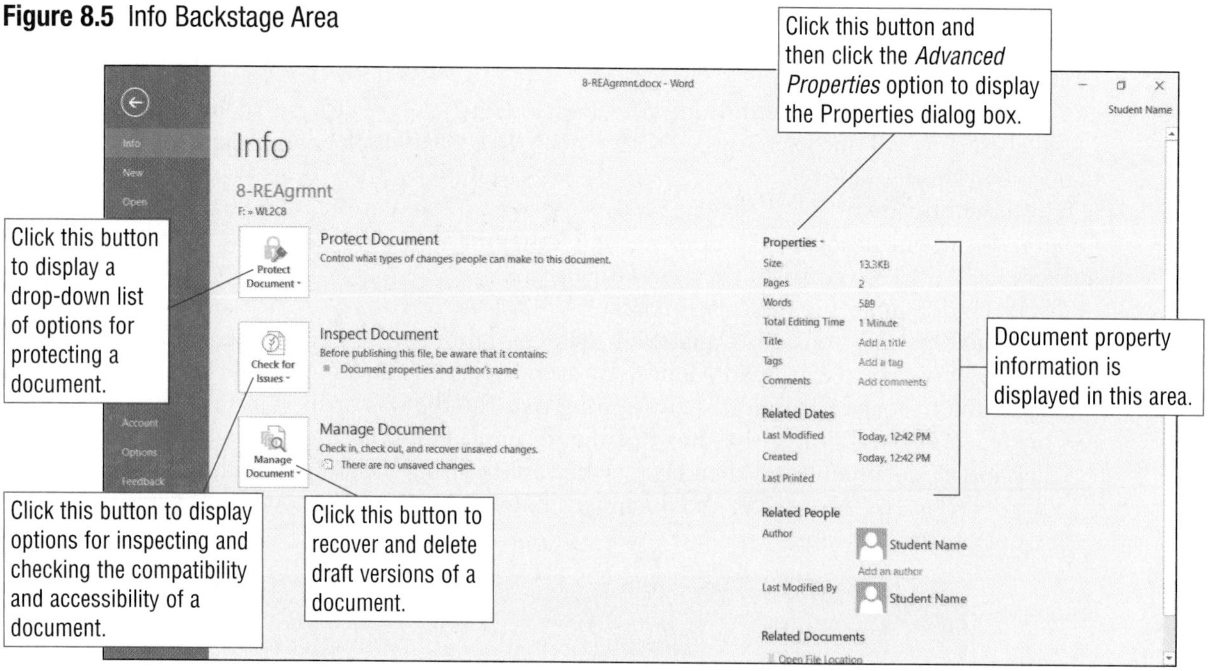

Click this button and then click the *Advanced Properties* option to display the Properties dialog box.

Click this button to display a drop-down list of options for protecting a document.

Document property information is displayed in this area.

Click this button to display options for inspecting and checking the compatibility and accessibility of a document.

Click this button to recover and delete draft versions of a document.

Quick Steps

Display the Properties Dialog Box

1. Click File tab.
2. Click Properties button.
3. Click *Advanced Properties.*

In addition to adding or updating document property information at the Info backstage area, specific information about a document can be viewed, added, edited, and customized with options at the Properties dialog box, shown in Figure 8.6. (The specific name of the dialog box reflects the currently open document.) Open the dialog box by displaying the Info backstage area, clicking the Properties button, and then clicking *Advanced Properties* at the drop-down list.

The Properties dialog box with the General tab selected displays information about the document type, size, and location. Click the Summary tab to view fields such as *Title*, *Subject*, *Author*, *Company*, *Category*, *Keywords*, and *Comments*. Some fields may contain data and others may be blank. Insert, edit, or delete text in the fields. With the Statistics tab selected, information displays such as the number of pages, paragraphs, lines, words, and characters. With the Contents tab selected, the dialog box displays the document title. Click the Custom tab to add custom properties to the document. For example, a property can be added that displays the date the document was completed, information on the department in which the document was created, and much more.

Another method for displaying document properties is to display the Open dialog box, click the document in the content pane, click the Organize button, and then click *Properties* at the drop-down list. Or right-click the file name in the content pane and then click *Properties* at the shortcut menu. The Properties dialog box that displays contains the tabs General, Security, Details, and Previous Versions. Some of the information in this Properties dialog box is the same as the information in the Properties dialog box that is accessed through the Info backstage area while some of the information varies between the two Properties dialog boxes. Generally, consider using the Properties dialog box accessed through the Info backstage area to add, edit, and create custom properties and use the Properties dialog box accessed through the Open dialog box to view document properties.

Figure 8.6 Properties Dialog Box with General Tab Selected

The Properties dialog box displays information about the document. Click each tab to display additional document information.

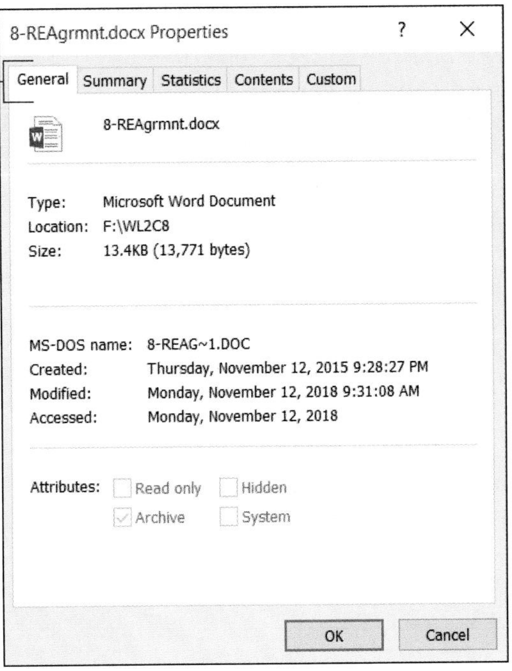

Project 3a Inserting Document Properties

Part 1 of 3

1. Open **REAgrmnt.docx** and then save it with the name **8-REAgrmnt**.
2. Make the following changes to the document:
   a. Insert page numbers that print at the top of each page at the right margin.
   b. Insert the footer *8-REAgrmnt.docx* centered on each page. (Do not set the footer text in italics. The footer text in this step was set in italics for emphasis only.)
3. Insert document properties by completing the following steps:
   a. Click the File tab. (Make sure the Info backstage area displays.)
   b. Hover the mouse pointer over the text *Add a title* that displays right of the *Title* document property, click in the text box that displays, and then type Real Estate Sale Agreement.
   c. Display the 8-REAgrmnt.docx Properties dialog box by clicking the Properties button and then clicking *Advanced Properties* at the drop-down list.
   d. At the 8-REAgrmnt.docx Properties dialog box with the Summary tab selected, press the Tab key to make the *Subject* text box active and then type Real Estate Sale Agreement.
   e. Click in the *Category* text box and then type Agreement.
   f. Press the Tab key and then type the following words, separated by commas, in the *Keywords* text box: real estate, agreement, contract, purchasing.
   g. Press the Tab key and then type the following text in the *Comments* text box: This is a real estate sale agreement between two parties.
4. Click OK to close the dialog box
5. Press the Back button to return to the document.
6. Save **8-REAgrmnt.docx** and then print only the document properties by completing the following steps:
   a. Click the File tab and then click the *Print* option.
   b. At the Print backstage area, click the first gallery in the *Settings* category and then click *Document Info* at the drop-down list.
   c. Click the Print button.
7. Save **8-REAgrmnt.docx**.

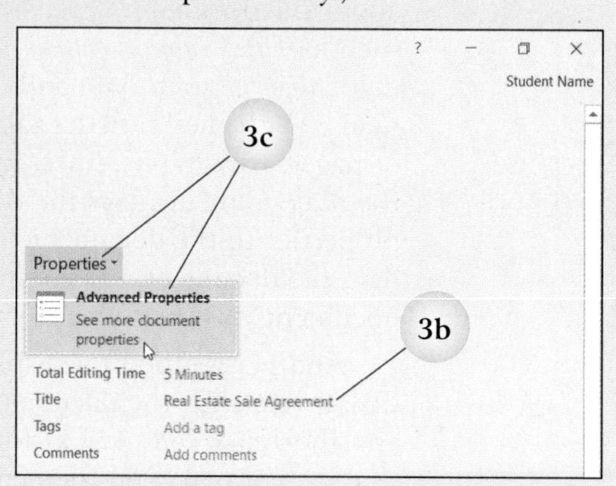

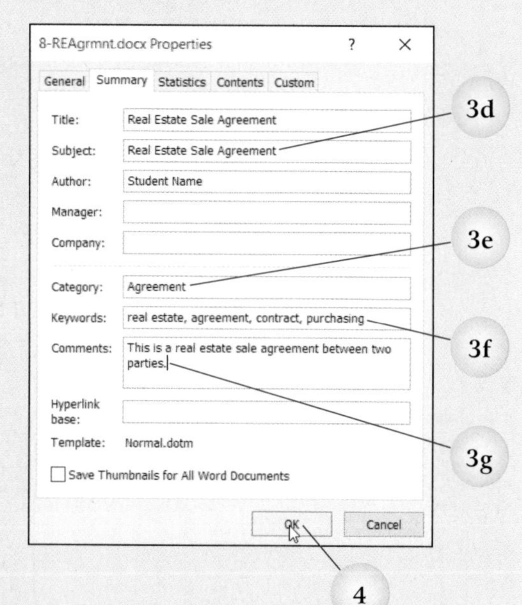

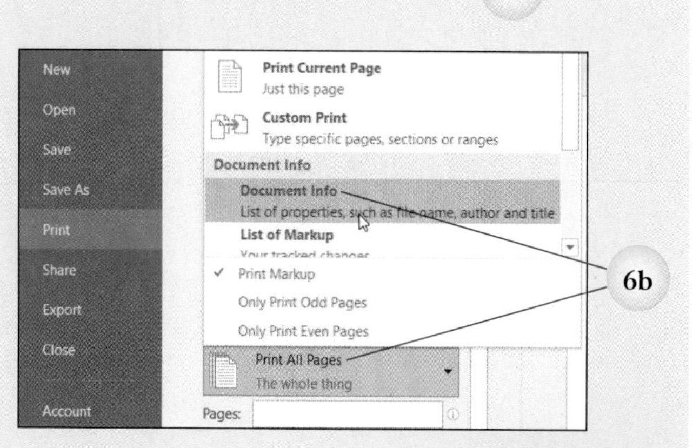

Check Your Work

Restricting Documents

The middle panel of the Info backstage area contains buttons for protecting a document, checking for issues in a document such as personal data and accessibility, and managing versions of a document. Click the Protect Document button in the middle panel and a drop-down list displays with the following options: *Mark as Final*, *Encrypt with Password*, *Restrict Editing*, and *Add a Digital Signature*.

Marking a Document as Final

Click the *Mark as Final* option to save the document as a read-only document. Click this option and a message displays stating that the document will be marked and then saved. At this message, click OK. This displays another message stating that the document is the final version of the document. The message further states that when a document is marked as final, the status property is set to *Final*; typing, editing commands, and proofing marks are turned off; and the document can be identified by the Mark as Final icon, which displays on the Status bar. At this message, click OK. After a document is marked as final, the message *This document has been marked as final to discourage editing* displays to the right of the Protect Document button at the Info backstage area.

Project 3b Marking a Document as Final **Part 2 of 3**

1. With **8-REAgrmnt.docx** open, mark the document as final by completing the following steps:
   a. Click the File tab.
   b. Click the Protect Document button at the Info backstage area and then click *Mark as Final* at the drop-down list.
   c. At the message stating that the document will be marked and saved, click OK.
   d. At the next message that displays, click OK. Notice the message that displays right of the Protect Document button.
   e. Click the Back button to return to the document.

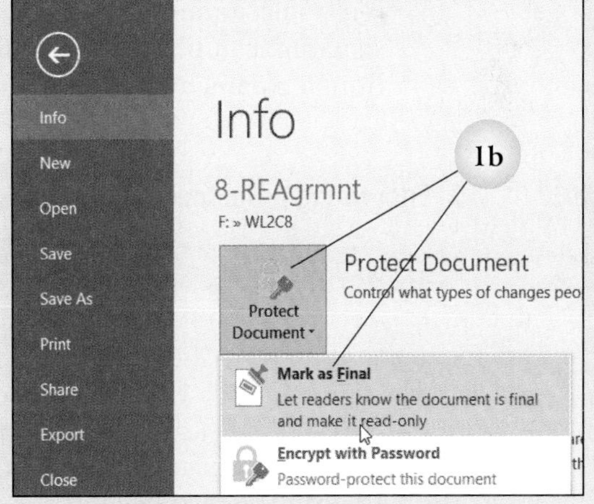

2. In the document window, notice the message bar that displays at the top of the screen and then close the document.
3. Open **8-REAgrmnt.docx** and then click the Edit Anyway button on the yellow message bar.

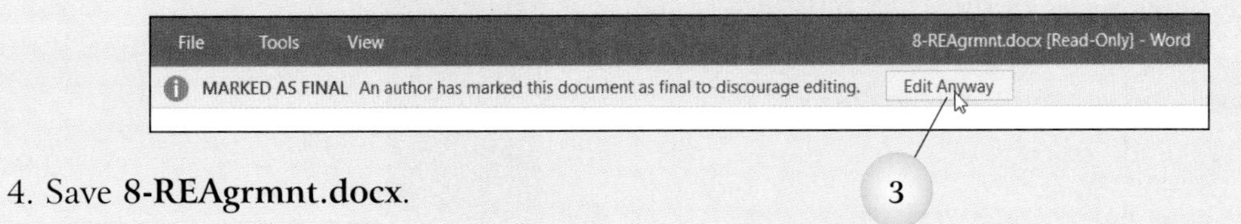

4. Save **8-REAgrmnt.docx**.

Tutorial

Encrypting and Inspecting a Document

Quick Steps

Encrypt a Document

1. Click File tab.
2. Click Protect Document button.
3. Click *Encrypt with Password.*
4. Type password and then press Enter.
5. Type password again and then press Enter.

Encrypting a Document

Word provides a number of methods for protecting a document with a password. As previously discussed in this chapter, a document can be protected with a password using options at the Start Enforcing Protection dialog box and the General Options dialog box.

In addition to these two methods, a document can be protected with a password by clicking the Protect Document button at the Info backstage area and then clicking the *Encrypt with Password* option at the drop-down list. At the Encrypt Document dialog box that displays, type a password in the text box (the text will display as bullets) and then press the Enter key or click OK. At the Confirm Password dialog box, type the password again (the text will display as bullets) and then press the Enter key or click OK. When a password is applied to a document, the message *A password is required to open this document* displays right of the Protect Document button.

Restricting Editing

Click the Protect Document button at the Info backstage area and then click the *Restrict Editing* option at the drop-down list and the document displays with the Restrict Editing task pane open. This is the same task pane discussed previously in this chapter.

Adding a Digital Signature

Use the *Add a Digital Signature* option at the Protect Document button drop-down list to insert an invisible digital signature in a document. A digital signature is an electronic stamp that verifies the authenticity of the document. Before a digital signature can be added, it must be obtained. A digital signature can be obtained from a commercial certification authority.

Project 3c Encrypting a Document with a Password

Part 3 of 3

1. With **8-REAgrmnt.docx** open, encrypt the document with a password by completing the following steps:
   a. Click the File tab, click the Protect Document button at the Info backstage area, and then click *Encrypt with Password* at the drop-down list.
   b. At the Encrypt Document dialog box, type your initials in uppercase letters in the *Password* text box. (The text will display as bullets.)

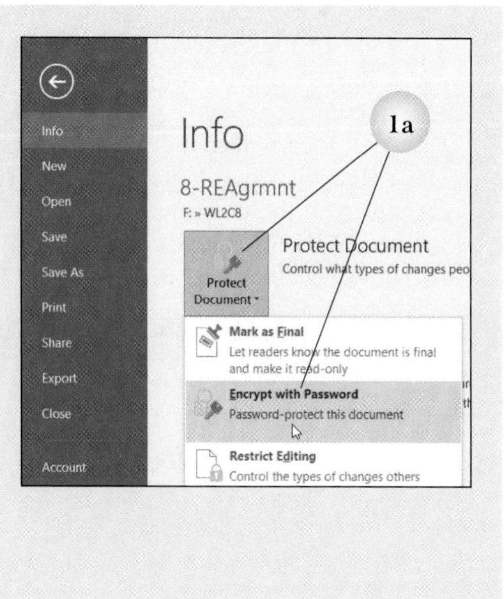

   c. Press the Enter key.
   d. At the Confirm Password dialog box, type your initials again in uppercase letters in the *Reenter password* text box (the text will display as bullets) and then press the Enter key.
2. Click the Back button to return to the document.
3. Save and then close the document.
4. Open **8-REAgrmnt.docx**.
5. At the Password dialog box, type your initials in uppercase letters in the *Enter password to open file* text box and then press the Enter key.
6. Save, print, and then close **8-REAgrmnt.docx**.

Check Your Work

Project 4 Prepare and Inspect a Lease Agreement **1 Part**

You will open a lease agreement document, make tracked changes, hide text, and then inspect the document.

Preview Finished Project

Inspecting Documents

Use options from the Check for Issues button drop-down list at the Info backstage area to inspect a document for personal and hidden data along with compatibility and accessibility issues. Click the Check for Issues button at the Info backstage area and a drop-down list displays with the following options: *Inspect Document*, *Check Accessibility*, and *Check Compatibility*.

Using the Document Inspector

Use Word's Document Inspector feature to inspect a document for personal data, hidden data, and metadata (data that describes other data, such as document properties). In certain situations, some personal or hidden data may need to be removed before a document is shared with others. To check a document for personal and hidden data, click the File tab, click the Check for Issues button at the Info backstage area, and then click the *Inspect Document* option at the drop-down list. This displays the Document Inspector dialog box, shown in Figure 8.7.

By default, the Document Inspector checks all the items listed in the dialog box. To control what items are inspected in the document, remove the check marks preceding items that are not to be checked. For example, if the headers and footers in a document do not need to be checked, click the *Headers, Footers, and Watermarks* check box to remove the check mark. To scan the document to check for the selected items, click the Inspect button at the bottom of the dialog box.

When the inspection is complete, the results display in the Document Inspector dialog box. A check mark before an option indicates that the Document Inspector did not find the specific items. If an exclamation point displays before an option, it means that the items were found and a list of the items displays. To remove the found items, click the Remove All button right of the option. Click the Reinspect button to ensure that the specific items were removed and then click the Close button.

Figure 8.7 Document Inspector Dialog Box

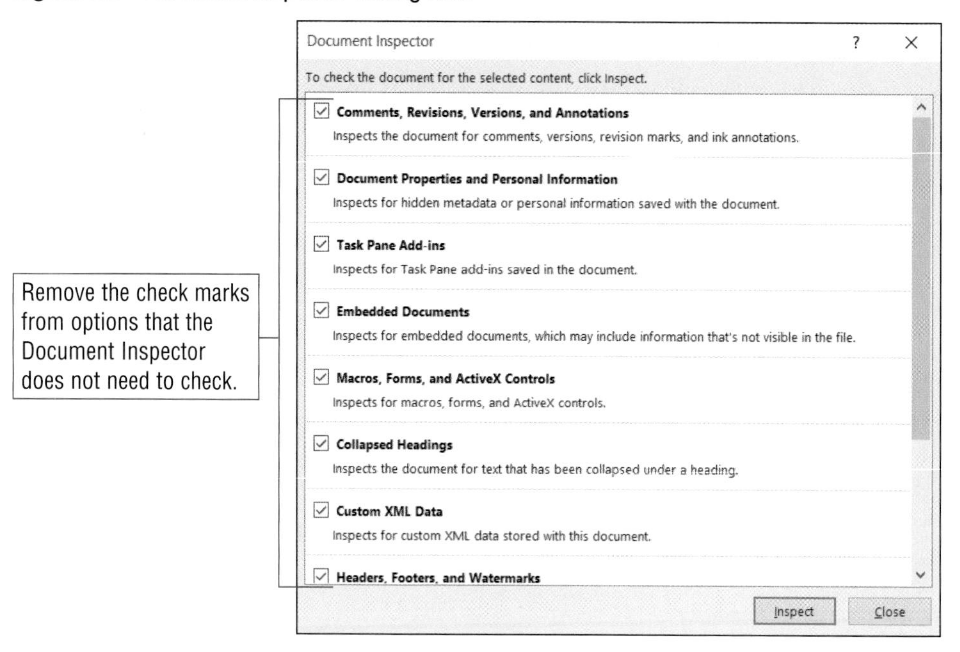

Project 4 Inspecting a Document

Part 1 of 1

1. Open **Lease.docx** and then save it with the name **8-Lease.docx**.
2. Make the following changes to the document:
   a. Turn on the Track Changes feature.
   b. Select the title *LEASE AGREEMENT* and then change the font size to 14 points.
   c. Delete the word *first* in the second numbered paragraph (the *RENT* paragraph) and then type fifteenth.
   d. Move the insertion point to the beginning of the text *IN WITNESS WHEREOF* (located on page 2) and then press the Tab key.
   e. Turn off Track Changes.
3. Hide text by completing the following steps:
   a. Move the insertion point to the end of the first paragraph of text in the document (one space after the period at the end of the sentence).
   b. Type The entire legal description of the property is required for this agreement to be valid.
   c. Select the text you just typed.
   d. Click the Home tab.
   e. Click the Font group dialog box launcher.
   f. At the Font dialog box, click the *Hidden* option in the *Effects* section.
   g. Click OK to close the dialog box.
4. Click the Save button on the Quick Access Toolbar.

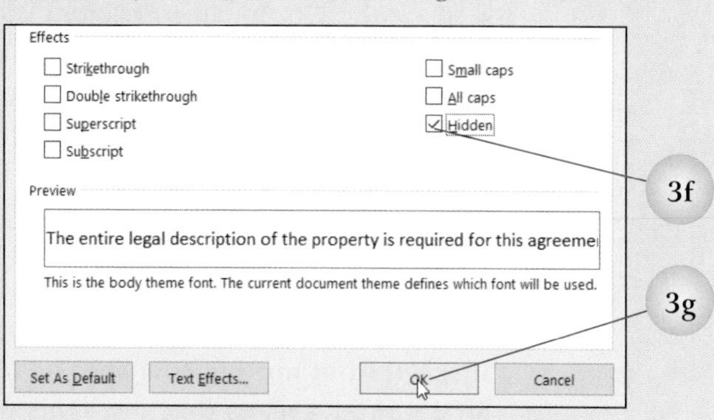

5. Inspect the document by completing the following steps:
   a. Click the File tab.
   b. Click the Check for Issues button at the Info backstage area and then click *Inspect Document* at the drop-down list.
   c. At the Document Inspector dialog box, specify not to check the document for extensible markup language (XML) data by clicking the *Custom XML Data* check box to remove the check mark.
   d. Click the Inspect button.

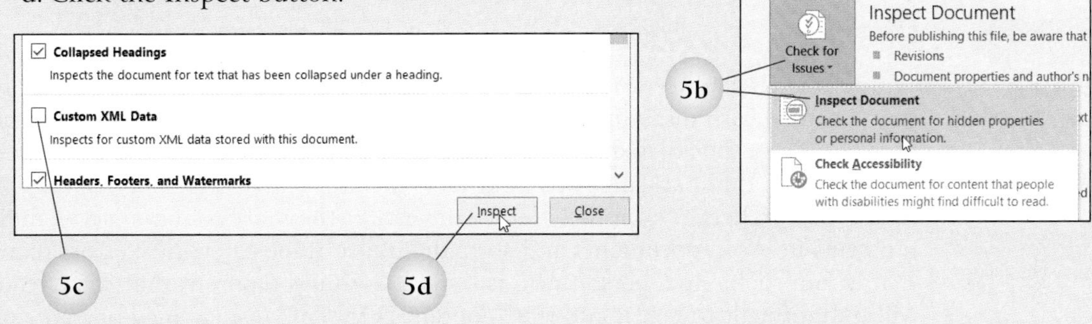

   e. Read the inspection results and then remove all the hidden text by clicking the Remove All button at the right side of the *Hidden Text* section. (Make sure that a message displays below *Hidden Text* stating that the text was successfully removed.)

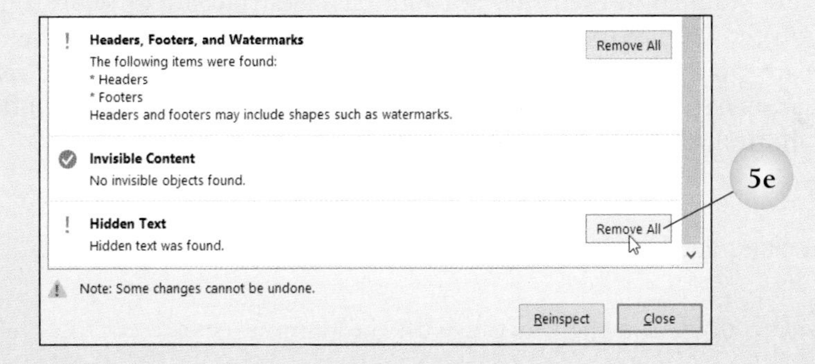

   f. Click the Reinspect button.
   g. To keep the header and footer text in the document, click the *Headers, Footers, and Watermarks* check box to remove the check mark.
   h. Click the Inspect button.
   i. Read the inspection results and then remove all the revisions by clicking the Remove All button at the right side of the *Comments, Revisions, Versions, and Annotations* section.
   j. Click the Reinspect button.
   k. To leave the remaining items in the document, click the Close button.
6. Click the Back button to return to the document.
7. Save, print, and then close **8-Lease.docx**.

Check Your Work

Project 5 Check the Accessibility and Compatibility of a Produce Document

3 Parts

You will open a document containing information on produce, check for accessibility issues, and check the compatibility of elements with previous versions of Word. You will also manage unsaved versions of the document.

Preview Finished Project

Tutorial

Checking the Accessibility and Compatibility of a Document

Quick Steps

Check Accessibility

1. Click File tab.
2. Click Check for Issues button.
3. Click *Check Accessibility*.

Checking the Accessibility of a Document

Word provides the Accessibility Checker feature to check a document for content that a person with disabilities (such as a visual impairment) might find difficult to read. Check the accessibility of a document by clicking the Check for Issues button at the Info backstage area and then clicking *Check Accessibility*. The Accessibility Checker examines the document for the most common accessibility problems in Word documents and sorts them into three categories: errors (content that is unreadable to a person who is blind); warnings (content that some readers will find difficult to read); and tips (content that some readers may or may not find difficult to read). The Accessibility Checker examines the document, closes the Info backstage area, and then displays the Accessibility Checker task pane.

In the Accessibility Checker task pane, passages of text that are unreadable are grouped in the *Errors* section, passages that are difficult to read are grouped in the *Warnings* section, and passages that may or may not be difficult to read are grouped in the *Tips* section. Select an issue in one of the sections, and an explanation of why it is an issue and how it can be corrected displays at the bottom of the task pane.

Project 5a Checking the Accessibility of a Document

Part 1 of 3

1. Open **PremPro.docx** and then save it with the name **8-PremPro**.
2. Complete an accessibility check by completing the following steps:
   a. Click the File tab.
   b. At the Info backstage area, click the Check for Issues button and then click *Check Accessibility* at the drop-down list.
   c. Notice the Accessibility Checker task pane at the right side of the screen, which contains an *Errors* section and a *Warnings* section. Click *Picture 4* in the *Errors* section and then read the information at the bottom of the task pane describing why the error should be fixed and how to fix it.

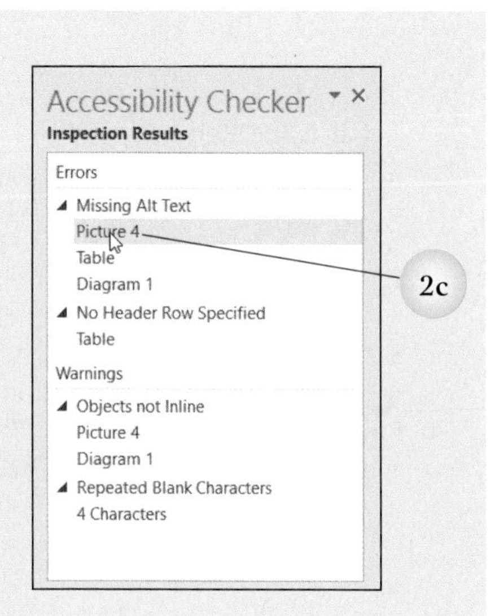

3. Add alternate text (a text-based representation of the image) to the image by completing the following steps:
   a. Right-click the selected image in the document and then click *Format Picture* at the shortcut menu.
   b. At the Format Picture task pane, click the Layout & Properties icon and then click *Alt Text* to expand the options.
   c. Click in the *Title* text box, type Cornucopia, and then press the Tab key. (This selects the default text in the *Description* text box.)
   d. Type Cornucopia of fruits and vegetables representing Premium Produce.
   e. Click the Close button to close the Format Picture task pane.
4. Click the first *Table* entry in the *Errors* section and then read the information at the bottom of the task pane about creating alternate text for a table. Add alternate text and repeat the header row by completing the following steps:
   a. With the table selected, click the Table Tools Layout tab.
   b. Click the Properties button in the Table group.
   c. At the Table Properties dialog box, click the Alt Text tab.
   d. Click in the *Description* text box and then type Produce table.
   e. Click OK to close the dialog box.
   f. Click anywhere in the first row in the table.
   g. Click the Repeat Header Rows button in the Data group on the Table Tools Layout tab.

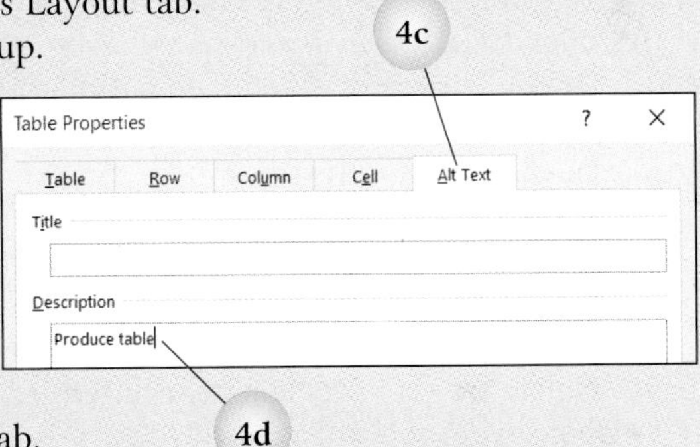

5. Click the *Diagram 1* entry in the *Errors* section and then add alternate text by completing the following steps:
   a. Right-click the selected SmartArt graphic and then click *Format Object* at the shortcut menu.
   b. At the Format Shape task pane, click the Layout & Properties icon and then, if necessary, click *Alt Text* to expand the options.
   c. Click in the *Title* text box, type Graphic, and then press the Tab key.
   d. In the Description text box, type SmartArt graphic with three shapes containing text on no pesticides, no herbicides, and organically grown produce.
   e. Click the Close button to close the Format Shape task pane.

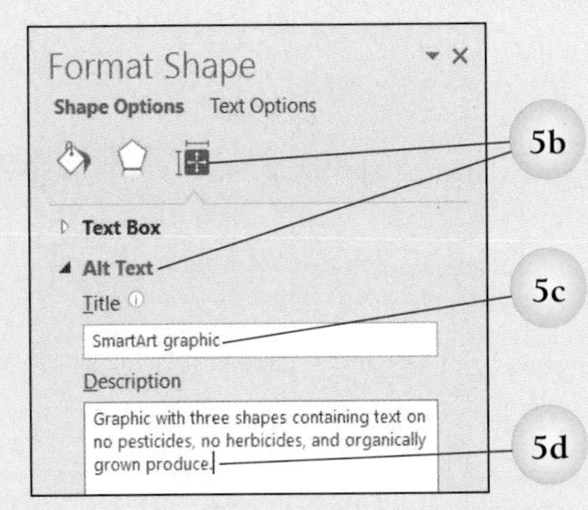

6. Click *Picture 4* in the *Warnings* section and then read the information about objects that are not inline with text. Do not make the change suggested because it will move the image to a different location on the page.
7. Click *Diagram 1* in the *Warnings* section and notice that the same information displays about objects that are not inline with text.
8. Close the Accessibility Checker task pane by clicking the Close button in the upper right corner of the task pane.
9. Save **8-PremPro.docx**.

Checking the Compatibility of a Document

Quick Steps

Check Compatibility

1. Click File tab.
2. Click Check for Issues button.
3. Click *Check Compatibility*.
4. Click OK.

Use one of the Check for Issues button drop-down options, *Check Compatibility*, to check a document and identify elements that are not supported or will function differently in previous versions of Word from Word 97 through Word 2010. To run the Compatibility Checker, open a document, click the Check for Issues button at the Info backstage area, and then click *Check Compatibility* at the drop-down list. This displays the Microsoft Word Compatibility Checker dialog box, which includes a summary of the elements in the document that are not compatible with previous versions of Word. This box also indicates what will happen when the document is saved and then opened in a previous version.

Project 5b Checking the Compatibility of Elements in a Document **Part 2 of 3**

1. With **8-PremPro.docx** open, check the compatibility of elements in the document by completing the following steps:
   a. Click the File tab, click the Check for Issues button at the Info backstage area, and then click *Check Compatibility* at the drop-down list.
   b. At the Microsoft Word Compatibility Checker dialog box, read the information that displays in the *Summary* text box.
   c. Click the Select versions to show button and then click *Word 97-2003* at the drop-down list. (This removes the check mark from the option.) Notice that the information about SmartArt graphics being converted to static objects disappears from the *Summary* text box. This is because Word 2007, 2010, and 2013 all support SmartArt graphics.

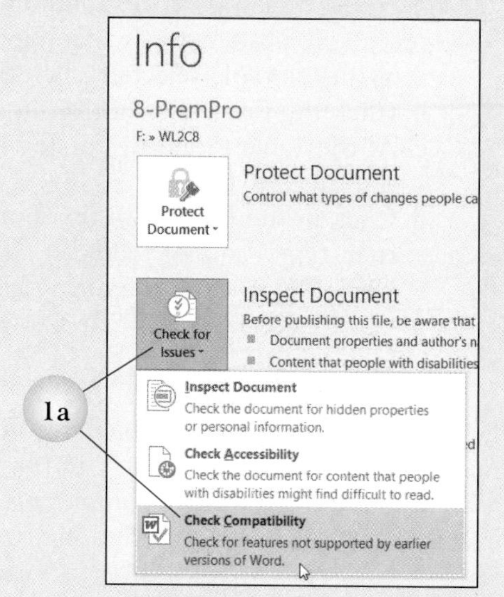

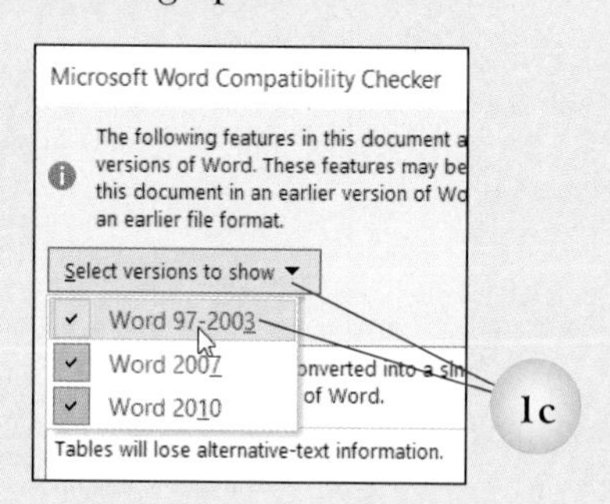

   d. Click OK to close the dialog box.
2. Save the document in Word 2003 format by completing the following steps:
   a. Press the F12 function key to display the Save As dialog box with WL2C8 the active folder.
   b. At the Save As dialog box, click the *Save as type* option box and then click *Word 97-2003 Document (*.doc)* at the drop-down list.
   c. Select the text in the *File name* text box and then type 8-PremPro-2003format.
   d. Click the Save button.
   e. Click the Continue button at the Microsoft Word Compatibility Checker dialog box.
3. Close **8-PremPro-2003format.doc**.

Tutorial

Managing Document Versions

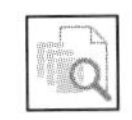 Manage Document

Managing Document Versions

When a document is being worked in, Word automatically saves it every 10 minutes. This automatic backup feature can be very helpful if the document is closed accidentally without saving it or the power to the computer is disrupted. As backups of the open document are automatically saved, they are listed right of the Manage Document button at the Info backstage area, as shown in Figure 8.8. Each autosave document displays with *Today*, followed by the time and *(autosave)*. When the document is saved and then closed, the autosave backup documents are deleted.

To open an autosave backup document, click the File tab and then click the autosave backup document. (Backup documents display right of the Manage Document button.) The document opens as a read-only document and a message bar displays with a Compare button and Restore button. Click the Compare button and the autosave document is compared to the original document. Review the comparison to decide which changes to accept and reject. Click the Restore button and a message displays stating that the selected version will overwrite the saved version. At this message, click OK.

When a document is saved, the autosave backup documents are deleted. However, if a document is closed without being saved (after 10 minutes) or the power is disrupted, Word keeps the autosave backup files in the UnsavedFiles folder on the hard drive. Access this folder by clicking the Manage Document button at the Info backstage area and then clicking *Recover Unsaved Documents*. At the Open dialog box, double-click the backup file to be opened. The UnsavedFiles folder can also be displayed at the Open dialog box by clicking the File tab, clicking the *Open* option, and then clicking the Recover Unsaved Documents button below the *Recent* option list. Files in the UnsavedFiles folder are kept for four days after a document is created. After that, they are automatically deleted.

Delete an autosave backup file by displaying the Info backstage area, right-clicking the autosave file (to the right of the Manage Document button), and then clicking *Delete This Version* at the shortcut menu. At the confirmation message that displays, click the Yes button. To delete all unsaved files from the UnsavedFiles folder, display a blank document, click the File tab, click the Manage Document button, and then click the *Delete All Unsaved Documents* option at the drop-down list. At the confirmation message that displays, click the Yes button.

As mentioned previously, Word automatically saves a backup of an unsaved document every 10 minutes. To change this default setting, click the File tab and then click *Options*. At the Word Options dialog box, click *Save* in the left panel. Notice that the *Save AutoRecover information every* measurement box is set at 10 minutes. To change this number, click the measurement box up arrow to increase the number of minutes between autosaves or click the down arrow to decrease the number of minutes.

Quick Steps

Display the UnsavedFiles Folder

1. Click File tab.
2. Click Manage Document button.
3. Click *Recover Unsaved Documents*.

OR

1. Click File tab.
2. Click *Open* option.
3. Click Recover Unsaved Documents button.

Delete an Autosave Backup File

1. Click File tab.
2. Right-click autosave backup file.
3. Click *Delete This Version* at shortcut menu.

Delete All Unsaved Files

1. Click File tab.
2. Click Manage Document button.
3. Click *Delete All Unsaved Documents*.
4. Click Yes.

Change the AutoRecover Time

1. Click File tab.
2. Click *Options*.
3. Click *Save*.
4. Type minutes in *Save AutoRecover information every* measurement box.
5. Click OK.

Figure 8.9 Autosave Documents at Info Backstage Area

Word automatically creates backups of a document; these backups are deleted when the document is saved. To open a backup document, click an autosave version.

Project 5c Opening and Deleting an Autosave Document

Part 3 of 3

1. At a blank screen, decrease the autosave time to 1 minute by completing the following steps:
   a. Click the File tab and then click *Options*.
   b. At the Word Options dialog box, click *Save* in the left panel.
   c. Click the *Save AutoRecover information every* measurement box down arrow until *1* displays.

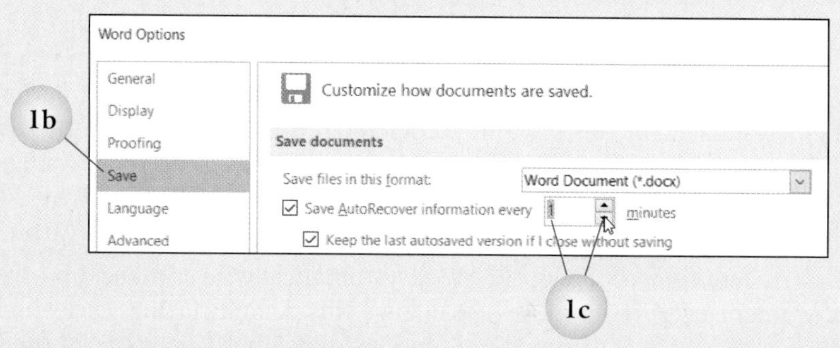

   d. Click OK to close the dialog box.
2. Open **8-PremPro.docx**.
3. Press Ctrl + End to move the insertion point to the end of the document and then type your first and last names.

4. Leave the document open for more than one minute without making any changes. After at least one minute has passed, click the File tab and then check to see if an autosave document displays right of the Manage Document button. (If not, click the Back button to return to the document and wait a few more minutes.)
5. When an autosave document displays at the Info backstage area, click the Back button to return to the document.
6. Select the SmartArt graphic and then delete it.
7. Click the File tab and then click the autosave document that displays right of the Manage Document button. If more than one autosave document displays, click the one at the top of the list (the most recent autosave document). This opens the autosave document as read-only.
8. Restore the document to the autosave version by clicking the Restore button in the message bar.

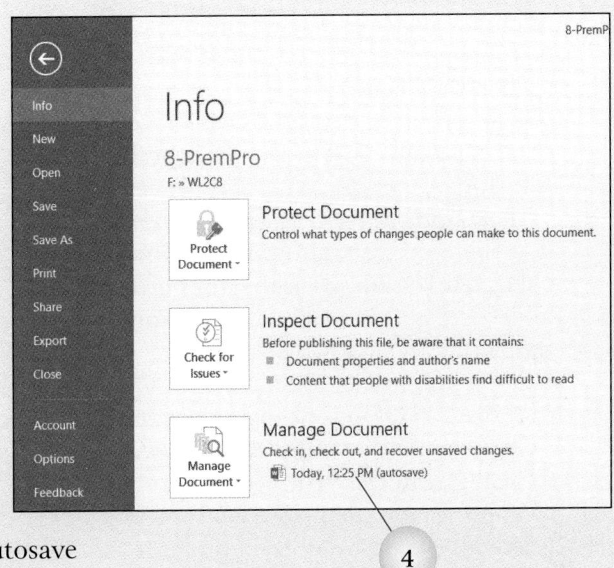

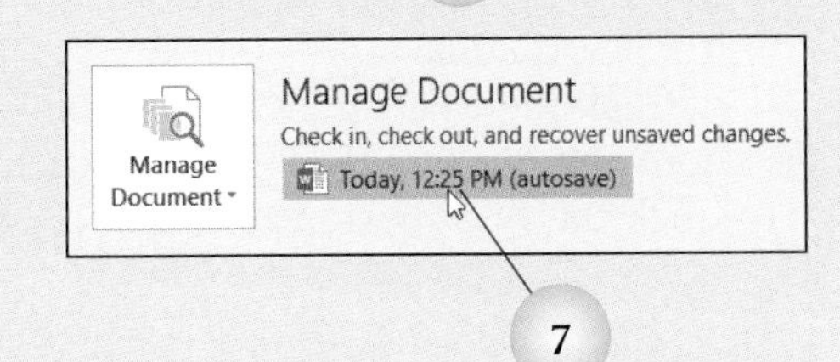

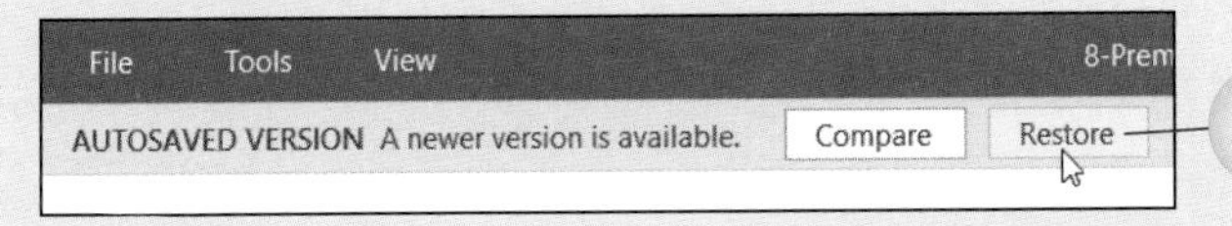

9. At the message that displays stating that the last saved version is about to be overwritten with the selected version, click OK. (This saves the document with the SmartArt.)
10. Press the Esc key to display the document in Normal view.
11. Check to see what versions of previous documents Word has saved by completing the following steps:
    a. Click the File tab.
    b. Click the Manage Document button and then click *Recover Unsaved Documents* at the drop-down list.
    c. At the Open dialog box, check the documents that display in the content pane.
    d. Click the Cancel button to close the Open dialog box.

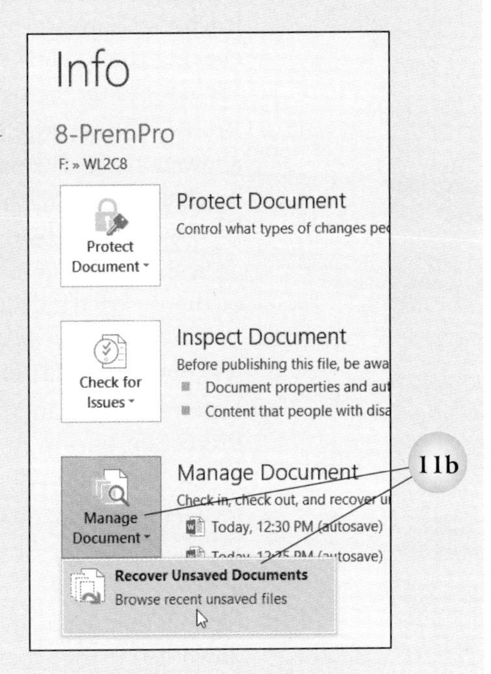

12. Delete an autosave backup file by completing the following steps:
    a. Click the File tab.
    b. Right-click the first autosave backup file name that displays right of the Manage Document button.
    c. Click *Delete This Version* at the shortcut menu.
    d. At the message asking whether to delete the selected version, click the Yes button.

13. Return the autosave time to 10 minutes by completing the following steps:
    a. At the Info backstage area, click *Options*.
    b. At the Word Options dialog box, click *Save* in the left panel.
    c. Click the *Save AutoRecover information every* measurement box up arrow until *10* displays.
    d. Click OK to close the dialog box.
14. Save, print, and then close **8-PremPro.docx**.
15. Delete all the unsaved backup files by completing the following steps:
    a. Press Ctrl + N to display a blank document.
    b. Click the File tab.
    c. Click the Manage Document button and then click *Delete All Unsaved Documents*.
    d. At the message that displays, click Yes.
16. Click the Back button to return to the blank document.

Check Your Work

Chapter Summary

- Restrict formatting and editing in a document and apply a password to protect it with options in the Restrict Editing task pane. Display this task pane by clicking the Review tab and then clicking the Restrict Editing button in the Protect group.
- Restrict formatting in a document by specifying what styles are and are not allowed at the Formatting Restrictions dialog box. Display this dialog box by clicking the Settings hyperlink in the *Formatting restrictions* section in the Restrict Editing task pane.
- To restrict editing in a document, use options in the *Editing restrictions* section of the Restrict Editing task pane. Insert a check mark in the *Allow only this type of editing in the document* check box, click the option box arrow at the drop-down list, and then click a specific option.
- Enforce editing and formatting restrictions by clicking the Yes, Start Enforcing Protection button in the Restrict Editing task pane and then enter a password at the Start Enforcing Protection dialog box.
- Protect a document with a password using options at the Start Enforcing Protection dialog box, the General Options dialog box, or the Info backstage area.
- Open a document in different views with options at the Open button drop-down list at the Open dialog box.
- Review and modify document properties at the Info backstage area.

- Display the Properties dialog box by clicking the Properties button at the Info backstage area and then clicking *Advanced Properties* at the drop-down list.
- When a document is marked as final, it is saved as a read-only document. Mark a document as final by clicking the Protect Document button at the Info backstage area and then clicking *Mark as Final* at the drop-down list. Typing, editing commands, and proofing marks are turned off when a document is marked as final.
- Another method for displaying the Restrict Editing task pane is to click the Protect Document button at the Info backstage area and then click *Restrict Editing* at the drop-down list.
- Insert a digital signature (an electronic stamp that verifies the authenticity of a document) in a document using the *Add a Digital Signature* option at the Protect Document button drop-down list. A digital signature can be obtained from a commercial certification authority.
- Inspect a document for personal data, hidden data, and metadata with options at the Document Inspector dialog box. Display this dialog box by clicking the Check for Issues button at the Info backstage area and then clicking *Inspect Document* at the drop-down list.
- The Accessibility Checker checks a document for content that a person with disabilities might find difficult to read. Run the Accessibility Checker by clicking the Check for Issues button at the Info backstage area and then clicking *Check Accessibility* at the drop-down list.
- Run the Compatibility Checker to check a document and identify elements that are not supported or that will function differently in previous versions of Word. To determine the compatibility of the features in a document, click the Check for Issues button at the Info backstage area and then click *Check Compatibility* at the drop-down list.
- By default, Word automatically saves a backup of an unsaved document every 10 minutes. A list of autosave backup documents displays right of the Manage Document button at the Info backstage area. Click the document name to open the autosave backup document.
- When a document is saved, Word automatically deletes the autosave backup documents. However, if a document is closed without saving it or the power to the computer is disrupted, Word keeps backup files in the UnsavedFiles folder on the hard drive. Display this folder by clicking the Manage Document button at the Info backstage area and then clicking *Recover Unsaved Documents* at the drop-down list.
- Delete an autosave backup file by displaying the Info backstage area, right-clicking the autosave backup file, and then clicking *Delete This Version* at the shortcut menu.
- Delete all the unsaved backup files by displaying a blank document, clicking the File tab, clicking the Manage Document button, and then clicking *Delete All Unsaved Documents*. At the confirmation message that displays, click the Yes button.
- Change the 10-minute autosave default setting by changing the *Save AutoRecover information every* measurement at the Word Options dialog box with *Save* selected in the left panel.

Commands Review

FEATURE	RIBBON TAB, GROUP/OPTION	BUTTON, OPTION
Accessibility Checker	File, *Info*	, *Check Accessibility*
Compatibility Checker	File, *Info*	, *Check Compatibility*
Document Inspector dialog box	File, *Info*	, *Inspect Document*
Encrypt Document dialog box	File, *Info*	, *Encrypt with Password*
Formatting Restrictions dialog box	Review, Protect	, *Settings*
General Options dialog box	File, *Save As, Browse*	*Tools, General Options*
Properties dialog box	File, *Info*	Properties, *Advanced Properties*
Restrict Editing task pane	Review, Protect	
UnsavedFiles folder	File, *Info*	, *Recover Unsaved Documents*

Workbook

Chapter study tools and assessment activities are available in the *Workbook* ebook. These resources are designed to help you further develop and demonstrate mastery of the skills learned in this chapter.

Unit assessment activities are also available in the *Workbook*. These activities are designed to help you demonstrate mastery of the skills learned in this unit.

Index

D

E

F

G

H

I

K

L

M

N

O

P

Q

R

S

T

U

V

W

COMMON COMMANDS FOR MICROSOFT 2016 OFFICE SUITE

WORD, EXCEL, POWERPOINT

Feature	Ribbon Tab, Group/*Option*	Button	Keyboard Shortcut
bold text	Home, Font	B	Ctrl + B
Clipboard task pane	Home, Clipboard		
close	File, *Close*		Ctrl + F4
close program			Alt + F4
copy	Home, Clipboard		Ctrl + C
cut	Home, Clipboard		Ctrl + X
Find	Home, Editing		Ctrl + F
font	Home, Font	Calibri (Body)	
font color	Home, Font	A	
font size	Home, Font	11	Ctrl + Shift + P
Format Painter	Home, Clipboard		Ctrl + Shift + C
Help			F1
Insert Hyperlink dialog box	Insert, Links		Ctrl + K
italicize text	Home, Font	I	Ctrl + I
New backstage area	File, *New*		
Open backstage area	File, *Open*		Ctrl + O
paste	Home, Clipboard		Ctrl + V
Print backstage area	File, *Print*		Ctrl + P
Save As backstage area	File, *Save* OR *Save As*		Ctrl + S
Save As dialog box			F12
shapes	Insert, Illustrations		
SmartArt	Insert, Illustrations		
table	Insert, Tables		
Tell Me		Tell me what you want to do	
text box	Insert, Text		
underline text	Home, Font	U	Ctrl + U
WordArt	Insert, Text		

WORD

Feature	Ribbon Tab, Group/*Option*	Button	Keyboard Shortcut
align left, center, or right	Home, Paragraph		Ctrl + L, E, or R
bullets	Home, Paragraph		
columns	Layout, Page Setup		
Envelopes and Labels dialog box	Mailings, Create		
header or footer	Insert, Header & Footer		
line spacing, single or double	Home, Paragraph		Ctrl + 1 or 2
Navigation pane	View, Show		Ctrl + F
numbering	Home, Paragraph		
online pictures	Insert, Illustrations		
page break	Insert, Pages		Ctrl + Enter
page number	Insert, Header & Footer		
Page Setup dialog box	Layout, Page Setup		
pictures	Insert, Illustrations		
section break	Layout, Page Setup		
Spelling & Grammar	Review, Proofing	ABC	F7
themes	Design, Document Formatting		

POWERPOINT

Feature	Ribbon Tab, Group/*Option*	Button	Keyboard Shortcut
add animation	Animations, Advanced Animation		
audio file	Insert, Media		
Font size, increase or decrease	Home, Font	A A	Ctrl + Shift + > Ctrl + Shift + <
layout	Home, Slides		
list level, increase or decrease	Home, Paragraph		Tab or Shift + Tab
new slide	Home, Slides		Ctrl + M
screenshot	Insert, Images		
Slide Sorter view	View, Presentation Views		
video file	Insert, Media		F7

EXCEL

Feature	Ribbon Tab, Group/*Option*	Button	Keyboard Shortcut
Accounting format	Home, Number		
align left, center, or right	Home, Alignment		
borders	Home, Font		Ctrl + Shift + &
cell formulas	Formulas, Formula Auditing		Ctrl + `
change margins	Page Layout, Page Setup OR File, *Print*		
column width or row height	Home, Cells		
Comma format	Home, Number		
create column, line, or pie chart	Insert, Charts		F11
decimal, increase or decrease	Home, Number		
delete cell, column, row, or worksheet	Home, Cells		
fill color	Home, Font		
format, move, copy, or rename worksheet	Home, Cells		
indent, increase or decrease	Home, Alignment		
insert cell, column, row, or worksheet	Home, Cells		
insert comment	Review, Comments		Shift + F2
insert function	Formulas, Function Library		
merge and center	Home, Alignment		
scale page width and/or height	Page Layout, Scale to Fit OR File, *Print*		
sort	Home, Editing		
Spelling or Thesaurus	Review, Proofing		F7; Shift + F7
SUM function	Home, Editing		Alt + =
theme	Page Layout, Themes		
wrap text	Home, Alignment		

ACCESS

Feature	Ribbon Tab, Group/*Option*	Button	Keyboard Shortcut
add fields to a form	Form Layout Tools Design, Controls		
add or delete records	HOME, Records		Ctrl + +; Delete
change margins	Print Preview, Page Size OR Page Layout		
column width	Home, Records		
conditional formatting in form or report	Form Layout Tools Format, Control Formatting OR Report Layout Tools Format, Control Formatting		
create form	Create, Forms		
create query with wizard or in Design view	Create, Queries		
create report	Create, Reports		
create table in Datasheet view or Design view	Create, Tables		
filter	Home, Sort & Filter		
Find	Home, Find		Ctrl + F
Group, Sort, and Total pane	Report Layout Tools Design, Grouping & Totals		
insert or delete fields	Table Tools Design, Tools		Delete
Labels Wizard	Create, Reports		
landscape orientation	Print Preview, Page Layout		
primary key field	Table Tools Design, Tools		
Print Preview	File, *Print*		Ctrl + P
property sheet in query	Query Tools Design, Show/Hide		Alt + Enter
relationships	Database Tools, Relationships		
run a query	Query Tools Design, Results		
sort ascending or descending order	Home, Sort & Filter		
Total row	Home, Records		

ParadigmEducation.com | 800-535-6865

PARADIGM EDUCATION SOLUTIONS